SURVEYING THE GREAT DIVIDE

01 02 03 04 05 21 20 19 18 17

Caitlin Press Inc.
8100 Alderwood Road,
Halfmoon Bay, BC V0N 1Y1
www.caitlin-press.com

Copy edited by Meg Yamamoto
Text design and cover by Vici Johnstone
Front cover image courtesy Library and Archives Canada e011183810
Back cover and title page image courtesy Library and Archives Canada e011166493

Printed in Canada

Caitlin Press Inc. acknowledges financial support from the Government of Canada and the Canada Council for the Arts, and the Province of British Columbia through the British Columbia Arts Council and the Book Publisher's Tax Credit

Canada Council for the Arts Conseil des Arts du Canada BRITISH COLUMBIA ARTS COUNCIL Funded by the Government of Canada Canada

Library and Archives Canada Cataloguing in Publication

Sherwood, Jay, 1947-, author
Surveying the great divide : the Alberta/BC boundary survey, 1913-1917 / Jay Sherwood.

ISBN 978-1-987915-52-5 (softcover)

1. Alberta—Boundaries—British Columbia. 2. British Columbia—Boundaries—Alberta. 3. Alberta--Surveys—History—20th century. 4. British Columbia—Surveys—History—20th century. I. Title.

FC208.S54 2017 971.23'02 C2017-904597-0

SURVEYING THE GREAT DIVIDE

The Alberta/BC Boundary Survey, 1913-1917

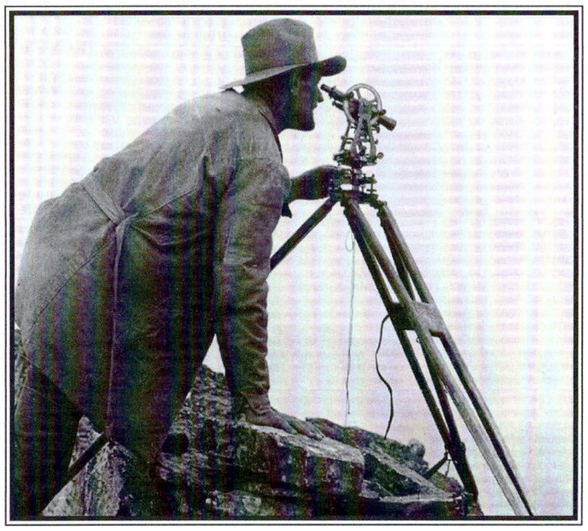

JAY SHERWOOD

CAITLIN PRESS

Contents

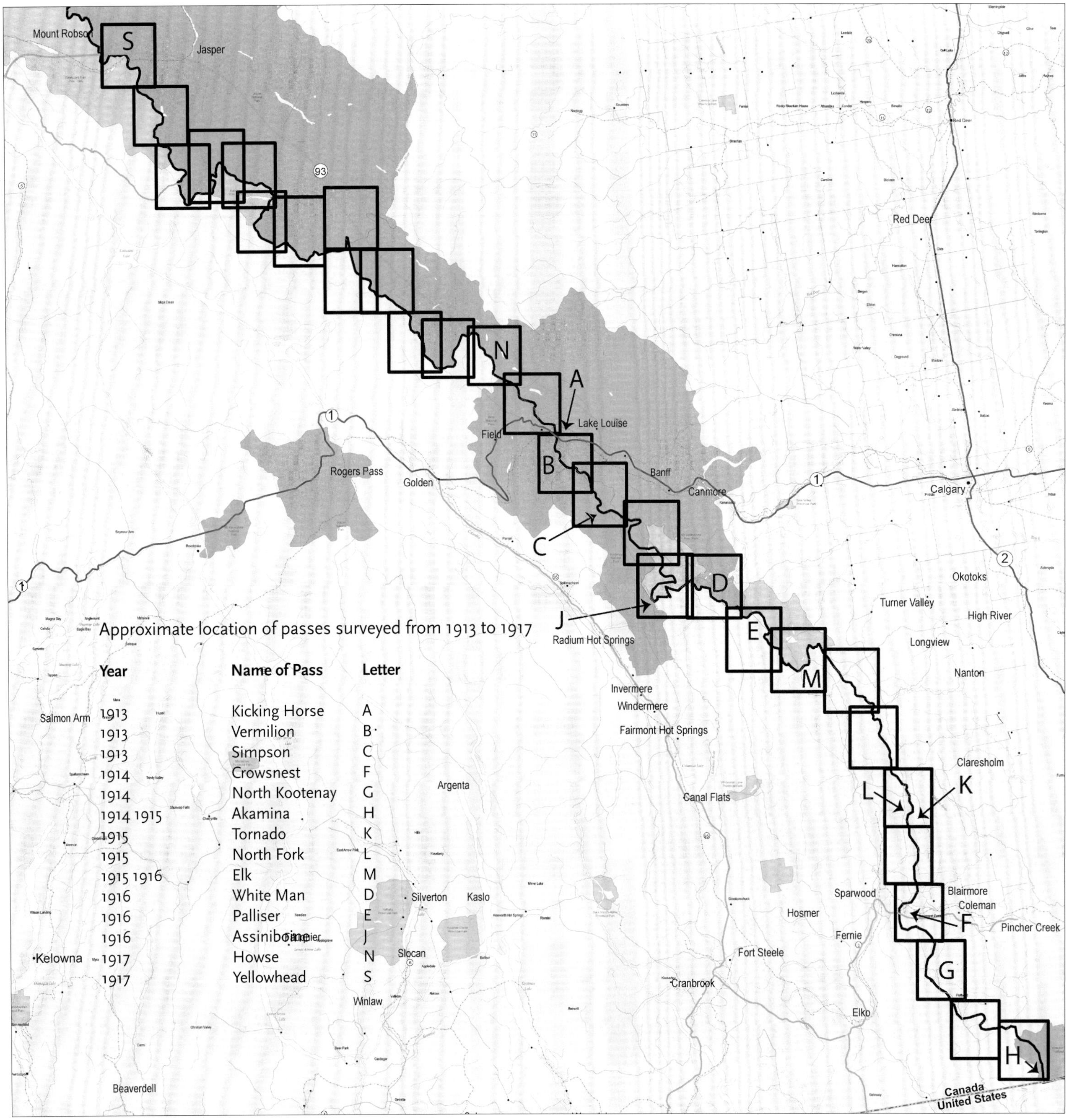
Approximate location of passes surveyed from 1913 to 1917
Year / Name of Pass / Letter
1913 Kicking Horse A
1913 Vermilion B
1913 Simpson C
1914 Crowsnest F
1914 North Kootenay G
1914 1915 Akamina H
1915 Tornado K
1915 North Fork L
1915 1916 Elk M
1916 White Man D
1916 Palliser E
1916 Assiniboine J
1917 Howse N
1917 Yellowhead S
Mount Robson
Jasper
Lake Louise
Field
Rogers Pass
Golden
Banff
Canmore
Calgary
Red Deer
Okotoks
Turner Valley
High River
Longview
Nanton
Radium Hot Springs
Invermere
Windermere
Fairmont Hot Springs
Canal Flats
Claresholm
Argenta
Salmon Arm
Silverton
Kaslo
Slocan
Winlaw
Kelowna
Beaverdell
Sparwood
Blairmore
Coleman
Pincher Creek
Hosmer
Fernie
Fort Steele
Cranbrook
Elko
Canada
United States

The Rocky Mountains 1917

In 1917 Canada commemorated its 50th anniversary as a nation. But it was not a time for the country to celebrate. Canada was entering its fourth year of involvement in World War I. Although there were battles like Vimy Ridge in which Canada played a significant role, the war remained unresolved, casualties continued, and the government brought in conscription to maintain a supply of soldiers for the Allies. In Canada, the remaining population struggled to provide an adequate supply of food both at home and for the soldiers overseas, and to produce the materiel needed for the war. The federal and provincial governments focussed much of their financial resources on the war effort and retained only their basic activities.

A sign in Crowsnest Pass in 1914. e011166458, Library and Archives Canada

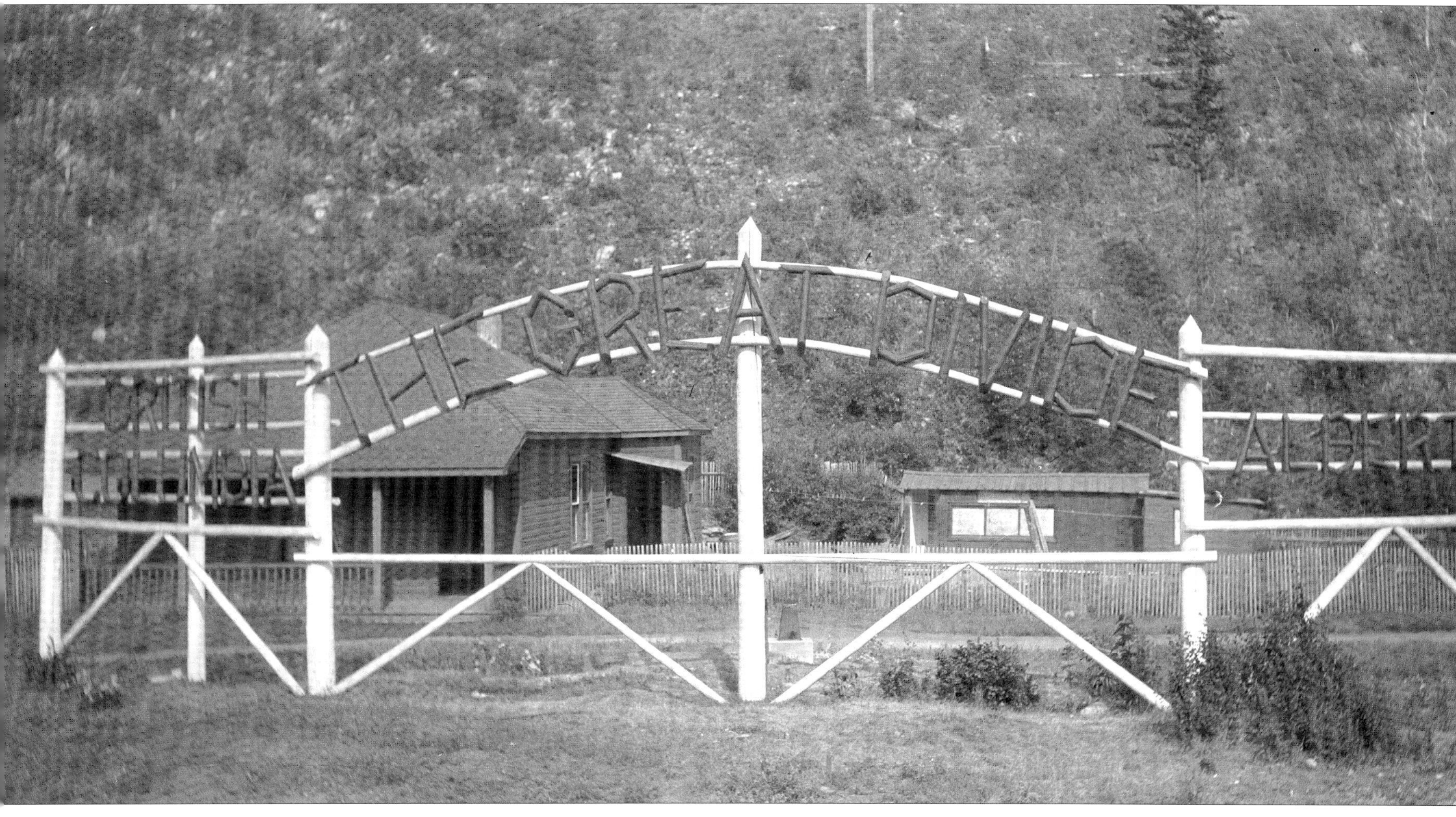

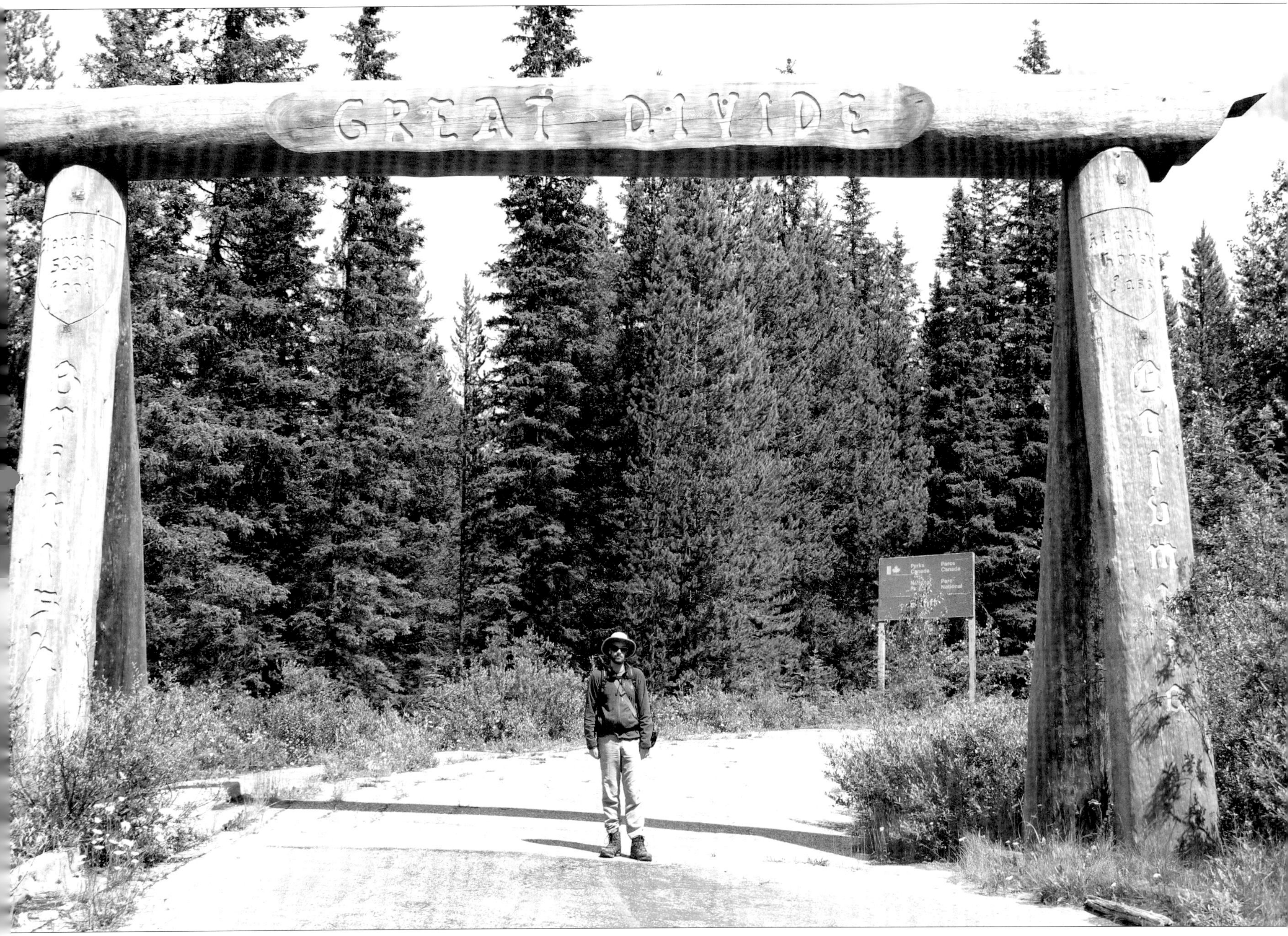

In 2016 this sign still remains on the original highway through Kicking Horse Pass. Photo Jay Sherwood

Despite the cutbacks necessitated by the war, a few projects continued. In the Rocky Mountains, two survey crews, funded by the governments of British Columbia, Alberta and Canada, defined the boundary between the two provinces along the Great Divide. The Alberta-BC boundary survey had started in 1913 during an economic boom in western Canada and was considered of sufficient importance that it received funding (on a slightly reduced scale) throughout the war. It was a quintessentially Canadian project—talented Canadian surveyors using the most modern equipment available, transported by horses and humans through rugged wilderness country to mountain passes and the summits of peaks along the Great Divide. It is also a testimony to the fortitude of the survey crews who spent months each year working in remote, mountainous terrain, often in inclement weather, travelling over trails that were generally poor or non-existent and occasionally fording rivers.

The Alberta–British Columbia boundary is the longest interprovincial boundary in Canada, extending for 1,842 kilometres. It consists of two parts: the Great Divide (more commonly called the Continental Divide today), a natural feature; and the 120th meridian, a man-made feature. The initial Alberta-BC boundary survey, which lasted from 1913 to 1924, delineated all but the northern quarter. Along the Great Divide it marked the boundary between the two provinces in the main passes and produced the first detailed maps of the Canadian Rockies. The 120th meridian (which the Alberta crew surveyed beginning in 1918) defined the boundary from its intersection with the Continental Divide in present-day Willmore Wilderness Park, through the Peace River district and farther north. The Alberta survey crew used concrete monuments to delineate and map the boundary through the economically important passes of the Rocky Mountains, while the British Columbia crew surveyed and mapped the area along the peaks. Today the Alberta-BC Boundary Commission maintains the surveying stations established a century ago.

The phototopographic part of the project was the lengthiest and most extensive of its kind in North America. From 1913 to 1924 the British Columbia survey crew took several thousand photographs of the terrain along the Great Divide, and these pictures were used to map the Rocky Mountains. The work was often arduous and dangerous. Carrying equipment, the crew usually took a few hours to reach the survey station on a mountain. Sometimes the weather became cloudy or rainy, necessitating a second, and sometimes third, trip up the mountain. The location where they surveyed was often on a precarious ridge or mountain peak, windy and sometimes subject to rain, snow and thunderstorms. On the mountain it usually took three to four hours to make the surveying measurements and take phototopographic pictures, and afterwards a cairn had to be built so the station could be recognized when surveying from other locations.

Because the photographs were taken at defined survey stations, it is possible to find their location and take pictures at the same place today. (At several stations the original cairns still remain.) In most locations along the Great Divide, the photographs taken during the boundary survey are the first pictorial record of that area. Thus the phototopography of the Alberta-BC boundary survey continues to have relevance a century later.

During the past decade the Mountain Legacy Project, under the direction of Dr. Eric Higgs of the University of Victoria, has returned to many of these survey stations. The repeat photographs that they have taken are being used by scientists are to document a variety of changes that have occurred in the landscape during the past century. This includes recession of glaciers; human impact on the landscape; changes in vegetation; and advancement of tree line to higher elevation. In turn, these photographs along with the ones taken on the original boundary survey, will provide reference for future scientists.

This book covers the Alberta-BC boundary survey from 1913 to 1917, when the Alberta and BC crews mainly worked together along the Rocky Mountains. Canada's 150th anniversary is an appropriate time to recognize an important Canadian surveying project that was in progress a century ago.

Background

The main boundaries of British Columbia were established while it was still part of Great Britain. The Oregon Treaty of 1846 extended the 49th parallel as the boundary between American and British territory from the Rocky Mountains to the Pacific Ocean. (The Treaty of 1818 had set the 49th parallel as the boundary from the northwesternmost point of the Lake of the Woods to the Rocky Mountains.) Along the Pacific Ocean the treaty defined the boundary as the main channel through the Strait of Juan de Fuca. This led to a dispute between Great Britain and the United States that was not settled until the Treaty of Washington in 1871. Great Britain retained all of Vancouver Island even though the southern part was below the 49th parallel. The boundary along the mainland part of the 49th parallel was surveyed between 1857 and 1861.

During the first half of the 19th century British Columbia remained land mainly inhabited by indigenous people, with Hudson's Bay Company trading posts and a few settlements. In 1849 Britain created the Colony of Vancouver Island. After gold was discovered along the Fraser River and miners came to the area, Great Britain established the Colony of British Columbia in 1858. Eight years later the British Columbia Act, 1866, united the Vancouver Island and British Columbia colonies into one jurisdiction called the Colony of British Columbia.

The act defined the colony's boundary: "to the South by the Territories of the United States of America, to the west by the Pacific Ocean and the frontier of the Russian Territories in North America, to the North by the Sixtieth Parallel of North Latitude, and to the East from the Boundary of the United States Northwards by the Rocky Mountains and the One hundred and twentieth Meridian of West Longitude." These boundaries remained unchanged when British Columbia became Canada's sixth province in 1871, although the United States now owned Alaska after purchasing it from Russia in 1867. When Alberta became a province in 1905, the Alberta Act affirmed that the province's western boundary was British Columbia's existing eastern boundary.

As part of the terms of Confederation, British Columbia received control over its lands, except for the Railway Belt (and later the Peace River Block). These were ceded to the federal government as part of the agreement for construction of the transcontinental railway to connect the province with the rest of Canada. At the same time, the British Columbia provincial government had responsibility for the costs involved in any surveying that it did. For almost all of the remainder of the 19th century the British Columbia government was in debt and budgeted only a small amount of money on basic surveying. As late as the 1905–06 fiscal year, the provincial government spent less than $7,000 on surveying. Consequently, there was no initiative for defining the eastern, northern or northwestern boundaries of the province.

Toward the end of the 19th century the situation changed when the Klondike gold rush into the Yukon Territory brought a large number of people to that area. Some of the major routes to the Klondike went from the Pacific Ocean through Alaska. This necessitated a decision on the disputed location of the boundary between the United States and Canada in the Alaska Panhandle area. After the arbitration committee made its decision in 1903, the survey of this portion of the boundary started. Some routes to the Yukon went through British Columbia, and this made it imperative to survey a portion of the 60th parallel along the BC-Yukon border. Work on this survey occurred from 1901 to 1903 and from 1907 to 1908.

Around the same time, the BC government expressed its first interest in having its eastern border surveyed. Economic development, particularly the location of coal in the Crowsnest Pass, spurred BC's interest in defining its boundary. The government wanted to obtain all the revenue from coal and timber royalties to which it was entitled. The peaks along the Great Divide made it easy to define the boundary in

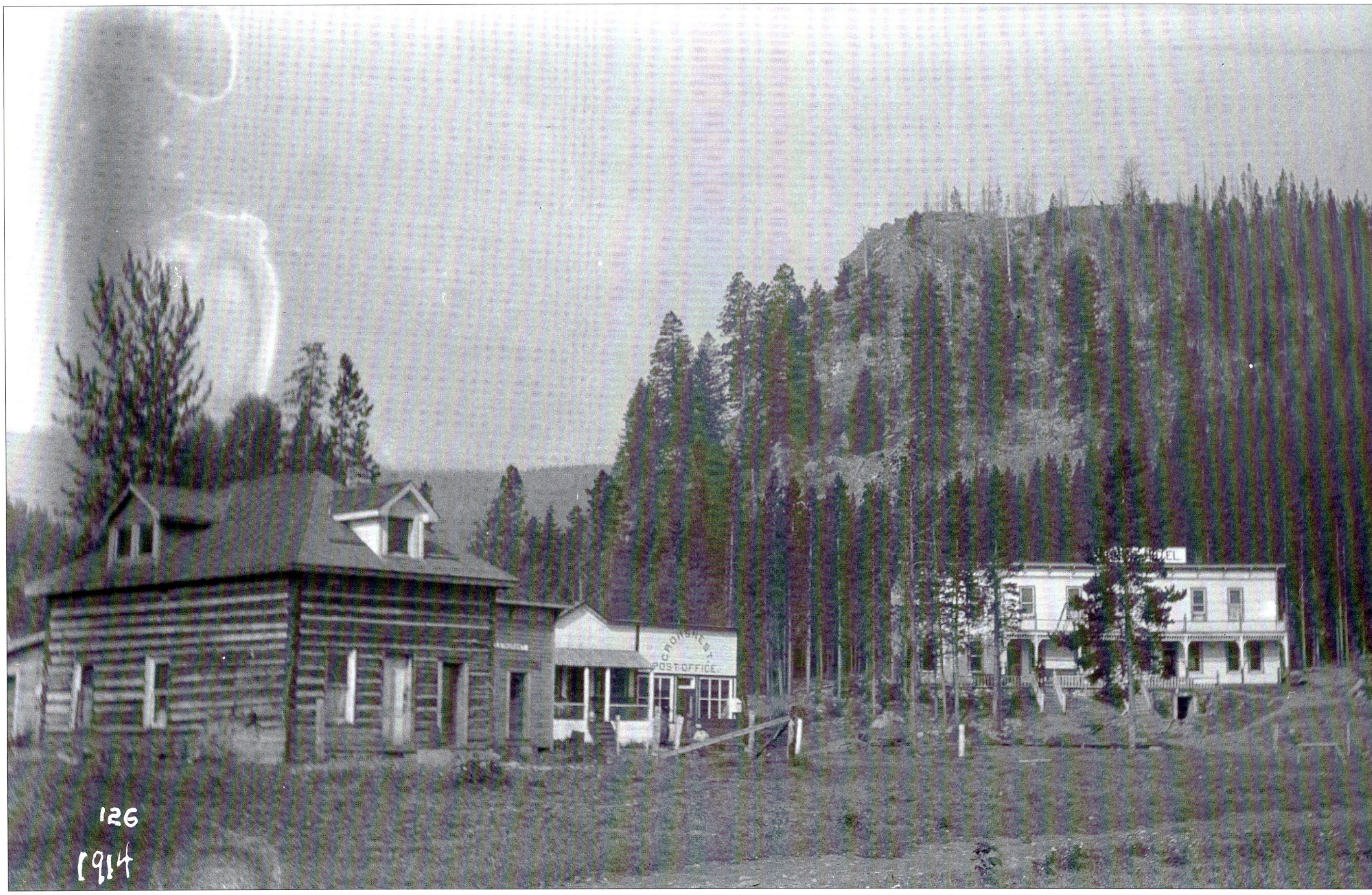

R.W. Cautley took this photograph of the original Summit Hotel along the Great Divide in the Crowsnest Pass in 1914. The picture was taken close to Station 1F. The creek that flowed into Alberta is behind the hotel. e011166456, Library and Archives Canada

most places, but the boundary line through the passes was often more difficult to determine.

In a letter dated January 8, 1904, J.S. Dennis, BC land commissioner for the Canadian Pacific Railway (CPR), wrote to British Columbia's surveyor general. The CPR had received land grants from the BC government for construction of the British Columbia Southern Railway, and for two of the lots the eastern boundary was the boundary between the province and the Alberta district of the Northwest Territories.

Dennis explained why the province needed to survey the boundary in the Crowsnest Pass: "The survey of the boundaries of these land grant blocks has to be made by the Railway Company, and we have had three parties in the field during the past season completing the work. The portion of the provincial boundary cannot, of course, be defined or marked by our surveyor, and I have, therefore, respectfully to request that the necessary steps may be taken to have it properly defined and marked."

Dennis also noted the importance of knowing the location of the boundary for both economic and jurisdictional reasons. "The boundary at the point mentioned will come into question at once in connection with the coal and timber areas which are being developed and which adjoin it on either side, and the portion marked on the attached map is particularly needed in connection with the settlement of outstanding questions between the British Columbia Southern Railway Company and the Crow's Nest Pass Coal Company."

The next month the CPR applied more pressure by sending a letter to the secretary of the federal Department of the Interior requesting that a proposal for a boundary survey be referred to the federal commissioner of lands and works. R.F. Green, BC's chief commissioner of lands and works, wrote to Clifford Sifton, minister of the interior.

> I have much pleasure in supporting Mr. Dennis' application, and in that connection beg to point out that the country lying between the point where the British Columbia Southern Railway crosses the summit of the Rocky Mountains and the International Boundary Line is likely in the near future to be opened up to settlement, and a large influx of people to that section may be expected with a view to exploit coal and oil lands; and in order that there may be no conflict between this province and Alberta in the administration of these lands it is highly desirable that the boundary line referred to should be defined and marked on the ground during this coming season.

In a memorandum written on April 6, Édouard Deville, the Dominion surveyor general, suggested that the survey be done jointly by the federal government (which was responsible for administration of the Northwest Territories) and the province of BC. "Authority will of course be required from Parliament and from the Legislature of the Province, vesting in the Commissioners the power to define the boundary." In a letter written in October 1907, Deville commented that for unknown reasons, the proposed survey did not proceed any further. The next month the new federal minister of the interior, Frank Oliver, wrote to BC's chief commissioner of lands and works in an effort to restart work on the boundary survey. However, the chief commissioner was not interested.

On August 10, 1909, Royal North-West Mounted Police Commissioner A.B. Perry wrote to the attorney general of Alberta. He provided a reason for surveying the Alberta and British Columbia boundary that evoked the spirit of the Wild West.

> At the summit of the Crow's Nest Pass, presumably in British Columbia side, Mr. Andy Good has a license for a hotel. It has been reported to me that this is a resting place for crooks and toughs. I am informed that when the police of British Columbia [BC had its own provincial police force] visit this hotel, all the crooks come into Alberta and go into camp, and when this force goes they all return to British Columbia.
>
> Supt. Primrose is of the opinion that the hotel is situated in Alberta. The CPR have marked the summit of the grade on the pass, and this is taken as on the boundary line. I doubt that this is correct....
>
> I would ask that the true boundary be ascertained and suitably marked.

The letter was sent to the Dominion surveyor general. Two months later Deville replied: "The British Columbia government have been invited several times to join us in the delimitation of the boundary but they have not yet accepted the invitation. The concurrence of the Dominion and of the Provinces of Alberta and British Columbia will of course be required for the establishment of the line."

In 1903 Richard McBride was elected premier of British Columbia, and during his administration the province experienced several years of prosperity. There was considerable economic development in western Canada. In British Columbia the growth was fuelled by mining activities and logging. Government revenue increased dramatically and there were funds to pay for long-neglected survey projects. From 1909 to 1913 the provincial government spent an average of over 5 percent of its budget on surveys. In April 1912, shortly after McBride won his fourth election, the BC government decided to make a commitment to survey its eastern boundary with Alberta. BC's surveyor general, G.H. Dawson, contacted his federal counterpart. During the following months they exchanged several letters pertaining to the proposed survey, and in October Deville came to Victoria for official meetings. In a memorandum dated December 2, 1912, Deville wrote to the minister of the interior:

> The Government of British Columbia have expressed the desire that steps should be taken at an early date for the delimitation of the boundary between British Columbia and Alberta.... It is proposed by the Provincial authorities that a joint survey be made and that work be commenced in the vicinity of the main passes where it is more urgently needed. Mr. A.O. Wheeler, who is a Dominion as well as a British Columbia Land Surveyor, is suggested to represent the Province upon the survey.

Deville supported this request and also noted the legal process that was necessary for this type of survey.

> It is recommended that the request of the Province be acceded to and that a joint survey be undertaken. After the boundary has been surveyed and marked on the ground, it will have to be accepted by the Legislatures of British Columbia and Alberta; when so accepted, the Parliament of Canada can by virtue of the provisions of the British North America Act, 1871, pass an Act declaring that line to be the boundary between the two Provinces. The Province of Alberta must, therefore, be invited to concur in the arrangements for the joint survey and to send a representative on the survey if the Provincial authorities so desire.

The surveyor general outlined the main features of the survey.

> The following arrangements are suggested for the consideration of the two Provinces:
>
> 1. Between the International Boundary and the 120th degree of longitude, the Interprovincial Boundary is the line dividing the waters flowing into the Pacific Ocean from those flowing elsewhere. This line may cross several times the meridian of the 120th longitude....
> 2. Places may be found where the water of a stream, of a glacier or of a lake divides and flows on one side towards the Pacific Ocean and on the other side towards the Arctic Ocean or the Gulf of Mexico. The stream, from the point where it separates in two directions should be followed up to that one of its sources which more nearly divides the basin of the stream into two parts of equal area. Should any place be found where water originally flowing to one side has been diverted to the other side, it must be understood that the boundary is to be defined as if the stream had never been diverted and were still flowing in its original channel.
> 3. Where the watershed line is sharp and well defined, it shall be adopted, but where the land is flat or rolling and the watershed line indistinct, it shall be defined by a series of straight lines marked by monuments.

The surveyor general listed the locations that he believed were the highest priority. This included Crowsnest Pass, owing to proximity of mining properties; Vermilion Pass, because of the construction of the highway from Banff to Windermere; Howse Pass, owing to proximity of timber claims; and Kicking Horse, Simpson and White Man Passes, owing to their lying within or adjacent to populated areas. Other passes that Deville thought should be surveyed included Athabasca, which might possibly become a railroad route, South Kootenay, North Kootenay, North Fork and Kananaskis. In the northern part of the Rockies, Deville thought that Moose Pass should be surveyed because it might become important as a route to the north, along with Robson Pass, which was a scenic location for tourists.

In addition to surveying the major passes, Deville proposed that "a topographical survey shall be made extending a few miles on each side of the line. A photograph of each monument shall be taken and attached to the field notes of the survey as a further means of identification.…The topographical survey may, if agreeable to the Provinces, be expanded in cases where the scenery is especially attractive." In addition, maps produced from the survey could be used to promote tourism.

Deville contacted the Alberta government, and it agreed to the survey. In January 1913 he wrote a draft of a report to the federal cabinet "recommending that the Provinces of Alberta and British Columbia be invited to join in the delimitation of the boundary between the two provinces." On February 18, the Dominion government passed an order-in-council formally inviting these provinces. Alberta's acceptance was delayed for a few months because there was a provincial election in April. The BC government decided not to proceed until it knew that the Alberta government still wanted to participate in the boundary survey. After the Liberal party was re-elected, arrangements for establishing the survey proceeded. On June 2 the Executive Council of British Columbia officially accepted the federal government's offer, and two weeks later Alberta followed the same procedure. All three governments agreed to share costs equally. British Columbia appointed A.O. Wheeler as its commissioner for the boundary survey. Wheeler, who had worked on phototopographic surveys for the Dominion government for several years, would be in charge of surveying the Great Divide along the mountains. R.W. Cautley, Alberta's representative, had the responsibility for surveying the major passes. Deville selected J.N. Wallace from Calgary as the Dominion representative. The boundary commissioners would receive a salary of $15 per day, the highest wage of any government surveyors in Canada. Wheeler and Cautley would work almost year-round on the survey, with approximately five months in the field and an equal amount of time in the office copying notes, making calculations, producing maps and preparing for the next field season.

Wheeler, Cautley and Wallace met at Banff and on June 9 signed a memorandum outlining the organization of the survey and the scope of the work that Cautley and Wheeler would each do. Wheeler was to "be in charge of the topographical portion of the survey and the establishment of boundary monuments on the peaks adjacent to the passes." Cautley would "be in charge of the surveying party required to take levels and make the preliminary survey of the boundary in the various passes and the erection of permanent boundary monuments therein." Wallace's role was to be an adviser, check the accuracy of the work and be an arbitrator if there was any disagreement about the location of the boundary line. His position was only part-time. Deville used this memorandum as the basis for issuing an official set of instructions to the commissioners on June 18.

It was already June, and it was imperative to begin the survey during the summer of 1913. Wheeler and Cautley, who had previously started to assemble their survey crews and supplies, needed to begin field operations quickly. The Alberta-BC boundary survey was ready to begin.

Cast of Characters

The first Alberta-BC boundary survey lasted from 1913 to 1924. The major characters involved with the project were some of Canada's most talented surveyors of that time period, and all but one of them worked for the entire 12 years of the boundary survey. For these people, it was one of the major activities of their surveying career.

Édouard-Gaston Deville, Surveyor General of Canada

Born in France in 1849, Deville began his career with the French navy and was in charge of hydrographic surveying projects throughout the world. He immigrated to Canada in 1874. Initially he was appointed to the Quebec government in 1875 as inspector of surveys. In 1878 he obtained his Dominion land surveyor licence and started work for the federal government as a topographic surveyor. Three years later he became an inspector for the Dominion land surveys, and in 1882 he was appointed head inspector. In 1885 Deville was appointed the federal government's surveyor general, a position he held for 39 years.

Deville was particularly interested in phototopographical surveying and started applying it to conditions in western Canada soon after becoming surveyor general. He perfected techniques developed by Aimé Laussedat, a French army engineer, and developed equipment that could be used in mountainous terrain. Deville became one of the world's leading experts on phototopographic surveying, and by the time of the Alberta-BC boundary survey the importance of this technology had been proven. He wrote a book titled *Photographic Surveying* and is considered the father of photogrammetry in Canada.

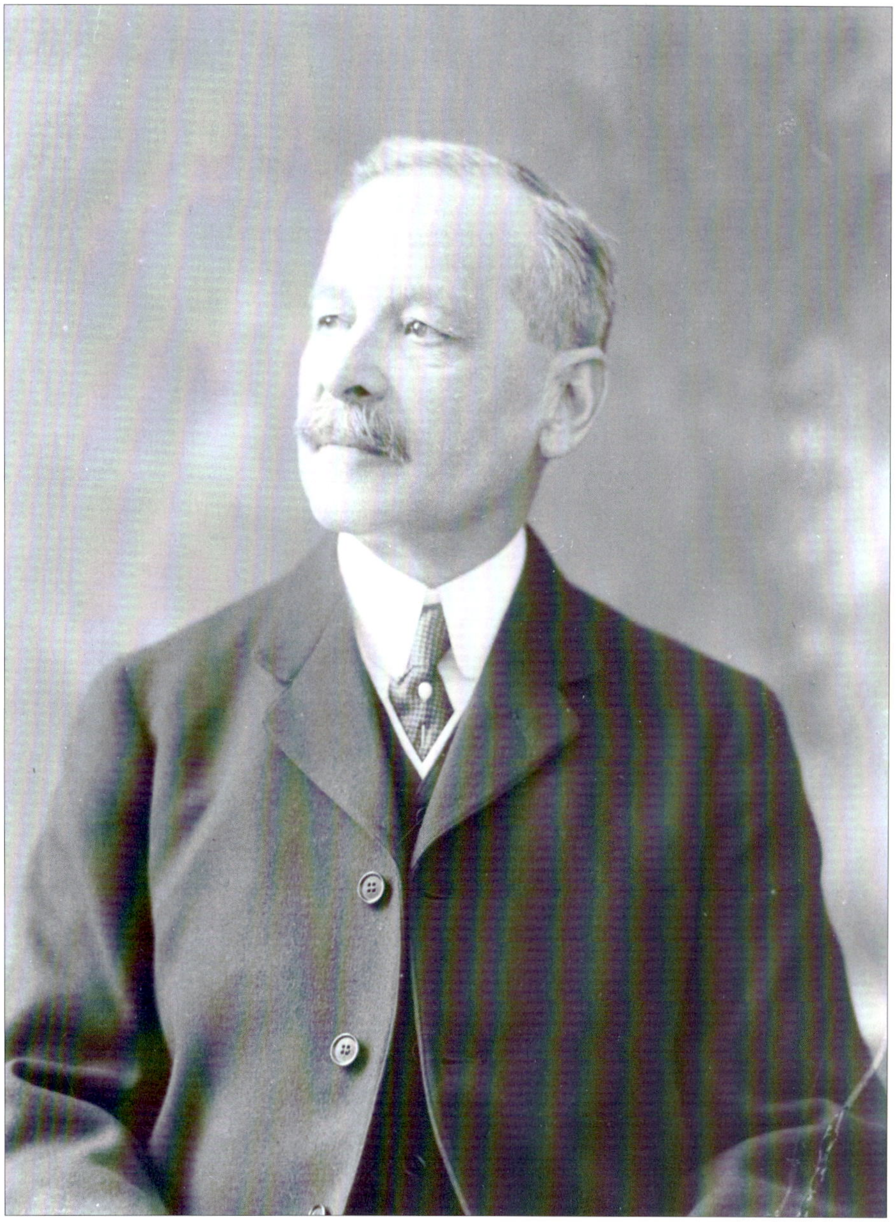

This photograph of Édouard Deville was taken around the time that the Alberta–British Columbia boundary survey started. PA-043041, Library and Archives Canada

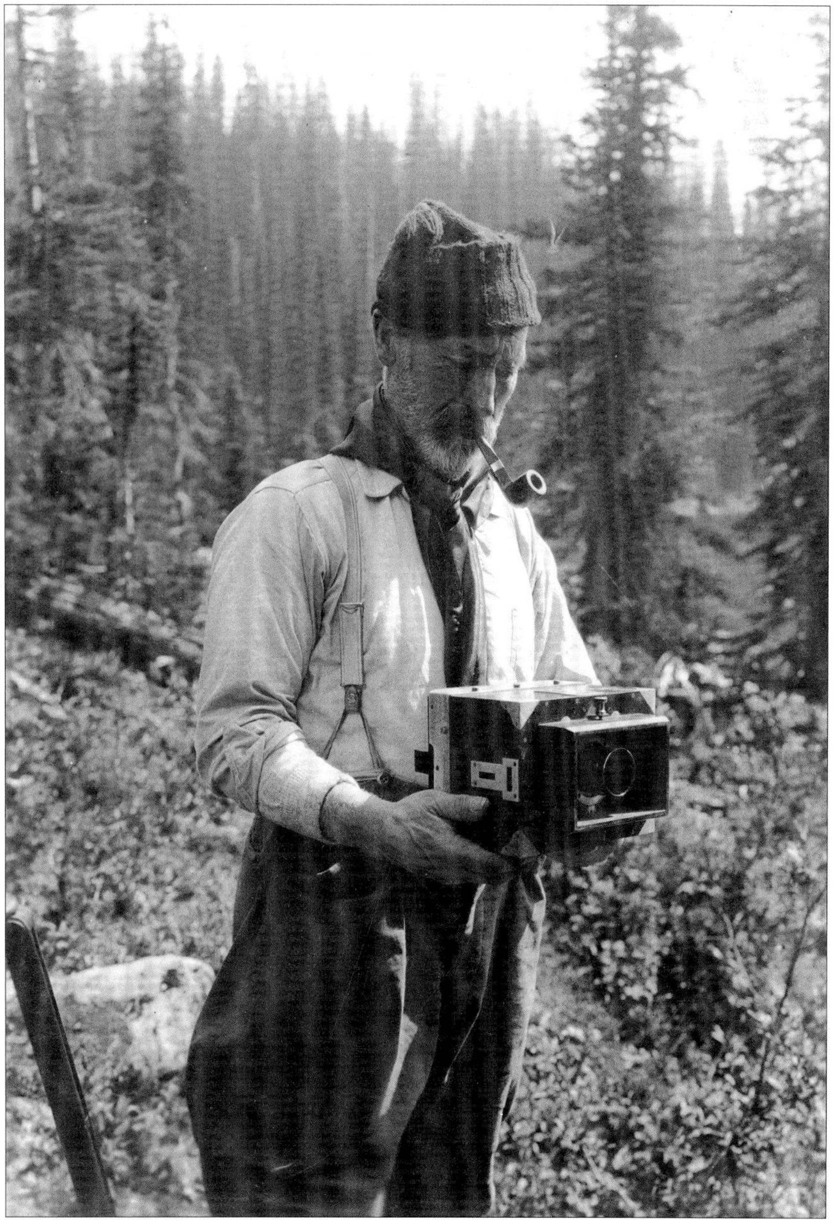

A.O. Wheeler with one of the phototopographic cameras.
V465-pd3-374, Whyte Museum of the Canadian Rockies

Arthur Oliver Wheeler, British Columbia Commissioner

A.O. Wheeler was born in Ireland in 1860 and immigrated with his family to Canada in 1876. He articled to be a surveyor in Ontario and received his licence in 1881. The following year he became both a Dominion and a Manitoba land surveyor. At the beginning of 1885 Wheeler began working in Ottawa as a surveyor for the Department of the Interior, and he learned about phototopographic surveying from Deville. That spring, during the North-West Rebellion, Wheeler served with the Dominion Land Surveyors' Intelligence Corps and was slightly wounded at the Battle of Batoche. Wheeler married Clara Macoun, the daughter of famous Canadian naturalist John Macoun, in 1888.

During the 1890s, most of Wheeler's surveying was in the western part of the Alberta district of the Northwest Territories on surveys for irrigation. Wheeler's work included the use of phototopography to assist with the maps that he produced. In 1900 he began working on phototopographic surveying projects in both the Selkirk and the Rocky Mountain ranges. Wheeler had a keen interest in the outdoors and mountaineering. In 1906 he was one of the founders of the Alpine Club of Canada and was elected president of the organization. During the following summers Wheeler took time from his surveying to organize and attend the Alpine Club's annual summer camp. Deville told Wheeler in 1910 that he could no longer attend the camps because it was interfering with his phototopographic surveying. Wheeler received an exemption for one more summer, and then he decided to resign and go into private practice. Dominion Land Surveyor Morris Parsons (M.P.) Bridgland then took over the federal government's phototopographic surveying in the Rocky Mountains. The boundary survey would utilize some of Bridgland's work done near the Great Divide.

When the Alberta-BC boundary survey was being organized, both Deville and the BC surveyor general, G.H. Dawson, selected Wheeler as their first choice to be the Pacific province's commissioner and in charge of the topographic and phototopographic surveying. Wheeler agreed, provided that he was allowed to attend the Alpine Club's summer camp. He hired A.J. Campbell, one of the men from his surveying company, to be his assistant and in charge of the surveying when Wheeler was absent.

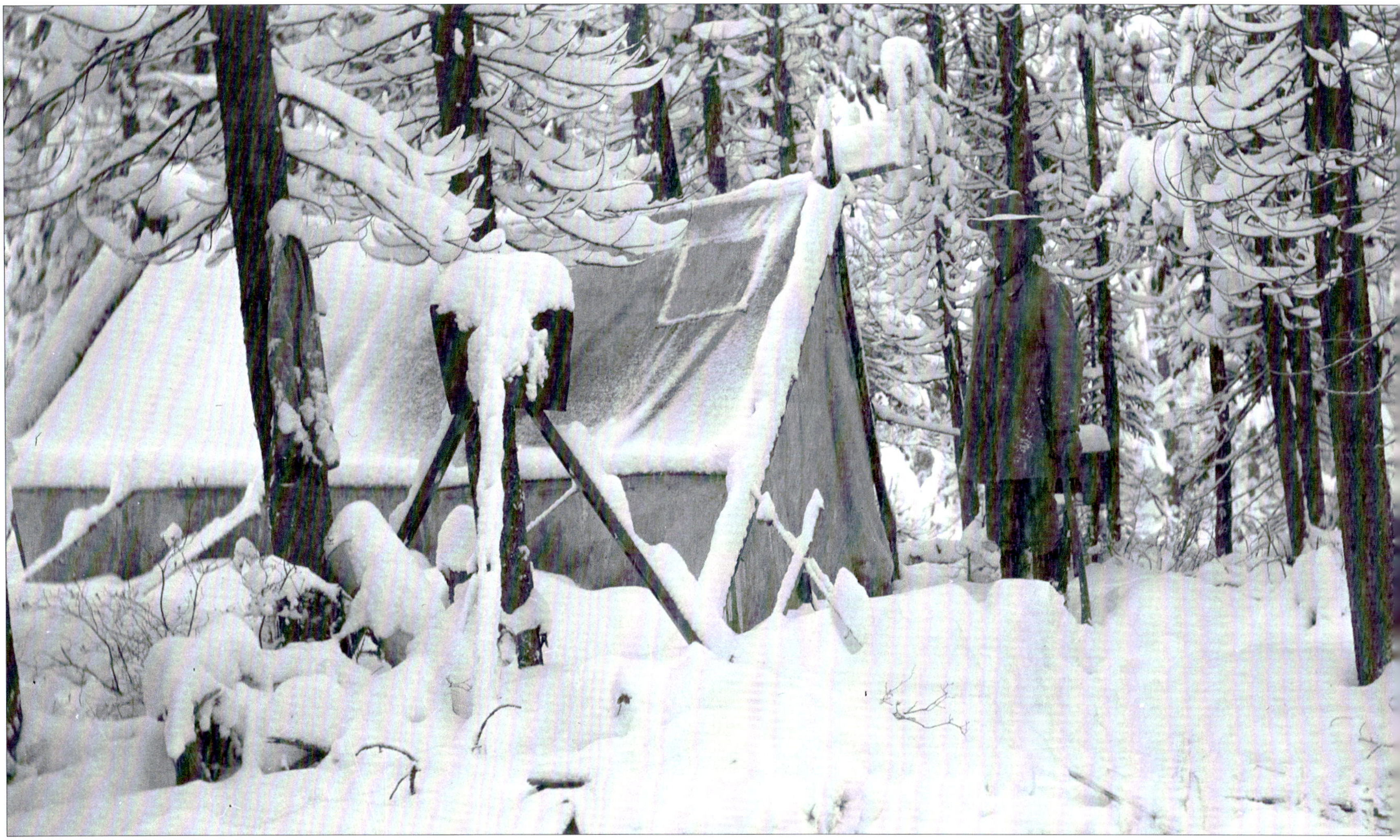

R.W. Cautley outside his office tent after a snowstorm in Akamina Pass. e011166460, Library and Archives Canada

Richard William Cautley, Alberta Commissioner, Dominion Commissioner (1915–24)

Born in England in 1873, Richard William (R.W. or Bill) Cautley immigrated to Vancouver when he was 17. In 1892 he began articling to be a surveyor with James F. Garden, a BC land surveyor who later became mayor of Vancouver. Cautley obtained both his provincial and his Dominion land surveying licences in 1896. The following year he was appointed one of the surveyors on the gold commissioner's staff for the Yukon Territory, and he spent six years there. His work included surveying the Dawson city townsite. In 1903 Cautley moved to Edmonton, and until 1909 he worked for the federal government making several surveys in the Prairie provinces. He also established a private surveying practice with his brother, Reginald. In 1909 Cautley was appointed surveyor for the Alberta government's land title office, a position he held until his appointment as Alberta's commissioner for the boundary survey. Cautley also wrote a textbook for surveying students that was used throughout Canada for many years.

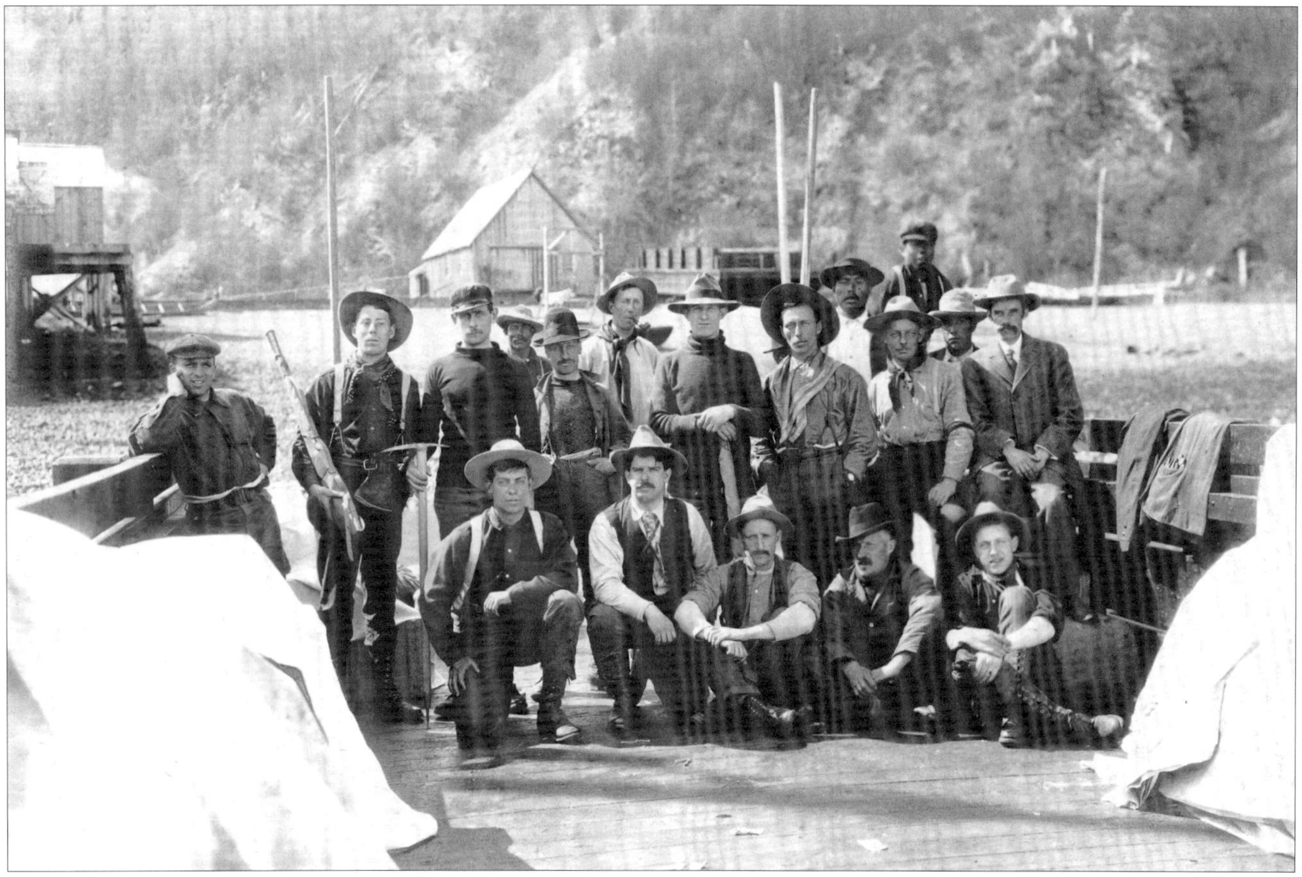

J.N. Wallace (second row, far right, wearing a suit) with his crew in 1908 on the BC-Yukon boundary survey. J-00810, Royal BC Museum and Archives

James Nevin Wallace, Dominion Commissioner (1913–14)

Wallace was born in Ireland in 1870 and graduated from Trinity College in Dublin with bachelor of engineering and bachelor of arts degrees. He immigrated to Canada in 1895, becoming an Ontario land surveyor in 1898 and a Dominion land surveyor two years later. In 1907 and 1908 he was in charge of the BC-Yukon boundary survey, and in 1911 he became head of the Levelling Office of the Topographical Survey of Canada.

Wallace was an ideal choice to be the federal government's commissioner for the boundary survey. His knowledge of levels was useful for measuring elevations, particularly for Cautley's work in the passes. He had experience working on a boundary survey. The federal commissioner worked only part-time, and Wallace was able to add this position to his existing work. Since his office was based in Calgary, it was relatively easy for him to visit the crews during the field season. In 1915, in an effort to reduce expenses during the war, Cautley became commissioner for both Alberta and the federal government, since the survey was proceeding without much difficulty. In the 1920s Wallace occasionally provided advice, particularly for Cautley's work on the 120th meridian.

Alan John Campbell, Assistant Surveyor, BC Crew

A.J. Campbell was born in Ontario in 1882 and grew up in that province. He obtained a diploma in civil engineering and a bachelor of applied science from the University of Toronto. While articling with W.J. Deans to be a surveyor, Campbell first came to western Canada in 1908, working on surveys in Manitoba and Saskatchewan. The next year he came to British Columbia and began surveying for A.O. Wheeler. In 1911 Wheeler formed a survey company with Campbell and R.D. McCaw. Campbell and McCaw spent much of that summer surveying a large number of lots in the Tetachuck Lake area of the upper Nechako headwaters.

In 1913, when A.O. Wheeler was appointed BC's commissioner for the Alberta-BC boundary survey, the company dissolved. McCaw began working for the BC government, initially on the Banff-Windermere Highway, and then in 1914 he started the provincial government's phototopographic surveying program, a lifelong project for him. Campbell became Wheeler's assistant and was in charge of the topographic survey during Wheeler's frequent absences. Campbell also worked for Wheeler during the winter, helping prepare the notes and maps made from the information gathered during the summer's work. Wheeler was known to be a difficult person to work with, but the quiet, soft-spoken Campbell remained for the entire project, and for those 12 years was the person who worked most closely with Wheeler.

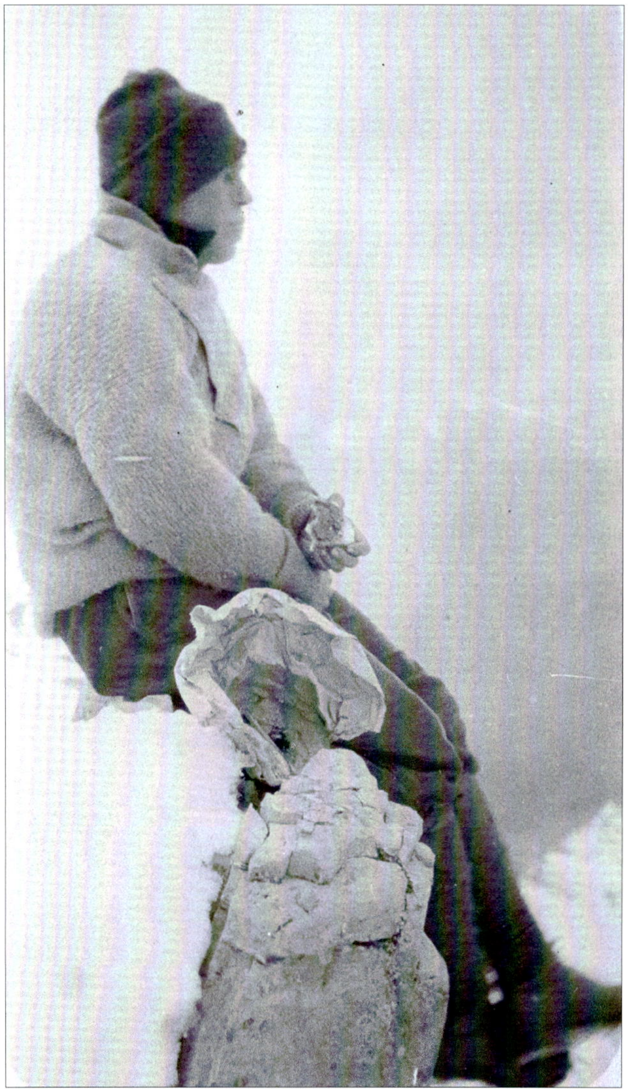

"Lunch at 10,000 feet" Spike Thomson took this photograph of A.J. Campbell on one of the peaks between Lake Louise and Jasper. PR1973.0534.0007, Provincial Archives of Alberta

Surveyor General—British Columbia

The surveyor general for British Columbia during the first part of the boundary survey was George Herbert Dawson, a veteran surveyor who held this position until 1917. His replacement was Joshua Umbach, surveyor general from 1917 to 1930.

Director of Surveys—Alberta

The director of surveys held a position equivalent to the British Columbia and Dominion surveyor general. Lionel Charlesworth was appointed to this position when Alberta became a province in 1905. In 1915 he became deputy minister of public works, and Albert Belyea held the position until 1922. However, Charlesworth remained the main representative of the Alberta government for the boundary survey.

SURVEYING METHODS

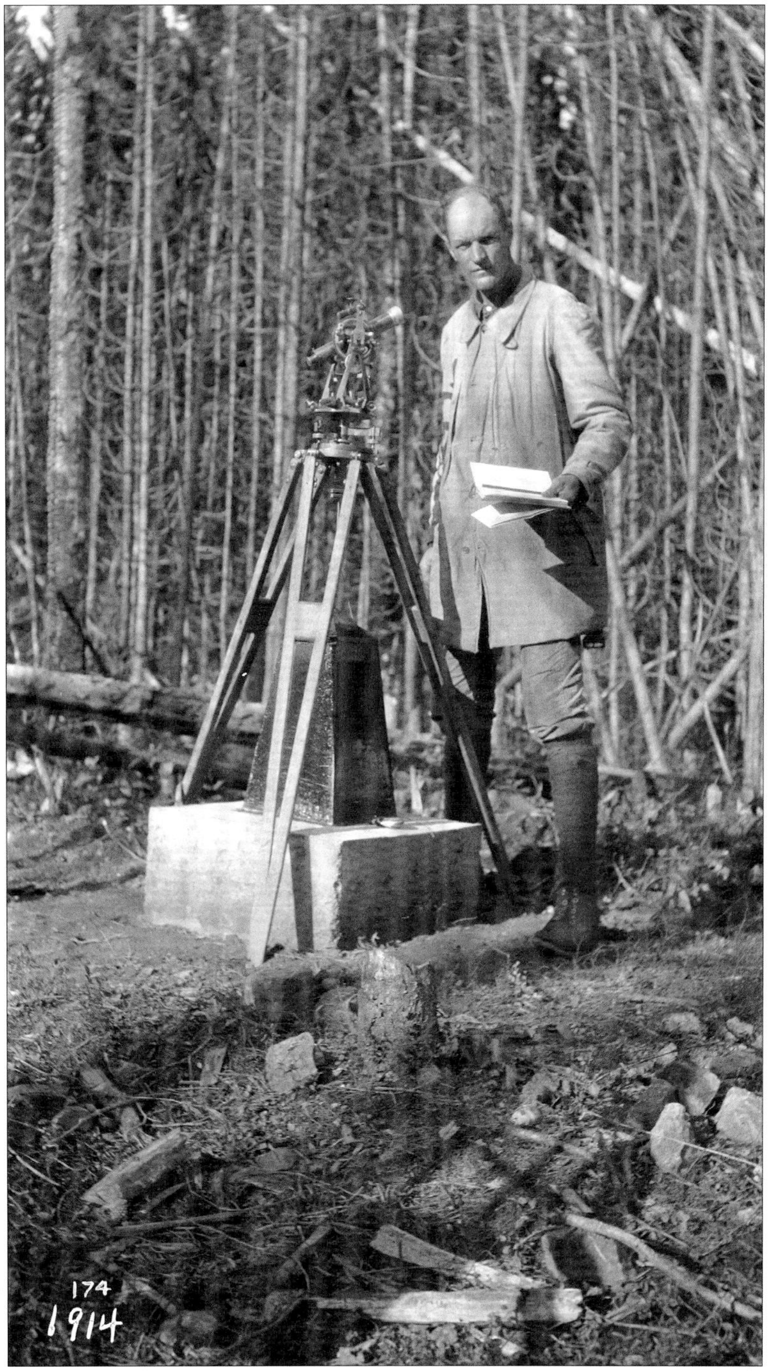

There were two main types of surveying used on the Alberta–British Columbia survey. Wheeler and Cautley employed separate methods because they were working on different parts of the boundary. Although the men worked independently, their surveying was interconnected. The first volume of *Report of the Commission Appointed to Delimit the Boundary between the Provinces of Alberta and British Columbia* has a chapter that includes a detailed description of the methods of surveying.

Cautley's surveying in the main passes through the Rocky Mountains was a basic traverse that included angles measured by a transit (also known as a theodolite) and distances measured with a steel chain. The purpose was to define the boundary as precisely as possible. A special feature of Cautley's survey was the use of concrete monuments to mark the survey stations across the pass.

The official report commented that it was "necessary to establish the Boundary as a series of straight lines which approximate the true position of the watershed. Thus the survey of the Boundary in the various passes consists of a number of concrete monuments placed by the Commissioners at such points of the watershed as may seem most suitable, with the special object in view that the connecting straight lines shall as nearly as possible coincide with the actual line of watershed, or shall at least equalize the areas cut off by such straight lines on either side of the watershed."

The line that Cautley surveyed was to follow the watershed through a pass as closely as possible and be delineated by concrete monuments. Although he could not place a monument at every change in direction in every pass, Cautley was encouraged to place sufficient stations to define the boundary as accurately as he could. The report noted the special nature of Cautley's basic traverse line and its main purposes.

R.W. Cautley surveying at a monument in the Crowsnest Pass in 1914. e011166459, Library and Archives Canada

"It is therefore an ordinary line survey made with great care and marked by very enduring monuments which fulfils two objects: first, it establishes an arbitrary boundary in the pass itself; secondly, it provides a carefully measured base for the system of triangles on which the work of the topographical section of the Commission depends, and for the trigonometrical connection with pre-existing surveys which provides the system of control."

The report noted that the survey of a pass usually extended from the lowest point in the pass to timberline on both sides, "because wherever there is timber the line of natural watershed is usually more or less obscure, and, secondly, because it is difficult to define the watershed by phototopographic methods with a sufficient degree of precision where the surface is timbered. In this connection it may be noted that practically all the lower passes of the Rocky Mountains are heavily timbered, and that timber line is found at an elevation above sea level of from 7000 to 7800 feet [2,133 to 2,377 metres]."

The report stated: "All the work in connection with the preliminary and final surveys in the passes is done by Mr. Cautley's party, but the location of the monuments is decided upon by the Commission as a whole, on the evidence adduced from the preliminary surveys."

It described the process of surveying a pass.

> The first work to be done consists in tracing the line of watershed right across the pass, surveying it by means of traverse lines and plotting it so that the Commissioners may realize what the position of the line of watershed is in relation to the lines of the preliminary traverse on the ground. In this way the Commissioners are able to decide where the monuments should be placed, although the sites chosen are often in the midst of thick woods, and to know how the straight line boundaries between monuments will lie in regard to the adjacent line of watershed, when they are cut out.

As commissioners representing Alberta and British Columbia, Cautley and Wheeler needed to agree on the location of the boundary line and monuments through a pass before Cautley made the final survey.

> The considerations which have to be taken into account are:
>
> 1. That all monuments shall be situated on the actual watershed.
> 2. That the monuments shall be so placed that the straight line connecting any two adjacent monuments may coincide as nearly as possible with the line of watershed, or, if the line of watershed is so crooked that this is not possible, that the areas cut off on either side of the straight line, between it and the line of watershed, may be compensated as nearly as possible.
> 3. That the monuments shall occupy naturally prominent positions, both on general grounds of advantage and so that, wherever practicable, every monument may be visible from the next one.
> 4. That no two adjacent monuments shall be more than half a mile [800 metres] apart, except in cases of practical necessity.

It is a testimony to the work of Cautley and Wheeler that during the 12 years of the boundary survey there was only one disagreement regarding the location of the line through a small portion of one pass. Eventually the commissioners decided to split the difference between the lines each claimed to be the boundary.

Once Wheeler and Cautley approved the proposed boundary line through a pass, Cautley completed the work, which included several operations. Vertical and horizontal angles had to be read at all of the stations. This would enable mapping of the boundary line through the passes and establishment of the elevation at each of these stations. The initial elevation for the boundary survey was derived from a station in Kicking Horse Pass that Wallace had established as part of his work as director of levels. There was a similar station in Crowsnest Pass. In addition, the International

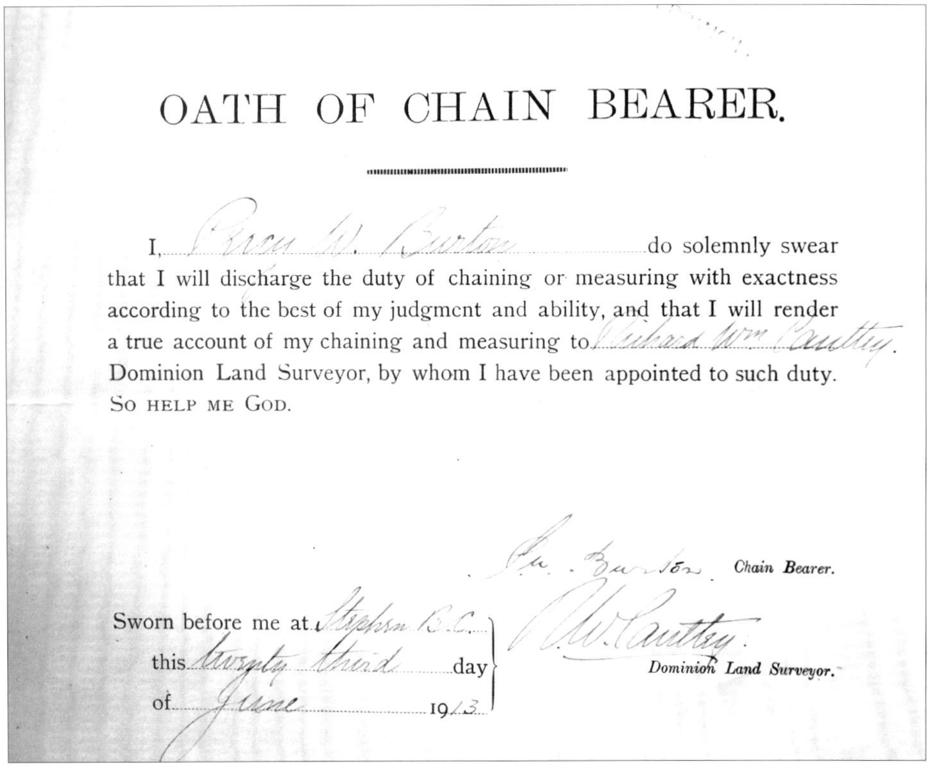

OATH OF CHAIN BEARER.

I, Percy W. Burton do solemnly swear that I will discharge the duty of chaining or measuring with exactness according to the best of my judgment and ability, and that I will render a true account of my chaining and measuring to Richard Wm Cautley. Dominion Land Surveyor, by whom I have been appointed to such duty. SO HELP ME GOD.

P.W. Burton. *Chain Bearer.*

Sworn before me at Stephen B.C.
this twenty third day
of June 1913

R.W. Cautley. *Dominion Land Surveyor.*

An accurate measurement of distance was crucial for the survey, so the crew members who did this work had to take an oath attesting to their work. Deville correspondence file 13668, Library and Archives Canada

Boundary Commission had established an elevation for Monument 272 at the intersection of Alberta, British Columbia and the United States. In surveying elevation from Crowsnest Pass to Monument 272, a direct distance of 85 kilometres, the final results showed an error of only 30 centimetres, a remarkable achievement.

The distance between the stations had to be measured and was "done with a 330 foot [100-metre] steel band tape and is all hypotenuse measurement, the angles of elevation or depression being measured with a transit and the chainage points being taken on a tripod." The survey crew tried to make the longest measurement possible, up to 100 metres, because fewer measurements usually produced more accurate results. The angle of slope was measured so that actual distance could be calculated. Every line between the

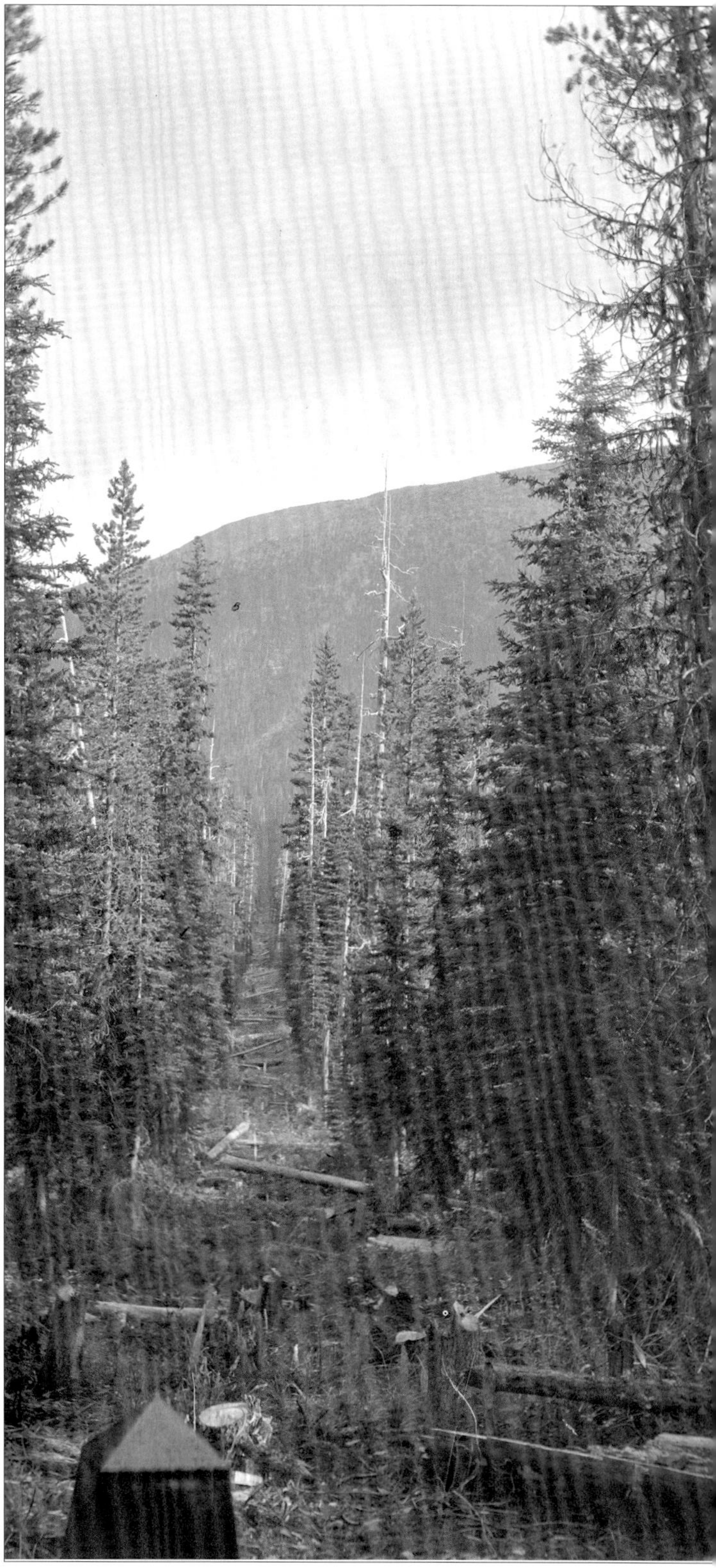

The cleared survey line on the north side of Akamina Pass. This line is still visible today. e011166465, Library and Archives Canada

monuments was chained twice, in opposite directions. The acceptable limit of error between the two measurements was one centimetre per 160 metres. If this was not achieved, the line would be measured a third time. Since the steel chain expanded and contracted depending on the temperature, thermometer readings were taken a few times during the day.

The survey line had to be cut out. "As a rule these lines occur in thickly timbered country, and they are cut out so as to give a clear opening to the sky of six feet [two metres], which means that they are from ten to fourteen feet wide [three to four metres] on the surface according to the nature of the timber."

The survey in each pass had to be connected with at least one survey post that was part of the Dominion land survey or the BC survey system. The Dominion land survey of townships, ranges, meridians and one-mile-square sections had been established across the Prairie provinces in the 19th and early 20th centuries. In most locations the Dominion land survey extended west across Alberta almost to the British Columbia border, so usually the surveyors did not have to go very far to connect the boundary survey. There were not nearly as many BC survey posts along the Great Divide, and these were primarily in the major passes.

In theory, the boundary survey stations would fit accurately with those of the Dominion land surveys. This occurred in almost all locations, but in a few places there was considerable discrepancy. The differences usually weren't found until Cautley and Wheeler were doing their winter office work. Then there would be considerable correspondence with Deville as to probable cause and how to handle the inaccuracy between the surveys.

Astronomical observations (particularly for Polaris to orient for true north), observing for the declination of the magnetic needle, and photographs of all the monuments and cleared lines were also part of Cautley's responsibilities.

The official report stated: "The system of control employed is dependent on the Dominion Lands System

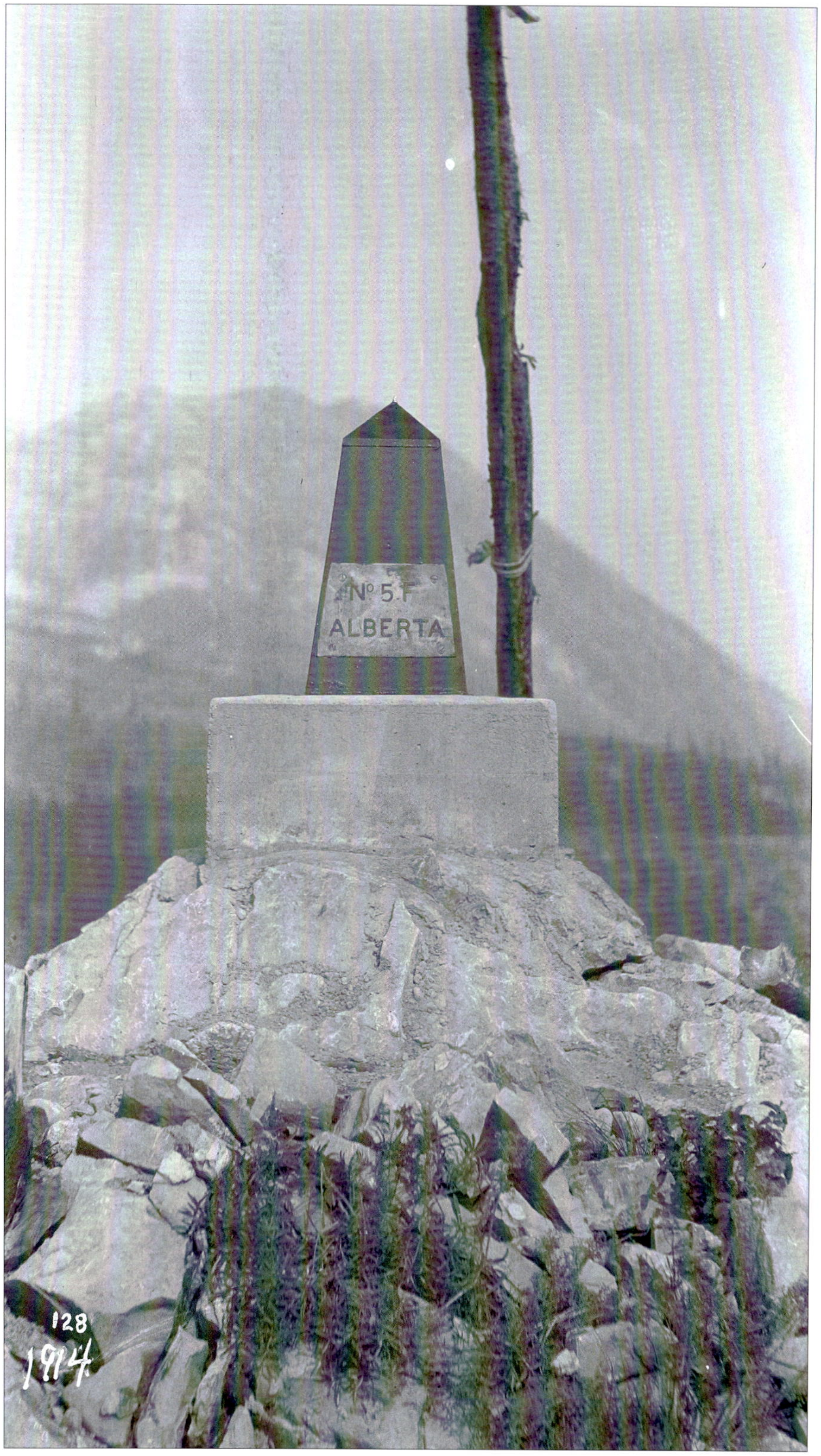

The Boundary Commissioners report used station 5F in the Crowsnest Pass as their example of a monument on the Alberta -BC boundary survey. e011166457, Library and Archives Canada

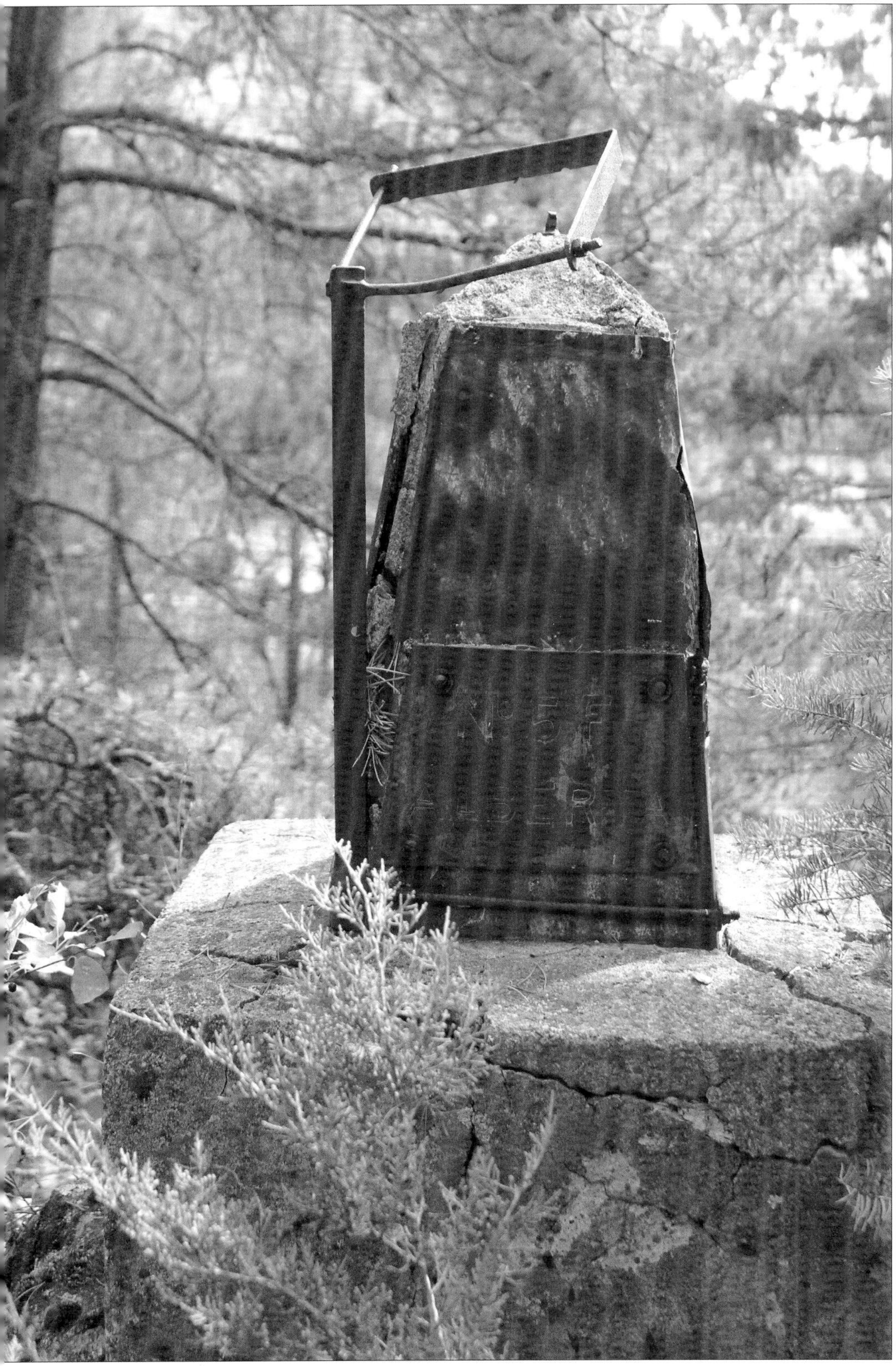

of Survey. The survey of the Boundary in almost every pass that has been surveyed has been connected with points of this System, and the latitude and longitude of the monument used as an observation station in each pass has been computed from the tables issued by the Surveyor General's office."

The distinctive feature of the survey in the passes was the construction of the monuments, and this aspect of the work was described in detail in the official report.

> The concrete monument which is erected in the passes was designed by Mr. Wheeler, and, with certain modifications suggested by Mr. Cautley, has proved to be entirely satisfactory.
>
> In essence the monument is a concrete monolith, consisting of a truncated pyramid 20 inches [50 centimetres] high, of which the bottom cross-section is 12 inches [30 centimetres] square and the top 7 inches [18 centimetres] square, having a flattish pyramidal top and set on a base 24 inches [60 centimetres] square which extends 10 inches [25 centimetres] above the ground and 36 inches [90 centimetres] into it.

If the base was filled entirely with concrete, its weight would be about 1,225 kilograms. If there was rock in the ground, all the loose rock was to be removed and the base built right on the rock. When the monument was in place it was only 90 centimetres high so the transit could be set over it.

The top part of the monument had a form made of zinc, which became the permanent outer covering. This form was filled with concrete. An iron bar protruded through the top of the zinc form and was secured in the concrete by a crosspiece [b]. Secured to the monument

The original 5F survey monument still existed in 2016. This photograph was taken at approximately the same location. In the past century trees have grown in the area, largely obscuring the mountain visible in the 1914 photograph. The amount of vegetation growth in the areas below timberline is one of the most noticeable changes in the landscape since the original boundary survey. Lodgepole pine is the tree species which has regenerated in many of these locations. Currently, the mountain pine beetle epidemic is affecting these lodgepole pine stands in many sections along the boundary, so in the coming years the landscape will change again. Photo Jay Sherwood

were brass plates with the names Alberta and British Columbia facing the province on the correct side.

The report commented that the monuments possessed great solidity and stability and were intended to resist fire and be enduring. Although many of the monuments have been replaced, some of the original ones still remain, having survived over a century in the mountains. The report noted that material for a monument could be carried piecemeal to the site. The gravel, which comprised four-fifths of the material, could usually be obtained nearby, along with the water. The bags of cement had to be transported. About 160 kilograms were used for each monument.

One of the members of Cautley's crew was designated as a monument builder. The report described the work this person did.

> The work of constructing the monuments is practically continuous, for the day after Mr. Cautley's party arrives in a new pass the packers either have to go back to the nearest railway point to bring up the cement or to find the nearest available source of good, clean gravel, and this work goes on throughout the time occupied by the preliminary survey and until the last monument is finished.
>
> Owing to the fact that the Boundary is situated on the watershed it is never possible to secure clean gravel on the spot, and it is necessary to get it from some point along one of the creeks running from the pass where the volume of water is sufficient to have caused the formation of gravel beds. Such a point can generally be found within three miles [five kilometres] of the pass at an elevation of from 600 to 1000 feet [183 to 305 metres] below it. The gravel is packed up to the pass in cement sacks.
>
> As soon as the Commissioners have determined the number and location of monuments to be built in a pass, the brass name plates have to be etched with the number of the monument and the characteristic letter of the pass in which it is built....
>
> The monument nearest to the lowest summit of a pass, i.e. the lowest point of its

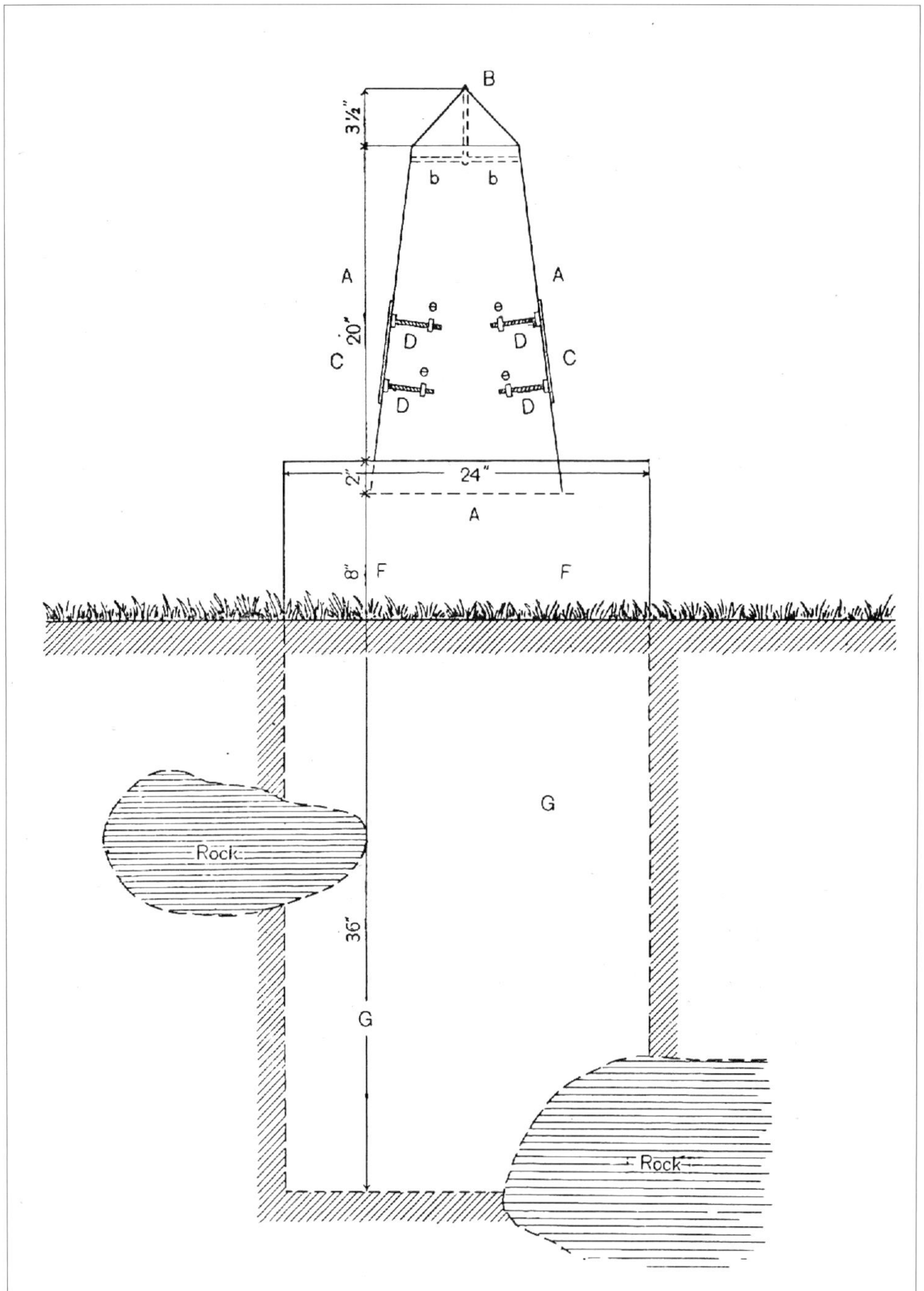

SHOWING CONSTRUCTION OF CONCRETE MONUMENT

This diagram of a monument was included in the first Boundary Commissioners report. Report of the Commission to Delimit the Boundary between the Provinces of Alberta and British Columbia

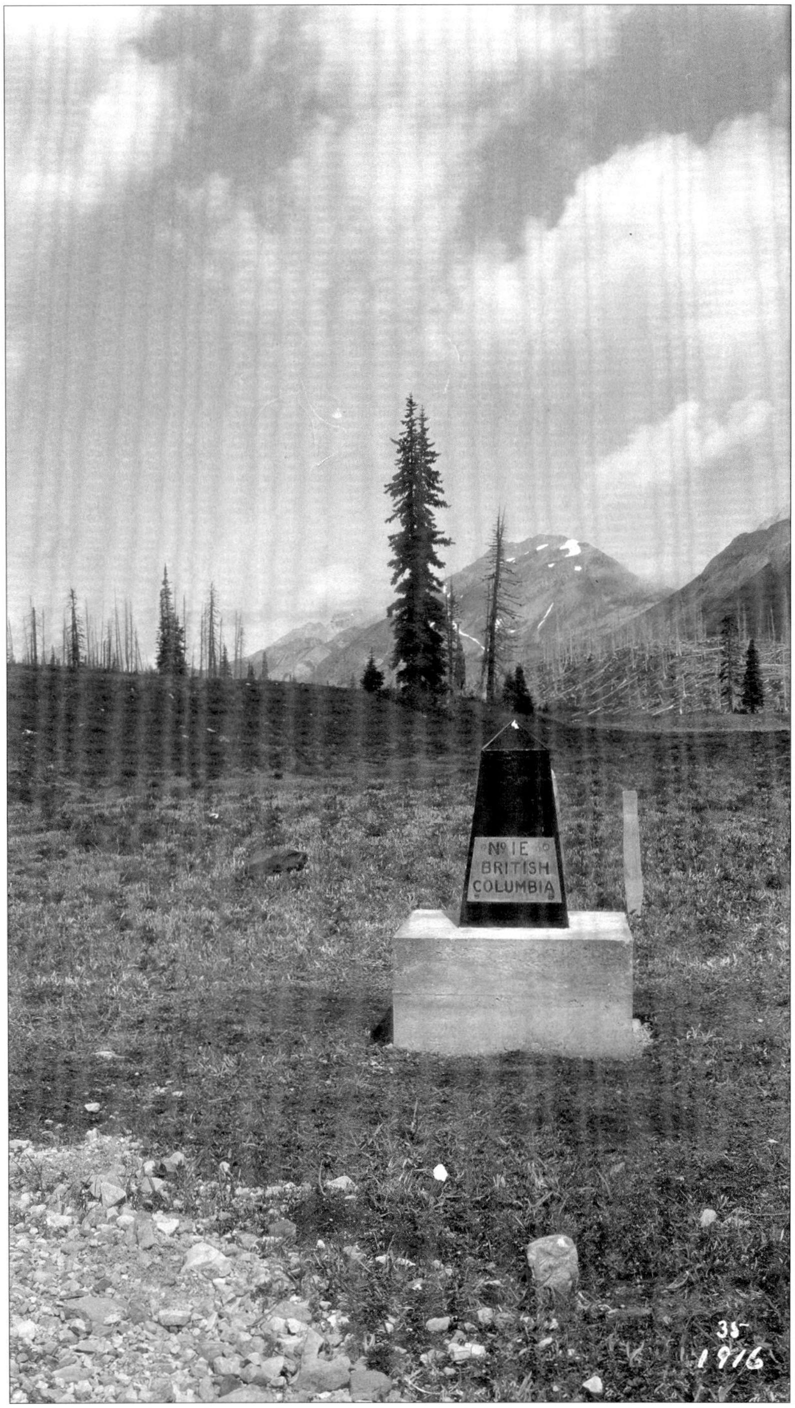

Monument 1E at the lowest point along the boundary in Palliser Pass. e011166477, Library and Archives Canada

cross-section along the watershed, is numbered 1. Proceeding from No. 1, those monuments that are built along the watershed on its course to the north boundary of the two Provinces are numbered consecutively 2, 4, 6, etc., and those that are built on its course to the International Boundary are numbered 3, 5, 7, etc.…

The brass plates are then bolted to one of the zinc forms and the iron bar, shown as B in Fig. 1, is soldered into position so that it will not move when the form is being filled with concrete. The zinc form is then taken to the monument site, fitted into a heavy wooden case, bottom up, and filled with concrete. On the same day the hole is excavated for the base of the monument in such a position that those sides of the monument which bear the name plates shall be at right angles to the lines which bisects the angle between the two adjacent courses of the Boundary. The monument builder then proceeds to another site so as to allow the concrete in the monument top to set, which, in good weather, only takes 24 hours. Next day the hole is filled with concrete to within two inches of ground level; the wooden form for the base is then set in position, by means of the reference picket set for that purpose, and filled with concrete. The monument top is then turned out of its wooden form and lifted into position on the wet concrete base, where it is worked down to a seat on four small wooden pegs which have been set, and levelled, to receive it two inches below the surface of the concrete in the wooden base form. The surface concrete is then trowelled smooth, and the monument is watched for a while to see that there is no likelihood of subsidence which might cause the top to set out of plumb.

The concrete is made in the proportion of one part of cement to four parts of gravel, and is well mixed and puddled; this mixture is

> somewhat richer than is ordinarily used, but has been adopted because the body of concrete in a monument is small, requiring greater power of cement than would be necessary in a larger body, and also with the idea of overcoming any defects in the gravel, which is not always as good as what would be used in ordinary concrete construction.
>
> When the concrete has set dry the wooden form is removed from the base, and the zinc cover is painted a bright red. This colour has been adopted by the Commission as being most distinctly visible, both against the green background of summer or the white background of winter.

Concrete monuments were used for all stations in a pass as long as it was possible to do so. However, on a few occasions it was necessary to use a brass bolt and cairn. One of the stations in Vermilion Pass was on top of a rock bluff that was inaccessible to horses. The report also described the situation at the highest stations in a pass.

> Usually the last straight course on either side of a pass is terminated by a bolt and cairn, because the terminal point selected by the Commission is generally inaccessible to horses. This is due to the feeling of the Commission that the straight line boundary should be carried beyond timber line to some prominent terminal point whence the position of the natural boundary, or watershed, is clearly defined, in all cases where such a line can be found which fairly conforms to the watershed.

The report also noted:

> Beyond the last course of the straight line boundary Mr. Wheeler uses bolts to mark dominating points of the watershed in the immediate vicinity of the passes. These bolts are used by him as triangulation stations, and are closely connected with all other monuments of the survey.

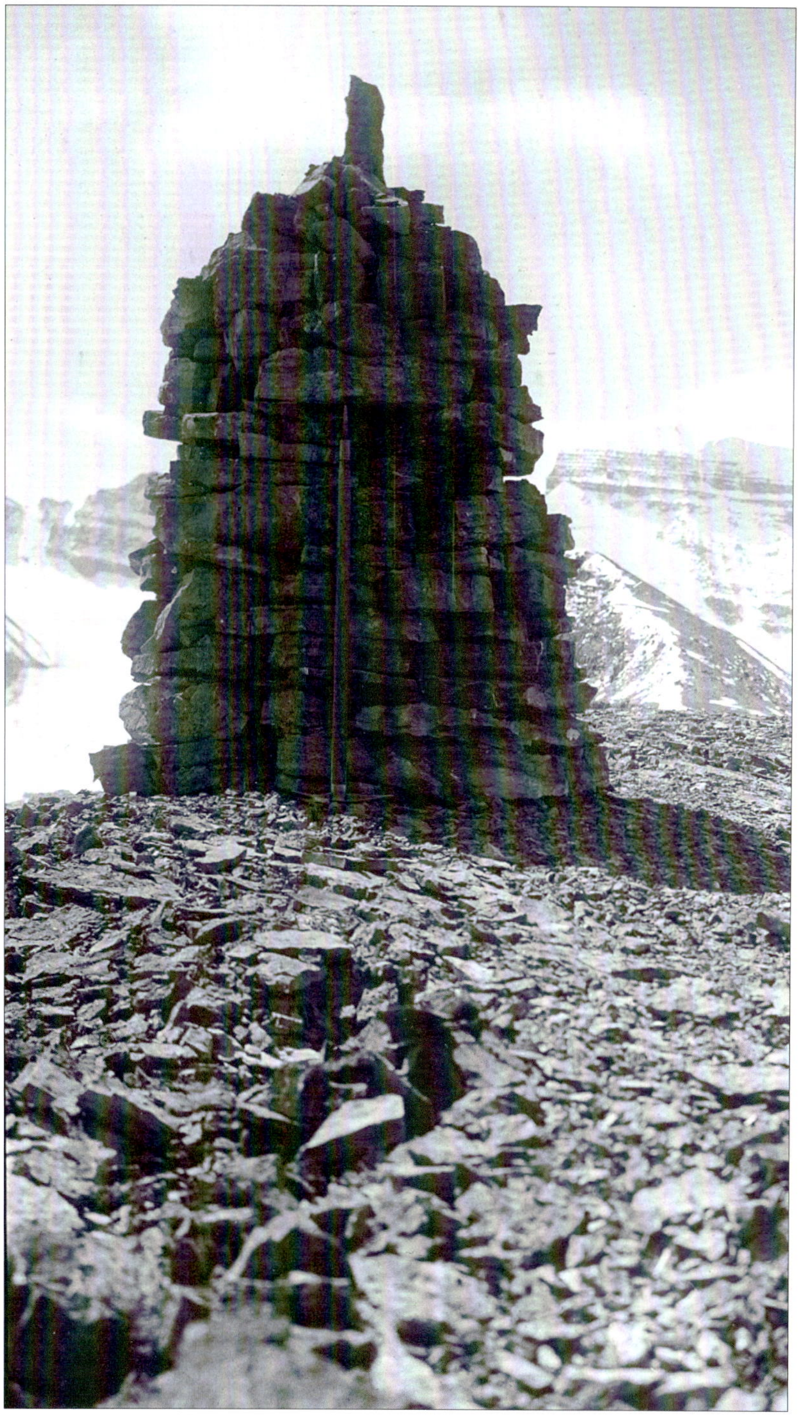

This bolt and cairn station is the highest and most southerly in Kicking Horse Pass. Wheeler 1913 photo album, Alberta surveyor general's office

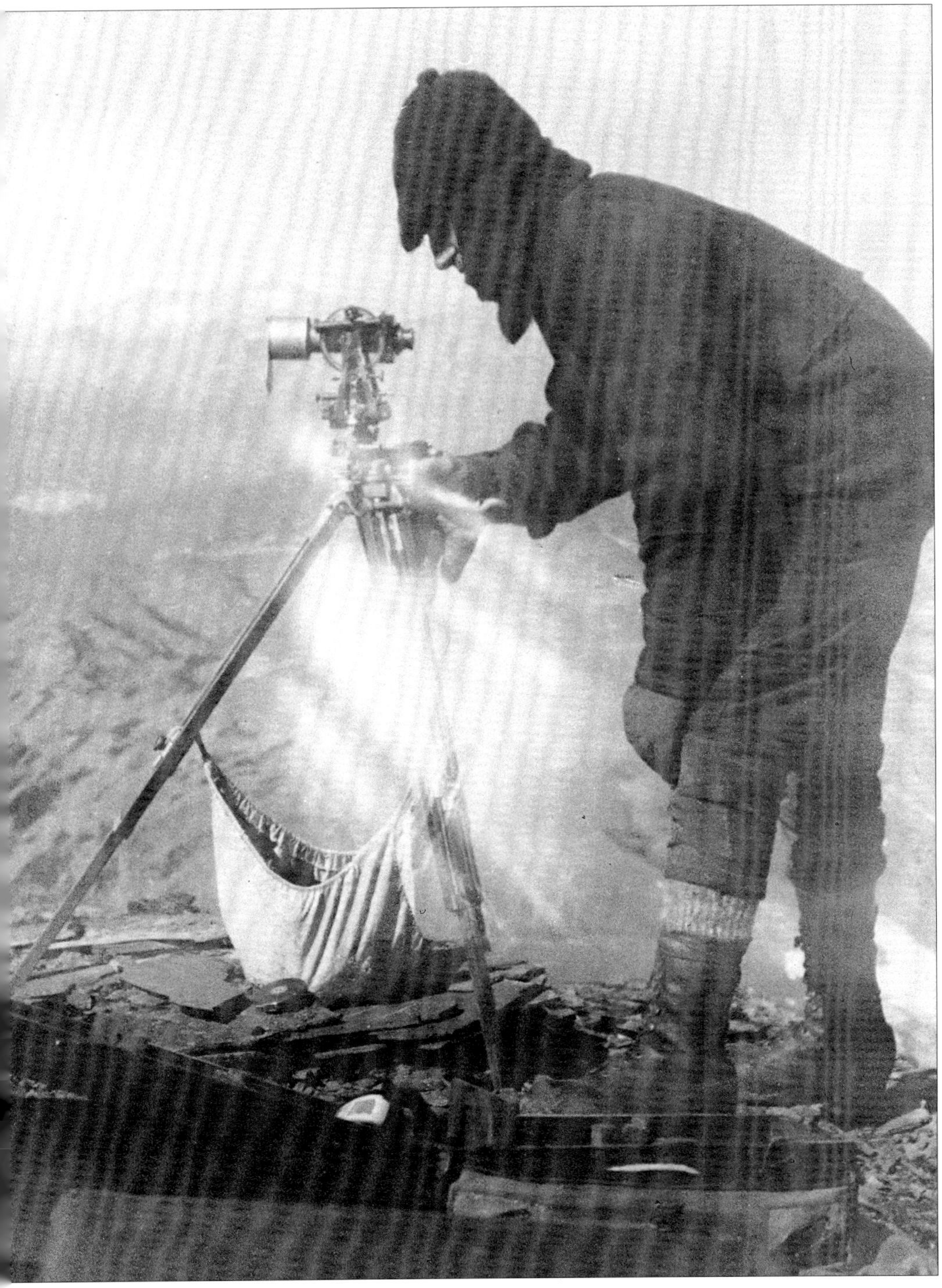

Spike Thomson took this photograph of the mountain transit in action. The small sack that was filled with stones to provide stability in windy conditions is visible. A10728, Provincial Archives of Alberta

> Since the position of bolts and cairns is accurately determined by the Commission, in relation to the other monuments of the Boundary survey, and to the points of the Dominion Lands System connected therewith, and the cairns are generally visible for miles on either side of a pass, it is possible for a surveyor employed to make land surveys within a reasonable distance of a pass to tie on to the Boundary survey by methods of a triangulation.…It is considered probable that these outlying bolts of the pass surveys will be found very useful, and will be extensively used in the years to come.

To construct a bolt, a hole was drilled into solid rock and a brass bolt cemented into it. The bolt had a shank 10 centimetres long with a rectangular top. A cross was stamped on the top, with the names Alberta and British Columbia stamped on the longer sides. Once the bolt was set and all of the surveying and phototopographic work was finished, a cairn about 1.5 metres high was built. Usually one or two of the crew would start constructing it while the surveyor was working, generally beginning on the windward side to provide some shelter.

To accomplish their surveying, Wheeler and Cautley (except for 1913) both had an assistant surveyor. Each crew had its own cook, packer and assistant packer. Cautley's work was more labour intensive, so he had a larger crew. There were two chainmen for measuring the survey line, and a monument builder. In addition, there were usually two axemen to clear the line. Wheeler had a small crew on the mountains. Normally, one or two men assisted Wheeler and Campbell with the surveying. During 1913 and the first part of 1914, Wheeler employed Conrad Kain to lead the mountain climbing.

While Cautley surveyed in the main passes, Wheeler worked on surveying and mapping along the course of the Great Divide. The report described the purpose of the BC commissioner's work.

> The survey of the Boundary beyond the passes is carried on as a topographical delineation of

> the watershed by means of photo-topography depending on an extended system of triangulation. The Boundary thus established is the natural watershed and is therefore not marked with monuments, but it is capable of being mapped with a greater accuracy than could possibly be attained in any other way. Besides this primary object of the topographical work, it supplies a wealth of detailed information in regard to the mountains, valleys, forests, lakes and watershed system on either side of the actual watershed which is, for the most part, quite original and invaluable to the geographer and scientist.

The report noted: "The topographical work of the Commission is entirely in the hands of Mr. Wheeler. It consists in the delineation of the watershed along the main range from the International Boundary northward to the final crossing of the 120th meridian of west longitude." There were two main aspects of Wheeler's work: the triangulation survey and the photography. In triangulation surveying, if two angles and a distance of a triangle are known, the remaining angle and distances can be computed. From mountain peaks Wheeler would survey to other stations and peaks in the area, creating a network of triangles. Wheeler would use Cautley's stations in the passes, with their known angles and distance to assist in his triangulation work. While the surveying provided the framework for mapping the Rocky Mountains, the phototopography enabled him to map the details. The report commented that "it was decided to adopt the method of phototopography as the one best suited to the mapping of the highly accentuated contours of mountain areas."

The report described the process.

> The work requires a specially constructed camera and mountain transit-theodolite. It is carried on by climbing to previously selected stations at the summits of peaks, or to high points on mountain ridges that command a view of the area to be mapped. From these a series of views is taken and their direction established by the use of the transit-theodolite, frequently entailing a precarious balancing over dizzy depths. Rock cairns are erected at the selected stations, either in advance or at the time they are occupied, and are used for identification purposes.
>
> The stations are fixed in position by a triangulation of a greater or less degree of precision, expanded from a given base and extended over the required area. This triangulation may be made independently or be carried on at the same time as the photographing.

Usually the triangulation surveying and phototopography were done at the same time, for the surveyors did not want to climb a mountain more than once unless necessary. In addition to the main surveying station, Wheeler or his assistant, Campbell, would occasionally establish a second station that was primarily for phototopography. Usually this station was at a lower elevation but with a better view of the terrain.

The phototopographic camera was designed to fit on the same tripod as the transit, so that both operations could be completed while working at a survey station. In addition to measuring angles, it was important to determine the elevation of the stations and the geographical features.

> The altitudes of the various points are obtained by reading angles of elevation or depression back and forth from point to point and applying the necessary corrections for curvature and refraction, a process known technically as trigonometric levelling.
>
> The chief advantage of the method is its rapidity for work in the field. It is much more rapid than any other that can be applied to the same class of country and the standard of accuracy is a high one. It is true that work can only be carried on in fine weather, when the stations are below the clouds and the landscape is sufficiently clear to be photographed, but the same limitation applies to any other method that can be used. Only a small party, generally a surveyor and one or two assis-

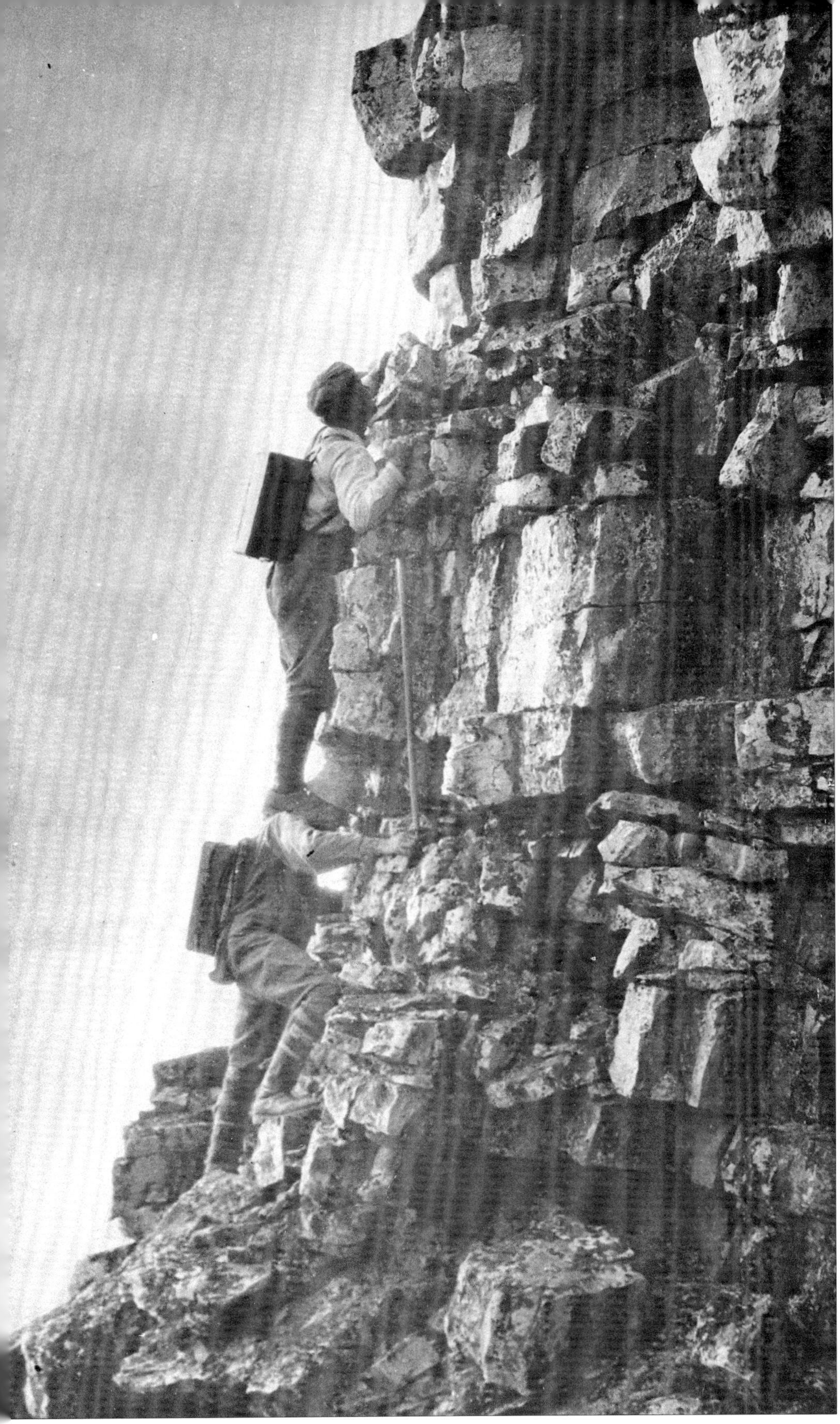

tants, is required to carry the instruments, take the views, record the transit reading and build the rock cairns or other signals that may be erected to mark the stations it is desired to perpetuate. The instrument outfit, adapted by Dr. Deville, weighs about 45 lbs. [20 kilograms], and is so disposed as to be easily carried, even when the climbing is dangerous.

The camera is of fixed focus and has a wide-angle lens covering about 52 degrees of arc for one view. It is adapted in two positions to a light, strong tripod with sliding legs, to which are attached levelling screws to bring the plate exposed in the camera to a vertical position, an absolute necessity to obtain suitable views. The same tripod fits the transit-theodolite. [Each photograph covered about 45 degrees of the landscape with a couple of degrees overlap on each side. A set of eight photographs would cover the entire scene.]

The size of the plate used is 6½" by 4¾" [16 by 12 centimetres], and the lens gives very nearly a true perspective. Later, in the office, the plates are developed and bromide enlargements, 9½ by 13 inches [23 by 33 centimetres], are made for mapping purposes. Practically speaking they are perspectives of the views and, by means of geometric and perspective constructions, the position and altitude of points seen in them can be obtained and the contour outlines of the various topographical features drawn on the plan.…In the mapping room, this chaotic condition soon resolves itself into orderly array.…

There are certain factors necessary to the conduct of a survey such as this, for instance: the triangulation on which the photographic work depends must start from a measured base and be expanded in sufficiently symmetrical proportions; the altitude above sea-level of one or both ends of the base must be known; and there must be independent checks on the expansion of the triangulation

Spike Thomson and A.J. Campbell climbing Mt. Fitzwilliam in 1917. PR1973.0534.0018, Provincial Archives of Alberta

at sufficiently close intervals to keep the work within bounds of the limit of accuracy.

The report concluded its discussion of Wheeler's work by stating:

> In the survey under discussion, the series of traverse lines accurately surveyed by Mr. Cautley's division across each pass furnishes a base from which to start and on which to check. These bases are connected with the Dominion system of land surveys and are as accurately fixed in position as those surveys will permit. The triangulation has been carried on at the same time as the photographing and the stations occupied have been fixed in position by reading horizontal angles, and in altitude by reading vertical angles, from one to the other.

In his 1913 report to the BC government, Wheeler wrote that the work of surveying on the mountains had both a routine and dangerous aspect. "Outside of the difficulties of carrying the survey instruments to the summits of commanding peaks, a process entailing all the delights and dangers of mountaineering of a high order, after a few years experience, the work becomes mechanical, except for the glories opened up by each new climb amidst the wonderful alpine scenery displayed by the Canadian Rockies." The vagaries of the weather in the mountains often produced difficulties. On many occasions the survey crews would leave camp in clear weather in the morning, only to find that conditions had changed by the time they reached the locations on the mountains where they planned to survey. Wheeler wrote: "To be perched on a high peak with standing room only when a tempest of snow scours over it is by no means a joy; neither is an electric storm, when your transit sings like a telegraph wire and to touch it gives you a sharp shock, when the rocks around you hum and your hair stands straight on end."

The surveying talents of both Cautley and Wheeler were essential for the success of the Alberta–British Columbia boundary survey. Each person had his own responsibilities, but they worked harmoniously and combined the information they gathered to produce a precise, comprehensive survey

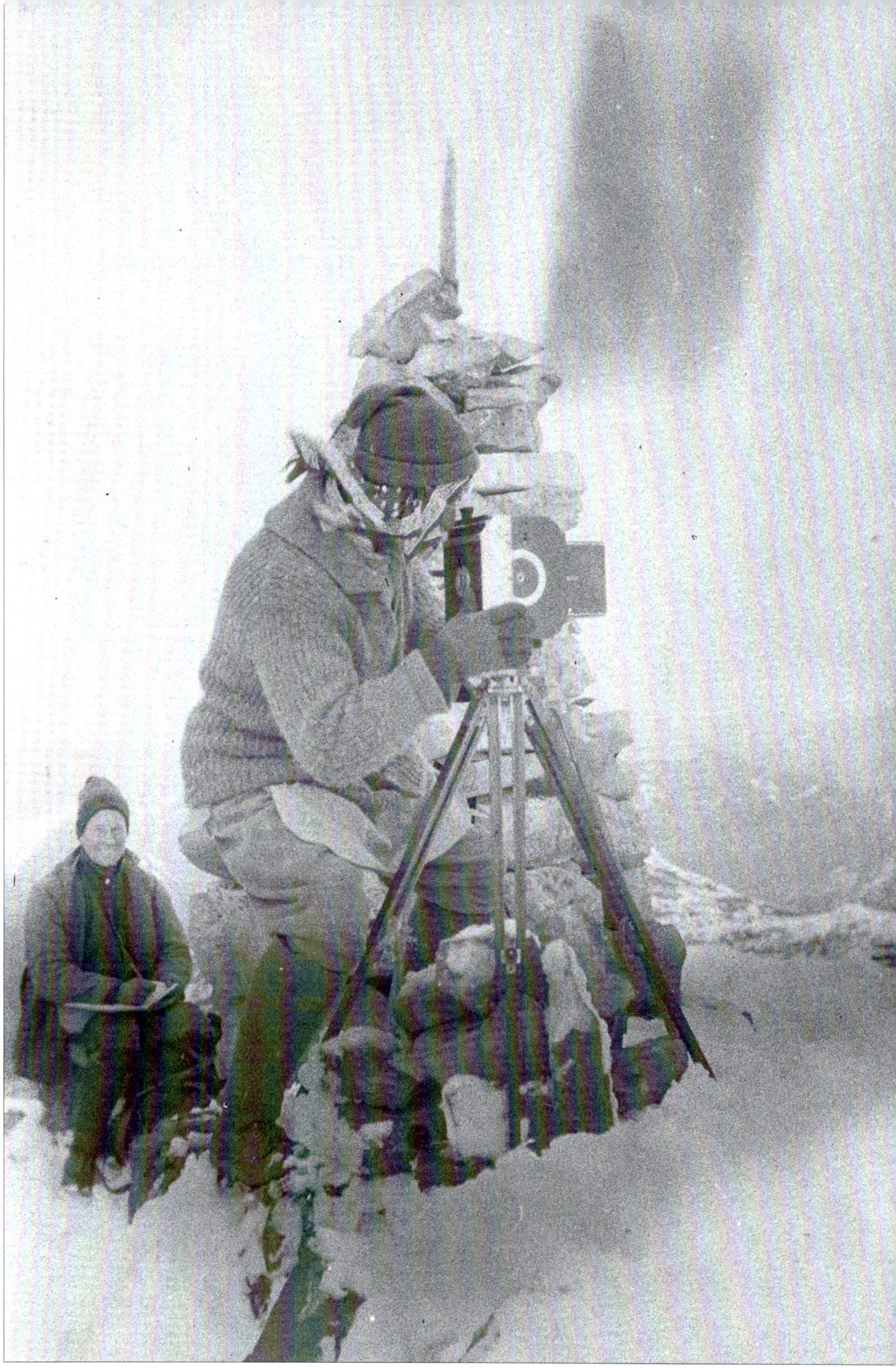

Spike Thomson took this photograph of Wheeler using the phototopographic camera which is set up beside the cairn for one of the stations. The man in the background (probably A.J. Campbell) is recording Wheeler's survey measurements. A10726, Provincial Archives of Alberta

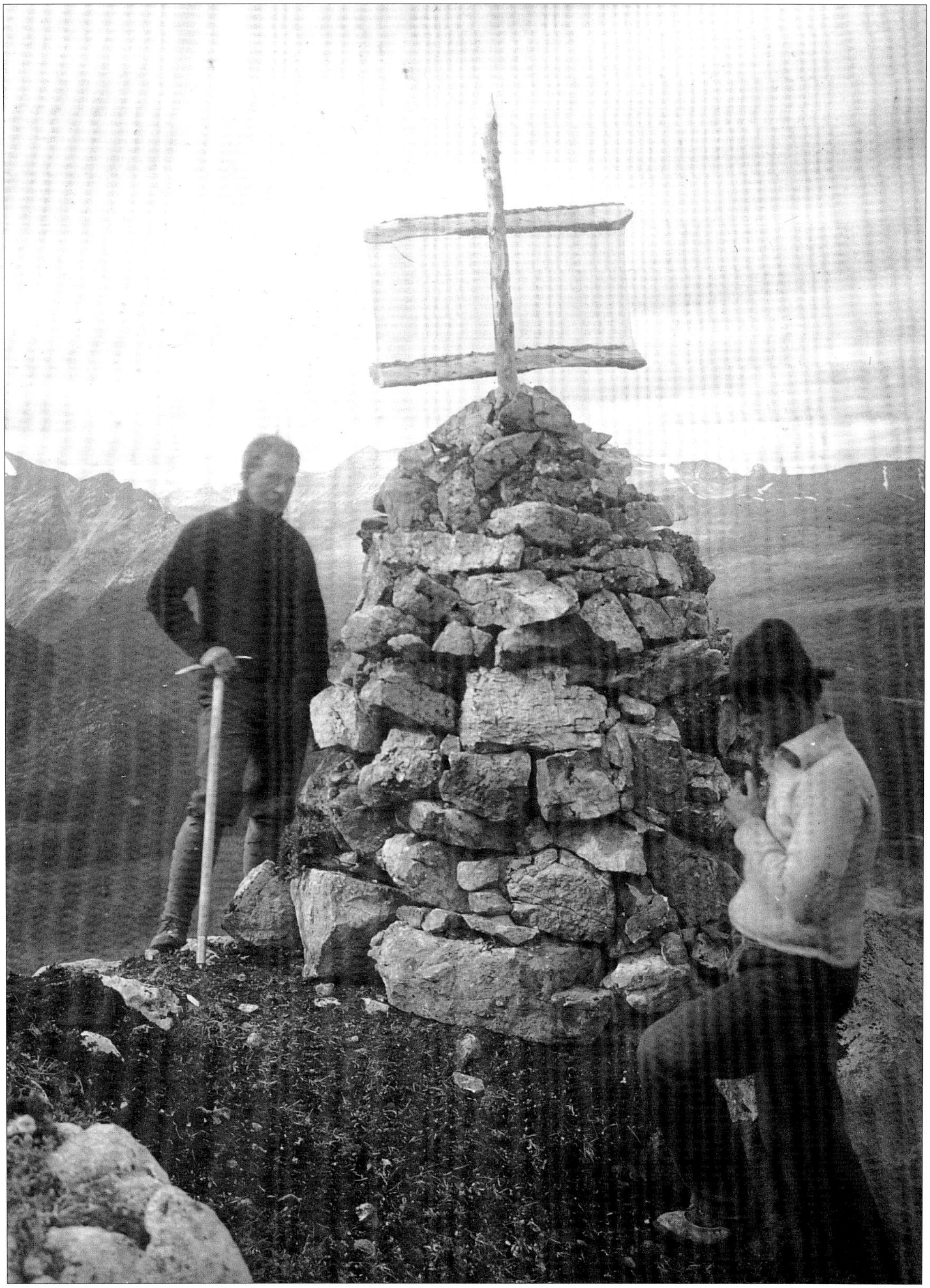

A.H. (Alfred Henry) Brinkman (left) and Conrad Kain (right) at Station 11A near the top of the south side of Kicking Horse Pass.

In 1908 Brinkman immigrated to Canada from England with his wife and two children. He had a lifelong interest in collecting and identifying mosses and lichens, and became one of Canada's leading experts in this field. Through this work Brinkman met the famous Canadian naturalist, John Macoun, the father-in-law of A.O. Wheeler. Between 1909 and 1912 he worked on Wheeler's survey crews for a few summers, and for the Alpine Club of Canada. During the 1913 survey Brinkman spent time collecting material in the evenings or on days when the men were not surveying. There are several items from his collection that are identified with locations and dates that were on the 1913 boundary survey. Today Brinkman's extensive collection is housed at some major universities and herbariums in the United States and Canada.

Conrad Kain, one of Canada's most famous mountaineering guides, made the first ascent of many peaks in the Canadian Rockies, including Mount Robson. Kain worked on the Alberta–British Columbia boundary survey in 1913, part of 1914, and in 1919. Mount Nasswald, in the Mount Assiniboine area, is named for Kain's home village in Austria. Wheeler 1913 photo album, Alberta surveyor general's office

1913

Confident that the boundary survey would begin during the 1913 field season, A.O. Wheeler began planning several months in advance. It was going to be an important summer, and there was one person that he needed to assist him. Conrad Kain, the famous Austrian mountain climber and guide, came to Canada in June 1909. During the next three summers he guided climbs for Wheeler's Alpine Club of Canada members. Then, in the spring of 1912, Kain left on a trip around the world and was now climbing the highest peaks in New Zealand. On January 27, 1913, Wheeler wrote to Kain:

> Are you coming back to Canada this summer? I can offer you a job on photo-survey work along the Continental Divide for the full summer, if you care to have it! At $3 per day. It will be a new territory. Mt Assiniboine and south. I would need you by 1 June. We are holding two camps this summer, one at Lake O'Hara and one at Robson Pass. I should want you for Robson camp. There will be several attempts to make the ascent of Robson from the east side. How does this prospect strike you, old boy? If you come back by 1 of May, we can get to work at the clubhouse until we are ready to start in June. I expect you will know something about New Zealand Alps before you return. We miss you from the Rockies and we all hope you will come back. You know you're welcome at any hour and we do our best for you. Auf Wiedersehen! Yours faithfully, A.O. Wheeler.

Kain's 27-year correspondence with Amelie Malek, who was an Austrian guiding client and friend, has survived, and it contains several letters from 1913. Kain shared the contents of Wheeler's letter with Malek and wrote: "Well, what do you say to that? It pleases me a little that one misses me there! I also know why!! So I have to go back to Canada. The wages are not bad, $3 and free room and board. Maybe I'll earn a little on the side."

In 1909 Rev. George Kinney and guide Curly Phillips claimed the first ascent of Mount Robson, the highest peak in the Canadian Rockies. However, the weather was cloudy, and there was doubt as to whether the two men had reached the actual summit. Kain had been with Wheeler on the 1911 Smithsonian expedition to Mount Robson, and though they looked at the route that Kinney and Phillips had followed, there was no attempt to have a group of climbers reach the summit, despite several days of good weather. For the summer of 1913 Wheeler planned to have an Alpine Club of Canada (ACC) camp at Mount Robson, and to have a group climb the peak for the first verified ascent. He wanted Kain to be the guide.

In addition, Wheeler would be away from the boundary survey for a few weeks, leaving A.J. Campbell, his assistant, in charge. Campbell had no experience with mountain climbing, and Wheeler wanted Kain to tutor him, getting him to be comfortable on mountain terrain.

Other members of Wheeler's talented and diverse crew included A.H. Brinkman, an avid bryophyte collector; Paul Wallace (no relation to J.N. Wallace), who became a university professor in the United States; cook Jack Stelfox, who wrote reminiscences of his three years on boundary survey crews; and packer Bob Logan.

Even though Crowsnest Pass was considered to have the most economic importance, the boundary commissioners decided to begin the survey at Kicking Horse Pass. It was not nearly as extensive as Crowsnest Pass, but it was one of the major passes and the commissioners considered it a good location for Wheeler and Cautley to survey together. The pass had railroad access, making it easy to transport people and supplies. It was close to Calgary and Banff, where J.N. Wallace and Wheeler lived, and Cautley was able to travel to the site by train. Unfortunately, forest fires had burned much of the vegetation in the

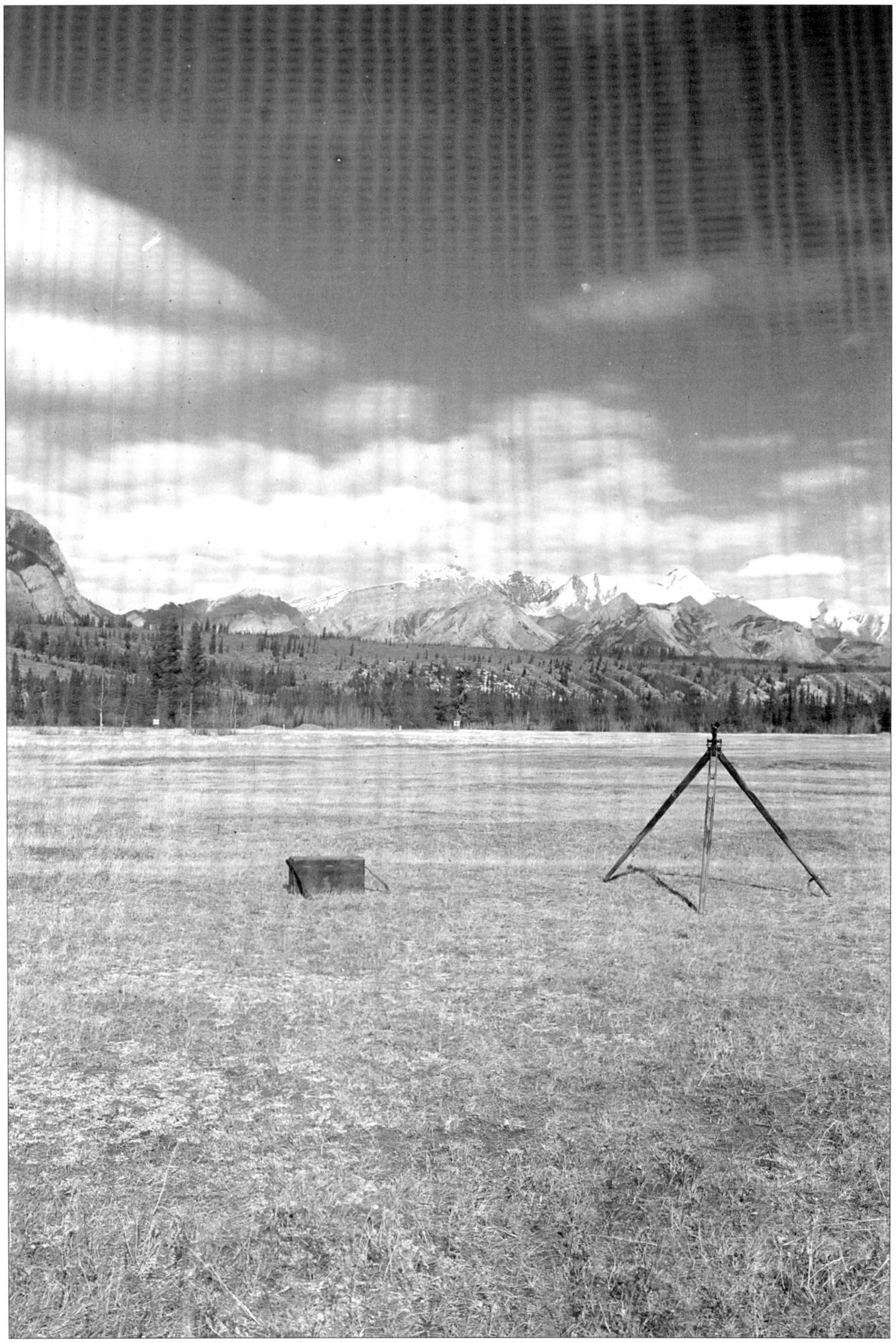

Testing the phototopographic cameras at the Banff golf course. The targets appear in the background at ground level as two bright dots. (The one on the left is at the base of a tall tree.) It was important that the cameras were properly adjusted and level. e007140299, Library and Archives Canada

pass, but this made it easier for the surveyors to define the boundary and survey the monuments. The gravel and water needed for the monuments was readily available, and the bags of cement would not have to be transported far.

For the summer of 1913 Wheeler hired Paul Wallace to be his personal secretary and assist in organizing both the boundary survey and the summer ACC camps. Wallace was a young university student from Ontario who had come to the 1912 ACC camp, although he hadn't done any mountain climbing. Wallace, who arrived at Banff on May 25, kept a diary and wrote letters to his family. On May 28 he wrote in his diary:

> Left at 10:10 for Stephen with Mr. Campbell.... The train did not stop at Stephen, but crossed the divide and slid down to Hector, two miles below. There we tried to get a hand car to carry about 200lbs [90 kilograms] of stuff back to Stephen. We did not succeed. We waited for a freight train that came along at noon, but did not succeed in getting a lift even on it.
>
> Just then a man came tramping up the track from Field, with an old valise in his hand. He offered to help us carry our things up to the pass. We broke open the large box of provisions and shared lunch with him. After lunch, as we were rearranging everything in bundles as conveniently as possible for the two mile carry, two tramps came up the track. Campbell spoke to them, and they turned in to help us. So we five tramped up the railway track to the summit of the Kicking Horse Pass. I carried a bag with flour, rolled oats, and butter. Mr. Campbell made a tump line out of my belt and some rope, and thus equipped, carried a valise full of canned food. The first tramp, who is at this moment sitting with me by an evening fire in front of my tent, carried a camp stove that clanked at each step. One of the gentle desperados carried a bag of potatoes, a roll of his own clothes the size of a double load of bread, and a valise; the other carried an awkward roll of tents and bedding.

We reached Stephen and the two docile desperados, after being paid 50c each, departed down the track toward Laggan [now called Lake Louise]. The first tramp remained with us, helped put up the tent, and shared our supper in the evening. I rather think he is going to share my blanket, too.

Campbell caught the 6 o'clock train for the east, and I remained behind to look out for Mr. Wheeler's camp supplies that are to come by freight.

The mountains about here are bare except for patches of spring snow, rugged but not very beautiful.

The water we drink is from the Pacific branch of the famous stream that comes to the parting of the ways on the Great Divide, one branch flowing to the Pacific, the other to the Atlantic Ocean.

The tramp did share my blanket, as I expected, and he made himself useful washing dishes, chopping wood, and putting up the extra tent for the stores when they come....

There was a heavy frost during the night, and we got so cold that we found it more comfortable to build a large fire and keep close to it. I got about 2 hours sleep in short snatches....

Mr. Davis arrived at 12 o'clock, and I indulged in a sleep in the sun in place of lunch....

I caught the eastbound express at 6:10 and made a slow trip to Banff, arriving there at 8 o'clock. The sky was clear, and the slanting rays of the setting sun threw the mountains into strong relief, and gave the snow a radiant glow.

Wheeler needed to get the phototopographic cameras ready for the field season. Since it was the first year of the boundary survey, he required a large supply of plates. Deville tried to expedite this order by having them shipped directly from the Cranmer Dry Plate Company in St. Louis to Banff. Unfortunately, the express car in which they were being transported burned in Medicine Hat, so Deville had to rush a duplicate order. On June 1 Wallace accompanied Wheeler to the Banff golf course to test the phototopographic cameras. Wallace described the adventure.

We drove to the golf links (government owned). On the way we passed the Bow Falls, a broad chute of foaming water confined by regular, wooded banks of no great height.

Everything went wrong in the work. We got camera targets up on tree trunks, then found that one of them was overshadowed by a huge pine branch. So Campbell climbed up and cut it down. Then the wind was so strong that it was almost impossible to adjust the cameras. Something went wrong with a screw, and Campbell rushed off to get a new one. He made the journey from the centre of the links to the Alpine Club house and back inside 50 minutes. Five minutes before he returned, McCaw got the refractory screw to work. [R.D. McCaw was doing a phototopographical survey of the BC section of the Banff-Windermere Highway for the province's Public Works Department.]

Wheeler was beginning to mutter some theological language by this time as he struggled with the camera. The tripod was very carefully adjusted, and he was in the act of putting the camera in its place when his foot slipped, the camera slipped from his hand and rolled away, and he fell heavily on the tripod, knocking it quite out of position. Wheeler's theological language increased in strength and volume.

A few minutes later, after taking a photograph, he handed McCaw a plate. At the critical moment when McCaw's hand was closing on the plate and Wheeler's hand was letting go, McCaw's foot slipped and he and the plate fell in different directions.

To add to our discomfort, the air was full of golf balls. One went between the legs of the level, others dropped about our heads. While fixing a target, Campbell and I had the satisfaction of hearing two consecutive plunks,

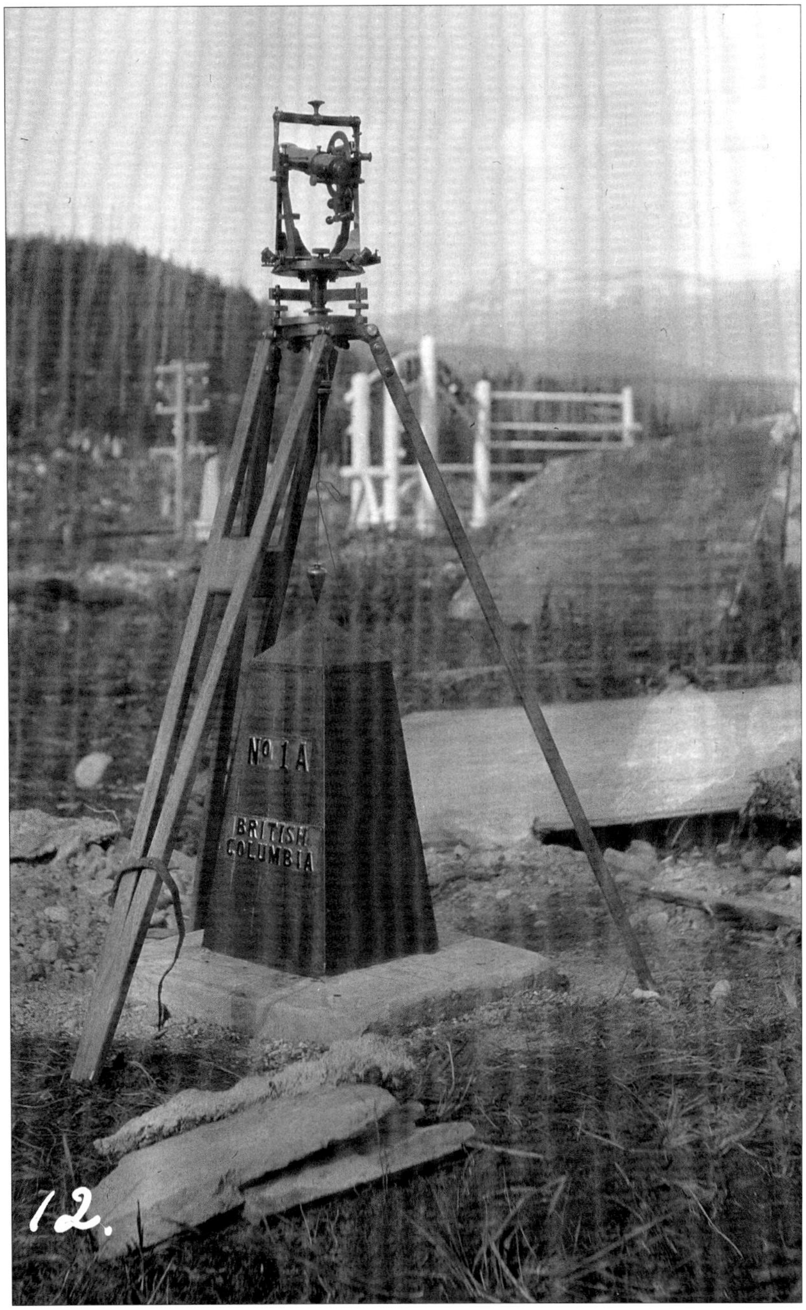

Cautley took this photo of Monument 1A at the lowest point along the boundary in Kicking Horse Pass. He described it as 'the first and worst' monument that his crew constructed. Cautley and his monument builder needed practice and experimentation to learn how to construct the monuments successfully. It is a testament to the work of Cautley and his crew that a large number of the monuments they constructed have survived for over a century in the rugged mountain conditions and weather. e011166491, Library and Archives Canada

> and seeing two balls floating in a pond beside us, just out of reach.

In a letter to his mother Wallace wrote: "'The old man', as everybody calls him, has been kindness itself to me—never varying once from what he was like when Muriel met him at the A.C.C. dinner. Everybody tells me how terrible he is, and I have to take it on faith."

In early June Campbell took Wheeler's crew and started some preliminary work in Kicking Horse Pass. Wheeler went to Victoria to meet the surveyor general, then returned to meet Cautley and J.N. Wallace on June 9 and 10 in Banff, where they developed their recommendations for surveying the Alberta–British Columbia boundary.

In his diary entry for June 12 Paul Wallace noted a visit from R.D. McCaw. The boundary survey would connect with McCaw's when they reached Vermilion Pass later in the summer. "Mr. McCaw came into Banff with the fire warden on his velocipede. He has made his first climb—up the eastern buttress of Mount Whymper."

Wallace also wrote about his visit to Kicking Horse Pass the previous day.

> Yesterday I was up to Stephen and back with letters for Campbell and his party. I reached there at 2:30 and met [Jack] Stelfox, the cook. He fired two shots with a revolver as a signal to Campbell, but nobody came. I sauntered up the low ridge north of the "Great Divide" sign and shouted—but with no effect.
>
> Stelfox told me that tramps were passing all day long. A couple began to get saucy, and he took a twelve-shooter automatic revolver, and persuaded them to move on.

On June 13 McCaw and Wheeler spent time working on the cameras to be used for both phototopographic surveys. During the next two days, Wheeler visited Campbell in Kicking Horse Pass and went to Lake O'Hara to check on preparations for the Alpine Club camp there. On June 17 he went to Vermilion Pass and spent three days with McCaw. Wheeler looked at some of the potential stations that Campbell would be surveying there while Wheeler was at the ACC camps.

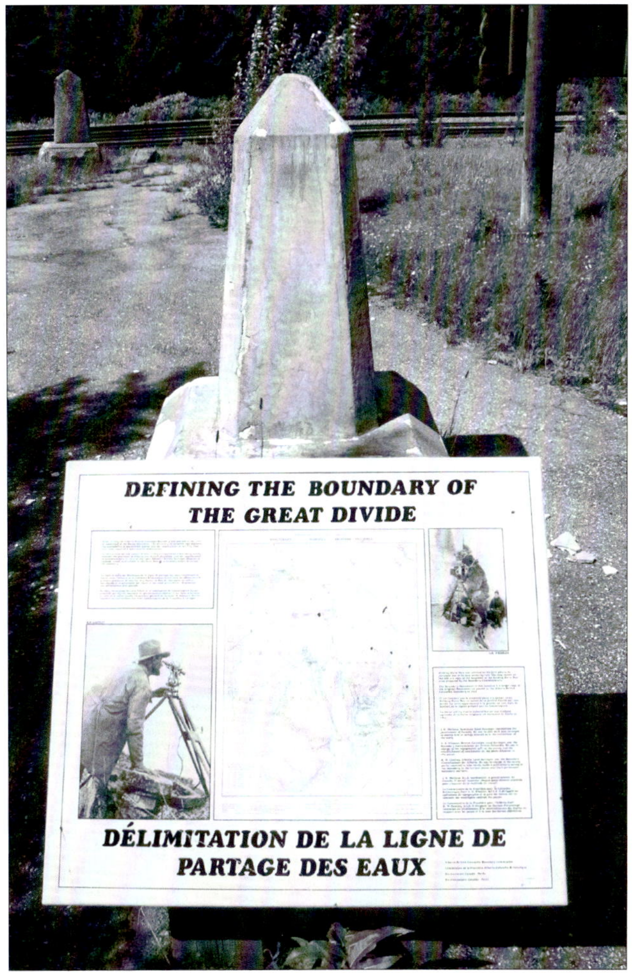

An interpretive display in Kicking Horse along the original highway describes the work of the boundary survey. Monument 1A (which has been moved to this site) is in the foreground. The monument by the train tracks is dedicated to the famous naturalist John Macoun. Photo Jay Sherwood

He and McCaw also climbed to the shoulder of Storm Mountain and took a set of photographs from the station there. On the train trip from Castle Mountain to Banff, Wheeler met Conrad Kain. Kain, who had left New Zealand on May 23, was just arriving in Banff.

After a short trip to Calgary and Edmonton, where he met Cautley and organized supplies for the Robson ACC camp, Wheeler returned to Banff. On June 25 Wheeler went to Kicking Horse Pass to begin working on the boundary survey. Cautley arrived a few hours later, and in the afternoon Cautley, Campbell and Wheeler spent time walking through the pass. It was raining the next day, so the two crews didn't accomplish much work.

Jack Stelfox recalled conditions. "The camp was in a swampy place across a small stream. There was quite a little snow on the ground at this time and the prospect of cooking with a small tin campstove to use was not very inviting." To make matters worse, "Mr. Cautley's supplies had arrived alright, but no equipment for his cook. This left myself to cook for both parties for two weeks."

The official report described the situation in Kicking Horse Pass: "The benches and slopes at lower levels of the summit of the pass have been practically denuded of forest by the action of fire and removal of material for railway purposes, and are now littered with brulé and windfall interspersed with second growth pine and spruce....In fact, the pass for several miles has been subject to the ravages of forest fires and what green timber exists is for the most part second growth pine with scattered bunches of spruce." The report also noted that a creek along the divide had been altered. "At the summit an artificial diversion has been made of the waters of the glacier stream, which originally flowed wholly to the east. This diversion has been arranged by the Canadian Pacific Railway by the construction of two concrete channels, one curving to the east and the other to the west. An artistic rustic sign marked 'The Great Divide' completes a realistic presentation of the division of the waters."

On June 27 Cautley started establishing the monument stations in Kicking Horse Pass. No one on either crew had any experience in constructing concrete monuments, so it was a trial-and-error process at the beginning. Rainy conditions added to the difficulty. In his diary that evening Wheeler wrote: "Made cement base for No. 3A. Also filled mould with cement and left both to set. C[autley] and party running preliminary line up hill. Rained off and on all afternoon. Mon[ument] 3A took 12 boxes of gravel and 1½ bags of cement. Will take ½ bag to complete."

The last days of June were rainy, so Wheeler took the train back to Banff and spent the time making preparations for the ACC camp at Lake O'Hara. On July 1 he returned, and the following day Wheeler

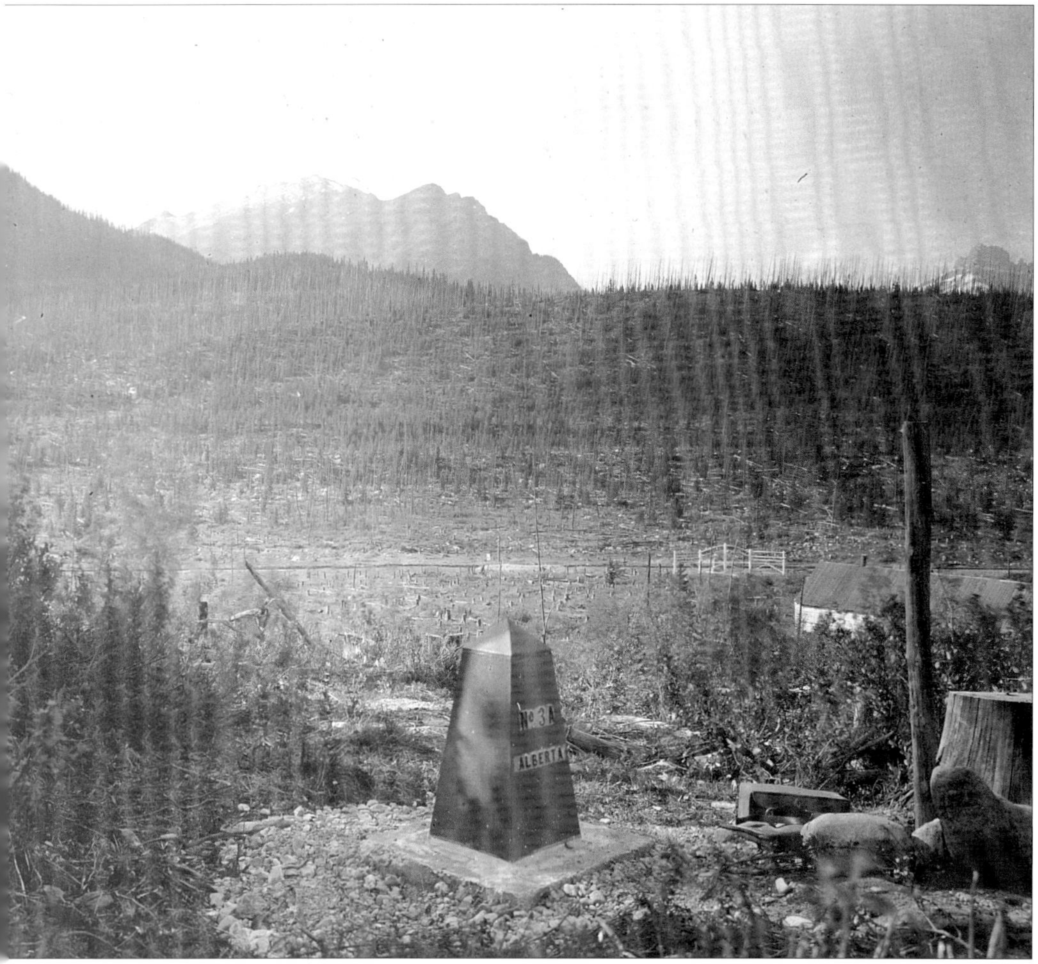

Monument 3A is the first monument above the pass on the south side. A fence and building are visible in the centre of the picture close to the pass. Wheeler 1913 photo album, Alberta surveyor general's office.

started his surveying. "Breakfast at 6am. Day fine. Got ready and started climbing at 7:45 am. First set, a signal on Cautley's plug near railway—No. 1A. Climbed to Niblock Shoulder and occupied same with camera and transit. Day cold but fine. Got several good views and posted Campbell in work. First day I could climb." While he was surveying on the mountain, Wheeler "sent Wallace and men with guide down to Jimmy Simpson's camp. They brought back box with paint, etc. Murphy came up with other packer & horses and carried gravel to Mon[ument] 7A." On July 3 Wheeler and his crew climbed again. "Up at usual time. Climbed to Divide Shoulder from Pope's Peak. Got good set of views and azimuth. Set brass bolt Monument 13A. Build 6 ft [2 metres] cairn on it. Got back to camp and found J.N. Wallace there. Day fine—good climb and rope. Got back in good shape." J.N. Wallace wanted to check on the progress of the survey and make sure it was going smoothly.

The same day Paul Wallace wrote a letter to his family. "Well, I am back at the Kicking Horse again, but this time not alone. The two parties of which the boundary survey is composed, under Mr. Wheeler and Mr. Cautley respectively, are engaged in phototopographical work, and the placing of monuments. I had the honor today of painting the first inter-provincial boundary monument erected in the Canadian Rocky Mountains."

On July 5 Wheeler and his crew climbed to the shoulder of Cathedral Mountain. Then he went to Banff, and for the next two days Campbell, along with Conrad Kain and a couple of the crew members, climbed to two stations. Kain wrote a letter to Malek.

> Great Divide, July 7, 1913
>
> Now I am in the mountains again. In the Rockies! It is spring in the mountains! For the first days in the camp I was the cook. Now I am working again on top of the mountains. I climb mountains again as a guide! I feel much better doing this, better than what I first arrived in Banff, but not quite 100 per cent yet. I get tired more easily than before, but I hope everything will be better again. The topographical survey will be done in order to establish precisely and correctly the border between Alberta and British Columbia. We all know each other in the group, and I am convinced they all are happy that I came back, because the people don't have the eye and the experience to choose good routes to the tops of mountains.

On July 8 Wheeler and Campbell went to Vermilion Pass. In his diary for July 9 Wheeler wrote: "Campbell and I climbed a shoulder of Boom Mountain to look over the ground. We divide and arrange a program of work while I am busy at ACC camps. We then went down to big valley head of Vermilion River and looked up feed." Wheeler and Campbell returned to Kicking Horse Pass. During the next two days Wheeler, Kain and Brinkman surveyed Bolt 10A on Mount Bosworth, along with Bolts 9A and 11A on the south side of Kicking Horse Pass. On July 12, after spending time conferring with Campbell, Wheeler left. He would be absent for over a month, first at the ACC camp at Lake O'Hara from July 13 to 25, and then at the ACC camp at Mount Robson from July 28 to August 10.

Cautley and Campbell completed surveying Kicking Horse Pass during the next few days. Altogether, eight concrete monuments were erected, along with four brass bolts and cairns. The total distance surveyed across the pass was about five kilometres. There was a Dominion land survey post in Kicking Horse Pass near the boundary, so it was easy to connect with an existing survey.

From Kicking Horse Pass, Cautley proceeded directly to Vermilion Pass) arriving there on July 18. Campbell surveyed along the divide between the two passes for about 50 kilometres. During that time Kain left to join Wheeler for the ACC Robson camp. Vermilion Pass was considerably different from Kicking Horse. There was more extensive forest cover. The pass was just four kilometres wide and more sharply defined. Only four concrete monuments were used for Vermilion Pass, while seven brass bolts and cairns were erected. From two of the stations, Campbell connected to monuments established by M.P. Bridgland in 1911. Campbell also occupied five camera stations in the vicinity of the pass. He and Cautley needed to make a triangulation survey to reach the nearest Dominion land survey post. Stelfox noted that there was a large construction crew working on the highway through Vermilion Pass while they were there.

Cautley and Campbell finished surveying in Vermilion Pass on August 13. Since Wheeler and Kain would be returning soon, both parties travelled to Simpson Pass. While Campbell and his crew returned to Banff and then proceeded to Simpson Pass, Cautley made the fateful choice to take a different route. His crew went from Vermilion Pass down the Vermilion River to its junction with the Simpson River. For the first 10 kilometres they followed the newly constructed highway. After that the trail was overgrown and obliterated in places. Heavy rain had swollen the waterways. While fording the Vermilion River, the horse carrying Cautley's transit and some other equipment lost its footing and was swept down the river. The horse was rescued but the pack that it was carrying fell off into deep water and could not be recovered.

The packer and the rest of the crew continued to Simpson Pass. Since Cautley was using his own personal transit he went back to Edmonton to get his spare instrument. Cautley had a home on Cooking Lake outside Edmonton, and it was the weekend, so he and his wife invited friends to visit. They took a boat trip on the lake and their craft overturned in windy weather. While the others clung to the boat, Cautley and a woman attempted to swim to shore. Cautley made it safely, but the woman drowned. The accident also waterlogged two watches that Cautley was using for his astronomic observations. It was 10 days before Cautley rejoined his crew at Simpson Pass.

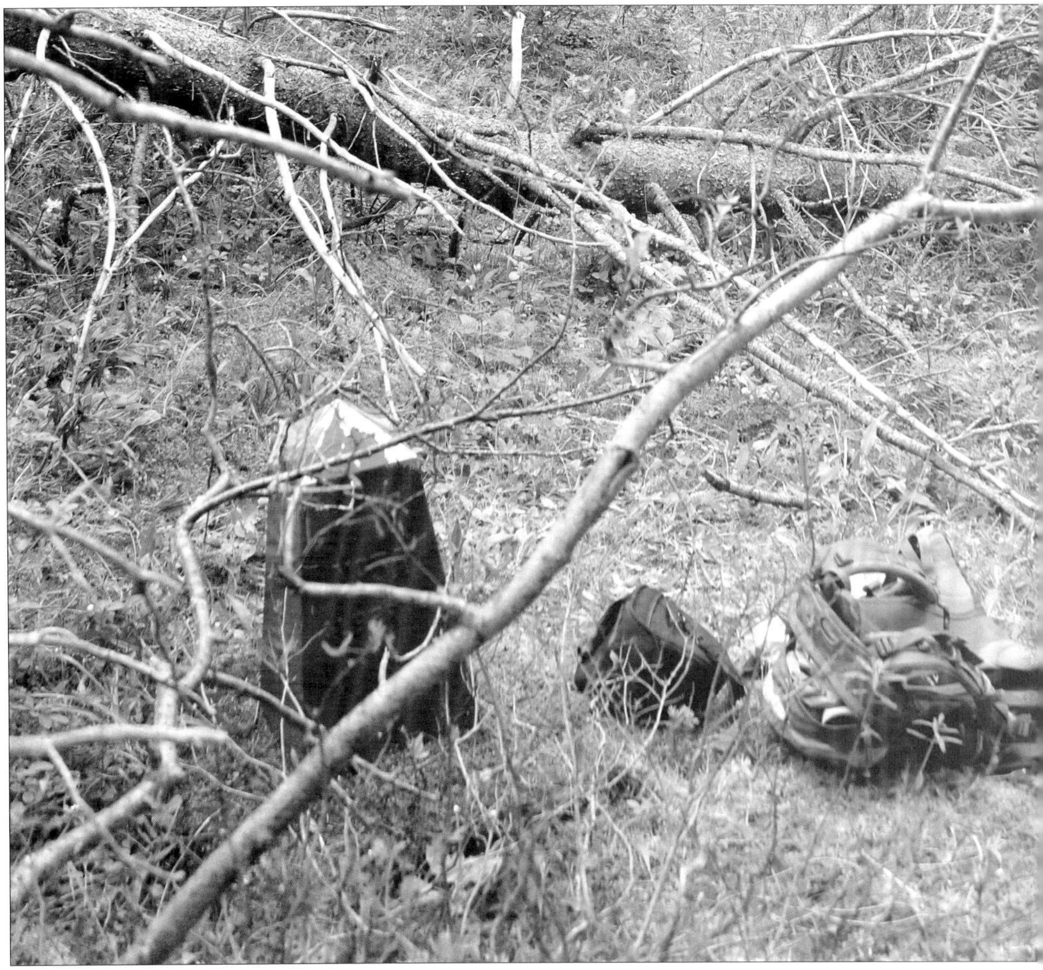

Monument 3A has been reconstructed. The vegetation growth that has occurred in the past century obscures the landscape and only the outline of the mountain on the left is visible. Most of the trees in the area are lodgepole pine and are being affected by the mountain pine beetle. The pine trees will probably die soon and the landscape will change again. Photo Jay Sherwood

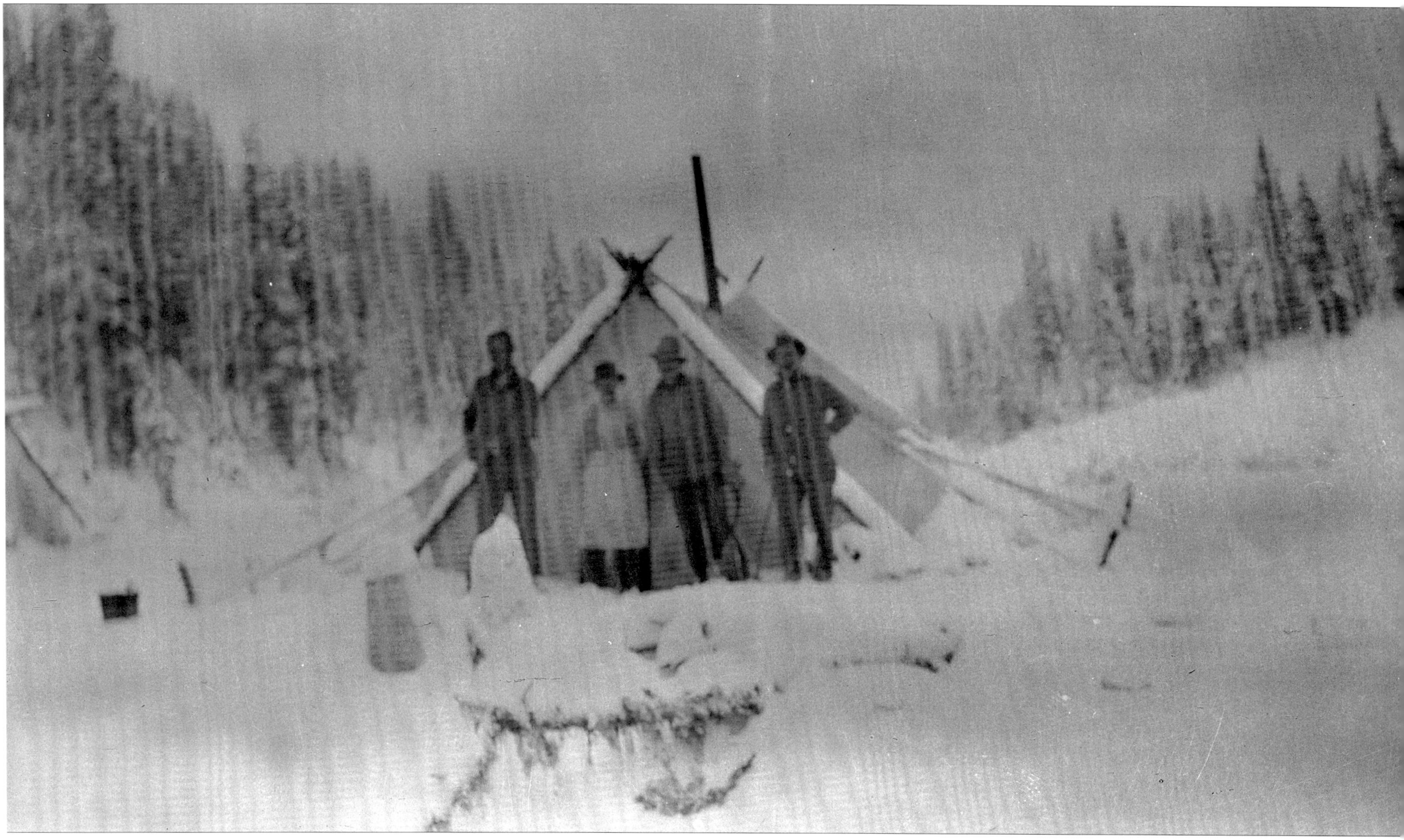

The snowstorm in Simpson Pass at the beginning of September. e011166495, Library and Archives Canada

I am sitting here under a larch tree at the shore of a splendid, deep blue lake between two Rocky Mountains. At the end of the lake is a waterfall, which comes down from another lake located a few feet higher, and even higher is a third lake. In the background are mountains with snow and ice: an indescribably beautiful picture of nature, added to it the fine sound of the bell, which one of the horses carries around its neck. I see some mountain goats on the grassy slopes above the edge of the forest. It is one of the most beautiful spots I have ever seen with my own eyes. I know that our views of nature and its beauty is almost the same and so I think of you while observing with joy....

If only you could sit under the nearest big larch tree next to me! I know you as a friend of nature and convinced that you, just like me, would see the mountain world is a paradise. Sorry, but I must interrupt and look after the horses. I don't hear the little bell anymore. Goodbye.

On the last day of August Kain noted that he had to go back to Simpson Pass to get a gun because the men needed fresh meat. That evening he wrote: "Was at Simpson Pass and am back now, went hunting, but could not see because of fog and storm. It is pretty cold. I have to crawl under the blanket, because I am wet through. We have no tent. This is only a mobile camp. Good night!"

On the first day of September Wheeler, Campbell and Brinkman climbed Pharaoh Peak South, and just finished their work before it started to snow. Kain described life in camp on the first day of September, after a snowstorm.

> Here I am, sitting under the larch tree again with a fire at my feet, meat hanging in the tree. Early in the morning I went hunting, and not far from the camp I shot a mountain goat. I have to bake bread and cook the meat. The others are on the mountain with the instruments. Don't know whether they can work in such fog? Excuse the interruption, I have to cook!!
>
> In the evening: my friends came back to camp early and half frozen. I improve their lives with a very good goat soup. The bread also turned out quite well. The weather foggy and cold.

Most of the first week of September was cold with rain and snow limiting the work that could be done. On September 5 Paul Wallace wrote to his family. He discussed conditions around camp and talked about Wheeler's process of naming some well-known geographic features in Banff National Park.

> We are having just now the kind of weather that seems to have been all the rage on Sundays at Go Home this summer. Two days cold rain has turned to snow. I am sitting in my tent, wrapped up in blankets, university sweater, and mitts, with my back supported by the ever useful typewriter. Conrad Kain, the great guide of the Rockies, is lying on his stomach beside me, attending to his extended correspondence. All the work I have done in three days is type—one letter, one receipt, two telegrams, so you can understand that I have time to get fat.

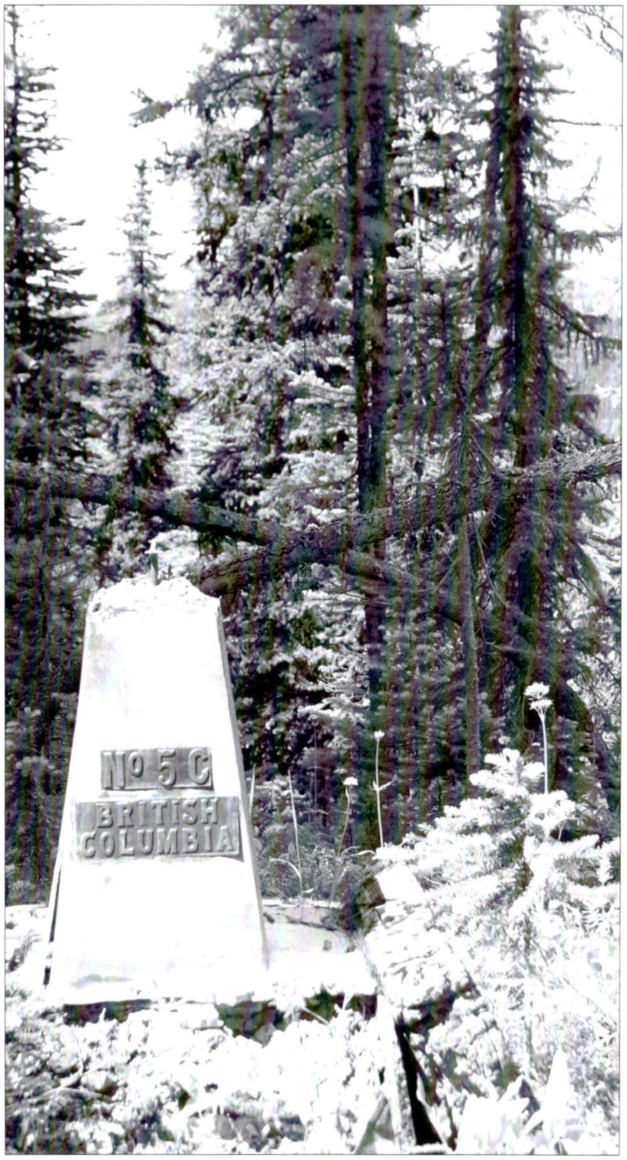

Monument 5C in Simpson Pass in 2016. In Cautley's photograph at this station the mountains in the background are clearly visible, so the trees must have started growing not too many years after the survey. Simpson Pass is in the subalpine zone, so there are not many lodgepole pine trees in the forested areas. Photo Jay Sherwood

> I am not going to get Mt. Assiniboine after all. The weather is too bad for an attack on the old citadel, and besides, Mr. Wheeler was not greatly impressed with the magnitude of my nerve on six inch ledges when we did

some scrambling the other day, and is probably glad enough to have the weather as an excuse for not taking me further south.

I had a magnificent view of the mountain from a small peak I climbed twice near here. Its resemblance to the Matterhorn is startling. It has two advantages over its Jura's brother; that it is incomparably higher than anything around it (though not actually as high as the Matterhorn), and it rises from snow fields and glaciers such as the Matterhorn cannot boast. Conrad Kain thinks it is a finer mountain.…

We spent a few days exploring a little corner of country, not many hours from the railway, that has never been visited except by trappers and prospectors. All the features were unnamed, and Mr. Wheeler set to work to name them.

We camped by the shore of an exquisite lake beneath two mountains of pyramid form, which were named Pharaoh and Ramses. The lake was called Egypt. Above this lake was another of a very vivid glacial green which was called Scarab Lake. Nearby are Mummy Lake and Mummy Mountain. Here Mr. Wheeler's Egyptian knowledge gave out, and we resorted to such names as—Whistling Valley (crowded by whistling marmots), Precipice Lake, Black Rock Lake, etc. Black Rock Lake is a fine example of the lakes that form such a distinctive feature of the Canadian Rockies. It lies with the woods on one side, and a sheer wall of black rock that's crowned by a rickety looking tower of more black rock that stretches about 2000 feet [610 metres] overhead. I was up Black Rock Peak with Mr. Wheeler one day, and we looked down, almost sheer, to the lake. At one place the cliff is more than sheer, and it is delightful to roll stones over, and wait for the echo from the neighboring hills—for the echo is much more distinct than the original sound of the rocks as they strike hundreds of feet below.…

Our tent is a very literary den, just now. Conrad his finished his correspondence, and is deep in an account of his climb on Mt. Robson, which I am to translate for him, and try to get published. He has already given me two of his favorite mountain stories which made such a hit at the campfire at Robson, and these too I am going to try to get published. I am practically Conrad's private secretary when Mr. Wheeler is too snug in his blankets to need me.

The boundary survey needed to make a connection with one of the stations of the Dominion land survey. On September 6 Wheeler wrote: "Campbell & Brinkman went down to the corral at Healy Creek gap to look for Tp [township] line and set signal.…Jack Warren took down their bedding & grub." Wheeler and Cautley spent the same morning looking over the boundary on the "north side of [Simpson] pass and arranged for places for monuments." During the second week of September Wheeler's crew surveyed stations on the mountains in a mixture of weather. They also tied their topographic survey to the Dominion station near the Bow River where Campbell set a target. Conrad Kain noted that he climbed a mountain to build a cairn and that there was a snowstorm along the way and lightning on top. A couple of days later, he, Campbell and Brinkman encountered a snowstorm on top of a mountain and had to leave because of electricity.

In another letter Kain wrote to Malek, he described how difficult it often was to write.

> Today, September 14th is a Sunday, day of rest.
>
> The night was very cold. Hoarfrost. Now it is sunny and warm. There is a beautiful autumn picture in front of us. The larch trees change colour. It has been a long time that I wrote you a long letter, and I know that I owe you many answers to various questions in your letter. The opportunity to write is not always there, and often it is too cold in the tent. You will notice the dirty writing paper, which one cannot keep clean. One interrupts, puts wood in the stove, etc. Often you finish the letter in a great rush, because the packer is going to ride into the village, etc.

On September 18 Kain had the opportunity to write a more detailed letter.

> I am sitting here under a big cliff on a ledge of a rather fine mountain near Simpson Pass. I am hunting for goats and I am quite alone by myself, nobody around me. Yet somebody is round me in my thoughts, with whom I am speaking now, while I am writing these lines. I think it is nice that we have a brain and can remember so many things in the past. This morning, I was sent out hunting, so I took the writing map along with me. I tried to write in English as nicely as I can. Let me tell you of my surroundings: here on the right is my rifle and pack. In front of me across the valley these big Alps. Below there is a fine timber with some larches in yellow colour amongst it. It gives a fine fall picture. The weather is not very good. There's lots of new snow on the higher mountains. Soon it will be snowing again. Till now I have not seen any sign of game. I do not feel too bad but a little homesick. I hope to get over it alright again. These days I have been thinking of you often and of your dear mother and Flora, as well as of my own people. You understand that. My heart is in good condition, and I can walk as always and go on hunting trips. I am often wondering if I can have sometimes so many happy hours again that I had in my old home? Well it is getting cold now, I have to move on a little.
>
> Now I can tell you more: I shot a goat round the mountains here!! Poor little thing! I do feel sorry for it, but we must have the meat!! I light a fire here in the woods; by-and-by my little teakettle will be boiling and I shall have a cup of hot tea. I wish I could say: "Miss Amelie, come on have a cup of tea with me, won't you?" Well the tea is made, and I have a good lunch for when I go back to the camp. A very bad storm is coming over the mountains from the south! Goodbye!
>
> In the camp, 3:30 PM. It took me some hours to reach the camp with my heavy load. Everybody had been pleased with my shooting! I got into the bad storm, and now it is snowing like in winter! Very bad weather for our work! If the weather keeps on like this, we shall soon go back to Banff. I am looking forward to my mail and hope there will be a letter from you waiting for me.

At the end of their work in Simpson Pass, Wheeler's crew surveyed a mining claim for the well-known Banff guide, park warden and adventurer Bill Peyto.

After Simpson Pass it was too late in the season for Cautley to go to Assiniboine, the next pass to the south, since he would not be able to finish it, and cold weather made it difficult to construct the monuments. In 1914 the boundary survey would work at Crowsnest Pass, so Cautley went there and spent a week starting the preliminary survey.

Meanwhile, on September 17, Wheeler's crew began working south along the Great Divide, heading toward the Mount Assiniboine area. Before leaving, Wheeler "packed up four boxes [of camera] plates for Peyto to take to McCaw." For his September 20 diary entry Wheeler wrote: "Darned porcupine squeaking around all night. Kept me awake some." They crossed Citadel Pass that day and descended to the Golden Valley.

Kain sent Malek his notes describing the trip. On September 20 there was a "descent of 500 feet [152 metres], trail very poor. Windfalls. Horses fall. At 3 PM stop for camp. Good meadow for horses, forest beautiful, green moss. Two small lakes, waterfall, fresh tracks of a moose. Good campfire." There was good weather the next morning so they went up a mountain. "I had a gun and went from the top to hunt for meat. At noon, we got a storm, fog and snow. Found nothing. Minor accident: broken rock fell 4 to 5 metres, minor injury to my hip. In my mind I thought and talked with Amelie." On September 22 the men remained in camp because it was snowing. The following day they "moved camp to the base of Mount Assiniboine. Snow. Trail poor. Passed a lake, nice view. Camp at foot of alpine meadow next to the lake, weather warm."

Bill Peyto and the Book Rest Mining Claim

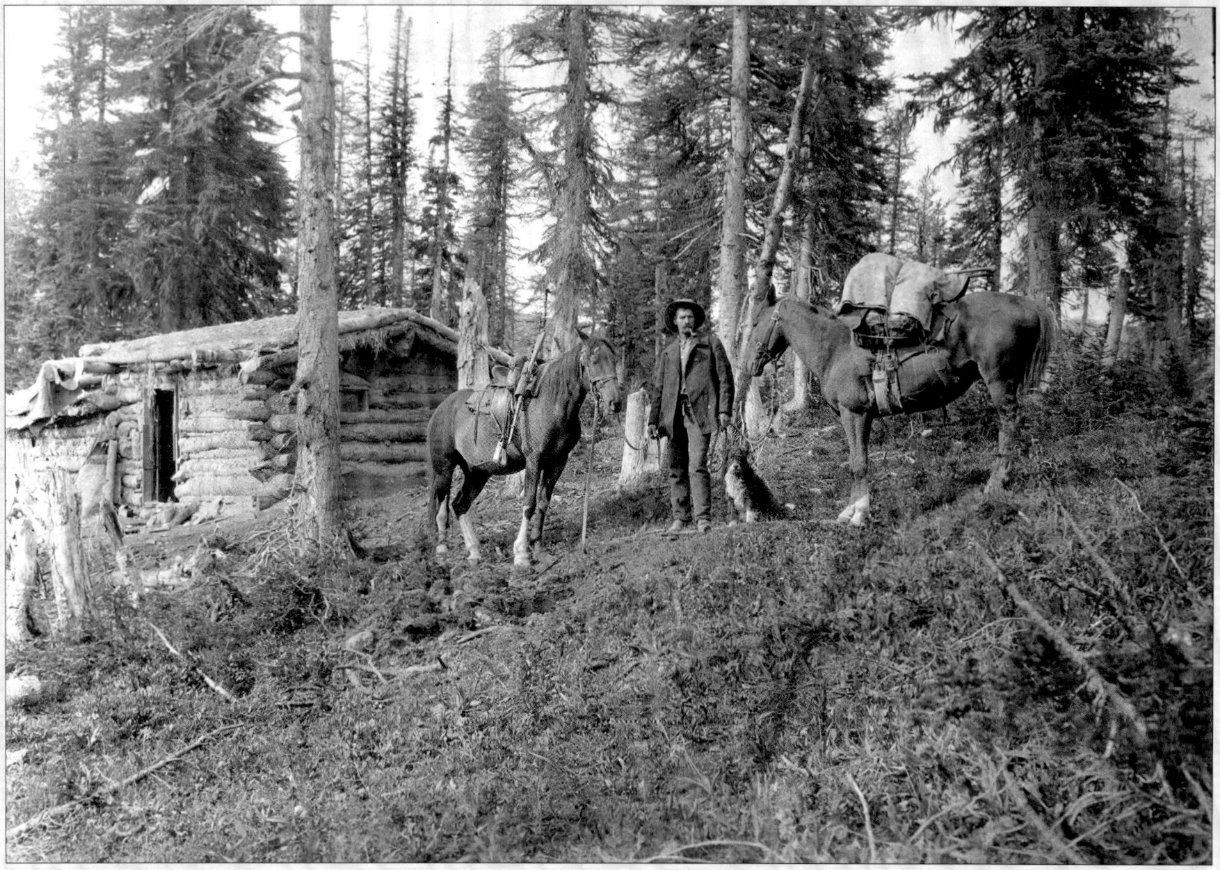

Abraham Knechtel, chief forester for the Dominion Park Service, and Norman Sanson spent a month collecting plants in the Simpson Pass area during the summer of 1913. Peyto provided assistance, and they used the cabin at Book Rest during their work. Knechtel took this photograph of Peyto during that time. V573 NA66-262, Whyte Museum of the Canadian Rockies

Ebenezer William (Bill) Peyto is one of the most famous and colourful characters in the early history of Banff National Park.

Peyto was born and raised in a rural area of Kent, England, not far from London. He immigrated to Canada in 1887 and came to the Banff area. In the early 1890s he began working as a guide and outfitter for Tom Wilson from Banff, and was a member of several well-known trips in the Rocky Mountains Park (as Banff was known at that time).

Peyto was also interested in prospecting, and in the late 1890s he located a rock outcrop with copper ore in the Simpson Pass area southwest of Banff. At that time the location was not part of the national park.

In 1900 Peyto enlisted in the Boer War and served for a year. Afterwards, he started his own guiding business and in 1902 married Emily Wood, the sister of a packer from Banff. Peyto also staked a mining claim called Book Rest in Simpson Pass, and he built a cabin there. Occasionally, Peyto used the cabin for some of his easy guiding trips into the area.

In August 1904 Peyto registered the Book Rest mining claim in Calgary (Alberta was still part of the Northwest Territories at that time). He needed to have the claim officially surveyed within 10 years.

In 1906 Emily died, and their only child was sent to live with a relative in Armstrong, BC. Peyto became more reclusive and used the cabin both for prospecting and as a retreat. In 1911 he joined the Park Warden Service. When the national park started assigning wardens to a district in 1913, Peyto and another warden received the assignment to the district that ran south of Banff to Mount Assiniboine and included the Simpson Pass area.

In September Peyto met A.O. Wheeler when he was in Banff getting supplies for the survey crews. Wheeler told him about the boundary survey, that they were working in the Simpson Pass area and that they needed to tie in any nearby mining claims to their survey. Peyto's claim had still not been surveyed because he did not have the money to do so, and it would have been expensive for a surveyor to come to Simpson Pass just for a mining claim. However, since Wheeler and Cautley were working in the area, Peyto realized that this was his opportunity to get the Book Rest claim surveyed, so he went to Simpson Pass.

Initially, Cautley started his location of the boundary in Simpson Pass and determined that the claim was in Alberta, as Peyto had registered it. This was unfortunate news for Peyto, since regulation changes in the national parks made mining activities more restrictive. In his diary entry for September 14 Wheeler wrote: "Went & saw Bill Peyto and arranged with him to get in my missing horses." The following day Campbell, Kain and Brinkman started to survey Bill Peyto's mining claim. On September 16 Wheeler recorded that Campbell and his crew finished Bill Peyto's claim. In the afternoon Wheeler worked at Bill Peyto's claim. "Marked all posts and took BTs [bearing trees]. Put stone mound around all posts. Bill came to supper. Arranged with him to go to McCaw's camp [Vermilion Pass area] and take letter."

Conrad Kain wrote a letter to Malek on September 18, and in it he described Peyto.

> The two days working near Peyto's camp near Simpson Pass were interesting. Bill is an old, honest man of the woods. He comes from Banff. Bill always has to tell something new. Luck has not always been with him all his life, but in spite of it he was happy. Eight years ago, he lost his wife. He said, "If she would still be alive, I would be 10 to 15 years further from the grave." I know from other people, too, that he was not the old Bill anymore for a long time. He looks rough and rugged like a wildcat! His eyes are unusually blue. If you look at him without talking to him you can easily understand that people are afraid of them. But this is only on the outside. I think I know him better. He is one of the Western characters: totally independent, doffs his hat to nobody, talks like he thinks, without any qualms. If somebody comes to him with problems, he will meet a soft-hearted man.

In his government report Wheeler wrote about Peyto: "Situated close by the watershed on the Alberta side he has a copper claim, which he has worked religiously for the past ten years. Its name, 'The Bookrest Claim,' is typical of the man. In his log cabin, close by a charming little tarn, he spends long periods in absolute solitude. This seems to weigh little on his mind, for the wilderness is to him an open book."

Over the winter of 1913 Wheeler completed the returns for the survey and sent them from his winter home in Sidney to Surveyor General Deville in Ottawa. In a letter dated April 2, 1914, Wheeler explained why he surveyed the Book Rest claim.

> While at the Simpson Pass last summer I found that close by the watershed line, on the Alberta side, there was a copper claim which was being worked by a man named Bill Peyto.
>
> Peyto is one of the oldest of the mountain guides and prospectors and has apparently been working this claim for a great many years. He appears to have taken it up under the regulations date August 13, 1908, but never had it surveyed, owing to the cost of bringing in a surveyor especially for that purpose.
>
> The claim was situated so close to the boundary line between the two provinces that I decided to make a survey of it; also with the object of helping out Bill Peyto, who is now one of the Rocky Mountain Park game guardians.

> Under the regulations approved by order in council dated August 13, 1908, Section 44, Clause c, it is necessary in order to acquire the title to have "had the claim surveyed at his own expense in accordance with instructions from the Surveyor General by an authorized Dominion Land Surveyor and the survey thereof approved."
>
> Although I made no actual charge to Peyto for this survey he practically gave value for the same by spending a couple of days hunting up horses belonging to my survey party that had gone astray, so it may be said to have been done at his own expense.
>
> The point at issue is that while the claim has been surveyed in accordance with the regulations mentioned, it has not been done under instructions received from you prior to such survey. Would you, therefore, be willing to accept the returns of my survey as a survey of the claim and thus enable Peyto to make application for title upon approval of the survey returns by you?
>
> The name of the claim is "The Book Rest" Claim and the corners have been properly posted and the line surveyed in accordance with the requirements of the regulations of Aug. 13, 1908.
>
> If you are willing to accept the returns of this survey I shall send them forward upon hearing from you to that effect.

Wheeler sent the returns on May 15 and explained: "I have not had much experience in surveying mining claims upon Dominion lands, and I am not sure that the plans are in order, but if, when you have had them examined, you will kindly send me a memorandum concerning the requirements....I shall be ready to supply all deficiencies."

Wheeler's lack of experience in this type of surveying must have been apparent, for Deville sent the survey back with a list of corrections. Wheeler replied from Banff on August 5.

> I have the honour to acknowledge the receipt of your letter of the 27th of July sending back the returns of the survey of the Bookrest mineral claim, situated near the Simpson Pass in Alberta, and informing me that the returns will not be accepted as they now stand; also that according to the departmental records the claim is in good standing till the 25th of August 1914, and that if the returns of the survey are not completed by that time it will be necessary that steps be taken to protect the interests of the owner, Mr. E.W. Peyto.
>
> In reply I beg to say that the survey was made by D.L.S. Campbell who is now at work in the Crowsnest Pass and I do not think it is possible that the returns can be amended to agree with the requirements by the date mentioned. I would therefore ask that an extension of three months be given in order to furnish time to make the returns in accordance with the requirements.
>
> It is now considerable time since the survey returns were filed and an earlier notification of the expiry would have enabled me to have had the returns made in accordance with the requirements. On these grounds, I beg to request, on behalf of Mr. Peyto, that the extension asked for be given.

Wheeler made the necessary corrections, but when he went to complete the survey he encountered another difficulty, as he told Deville in a letter from Crowsnest Pass on August 2, 1915.

> I beg to say that I have tried to get this matter straightened out, but E.W. Peyto has enlisted [in World War I] and is now on active service or in training for the same.
>
> I have fixed the survey on the ground so that it is made in accordance with the requirements, but I find I cannot get the plans and notes in proper order without consulting Peyto and I cannot get in touch with him.
>
> I now beg to make request that Peyto's right to the claims may be maintained until I can get at the records and so fill the requirements for the survey returns. This I cannot do while engaged with the boundary survey fieldwork.

> I have no doubt that under the circumstances of Peyto having enlisted in the defense of the Empire the department will keep his claim in good standing until the necessary survey returns can be filed. A six month extension would, I think, be sufficient. Please inform me where and when the original filing of the claim was made.
>
> There are no conflicting claims and, as far as I could learn, no other claims in the vicinity, and I do not think this one is of much value, but the old man sets great store by it and I think it would be a sad blow to him if he loses it through having filled what he considers to be his duty to his country.

Deville inquired about Peyto's situation and then wrote to Wheeler on August 21: "The Assistant Controller of Mining Lands states that by Order in Council mineral claims or mining leases held by persons on active service for the British Empire or her allies are protected from cancellation until six months after the termination of the war." However, Wheeler needed to "furnish evidence that Mr. Peyto [was] so engaged."

On June 6, 1916, Wheeler wrote to Deville "concerning the survey of the Book Rest Mineral Claim belonging to E.W. Peyto. I now forward the field notes and plan, having made corrections to the same in accordance with the copy of the instructions and specimen plan sent me." Wheeler was getting ready to start the 1916 field season and must have been in a hurry to finish the Book Rest survey, for Deville found some mistakes in copying the information, and once more the survey plan and field notes were returned to Wheeler.

On January 22, 1917, over three years after the survey in Simpson Pass, Wheeler sent a letter to the surveyor general in Ottawa. "I am sending, under separate cover, registered, the corrected copy of the Book Rest mineral claim. The field notes have been made in duplicate and there are three copies of the plan....I trust that this will close up the matter and that all requirements have now been filled."

Wheeler had also learned that he needed to return to the Book Rest claim, and in the same letter he asked Deville: "Is it absolutely necessary to post one of these plans upon the claim? There is no other claim within ten miles [16 kilometres] from it nor is there like to be, and in order to place this map upon the claim, it would require two days of travel into the heart of the mountains."

Deville wrote to Wheeler that he had kept one copy of the plan and was sending the other two back. Wheeler had to send one copy to the Mining Recorder and take the other to the mining claim in Simpson Pass. He told Wheeler why this was necessary. "The regulations require that a plan shall be posted on the claim: if it is not so posted, it is open to any one to dispute Mr. Peyto's title on the ground that he has not complied with the regulations. A permission from the Department to waive this requirement would be of no avail, as the Minister has not the power to authorize any one not to do what an Order in Council directs to be done. Any such dispute would go before the courts for decision, not before the Minister."

Wheeler eventually completed his final obligation and Peyto received his Book Rest mining claim. Peyto was wounded in June 1916 and sent home late that year. He returned to the Park Service in 1920 and remained with it until his official retirement in 1936. The Park Service constructed a cabin at Book Rest for the wardens to use while patrolling the area. The mining claim produced very little copper, but Peyto spent much time there enjoying the solitude and beauty of the area.

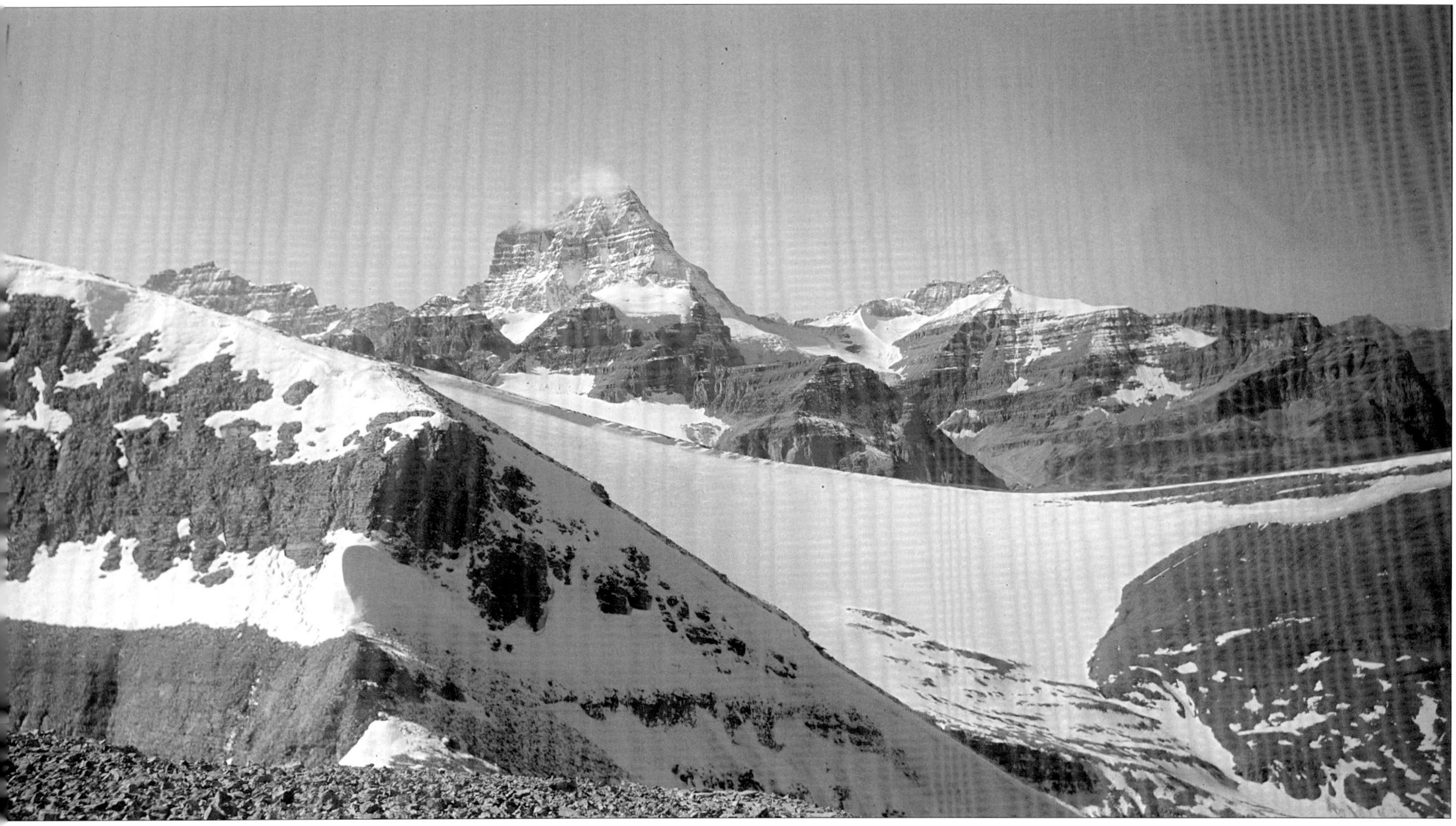

A view of Mount Assiniboine from the east. There is seasonal snow in the foreground and several glaciers are visible. WHE_1913_W13-282, Library and Archives Canada

On September 24 Kain accompanied Wheeler and the men, who surveyed from the top of one of the mountains. "Start 6:30 through forest. Snow on mountain north of the camp. Hard 3½ hour climb to mountaintop. View marvelous! Sun warm (sunbath). On top of the mountain continued writing the article The Lady Climber. 4:00 in the camp. Good fire. Talk about the war in Africa. Had disagreements. I and Brinkman were against the war." Kain, Brinkman and Wallace enjoyed having discussions about a variety of current affairs around the evening campfire.

On September 26, a beautiful early fall day, Kain, Wheeler and Campbell climbed Wonder Peak just east of Mount Assiniboine. Kain wrote to Malek.

There are many days in life when life isn't worth much. But today is a day when one can see wonders of nature and has joy in life! I am lying here on top of Mount Wonder. Some yards away, Mr. Wheeler and Mr. Campbell are working with their instruments. I only try to describe the beauty to you, I know it is impossible, but I have the goodwill! Already in the name of Mount Wonder must tell you a lot. Three hours ago, the mountain was still nameless. We were right to christen it Mount Wonder. The top is on the Great Divide. The water on the eastern side has a long trip to make to the Atlantic, on the southwestern side to the

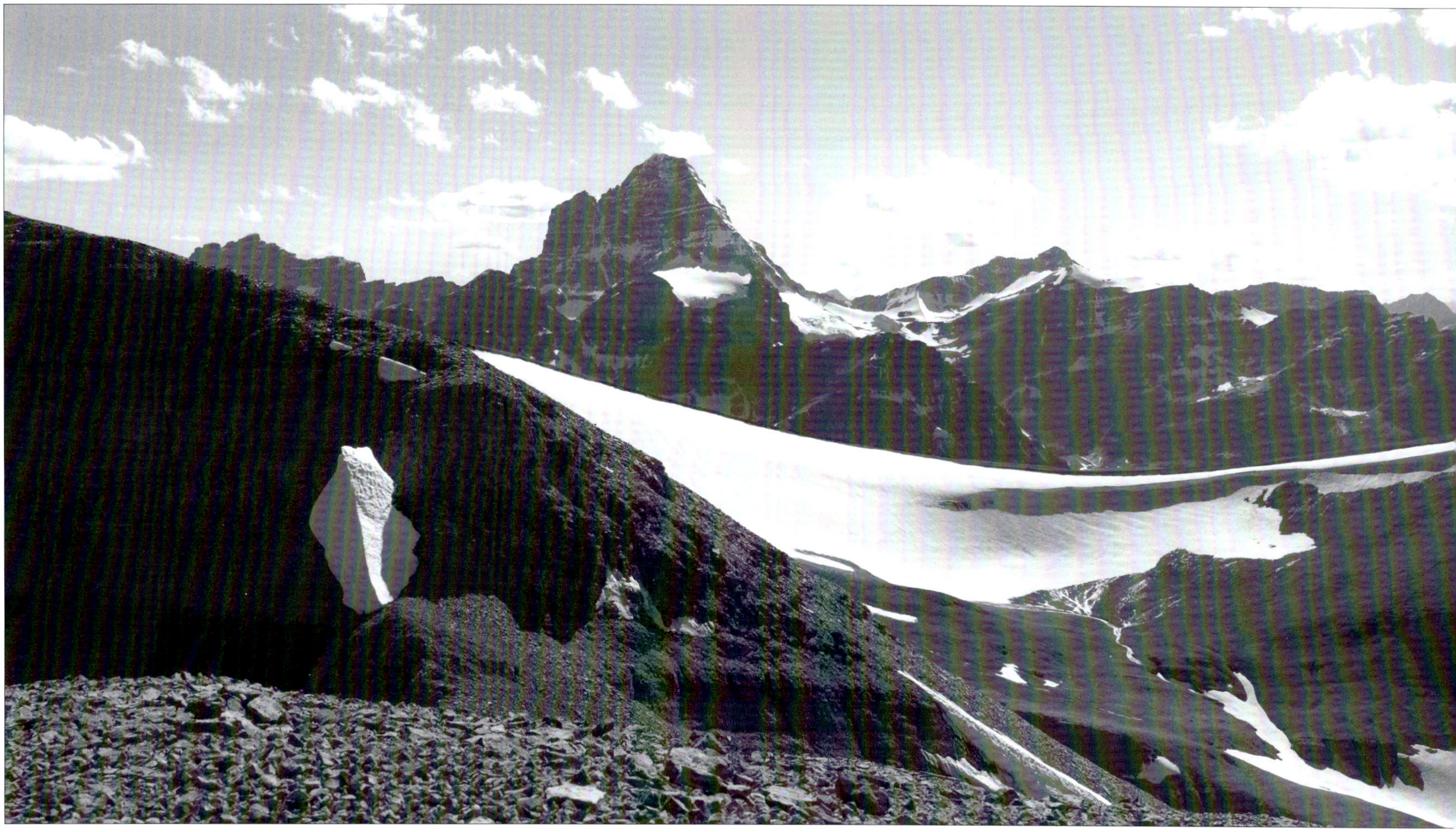

The Mountain Legacy picture was taken in late July, so there would be even less seasonal snow two months later. Most of the glaciers in the 1913 photography remain, but several have decreased in size. In the right foreground plant vegetation is beginning to grow. MLP2010_W13-282, Mountain Legacy Project

Pacific Ocean. On the Atlantic side are two lakes deep in the valley. One is one and a half miles long, the other a half-mile. We named both: The longer one Marvel Lake, the other Wonder [Gloria] Lake. The latter has an indescribably green-blue colour, hence the name. Marvel Lake is deep blue and has a few tiny isles. Around these, the water is not very deep, hence the varied colours. Both lakes have thick forests of fir and spruce around them. 600 metres below the top, three wild goats are lying in the grass, enjoying a sunbath. As far as the eye can see, nothing but mountains from 7000 feet to 11,000 feet [2,135 to 3,350 metres] high. Now the Pacific side: first I see mountain meadows and lower down I can count seven lakes; there's green forest and Mount Assiniboine, which in its shape resembles the Matterhorn very much! In the west and south I see high, snow-covered mountains. At the foot of Mount Assiniboine, there is a lake, perhaps one and a half miles long, and the glacier runs directly into it. Some little icebergs swim in it aimlessly. Our camp is at the shore of this lake in a forest of larch

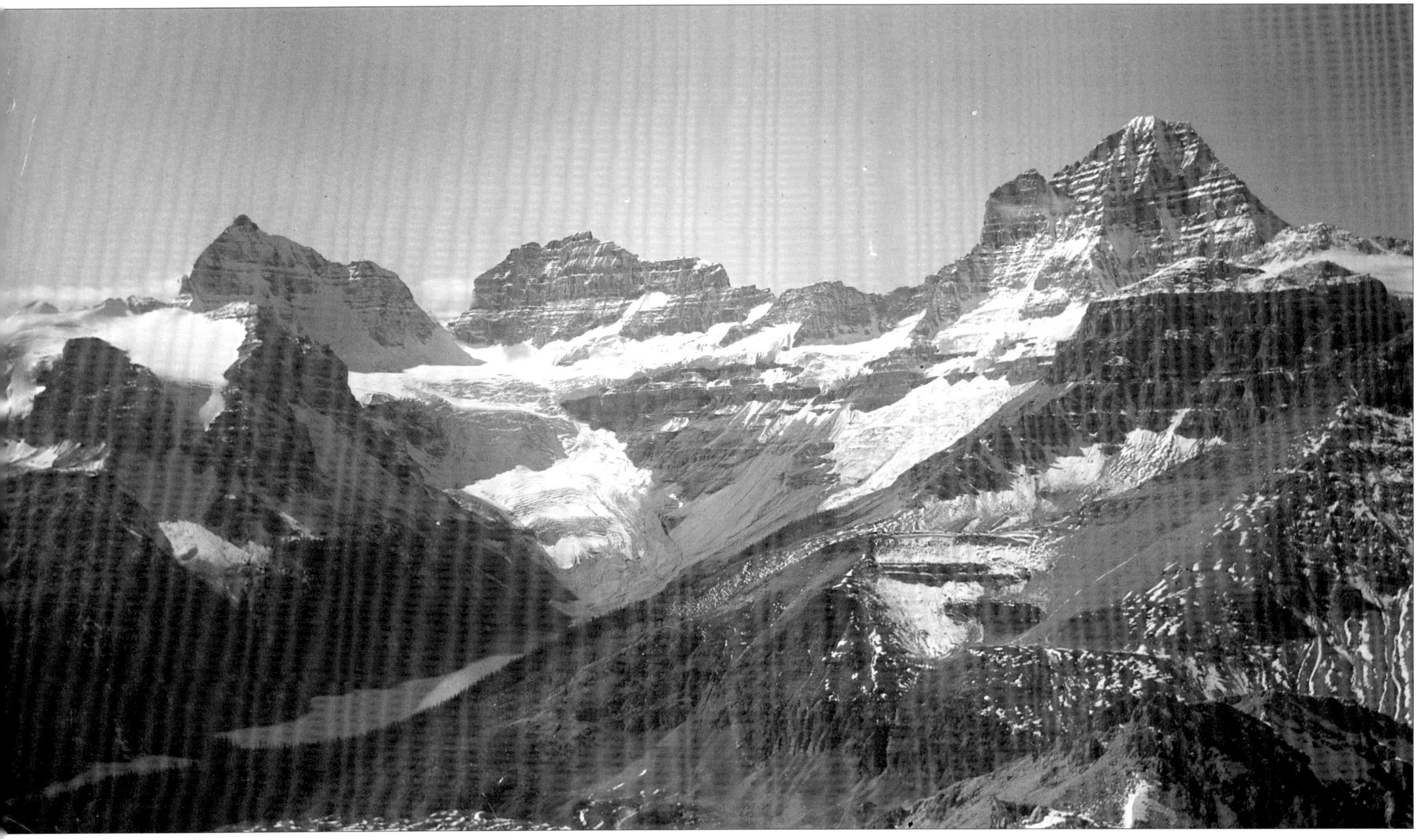

This photograph from Wonder Peak shows Mount Assiniboine and the glaciers on its southeast flank. The main lake in the picture is Gloria Lake. WHE_1913_W13-258, Library and Archives Canada

trees, which are all in the colourful fall foliage. Any man, any person, who can see such a picture would be truly happy about it. And I do feel happy in the peace and calmness of nature. I think of you and many other friends of nature. I wish everybody an opportunity to see such a wonderful scene. I will take two stones from this peak: one I send to you and one I will keep for myself. Once you have this rock in your hand and in your beautiful room, you will remember that your good friend far away had been thinking of you when he saw this miracle of nature, and that somebody travels in the big world who remembers you fondly at an area where the peace of the mountain reigns.…I have a few more minutes time, then I have to build a stone man [cairn]. In the evening I will continue writing. Tomorrow Mr. Wheeler goes to Banff and takes the letter along. We are three days away from Banff. In one week, we too will leave the mountains. So now I finish my lines on top of Mount Wonder. I look around once more and reread my lines.

Wheeler also wrote enthusiastically about the day in his diary: "Glorious view of Lakes Gloria & Marvel.

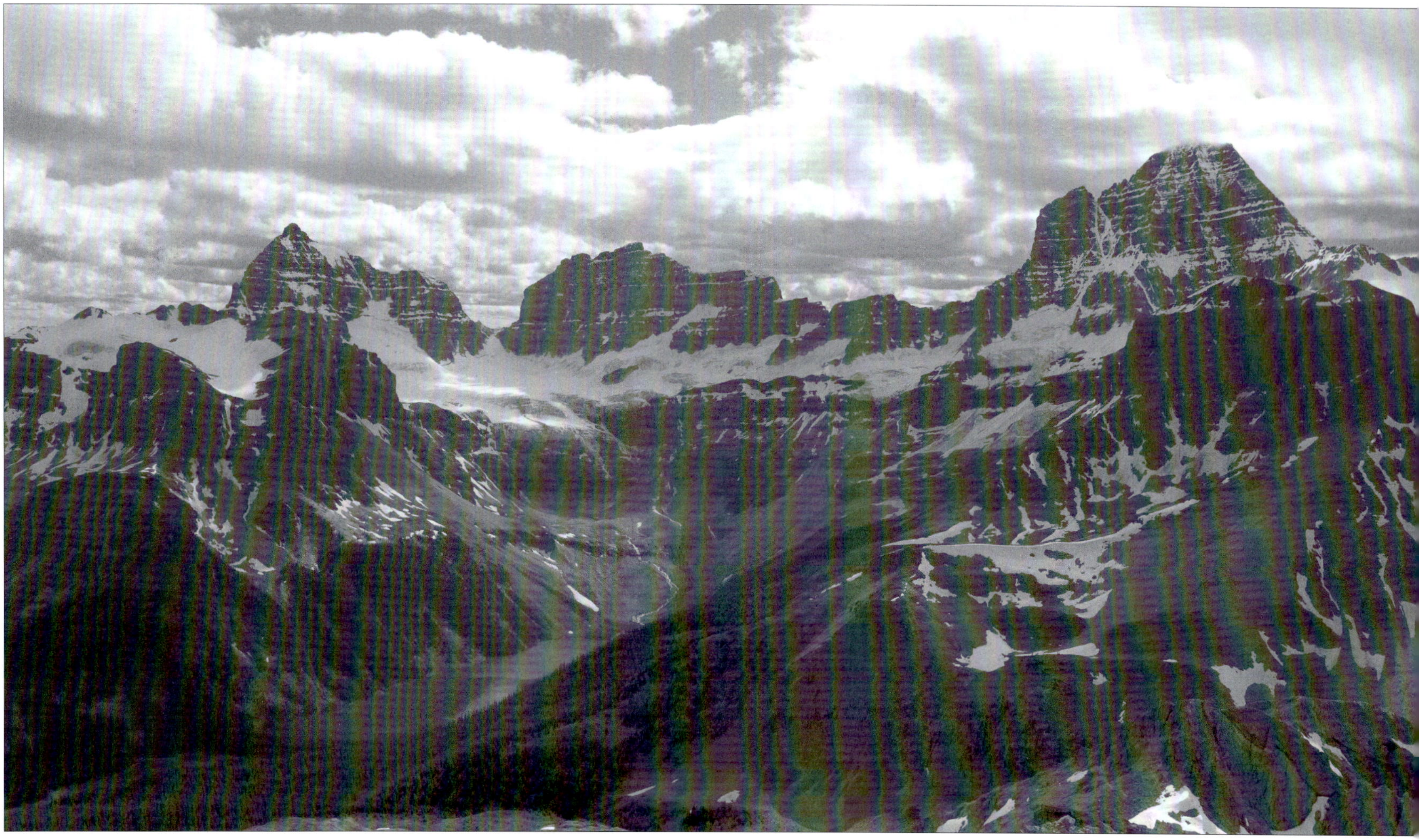

The main glaciers still exist, but the amount of landscape around Mount Assiniboine that is covered in glaciers has decreased significantly. The extent of vegetation in the foreground has increased. MLP2010_W13-258, Mountain Legacy Project

Located divide OK. Ten lakes in sight. Fine summer day. Magnificent views." The next day Wheeler started his return journey to Banff, leaving Campbell and the crew to finish the survey.

Kain wrote that they "climbed mountain northwest of Mount Assiniboine, reached top at 3:40, cold, windy, half frozen. Built two stone men. Descent to the lake across iced up rock. Very dangerous. Everybody tired in camp." September 28 was Sunday and a chance for the crew to rest, while rain and snow on Monday kept the men in camp. Good weather then returned, and the crew resumed surveying. In his diary Kain recorded: "September 30. Climbed mountain from Marvel Lake station. Ascent long and easy. Saw two goats and found a sheep's head with horns. View great. When I built a stone man, I had sad thoughts. Indescribably sad. Early in camp." The surveyors finished their work the next day. Kain wrote: "October 1. Station on mountain, named it Mount Hill. Built two stone men. Weather fine, view fabulous. View deep down to Spray valley. Early in camp."

The crew started their return trip on October 3. Kain recorded the journey: "Said farewell to these mountains. Via Grand Creek to Spray Lakes, snow,

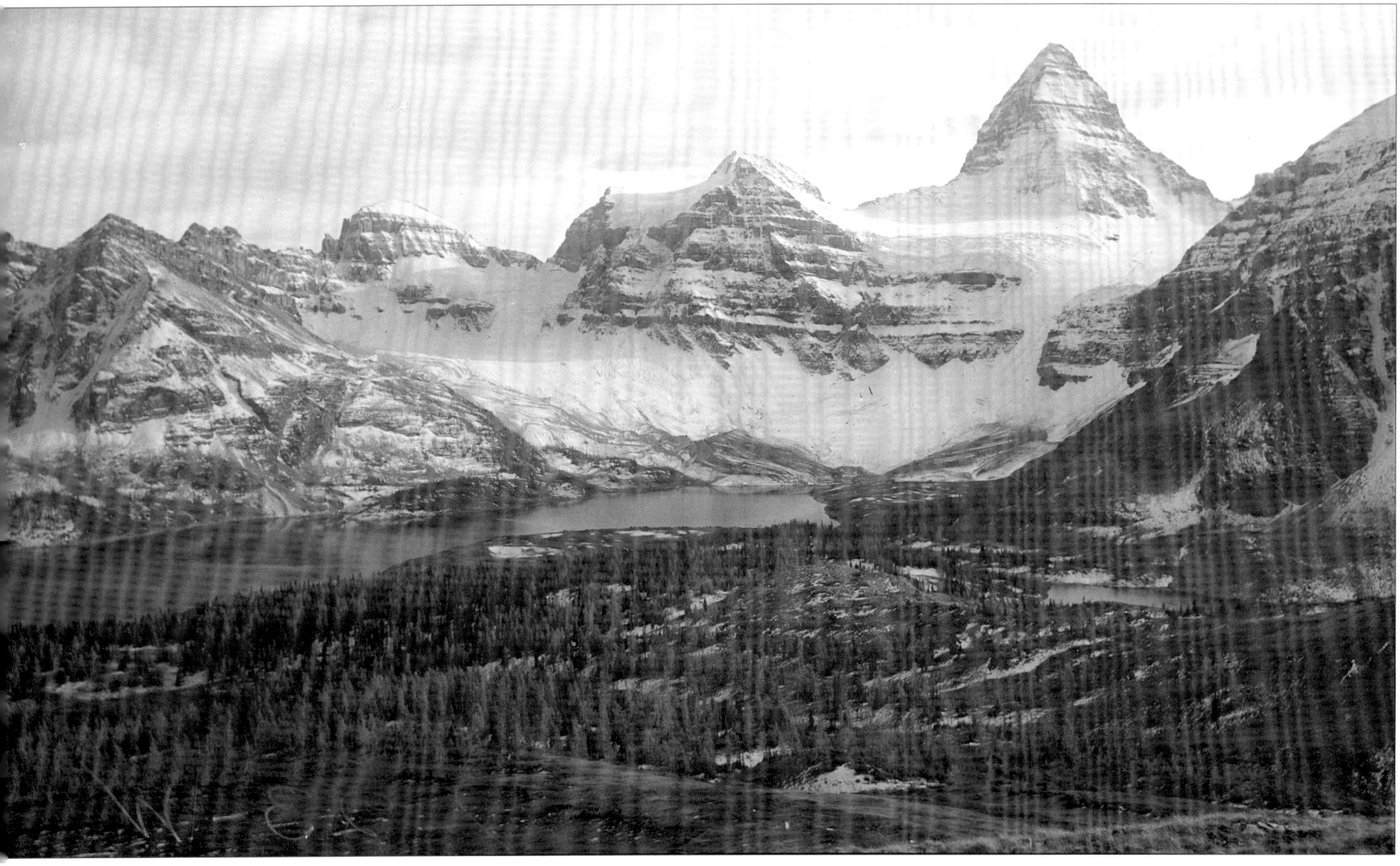

This classic view of Mount Assiniboine and Lake Magog from the Nub shows what the area looked like a century ago. There are reference points in the 1913 photograph that are visible in the repeat picture: the snow chute on the right; the rock outcrop in the centre foreground; the meadow in the front left. Along with several peaks behind Lake Magog, this photograph provides excellent comparisons of one of the most photographed mountains in the Canadian Rockies. WHE_1913_W13-247, Library and Archives Canada

path very poor, it snows like in winter, 6 pm camp at Spray Lake." Because it was snowing, they remained in camp the next day to rest the horses. The men resumed their trip on October 5. "Start 10 AM, past large lake, one foot of snow, very poor for walking. Winter scenery." They camped that evening at White Man Gap and made it back to Banff the following morning. "Start 9 AM. Last day with pack train, path good, 6 miles [10 kilometres] on road (Spray Road). Two hours."

Kain spent eight days in Banff before travelling to Calgary, where he met Wheeler and stayed overnight. After spending the day visiting friends, he and Wheeler took the train to Fort McLeod, arriving at 11:00 and staying at the American Hotel (a historic hotel that still remains). The men took the morning train to Crowsnest Pass and set up near Cautley's camp about 800 metres from the pass. J.N. Wallace, the Dominion's commissioner for the boundary survey, was also there. In preparation for the 1914 field season, the three men spent the next five days determining the location of the

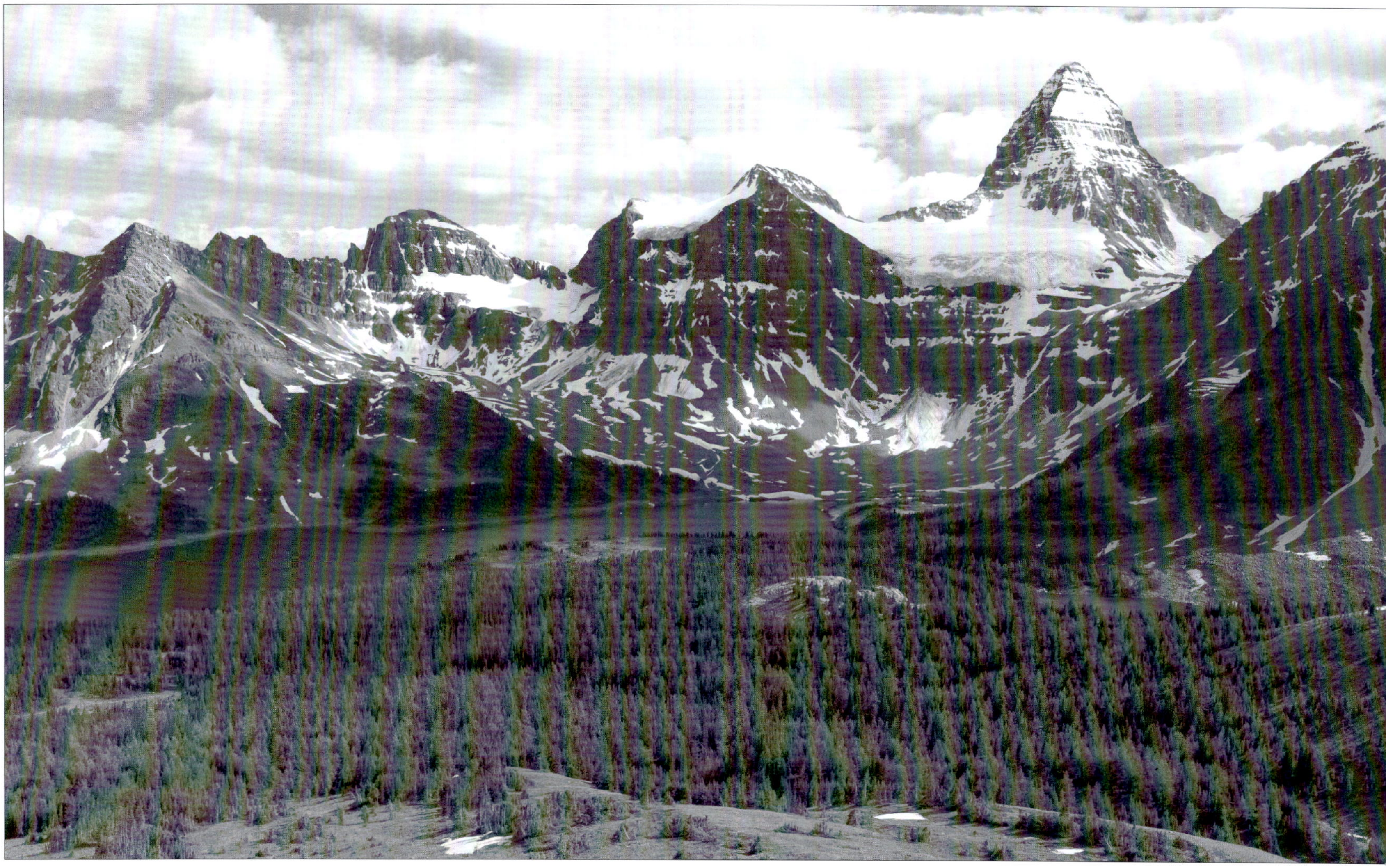

The glaciers on the lower slopes around Mount Assiniboine had almost disappeared by 2010. There is also an increase in the density of the forest. MLP2010_W13-247, Mountain Legacy Project

boundary through the Crowsnest Pass, while Kain did the cooking. In a letter to Malek he wrote: "This summer, Mr. Wheeler was a totally different person. Everybody says that. Never before had he been so good-humored and agreeable. This summer, I did not hear a single cross word from him!"

The 1913 field season was successful. The boundary survey completed three passes, started the preliminary survey of the largest pass along the Great Divide, and mapped the spine of the Rocky Mountains from Kicking Horse Pass to Mount Assiniboine. The two crews established efficient routines for their surveying, and their work interconnected effectively. Wheeler and Cautley developed a harmonious relationship, and Campbell managed the topographical crew well during Wheeler's absence.

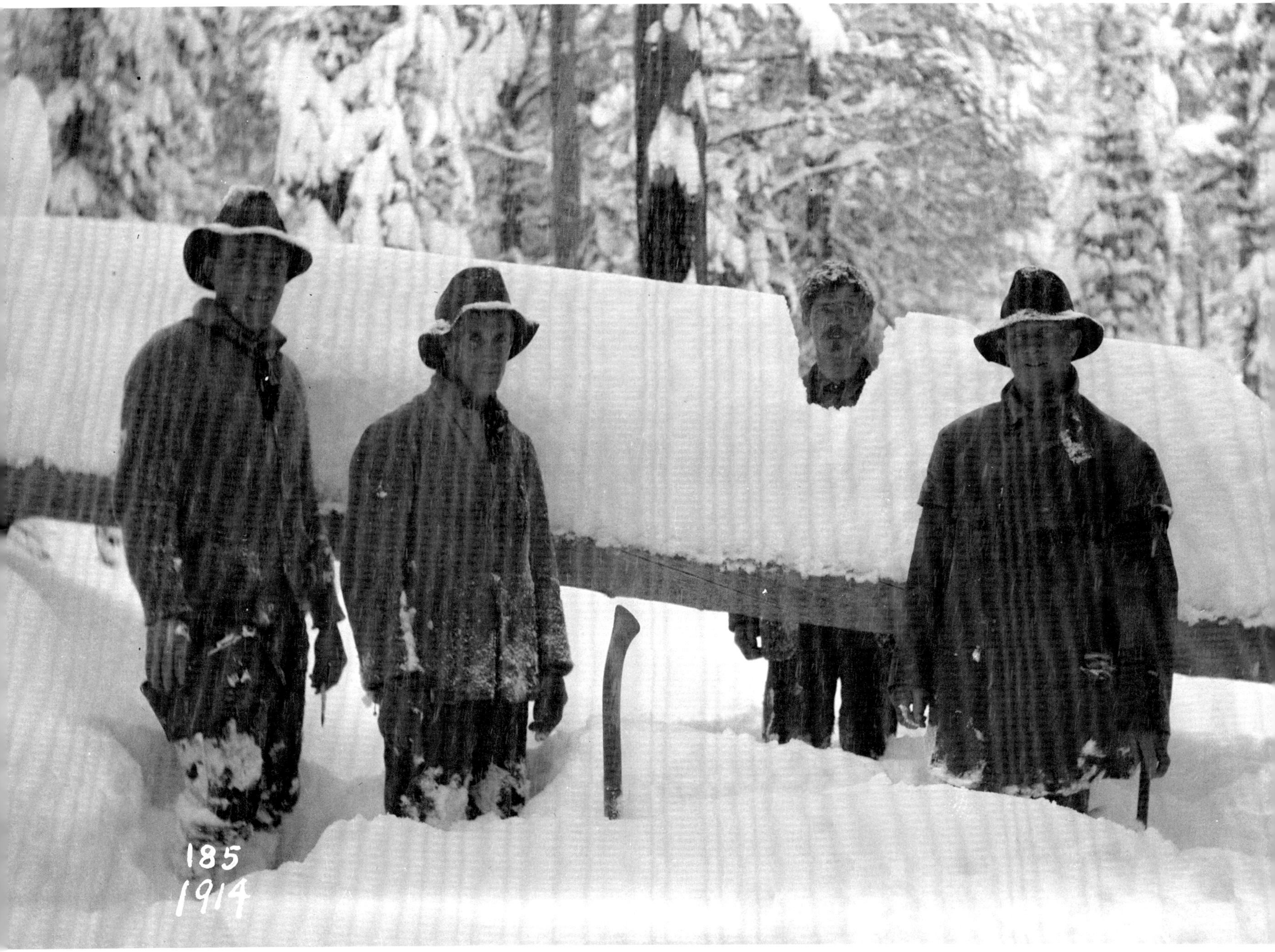

Members of R.W. Cautley's survey crew at Akamina Pass after a snowstorm in early October. Looking through the snow behind the log is Cautley's assistant, W.M. Carthew, who was killed during World War I. e011166461, Library and Archives Canada

1914

The fieldwork was only one part of the boundary survey. During the winter of 1913–14 Wheeler and Cautley needed to transform the information they gathered into usable data. Field notes had to be copied, calculations made and maps produced. Reports had to be written and photographs put into albums and labelled. Wheeler went back to his winter home at Sidney on Vancouver Island, while Cautley returned to Edmonton. As they did in the field, both men needed to develop procedures to work together in sharing information. Communication took time for mail was the main method for sending documents. The office work in the winter would take about the same amount of time to complete as the fieldwork. Cautley largely worked alone, for his calculations and maps were not as complex. A major part of Wheeler's office work was producing precise, detailed topographic maps of the Great Divide and adjacent terrain, and he employed Campbell and one or more draftsmen for this work. The pictures taken with the phototopographic camera were a vital part of the mapping, and the large-sized photographs were used to delineate the Great Divide and surrounding area. It was imperative to try to complete the office work before the next field season started, so there was always a sense of urgency to operations in the winter.

The main priority for the 1914 field season was surveying the Crowsnest Pass area. With extensive coal and timber resources, it was considered the most economically important section of the Alberta–British Columbia boundary survey. A road and railway went through the Crowsnest corridor. During their reconnaissance in the fall, Wheeler and Cautley decided that it would be advantageous to carefully delineate the boundary through the entire area, not just the main pass. There were two small passes, Tent and Ptolemy, a few kilometres to the south, and one small pass, Phillipps, about two kilometres to the north. In 1914 the railway went through the Crowsnest Pass, while the road (which was just beginning to have automobile traffic) went through Phillipps Pass. In his government report Wheeler provided an overview of the survey of the area.

> The Crowsnest Pass, or more correctly speaking, system of passes, is a somewhat complex proposition. It has been the practice of the Commission in the survey of passes made thus far to carry the delimitation of the boundary from the summit of the limestone peak dominating the pass on one side to the dominating summit on the opposite side. To do this in the case of the Crowsnest Pass entailed a distance of more than fifteen miles [24 kilometres], and necessitated the survey of three minor passes within that distance.
>
> In view of the fact that the entire area appears to be underlaid by extensive coal beds on both sides of the divide, and that large interests are involved, it was decided to delimit the boundary for the full distance from limestone peak to limestone peak. Fifty-four concrete monuments were constructed at points selected along the watershed. Where the watershed formed a natural boundary, nine brass bolts were sunk in the rock at suitable points and rock cairns built over them.

Wheeler had conducted a phototopographic survey of the western side of the Crowsnest Pass area in 1900. In addition, during 1913 and the first part of 1914, Bridgland made a phototopographic survey of the Crowsnest Forest Reserve on the Alberta side of the Great Divide. During the second half of the 1914 field season, Bridgland and his assistant surveyed Waterton Lakes National Park. Wheeler was able to use the information from these surveys to make his work on this section of the boundary survey easier. After meeting Bridgland in Calgary on July 8, Wheeler wrote to Deville.

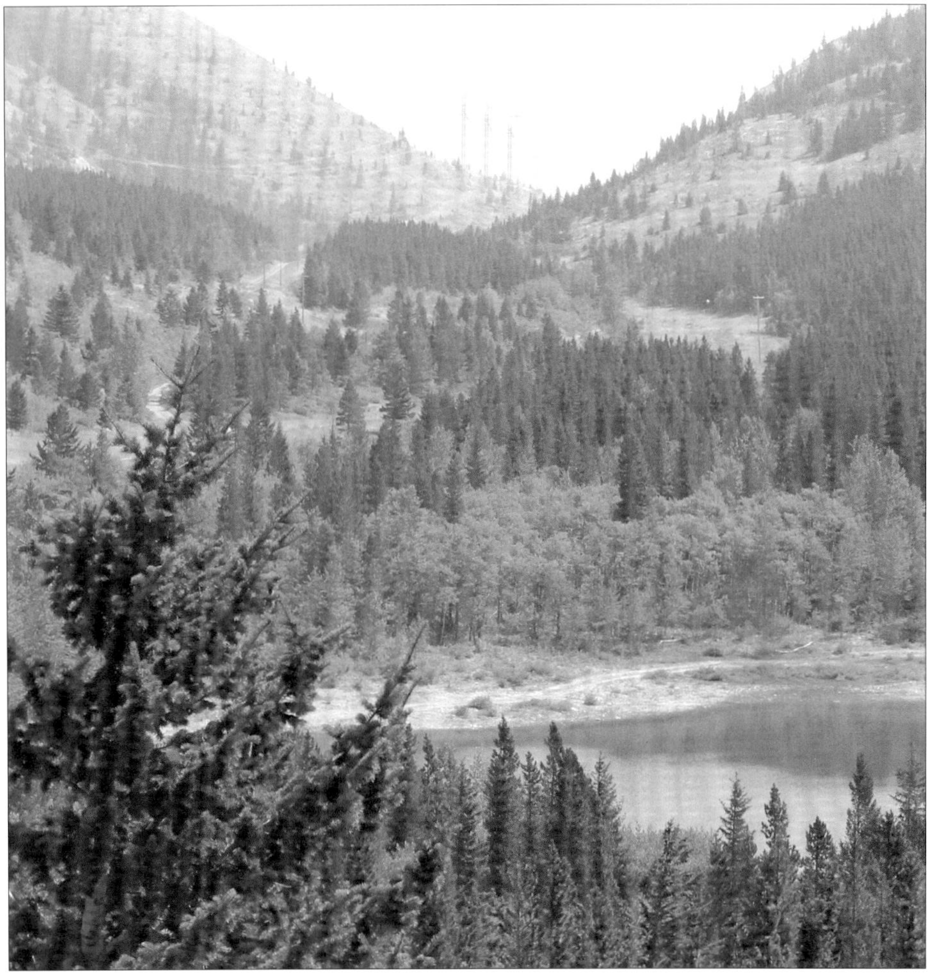

This is a view of Phillipps Pass and the small pond there looking east into Alberta. The route of the original automobile highway was through the pass. Today a power line and pipeline go through Phillipps Pass. Jay Sherwood photo

> Recently I met Mr. Bridgland in Calgary and discussed with him the survey he is making of the Forest Reserve on the east side of the Divide, south of Crowsnest Pass....
>
> I have arranged with him to co-operate in the matter of stations occupied, so that I can use his on the east side of the Divide and he can use a number of mine to supplement his work.
>
> It will be necessary, however, that we should be able to get together during the winter in order to use each other's enlargements.

Deville arranged for the two men to spend time sharing their data, and the two men found that the information gathered from their surveys was in agreement.

The reconnaissance of Phillipps Pass led to a disagreement between Cautley and Wheeler regarding the location of the boundary there, the only occasion during the entire boundary survey that there was any contention. There was a shallow pond 25 metres below the elevation of the main part of the pass. There were no apparent waterways flowing into the pond, no obvious outflow source and no evidence that the lake had risen any higher than the pass at any time in recent history. The pass was almost level, with the eastern end about 50 centimetres higher than the western entrance. Crowsnest Lake, which was in Alberta, was about one kilometre distant and below the lake from the western end of Phillipps Pass. Just above the lake there was a spring. The Alberta and federal commissioners believed that the water flowing out of the spring originated from Phillipps Lake and that all of the lake should be in Alberta. Wheeler, the BC commissioner, contended that there was no definitive evidence connecting the water from the lake and the spring. Because there was no surface outflow, and the eastern end of the pass was higher, Wheeler believed that the divide should be marked there.

During the winter of 1913–14 there was considerable correspondence among the three governments attempting to reach an agreement before the field season started. The Dominion commissioner, J.N. Wallace, wrote to Deville on January 26, 1914: "Owing, however, to the fact that Crowsnest Pass survey is not yet completed, and that it will be visited this coming season, and also to the fact that the main travelled route goes over the small pass and not over Crow's Nest Pass where the Canadian Pacific Railway crosses the summit, it seems desirable to have the boundary established in the small pass."

In a letter on April 9, 1914, Dawson, BC's surveyor general, wrote to Deville:

> It would appear that the matter might, with advantage, be left in abeyance and adjusted at some future date, probably in connection with other matters on which the Commissioners may disagree. As, however, the work for the coming season is to commence in the vicinity, the expenses in returning to the ground in or-

> der to set monuments would be avoided, could the matter be settled in the immediate future.
>
> Possibly the simplest way to solve this question out of hand is to divide the area between the two Provinces and I am prepared to accept this solution, provided it commends itself to yourself and the Director of Surveys for the Province of Alberta.

Deville agreed to this suggestion, but the Alberta government refused to compromise. Attempts to resolve the location of the boundary in Phillipps Pass during the summer of 1914 were unsuccessful. In a letter to Dawson on September 9 Wheeler wrote: "I would now recommend that no further action be taken in this matter for the present." This small section was not defined and surveyed until 1924, the final year of the initial Alberta-BC boundary survey, when the boundary line was placed through the middle of the pass.

In late February the three boundary commissioners met in Victoria, and on the 24th they issued a memorandum for the 1914 program.

> That it is advisable to first complete the survey of Crowsnest Pass, and then undertake the survey of as many as possible of the passes, specified in your instructions (18th June 1913), and situated between the International Boundary and Simpson Pass. While the Yellowhead Pass is an important one, we consider that the expense involved in moving some 400 miles [645 kilometres] to it from Crowsnest Pass would be detrimental to the general survey of the Boundary.
>
> That your instructions, dated 18th June 1913, be amended to include the establishing of the Boundary in any passes of small extent, which may be found to be immediately adjacent to, and not separated by any high mountain from, the passes already specified in your instructions of June 18th, 1913, provided that, in the unanimous opinion of the Commission, the survey of the Boundary in such small adjacent passes can be undertaken without due delay of the general progress of the Boundary Survey.

The composition of Wheeler's survey crew remained unchanged. To make Cautley's work more efficient, it was decided that he, like Wheeler, should have an assistant, preferably a person who was a Dominion land surveyor. One additional axeman was added to his crew.

There was a small change to the monuments. The thickness of the brass plates was increased and the bolts used to fasten them were also to be brass.

In preparations for the upcoming field season, there was a realization that determination of the boundary was urgently needed in two areas. One was in Elk Pass, north of Crowsnest. Wheeler believed that four BC lots surveyed there might be partially in Alberta. In his government report Wheeler wrote that this was a "pass of very considerable importance, owing to the fact that it [was] the projected route of the Grain Belt Construction and Development Company's railway from Calgary to Fernie via the Elk River valley." He added that "extensive location surveys" had been made by the company in the vicinity. The second area was south of Crowsnest Pass near the headwaters of the North Fork of the Flathead River. Wheeler decided to send Campbell and most of his crew to do a quick topographic survey in Elk Pass while en route from Banff to Crowsnest Pass with the pack train at the beginning of the field season (see map on page 62). The three coal lease lots south of Crowsnest Pass would be checked by Cautley during the summer.

Fortunately for the boundary survey, there was no conflict in Crowsnest Pass. As part of its construction of the BC Southern Railway from Crowsnest Pass to Kootenay Lake, the Canadian Pacific Railway received a land grant of some large lots in southeastern BC from the provincial government. In 1904 the CPR hired veteran surveyor John McLatchie to survey the east boundary of Lot 4589. The description of this lot defined the northeast corner as being on the BC Southern Railway line at the Alberta-BC boundary. Since the provincial boundary had not yet been surveyed, McLatchie had to make his best determination of the boundary. In their reconnaissance during the fall of 1913, Wheeler and Cautley accepted McLatchie's location for the northeast corner of Lot 4589.

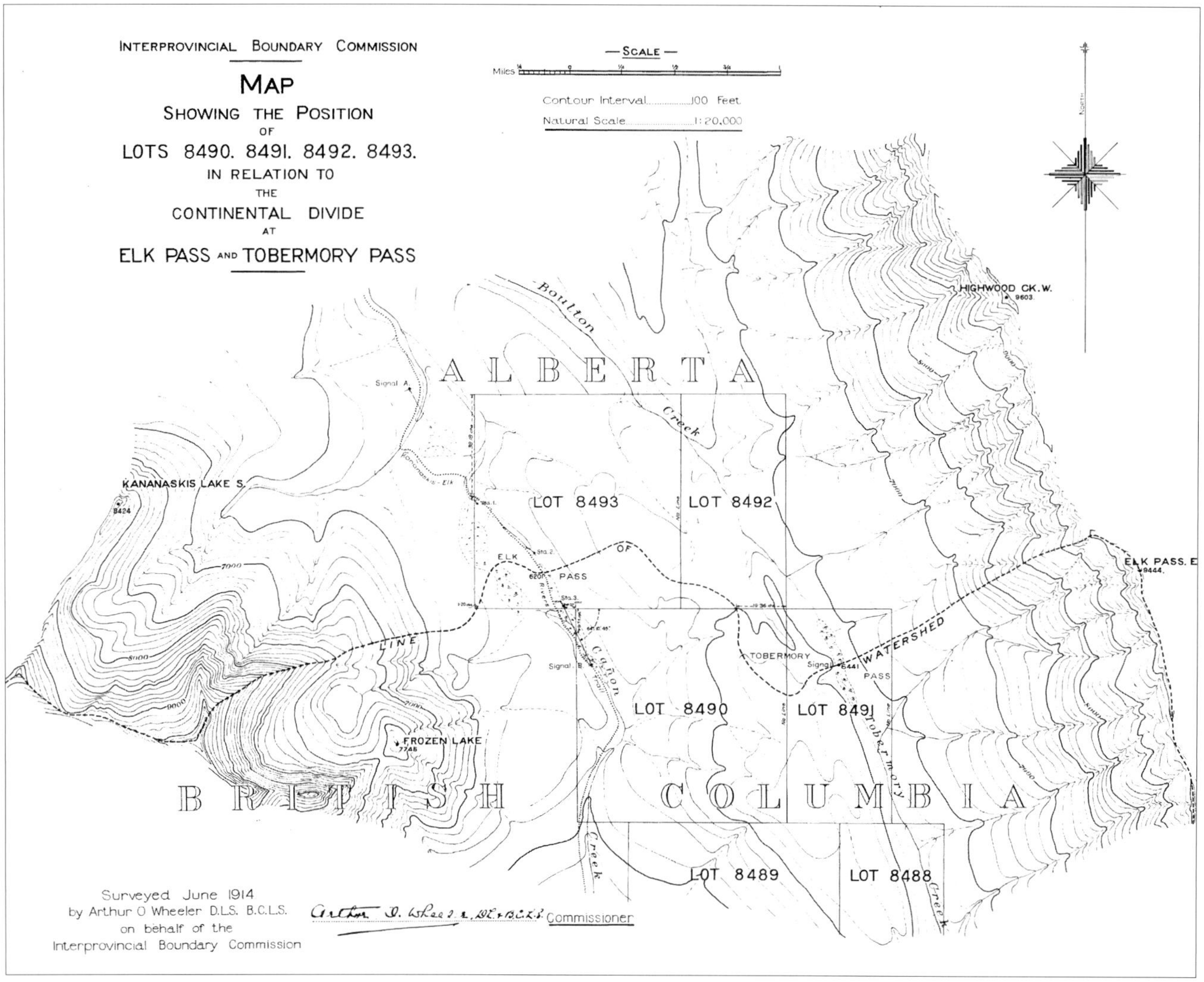

Wheeler's map shows that the four British Columbia lots they surveyed in Elk Pass all extended into Alberta. Commission Report. Part 1. Atlas

The east boundary of Lot 4589 was a true meridian line that ran directly south for over 43 miles (70 kilometres) to the International Boundary. Posts were established every mile (1.6 kilometres) and at other points. The boundary survey in 1914 connected to two of McLatchie's posts. For many years, lots surveyed in the southeast corner of British Columbia tied into McLatchie's line.

Cautley and his crew started the field season first. Since he had a larger crew and was carrying more supplies as well as the items for the monuments, Cautley wanted to have his own pack train so he didn't have to make arrangements for horses every year. He received permission, and in late May he went to Morley, east of Banff, where he purchased a pack train of 14 horses from Frank Wellman, a guide and outfitter. Cautley shipped the horses to Coleman in the Crowsnest Pass and sent his assistant, W.M. Carthew, to get their initial camp ready. Since there were a large number of monuments to establish in the Crowsnest Pass, Cautley also arranged for both the cement and gravel to be sent by rail, for he had not found a good source of gravel in the pass during the previous fall. Cautley travelled by train from Edmonton to Crowsnest Pass, and his crew assembled there on June 2.

During the winter, Conrad Kain had gone back to New Zealand for more mountain climbing. He returned to Banff in early June to work on the boundary survey for the first part of the 1914 season. From Banff he wrote to Malek on June 5. Kain told her that he had sprained his hand while chopping wood. He observed that there was an economic depression in Canada. "Unfortunately, I have to say that, at the moment, the conditions in Canada are not the best. Thousands of workers are out of work. Even in Banff, there are several hundred of them. For that reason, wages are low. You will be surprised to hear that my salary, too, was cut, lowered by 25 dollars per month. It is very annoying that the price of food is still as high as before."

One of the members of Wheeler's 1914 crew was Horace Westmoreland, a mountain climber from England who had been on Wheeler's 1912 survey crew and attended the 1912 and both of the 1913 Alpine Club of Canada camps. During the winter of 1913–14 he had worked as a draftsman for Wheeler at Sidney. Westmoreland wrote a brief recollection of his time on Wheeler's crew. Before departing from Banff, he noted that they tested the instruments on the golf course, as had been done at the beginning of the 1913 field season. "There was a string of perhaps six horses to go with us, a party which consisted of Alan Campbell, myself and Conrad plus a cook and a packer. We three took the train to Morley. There was open prairie there and we camped near the track to await the arrival of the horses which were coming down by trail."

From Morley, Kain wrote to Malek on June 14: "Today is my last day in civilization. Tomorrow, we will leave with our pack train. We are six men and ten horses. Morley is an Indian village. There is only a storage house and a station. We were here for several days. I waited in vain for your next mail. Now I have to wait until July 20th, until we get to the Crowsnest pass. I hope to find news from you there. First of all, I must say that I am healthy, only my hand is not yet totally as it should be. I still have to be very careful."

Westmoreland recalled: "After the horses arrived with the packer we loaded up and started up the trail to Elk Pass, eighty miles [128 kilometres]. The summit of Elk Pass is wide and boggy with sparse bushes." Campbell began his survey at the pass by taking observations on Polaris. "We ran a traverse, plotted it, and erected a signal at each end, and on a bright moonlit night Campbell completed his orientation." Although the boundary had yet to be officially determined, Campbell's surveying indicated that the four BC lots in Elk Pass extended into Alberta.

Westmoreland described the work at Elk Pass.

> The survey was phototopographic. We went up to timberline where we bivouacked, climbed the mountain we were to work from, set up the tripod which had a triangular sling between its three legs, put a big rock in the sling and then built it up with stone until a solid cairn, otherwise the vibration caused by the wind spoiled the photographs which we had to take. Nine exposures took us round the horizon with a bit of an overlap. We then replaced the camera with the theodolite and read angles in azimuth, and elevation or depression, of about 20 points in each of the nine photographs. From these the mountains were plotted in the winter in the office.

Westmoreland recounted hunting with Kain.

> On an off day Conrad and I walked up the slopes of Mount Fox looking for fresh meat and we saw some mountain goats at the foot of a crag about five or six hundred feet high to the left of us. We went across and hit the crag about half way up and traversed along a narrow ledge about a foot wide [30 centimetres]. I took my rifle and started to try and shoot one. I only had six cartridges and anyone who has used a rifle knows how difficult it is to fire downwards at an angle forty-five degrees and hit a target.
>
> The goats were disturbed by the first few shots and achieved the most beautiful ascent of the crag by leaping many feet in the air on to small protuberances again and again until they had passed us about one hundred feet [30 metres] away. I hit the last one and it fell two hundred and fifty feet [75 metres]. We went down and Conrad carried it back to camp. It must have been the grandfather of all mountain goats in the district. It was practically impossible to cut or chew the meat

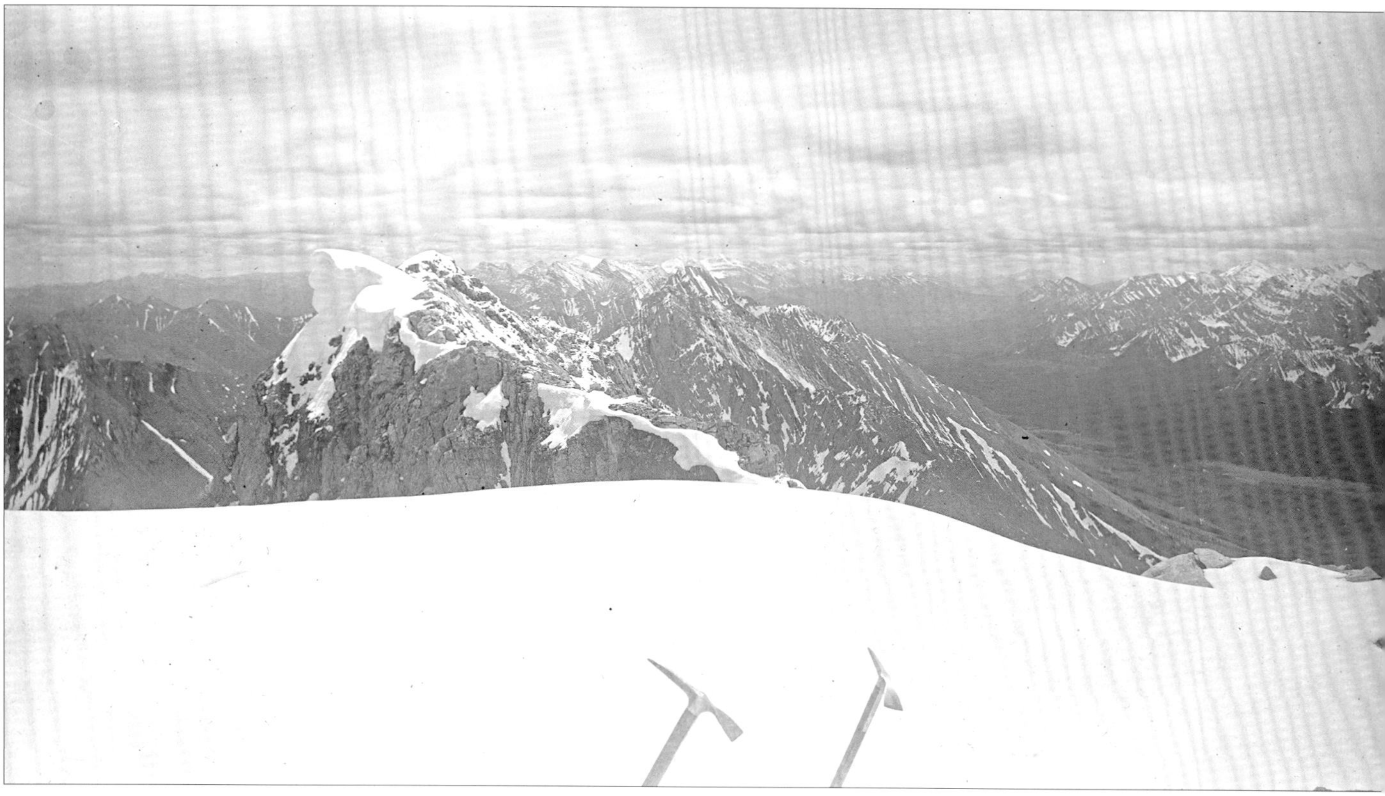

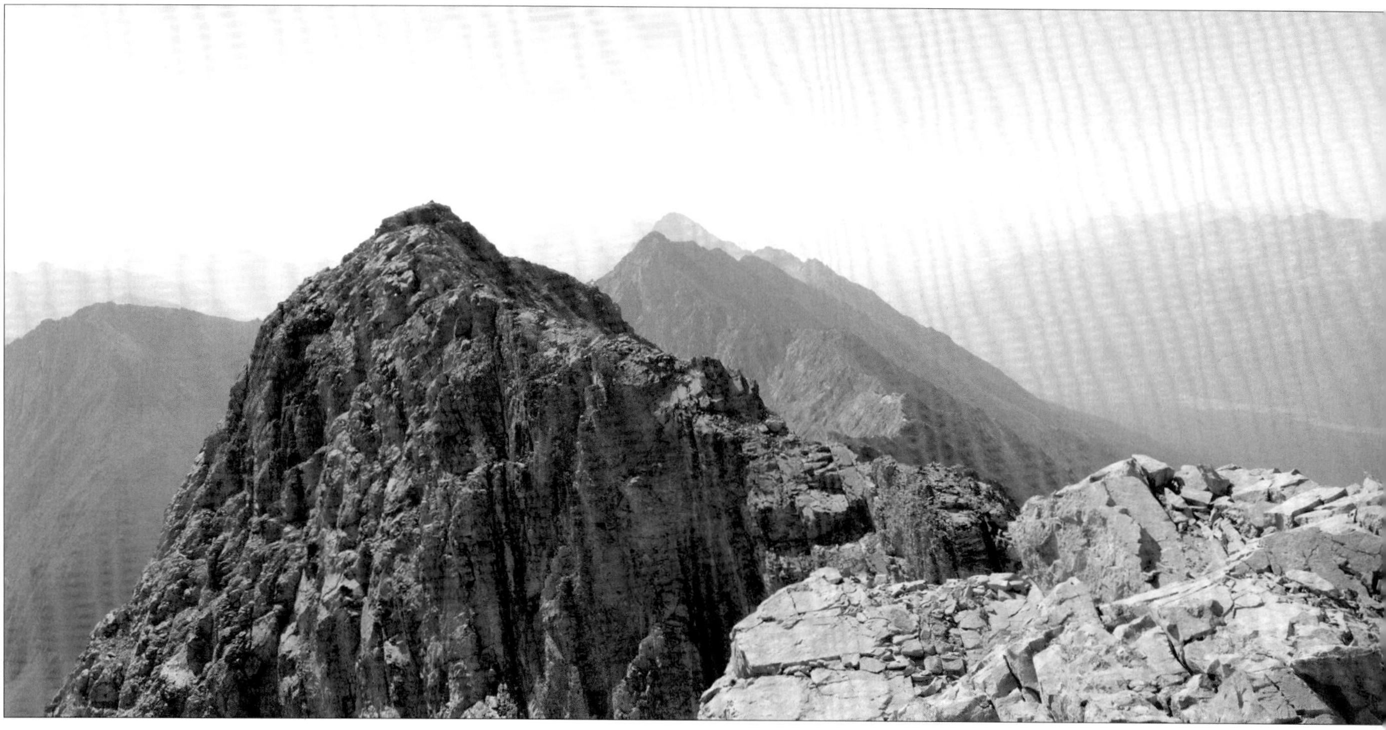

During the survey of Elk Pass in late June Campbell's crew climbed to this peak in the Highwood Range. From here Campbell had an excellent panorama of the Elk River valley, as shown in these two photographs. Since the picture was taken early in the field season, there is still a large amount of winter snow remaining on the peaks. WHE1914_31, WHE1914_32, Library and Archives Canada

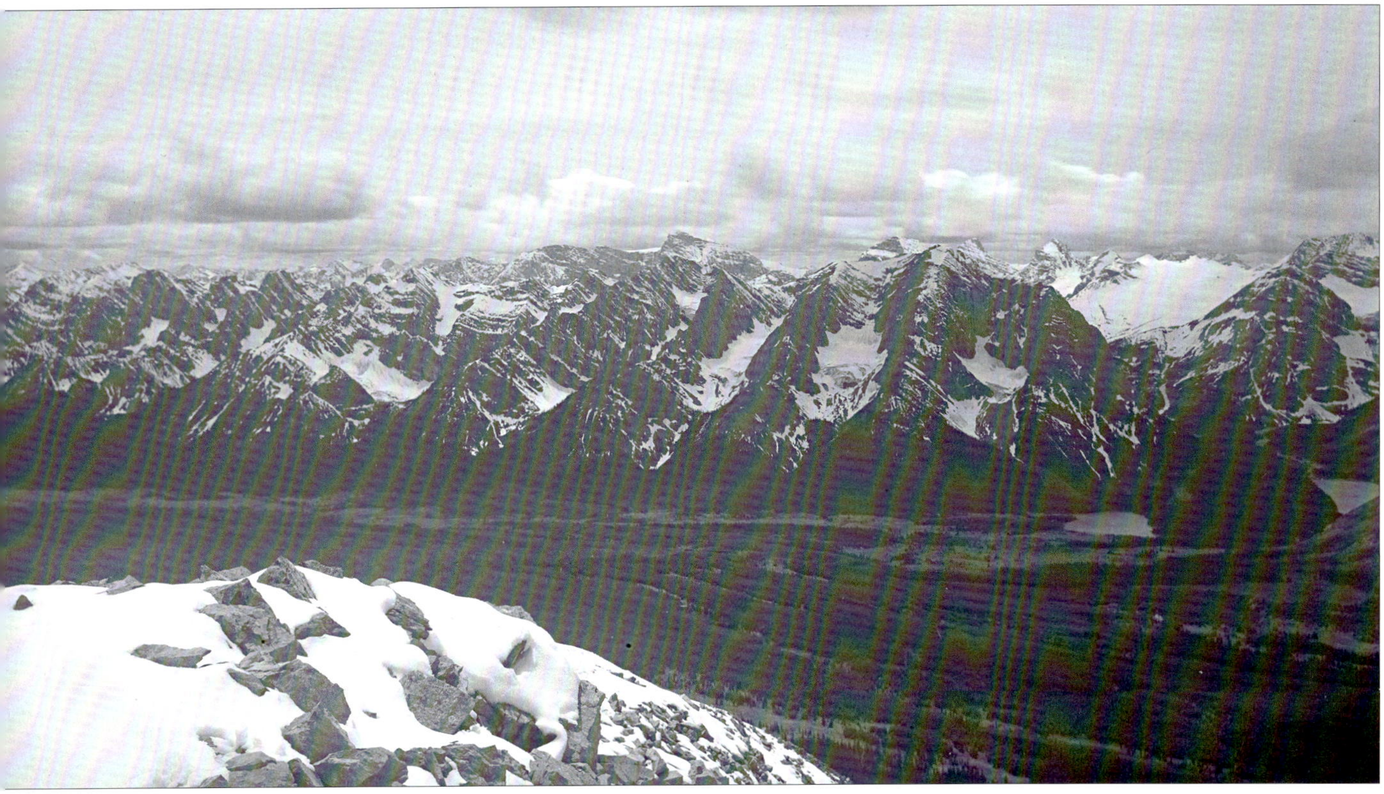

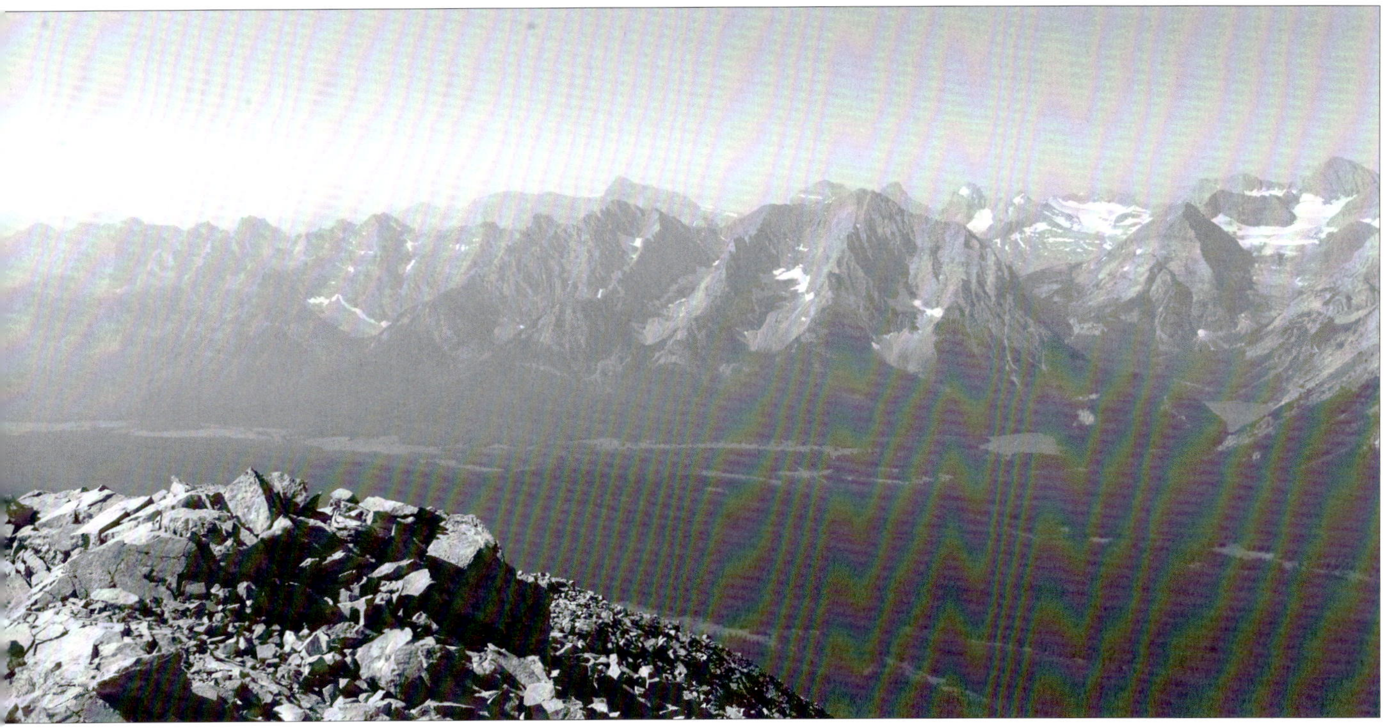

Smoke has affected the clarity of the repeat photograph, but snow is almost completely gone from the Elk valley by early August of 2007. The change in glaciation around the Elk Lakes is noticeable. MLP2007_W14-31, MLP W14-32, Mountain Legacy Project

> when cooked, but it made the most wonderful beef tea, we used to carry it in thermos flasks when we went to occupy stations on the peaks. It was wonderfully sustaining.

Kain wrote to Malek from an unnamed mountain near Elk Pass on June 25.

> I am sitting here on an unclimbed mountain top! It is not very high, but offers gorgeous views. The top is on the Great Divide. In the east and south, there are bare mountains like the Dolomites, only not so steep. On the scree below, I see wildlife tracks, but no goats or sheep. East of the top, the Elbow Pass can be seen. A week ago, there must have been snow on the pass. Now it is spring green. In the south, the mountains turned into hills. North of here, the two Kananaskis Lakes can be seen. The upper one is especially beautiful. The colour changes very distinctly. If the sun is shining the lake is light green, but in the shade it is deep blue. On the lake are four little isles and one tiny one with only three or four trees on it. Northwest, one sees the Elk Valley, at the end of which are two larger lakes and in between them, a small one. In the background, there are high mountains, without names, with hanging glaciers. North northwest, one can see a bit of Mount Assiniboine, that is to say we believe this beautiful mountain to be Mount Assiniboine. The forest consists of fir, spruce, and larch trees. The bottom of the valley is mossy and thus, many bad flies inhabit it! What can I tell you about the flowers? I cannot find the words! I wish only you could see this garden of flowers! You would be happy like a child, and I would be the happiest man to see you in such happy moments! The flowers are mostly in yellow or white colours. But there are also some red ones. This morning, I found the first forget-me-not in a blue colour for which I have no words. Yesterday we were in the forest all day. I thought of you almost all day, because I saw so many flowers, which brought such fond memories. I put some of the flowers in a book to press them for you. What a pity that the life of the flowers is so short! How beautiful it would be if the flowers could reach you fresh, just like picked. There is a cold wind. I have to stop writing and put on gloves. At this windy elevation, I say goodbye for today!

The next day, from their main camp, Kain wrote: "Today, we have snow and all the mountains are in fog. It is rather cold. We are going into the forest and hack out a baseline." Two days later, he mentioned the hunting trip that Westmoreland described. "Yesterday, we went up on a little mountain. It was terribly cold. We stayed on top for five hours! On the way back, Mr. West[moreland] shot a wild goat, so we will have a good goat soup today. Tomorrow, we will move on to Crowsnest pass. Perhaps for five to six days."

Kain wrote to Malek from Crowsnest Pass on July 7: "Trip is beautiful, much of it through forest." He also noted that his hand was still sprained and had gotten swollen after using an axe for a few days. Kain remained with the boundary survey until late July, when he went to the Alpine Club camp at Yoho National Park. Afterwards he left for New Zealand again.

At Crowsnest Pass Campbell inspected the controversial Phillipps Pass. Westmoreland wrote:

> On one of our days while surveying the area we came across a small lake. Here in the Lake District we would call it a tarn. The definition of whether it was Alberta or British Columbia depended on which way the water flowed, to the east or to the west.…This lake had no outlet to show us which way the water would flow but in an easterly direction on the railway track there was a stream gushing out of a rock face and Campbell had the idea that if we could colour the water in the lake sufficiently, then dash down to the gushing stream and it came out coloured, the small lake would belong to Alberta. However we had no colouring matter and so left it.

It took Cautley until August 24 to complete the survey of the boundary through the Crowsnest Pass.

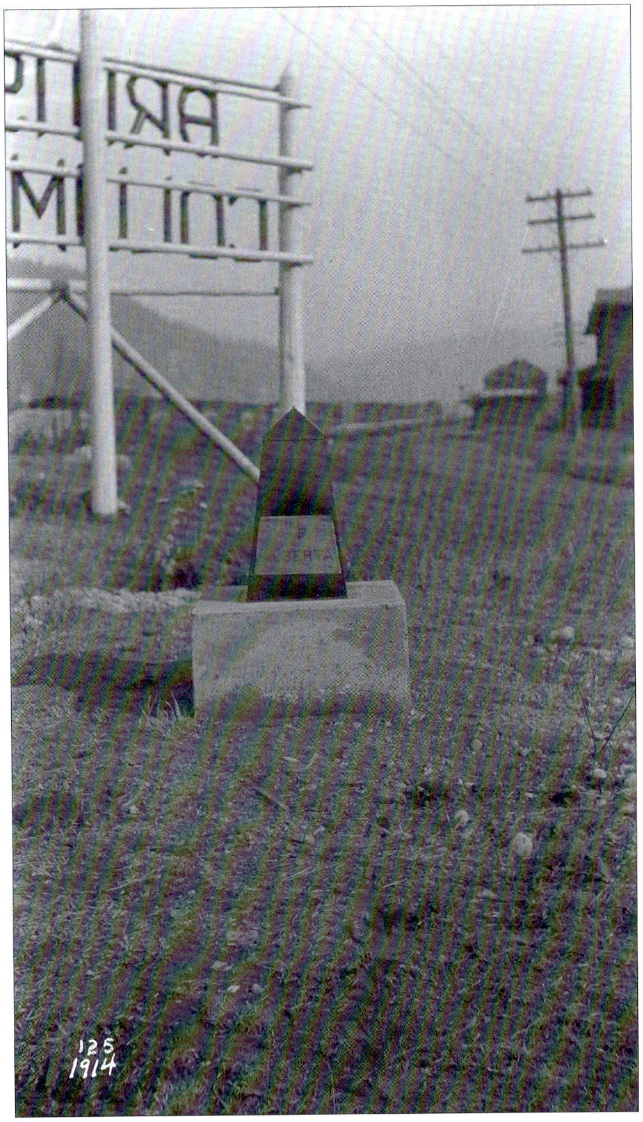

Looking east into Alberta from station 1F in Crowsnest Pass. The Great Divide sign is behind the monument, while the railroad line and train station are in the middle. Mountains are visible in the background. e011166455, Library and Archives Canada

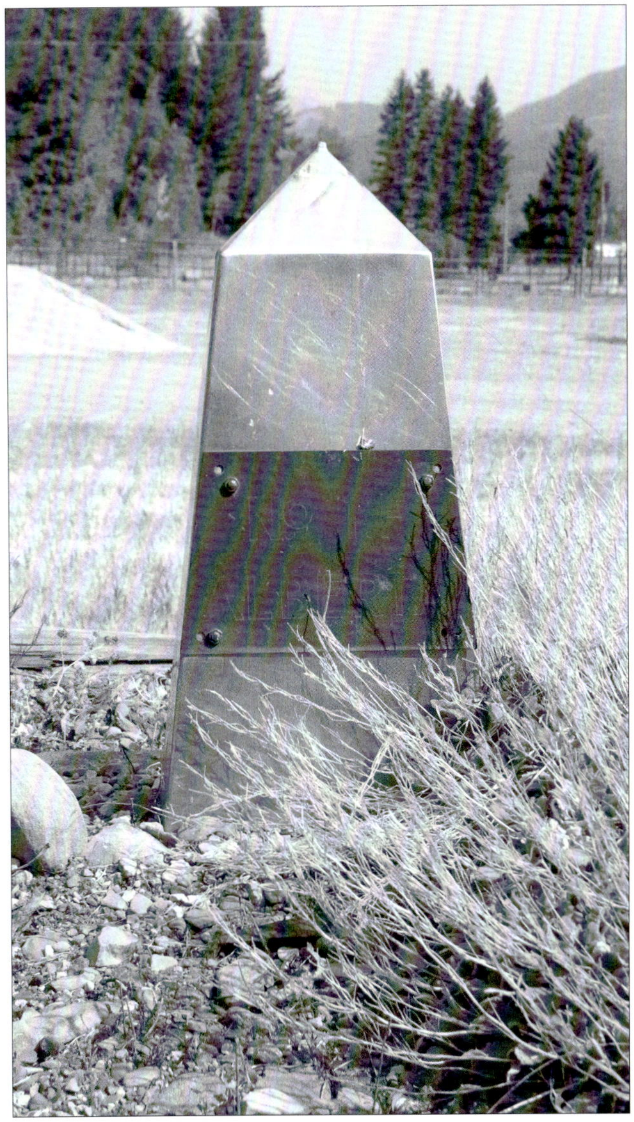

The present day Monument 1F shows the changes in human activity at Crowsnest Pass. Vegetation growth obscures part of the view of the mountains. Jay Sherwood photo

His primary station, 1F, was along the divide near the railway tracks. Crowsnest was a divisional point and had a railway station, hotel, post office and store, along with residences for the railway employees. The work went smoothly. The crew cut and surveyed 21 kilometres of boundary line, established 54 concrete monuments and set nine brass bolts with rock cairns. Seven of the concrete monuments were north of Crowsnest Pass, while the remainder were to the south and encompassed Tent and Ptolemy Passes. The government wagon road from the railway line to the International Boundary went through Tent Pass, while Ptolemy Pass had a trail. The boundary was hook-shaped, enabling Cautley to reach the most southerly monuments via these passes without having to traverse the entire

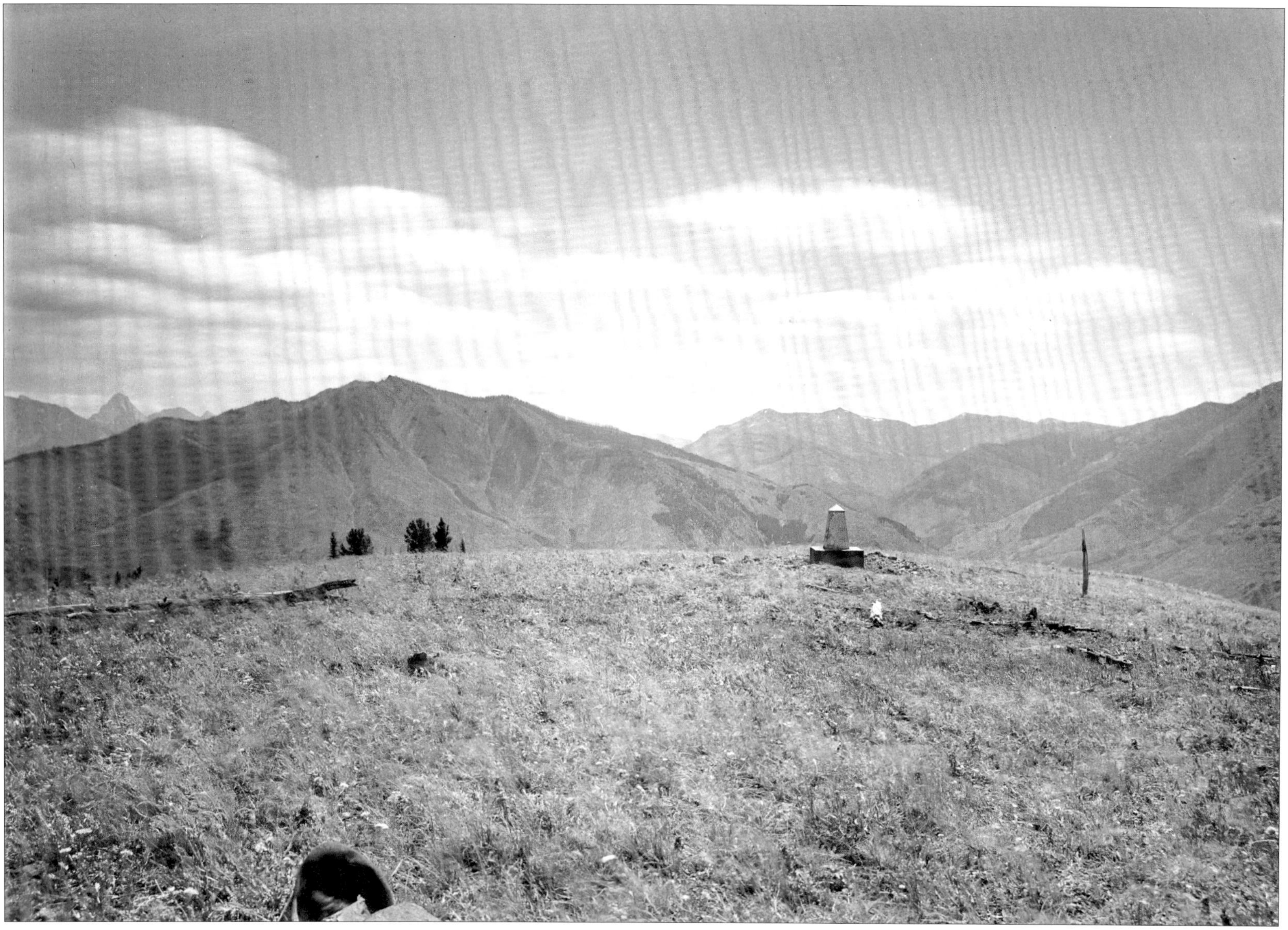

Station 57F in Crowsnest Pass. This picture shows the open landscape that was prevalent through much of the area in 1914. WHE1914_W14-122, Library and Archives Canada

boundary route. There were several Dominion land survey posts in the pass, so it was easy to make a connection from multiple stations. At the southern end of the Great Divide through the Crowsnest area, Cautley surveyed the north boundary of three coal lease lots that reached into the Flathead drainage. He marked the boundary through these lots and found that there was only a small variance. A portion of one lot was in Alberta, but that part had not been developed. The monumentation through the Crowsnest Pass area was the most extensive section of the entire boundary survey.

Wheeler's crew worked in the Crowsnest Pass area from early July until August 12. They established 22 stations, most of them done by Campbell. Only seven were over 2,000 metres and just three of these were higher than 2,500 metres. Wheeler remained in Banff

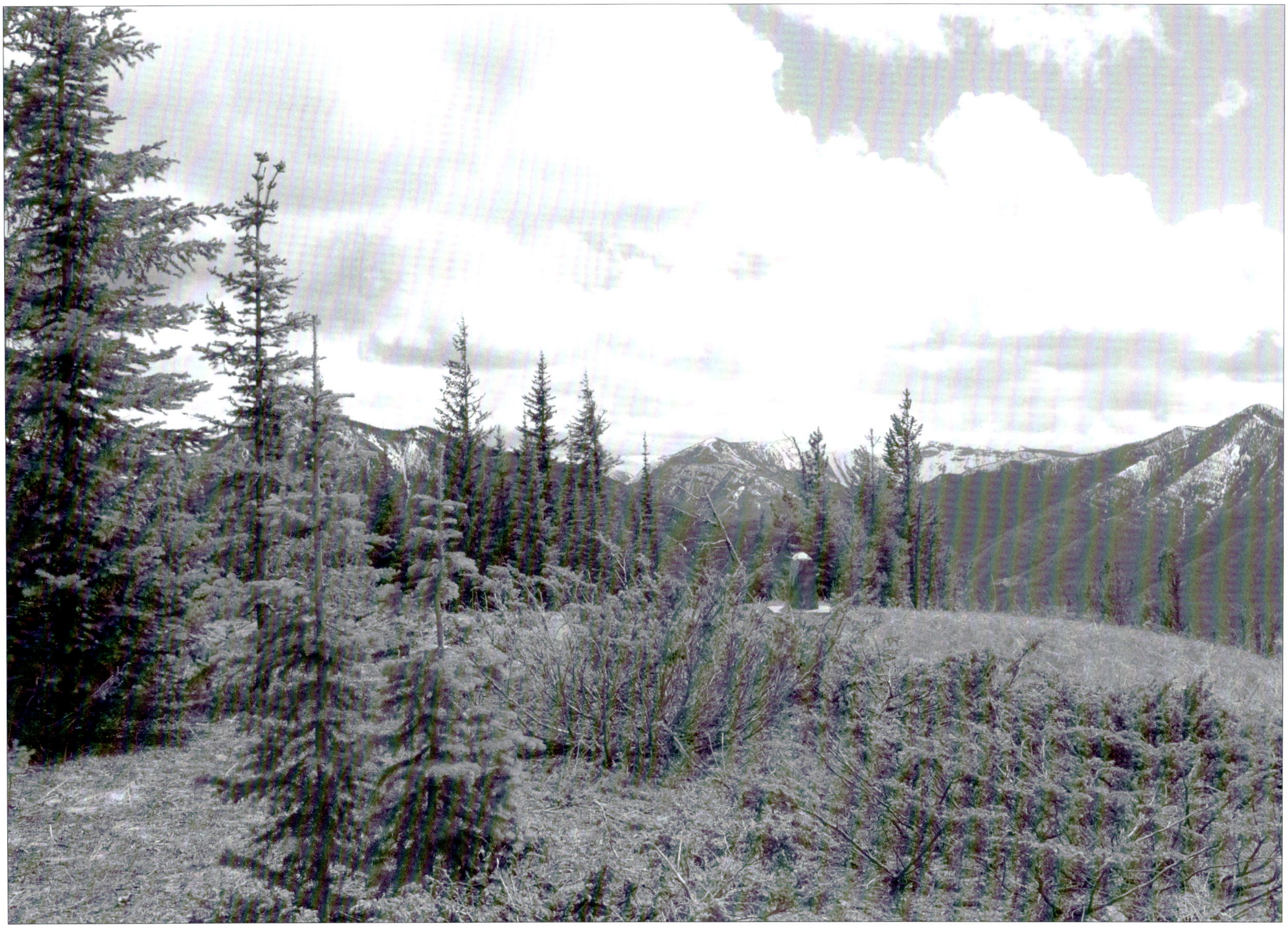

The original picture was taken in July, while the repeat photograph was made in mid-June when winter snow remained on the upper slopes of the mountains. The forest has become re-established in much of the Crowsnest Pass, although there are still partially open areas, like around this station. HB1_A0004834, Mountain Legacy

during June and early July, working on unfinished material from the 1913 season and preparing for the ACC camp. On July 7 he left Banff for Calgary on the evening train. The next day Wheeler met Bridgland, and the two men made arrangements to connect their surveys but keep the overlap to a minimum. On July 10 Wheeler left Calgary on the 6:00 a.m. train. Campbell and Westmoreland met him at the station and took him to the camp. Wheeler wrote in his diary: "Cautley came for lunch. Talked and looked over maps, etc.… Went with him & looked over ground at post office. Campbell with us. Cautley stayed for tea." J.N. Wallace came the following day, and the three commissioners and Campbell spent the afternoon looking at part of

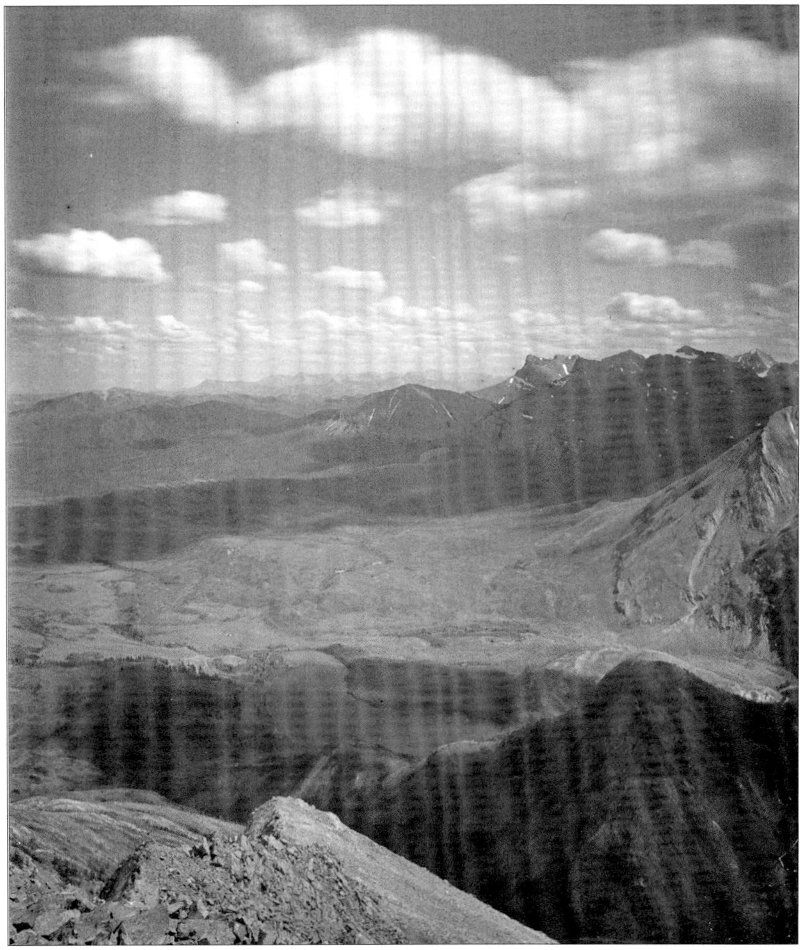

One of the pictures taken from a station on Mount Tecumseh shows the view south across the Crowsnest Pass region. Crowsnest Lake is in the picture. e06610706, Library and Archives Canada

Cautley's work. Since the Crowsnest Pass area was so extensive, the three commissioners spent a few days together inspecting the preliminary survey. On July 17 Wheeler returned to Banff, taking Kain with him. By the 29th Wheeler was back in the Crowsnest Pass, but he stayed there only until August 2, when he went back to the Alpine Club camp.

The commission report included some "general remarks on the boundary through the Crowsnest system of passes." It stated an attitude toward coal that was common at that time.

> All this section of country is underlain by valuable coal deposits, which outcrop on many of the ridges, and old prospect holes are seen right on the watershed. The same conditions are found on the Alberta side of the watershed, extending easterly throughout the foothills area of that region. So much coal has been discovered in this district and the market for it is, at present, so limited that many owners have to be content with doing development work only; but that the district will one day be a hive of industry, giving employment to many thousands of men, no one can doubt.

There was also a note on wildlife that was observed.

> Goats, moose, deer, bears, a great number of blue and ruffed grouse and ptarmigan on the rock slopes above timberline were seen on this part of the work: in fact, Mr. Cautley experienced some difficulty at one part of the line, where two bears would tumble sacks of cement into holes dug for monument bases, scatter gravel about and, on one occasion, dragged a full sack of cement more than a quarter of a mile [400 metres] through the woods.

World War I started on July 28, and Canada joined the conflict on August 4. There was a telegraph station in Crowsnest Pass, so the survey crews heard the news fairly quickly. Westmoreland had a commission with the 50th Highlanders. His regiment began mobilizing once the war started, so he left the crew. On August 12 Westmoreland telephoned Wheeler from Calgary to inform him that he had been called to join his regiment. Wheeler wrote to Deville regarding Westmoreland's status, and on September 15 the Dominion surveyor general replied:

> By Order in Council of the 11th August, 1914, employees of the Dominion Government, whether temporary or otherwise, who are called on military duty, are to be paid as if they had not left: accordingly Mr. Westmoreland will, until your field party is discharged, be entitled to the part of his salary which was being paid to him by the Dominion Government.

> This amount is only one-third of Mr. Westmoreland's full salary. The Surveyor General of British Columbia and the Director of Surveys of Alberta are being asked what they desire to be done as to the other two-thirds of the salary.

The BC government paid its share of Westmoreland's salary.

On August 14 Wheeler, accompanied by Wallace, returned to Crowsnest Pass. When the two men arrived they found the packer, Charlie Schultz, waiting for them with horses. The crew members were camped a short distance south toward Corbin, along the BC government road that went to the International Boundary. They were surveying toward North Kootenay Pass. From the campsite Wheeler and Campbell climbed Mount Ptolemy, the highest mountain in the area, and placed the last two bolts (105F and 107F) and cairns for Crowsnest Pass. Wheeler noted that the air was smoky, a problem that continued for several days. Wallace remained with Wheeler's crew for three days.

After Crowsnest Pass, there were two more passes that the boundary survey intended to monument as it headed south toward the International Boundary. Both North Kootenay and South Kootenay Passes were historic indigenous transportation routes between the prairies and the land west of the Rocky Mountains. Members of the Siksika First Nation travelled across these passes to trade at Tobacco Plains on the Kootenay River, and members of the Ktunaxa (Kootenay) journeyed to the prairie.

The survey crew worked south along the road past Corbin to Flathead Pass. Wheeler established two camera stations in the vicinity on August 22, and the men spent the next few days surveying from nearby peaks. On August 26 Wheeler noted that it was very smoky. While they were at the pass, Wheeler sent one of the packers ahead to explore the trail that went to North Kootenay Pass. Two days later they moved to Flathead townsite, about 20 kilometres south of Corbin. The commission report described this location: "Flathead Townsite—so called—is a level little prairie, interspersed with belts of pine, poplar and spruce, and surrounded by high mountains. It is situated opposite North Kootenay Pass, about four miles [6.5 kilometres] to the southwest. At some past date, during a mining boom, a townsite was laid out, but now it is only occupied by a mining development company and a few prospectors." Between Crowsnest and North Kootenay Pass, Wheeler and Campbell occupied 16 triangulation and camera stations. Almost all of them were over 2,000 metres in elevation, with Mount Darrah, at 2,755 metres, being the highest.

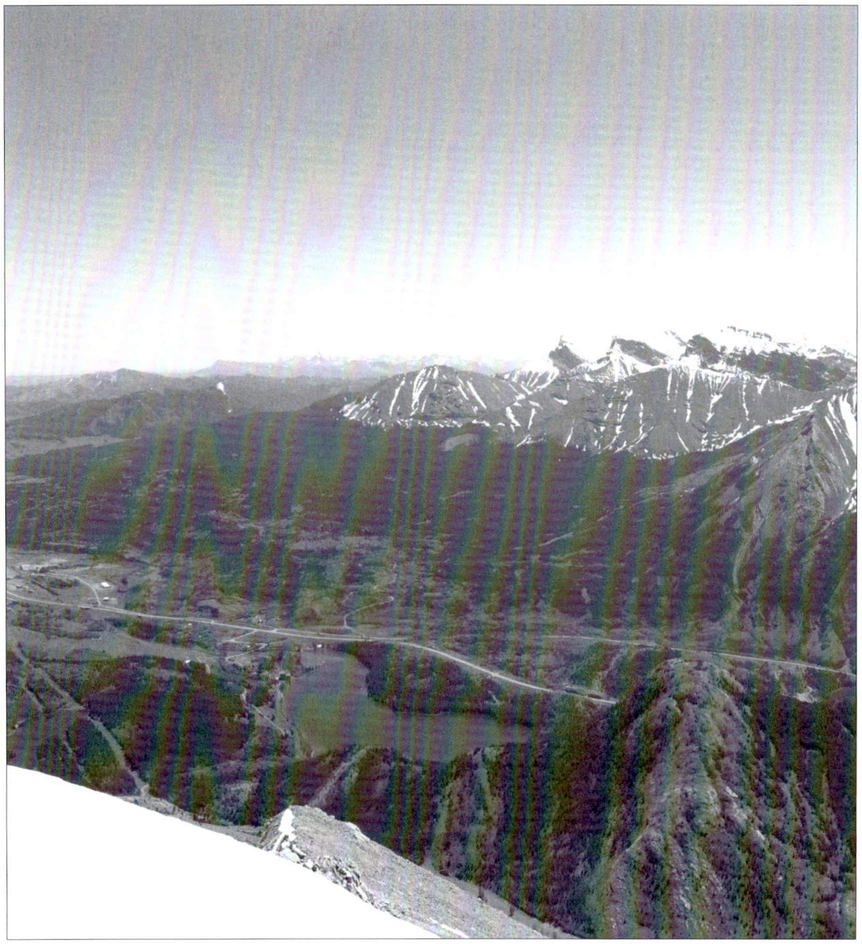

The Mountain Legacy Project photograph shows human activity around the lake, including Highway 3. The picture was taken in mid-June, so seasonal snow can be seen on the mountains. HB1_A0004921, Mountain Legacy Project

The next day Wheeler visited Cautley at North Kootenay Pass. From the government road it was about 6.5 kilometres up an overgrown trail to North Kootenay Pass. The two men examined the pass and determined the location of the boundary. Cautley wrote to Deville

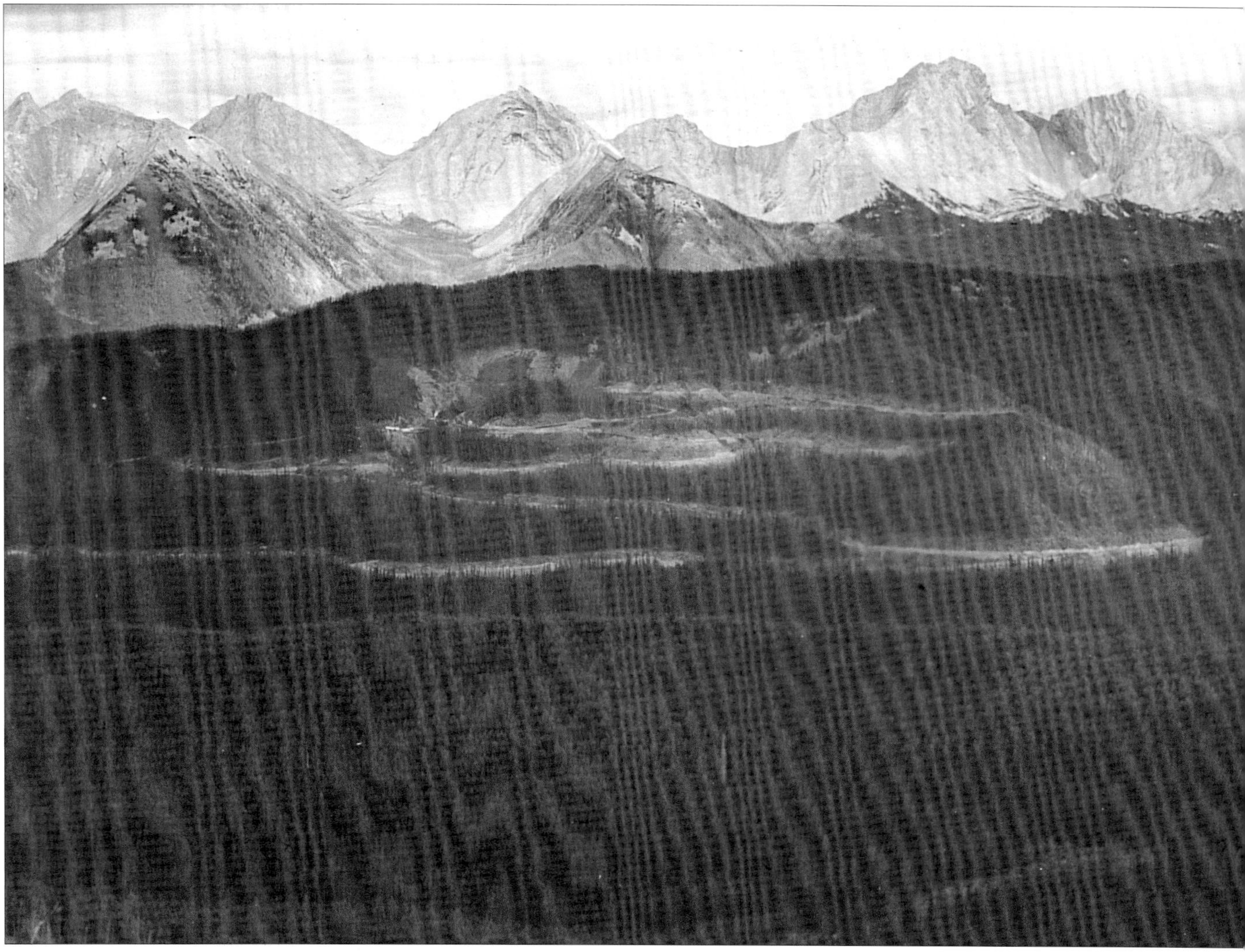

Wheeler's personal photo album had this panorama of the coal mine at Corbin. It also shows the Eastern British Columbia rail line that started at the Canadian Pacific Railway line west of Crowsnest Pass and switchbacked up the mountain to the mine site. The Corbin Coal and Coke Company started in 1908 and was named for Daniel Corbin, a Spokane businessman who had business ventures in the Crowsnest Pass area, including this mine. The rich coal deposits at or near the surface made it easy to start mining at the site. There was a large 60-metre coal seam at the surface called the "Big Showing." Operations continued until 1935 when a bitter strike resulted in the mine's closure. Wheeler 1914 photo album, Alberta surveyor general's office.

on August 31: "I am now camped in North Kootenay Pass, which however is a very small pass from a survey point of view, being composed of two narrow defiles, about ½ mile [800 metres] apart, separated by a bare hill about 500 feet [150 metres] high and bounded to north and south by precipitous peaks."

Five concrete monuments and four brass bolts were used to define the boundary in North Kootenay Pass. It took just under two weeks to complete the work there. Wheeler departed for Banff on September 5 and returned a week later, leaving Campbell to finish the topographic and phototopographic surveying of the pass. Although North Kootenay Pass had significance to the indigenous people, Wheeler and Cautley believed it did not have any potential as a 20th-century transportation route.

There was now one pass to survey before the US border at the 49th parallel. Unfortunately, neither Wheeler nor Cautley was familiar with the geography of the Rockies in this region, and they did not know that there were three more notable passes in the Flathead section of the boundary survey.

From North Kootenay Pass Cautley and his crew left for South Kootenay Pass on September 10. They returned to the government wagon road and followed it south. The commission report described the road.

After leaving Flathead Townsite, the government road crosses the river seven times in the first five miles

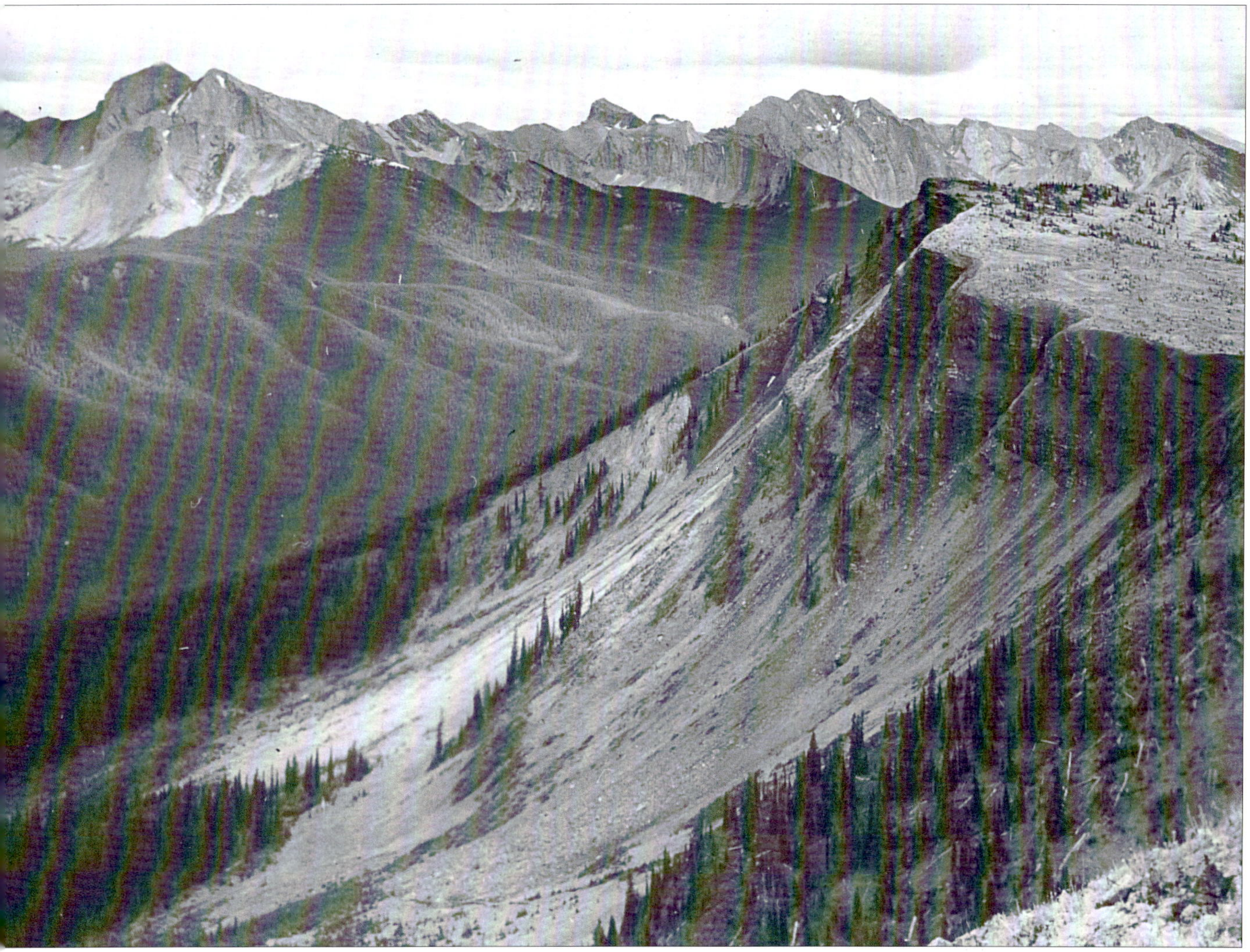

[eight kilometres] of its course. It then keeps on the west side on the benches above the river, which flows in a narrow trench presenting numerous cutbanks. At the time of the survey, several gangs of men were working on the construction of the road and it will be a fine one when finished. The road bed is very soft in places and will require a lot of surfacing; the grades are excellent but, owing to heavy rains, it was, at the time, a veritable bog where it winds through dense forest. The road furnishes a complete line of wagon travel from Crowsnest on the Canadian Pacific Railway to the International Boundary and is a good foundation for a future automobile road.

When Cautley inquired about the location of South Kootenay Pass, local residents assumed that he was referring to their name for Akamina Pass, rather than the historic pass used by the indigenous people. Consequently, Cautley and his crew travelled to the US border, and continued into Montana for a few kilometres until they reached Kishinena Creek. Then they travelled up Kishinena and Akamina Creeks to a pass through the Rocky Mountains that they thought was South Kootenay Pass, arriving there on September 19.

While Wheeler was gone, Campbell and his crew finished North Kootenay Pass and continued working south along the Rocky Mountains. After his return, Wheeler connected the survey with one of McLatchie's posts and a Geological Survey station. On September 15 they found a faint trail that led up Pass Creek. It snowed the next two days as they cut trail up the valley. On September 17 Wheeler wrote: "Campbell & I went ahead and explored trail up Pass Creek as far as Virgo's shack. Failed to find old trail going on owing to snow on ground." When they returned the next day they met Virgo, a local prospector, located the trail and cleared it almost to the pass. Wheeler also learned that this was Middle Kootenay Pass. In his government report, Wheeler noted that this pass was not marked on their maps. However, "by crossing the Middle Kootenay Pass the topographical party hoped to find a shorter route to South Kootenay Pass than had been taken by Mr. Cautley."

Heavy rain kept the crew in camp on the 19th, but the next day Wheeler and Schultz left to find South Kootenay Pass, taking two pack horses and one saddle horse with them. Campbell and the rest of the crew were to finish surveying the terrain around Middle Kootenay Pass and then join them. Wheeler and Schultz camped just below the pass. Near the summit they found a good trail. On September 21 the two men crossed the pass into Alberta. In his diary Wheeler wrote that they "followed trail down valley to old oil works now abandoned." He continued: "Here struck good road leading nearly due north up valley of branch of S. Branch of South Fork [Castle] River. Followed road almost to Prairie—about 14 miles [23 kilometres] from Summit. Here struck Forest Ranger Miller's Ranch and camped for the night. He gave me full information & find I was going to Pincher Creek.…Chickens, pigs and rabbits (hares) galore about Miller's place."

The next morning they left at 8:15, backtracking to the junction of the trail from Middle Kootenay Pass, and then heading south to the headwaters of the Castle River. "Traveled all day up S. Branch of South Fork River. At noon left good trail and took to river bed gravel bars. Left note here for Campbell re climbing Castle Mt. All afternoon traveled up river bed—must have crossed river a hundred times. Bits of old trail in places. Mostly followed Sheppard's horse tracks." (A.C.T. Sheppard from the Geological Survey of Canada was making a triangulation survey in the area.) Wheeler estimated that they travelled about 35 kilometres that day.

After leaving camp at 9:30 on September 23, Wheeler and Schultz "soon struck cutting on trail and a little lake. In two hours came to Miller's Meadow Cache [a forest ranger's camp]. Traveled on for ¾ hour and had lunch on a good trail going up from cache—at old campground, ½ hour after lunch climb to summit between the S. Branch South Fork River [Castle River drainage] and N. branch Blakiston Creek [in Waterton Lakes National Park]." There he found the camp of Alfred Hyatt, Bridgland's assistant, who was doing phototopographic surveying in the area. At the camp were Sheppard and his assistant. "Sheppard advised me not to try the Sage Creek pass over, but to go round by Blakiston Creek." Wheeler and Schultz accompanied him to his camp on North Blakiston Creek near the fork with South Blakiston Creek in the vicinity of Red Rock Canyon in Waterton Lakes National Park.

The next morning Sheppard provided breakfast to Wheeler and Schultz and also replenished their food supply, which was running low. Wheeler learned that Sheppard's packer had arrived and brought a message that Cautley was actually at Akamina Pass. The packer accompanied Wheeler and Schultz until he could show them a "short cut trail to road from Pincher Creek to Oil City—a good wagon road." This wagon road crossed Blakiston Creek and passed Crandell Lake. The men arrived at Oil City at 11:00 a.m. The commission report described Oil City as having "three or four log buildings and several borings for oil." There, by good fortune, Wheeler found Wallace, who was on his way to examine South Kootenay Pass with a guide from Glacier National Park named Robertson. Wheeler continued to Cautley's camp at Akamina Pass, arriving at 4:00 p.m.

Schultz returned to Campbell and his crew on September 25. Wheeler worked around camp and read about the war news. Wallace and his guide returned at supper. In his government report Wheeler wrote: "While at Akamina Pass J.N. Wallace crossed the South Kootenay by the old Indian pony trail. He reports the pass as difficult of approach on both sides. It is, he says, a mere 'crossing' of the range, and will never be a suitable route for a road. Owing to the steep and rugged ascent it is difficult and laborious even for pack ponies, and has evidently been used by the Indians as a direct line of travel

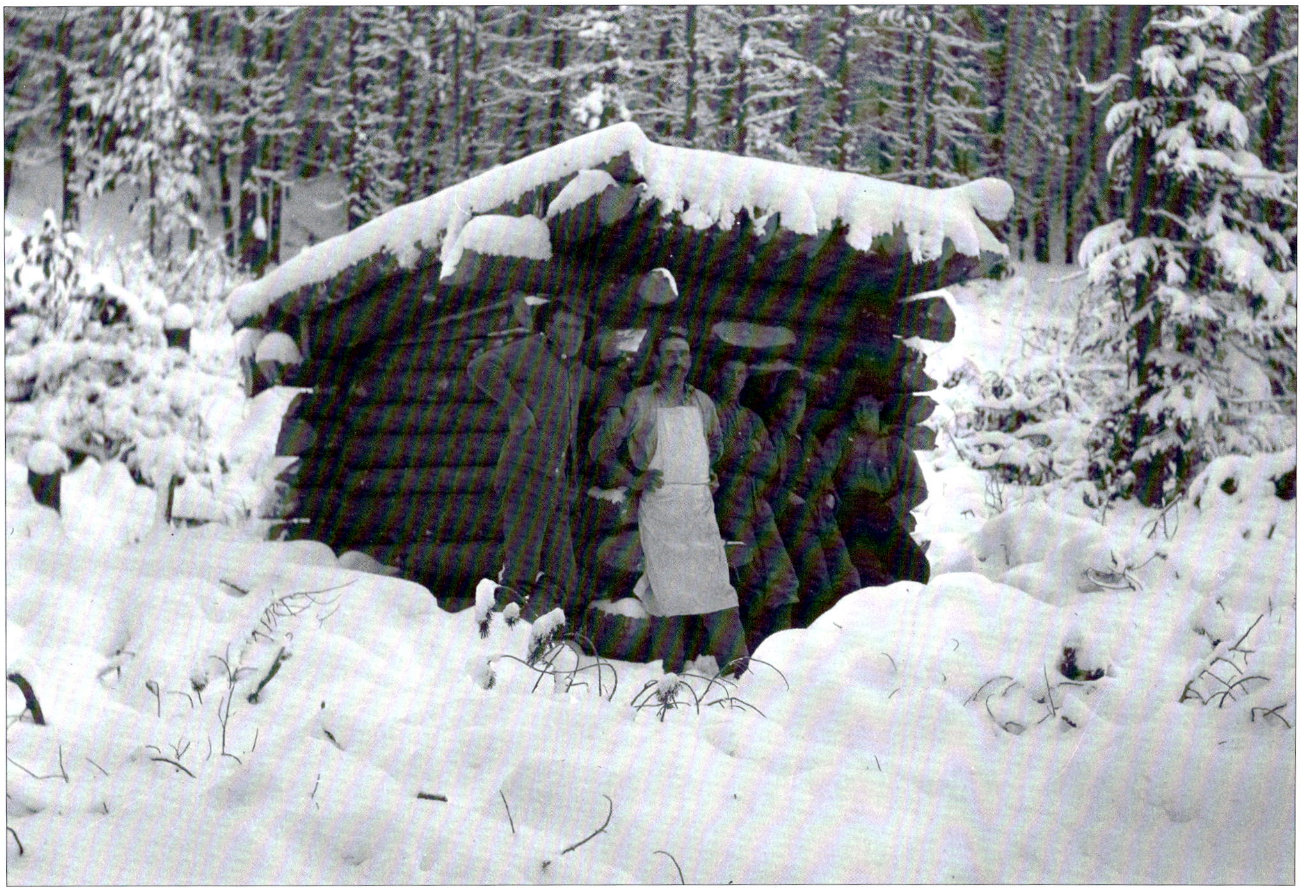

Cautley's crew built this cache after the prolonged snowstorm in early October. Cautley planned to return to Akamina Pass at the beginning of the 1915 field season, so he left a large amount of his supplies in this remote location. e011166462, Library and Archives Canada

between the plains of Alberta and the Kootenay Valley, via Blakiston Brook and Kishinena Creek."

On the 26th the three commissioners examined the work that Cautley had done in determining the boundary in Akamina Pass. The boundary commission provided some flexibility in selecting the passes to be monumented, as long as the three commissioners unanimously agreed. Cautley had already done a considerable amount of work there. The pass had economic and geographic significance, and it was merely a matter of exchanging South Kootenay for Akamina. Wheeler described the pass in his report.

> The pass is situated a mile and three-quarters [2.8 kilometres] north of the International Boundary. It is broad and well timbered, and is traversed by a good wagon road with a maximum grade of about 1 to 8. The road connects the prairies of Alberta with the Flathead River Valley, entering the latter south of the International Boundary. It is one of the two existing wagon thoroughfares across the main divide south of Crowsnest branch of the Canadian Pacific Railway....It is of considerable importance, owing to the easy grade across the Great Divide, and to the fact that oil prospects are now being worked at Oil City on the Alberta side and at Akamina Brook on the British Columbia side.

Akamina, an indigenous word meaning "high bench land," had been named by George Dawson of the Canadian Geological Survey during a study of the area in 1886. Dawson also named North and South Kootenay Passes at the same time. The commission report stated that Akamina Pass did not appear on any of the maps that they referenced, while South Kootenay did.

Since the International Boundary was so close to Akamina Pass, Wheeler decided to visit the location. On September 28, after a day of rain, he went there with Percy Burton, a member of Cautley's crew. Along the way they saw 13 goats and a bear. The next day Wheeler and Cautley examined the north side of Akamina Pass to select the location for the stations at the top of the pass. On the final day of September Wheeler "went on old trail to Oil [Cameron] Lake to see what feed is like. Trail good & open except near summit. Feed will hold horses for a while."

During the last four days of September, Cautley's crew began cutting the boundary line through Akamina Pass. On the first day of October it rained all day. Bad weather continued until the fifth of October, preventing further work on the boundary survey. On October 3 Cautley's packers arrived, bringing mail and the "latest war news to 26th September." By the morning of the fourth, Wheeler noted, there was 30 centimetres of snow on the ground. When the snow finished on October 5, Cautley recorded that they had over 80 centimetres.

While Cautley's crew and Wheeler were in Akamina Pass, Campbell and his men surveyed two stations south of Middle Kootenay Pass. Then they began following Wheeler's route to Waterton. The men were camped along Blakiston Creek when the inclement weather started and were only able to move down to the wagon road.

On October 6 Cautley's head packer went to see if he could find where Campbell was camped. On October 7 Ben, Wheeler's assistant packer, arrived with a pack horse and a saddle horse. In the afternoon Wheeler moved back to the Blakiston valley, where he met Campbell and the crew. The next day they began travelling to Pincher Creek. Shortly after they started they met two sleighs travelling to Oil City, so the road was packed for them. After about 20 kilometres of travel they reached the Thornton homestead and slept in the hayloft. On October 9 they continued along the road to Pincher Creek. "At Twin Butte post office picked up some mail.…Pushed on and made Dry Fork at 4 pm. Stayed there the night getting meals at Kinmans. Boys slept in store house—Campbell & I in the house." On October 10 Wheeler and his crew arrived at Pincher Creek, camping beside the creek on the property of former MP John Herron. On October 12, Thanksgiving, Wheeler paid the men and finished his accounts, and then went to Pincher Station, about four kilometres north on the rail line. Campbell went west to Crowsnest while Wheeler returned to Banff. In Calgary he visited both Bridgland and Wallace.

After the snowfall, Cautley remained at Akamina Pass for a week, waiting for the snow to melt and make it easier to get his pack train out. He decided to leave behind equipment and supplies that he would use at the beginning of the next field season. On November 13 Cautley wrote to Deville: "Owing to the very heavy snowstorm of the 2nd, 3rd, and 4th of October, during which 32 inches [80 centimetres] of snow fell in the South Kootenay [Akamina] Pass, and the consequent difficulty of transport, I was obliged to leave all the camp equipage I could spare in the Pass. I accordingly built a strong log cache at my camp." Most of his surveying equipment, except for the transit, as well as the bags of cement, was placed in the cache. Cautley left Akamina Pass on October 13 and arrived in Pincher Creek two days later.

In the conclusion to his government report, Wheeler wrote about the economic importance of the southernmost section of the boundary survey.

> Between the Canadian Pacific Railway through the Crowsnest Pass and the International Boundary is a wide area of country of immense economic value, owing to the vast beds of coal that lie hidden there, and the many indications of petroleum that have from time to time been discovered.
>
> A number of coal mines are now being worked and practical experimental prospecting for both coal and oil is being undertaken at various places. This is the more apparent since the recent oil boom south and west of Calgary, and the boring of several wells is in operation on both sides of and close to the divide, while nearly the entire area along the watershed on the British Columbia side has been taken up in either coal or oil leases.

William Morden Carthew

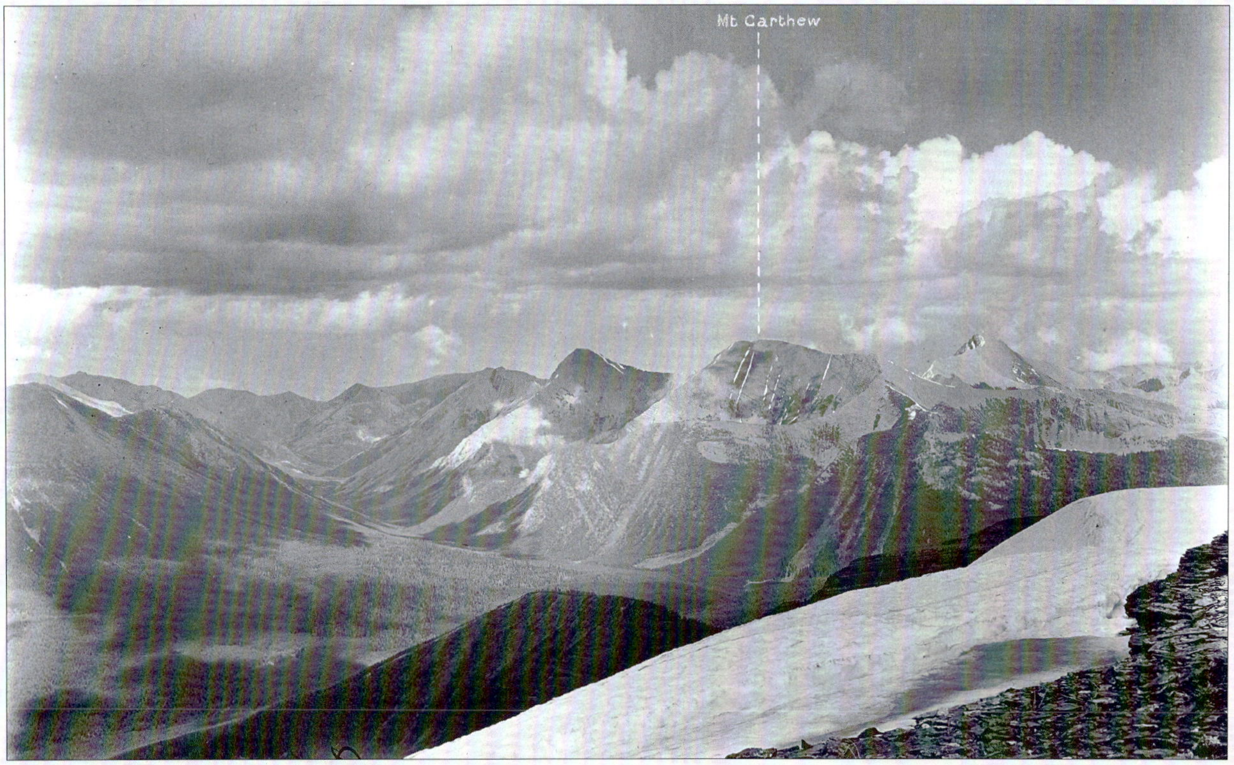

This photograph with Mount Carthew labelled on it is in Wheeler's personal photo album. Wheeler sent an enlargement of this picture to Carthew's parents. V771-pd4-11-1, Whyte Museum of the Canadian Rockies

Cautley's surveying assistant in 1914 was William Morden Carthew. Born in England in 1886, Carthew came to Canada in 1905, settling in Edmonton, where he became a land surveyor. He received his Dominion land surveyor commission in 1910 and became an Alberta land surveyor the following year. Carthew then went into partnership with Cautley until the latter started working on the boundary survey.

In January 1915 Carthew enlisted in World War I and was sent overseas, where he was killed at the battle of Mont Sorrel near Ypres in early June 1916. Wheeler named Mount Carthew in Waterton Lakes National Park for W.M. Carthew, who climbed this peak in 1914 as part of the initial survey of Akamina Pass. Carthew Lakes and Carthew Creek, at the base of the mountain, are also named for him. Carthew was one of three Alberta land surveyors who died during World War I, and the only one to have geographical features in the Rocky Mountains named for him.

In 1914 the boundary survey covered the region considered to have the most economic importance and placed monuments through the most extensive of the passes. Cautley wrote to Deville: "It is scarcely probable that I shall ever be able to make 59 monuments in one season again, because I do not expect that the Commissioners will have another pass to deal with like the Crowsnest." All but five of the monuments were in the Crowsnest Pass. For several reasons, the surveyors had been unable to complete the southern section and would have to return in 1915. Most importantly, World War I had started, a conflict that would impact the boundary survey in several ways, along with the personal lives of many of those who worked on the project.

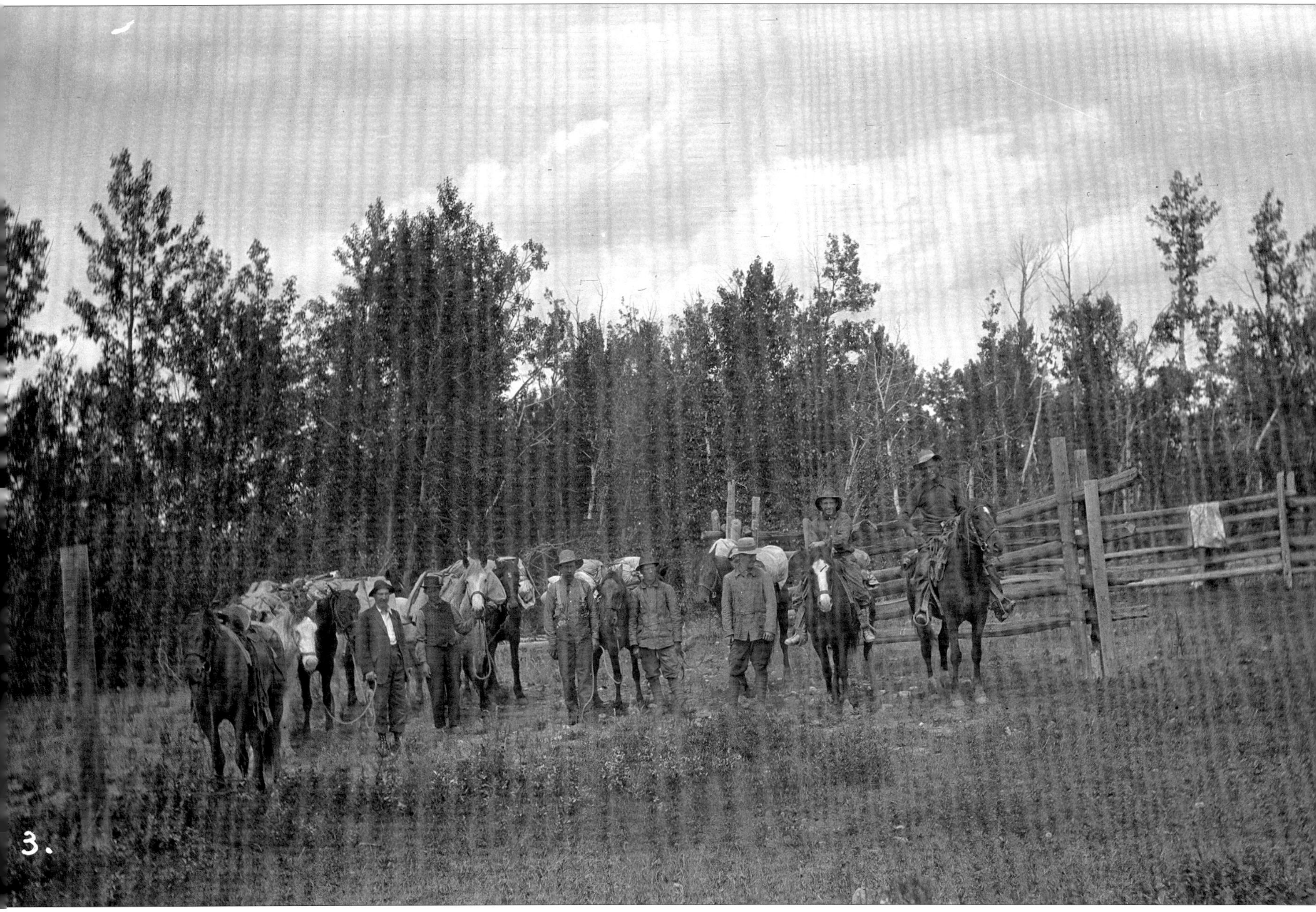

Cautley's crew departing Pincher Creek at the start of the field season. e011166466, Library and Archives Canada

1915

The third year of the boundary survey began in an atmosphere of uncertainty. World War I continued, and it appeared that the conflict would not end quickly. Both the federal and provincial governments were focussing more of their attention and spending more of their budget on items related to the war. Nevertheless, there was consensus among the three governments that the boundary survey should continue. The work of the first two years had demonstrated that defining the boundary on the ground was important, and there was a desire to retain the project, even if it was in a reduced role.

Within the boundary survey, some contentious issues emerged. On February 11, Alberta's director of surveys wrote to Deville. In a detailed letter, Lionel Charlesworth expressed a concern that he had from the beginning of the survey.

> The Alberta Government's understanding of the work contemplated was that the boundary was to be determined and marked by permanent monuments in the principal mountain passes. The remainder of the boundary was to be dealt with at a later date.
>
> It was considered, and carefully pointed out in my letter to you of May 20, 1913, that the important part of the work was the determination of the boundary line. It was understood that a topographical survey should be made, extending a few miles on each side of the established line, but that this part of the work was an entirely secondary consideration.
>
> It now appears that this secondary topographical work has been so much extended by Mr. Wheeler that instead of taking in a few miles around each pass where the boundary is established, he, in the season of 1913, took an area of approximately 500 square miles, and presumably covered a like area in 1914, and the cost of this secondary part of the undertaking not only exceeds the cost of the really vital part of the work but is very nearly up to the estimated cost of the whole survey, which estimate was made by Mr. Wheeler himself.
>
> It is considered that Mr. Wheeler has gone very far outside his instructions in extending the topographical portion of the work to so great an extent. It is accordingly the opinion of the Government of Alberta that that part of the survey should in future be kept within the limits originally intended, and I am directed to request that this be done.

Charlesworth reiterated that he wanted the survey to continue, but he believed the delineation of the boundary to be of primary importance. In a letter to BC's surveyor general on April 28, 1915, the Alberta director of surveys wrote: "I wish however to state clearly again that the question we have raised is not one of a change in arrangements, but is merely a request that the original arrangements be adhered to."

Charlesworth voiced his complaint because Wheeler's extended topography primarily benefitted British Columbia. In many areas along the boundary, the topography along the Alberta side quickly turned to hills or prairie. As president of the Alpine Club of Canada, Wheeler was most interested in the mountainous terrain near the boundary, and almost all of that was on the British Columbia side. Charlesworth also believed that a reduction in the scale of the topographic survey would be a way of reducing expenses. He did not mention that Bridgland's topographic survey of the Crowsnest Forest Reserve and Waterton Lakes National Park in 1913 and 1914 primarily covered the southern part of the Alberta side of the Great Divide, or that Wheeler incorporated this information into his work.

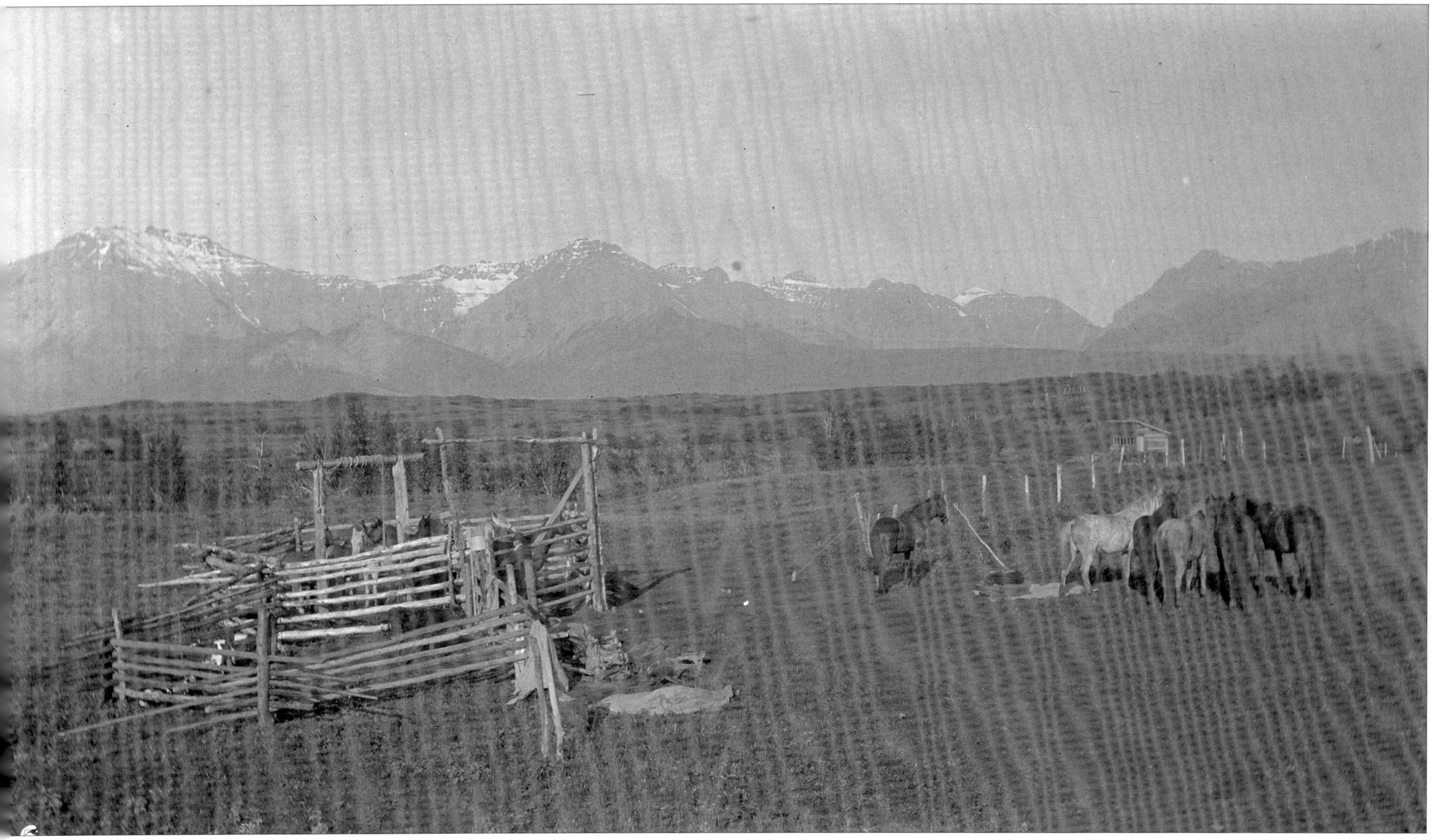

En route to Akamina Pass. e011166469, Library and Archives Canada

Deville wrote to Dawson on May 3, 1915:

> Paragraph 10 provides that a topographical survey shall be made extending a few miles on each side of the boundary and Paragraph 11 that Mr. Wheeler shall be in charge of the topographical portion of the survey and the establishment of survey monuments on the peaks. Mr. Wheeler has given a broad interpretation to these instructions which he considers warranted by the usefulness of a topographical survey for economic and other purposes. I regret to say that I cannot quite agree with this view: the survey of the boundary should, it seems to me, be made for boundary purposes only and be dissociated from other considerations....
>
> I am inclined to think that the most satisfactory solution of the delimitation problem would be to have a continuous topographical survey extending for a mile or so on each side of the boundary.

Deville had a suggestion: "Whether the survey is or is not continued this year, would it not be advisable, after the Commissioners have exchanged ideas among themselves, that we should have a meeting with Mr. Charlesworth and discuss the whole subject from our

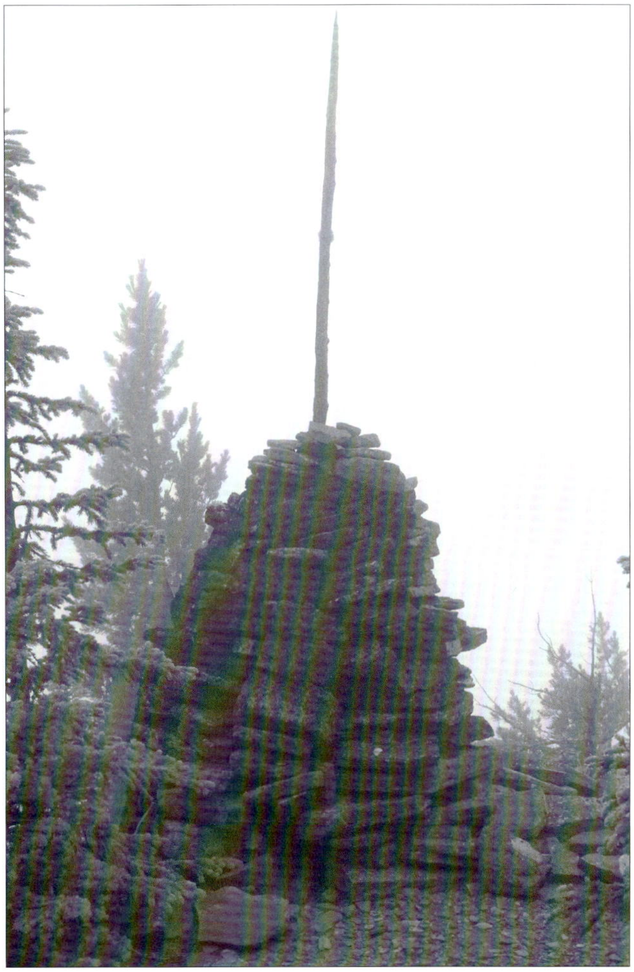

Monument 10H in the fog. The tree line has now moved above the monument and shelters this station. Many of the rocks in the 1915 photograph can still be identified. Along with the growth of lichen on the rocks, it is apparent that this monument has been largely undisturbed during the past century. Jay Sherwood photo

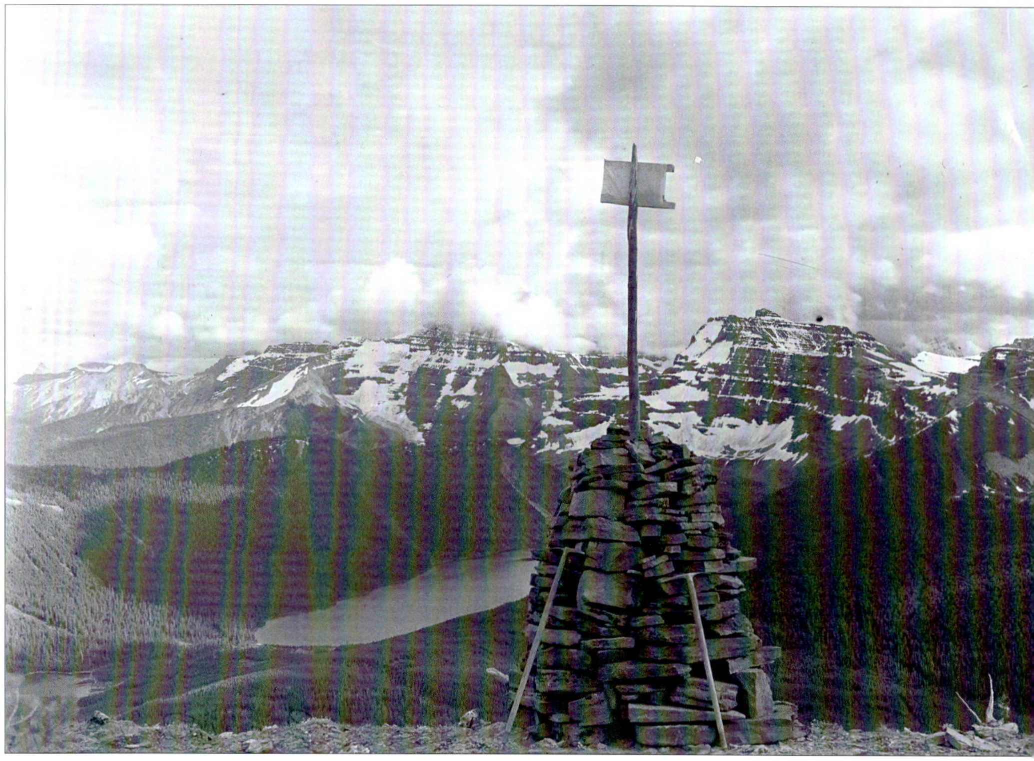

Monument 10H on the north side of Akamina Pass. Cameron Lake is in the centre. On the right is the ridge line that defines the interprovincial boundary on the south side of the pass up to Forum Peak. WHE1915_W15-30, Library and Archives Canada

own point of view? It is so much more easy to come to an understanding through verbal discussion than by correspondence."

On May 27 Wheeler arrived in Calgary, where he met Wallace and Bridgland before taking the night train to Edmonton. The next day he met Deville, Dawson and Charlesworth, and spent time with Cautley while the three surveyor generals met and came to an amicable arrangement. The three governments involved approved the survey, but the expenditure was reduced from $29,000 to $18,000. Cautley received around $10,000 because of the expenses for constructing the monuments. As a means of reducing the expenses of the boundary survey, they decided to make Cautley commissioner for both the Alberta and Dominion governments. Except for the disagreement about the boundary through Phillipps Pass, the survey had proceeded smoothly. Wheeler did not like this arrangement, but the surveyor generals believed it would work, which it did. Privy Council No. 2147 on September 20, 1915, made the official announcement.

The surveyor generals also reduced the work in the field by a few weeks. This not only saved money but also gave Wheeler and Cautley time to get all of their maps, reports and photographs finished. The boundary commission needed to publish a detailed report once the first section of the boundary survey was completed in 1916. Since this was the first volume, there would be ongoing discussion during 1915 and

Monument 272—A Monument through Time

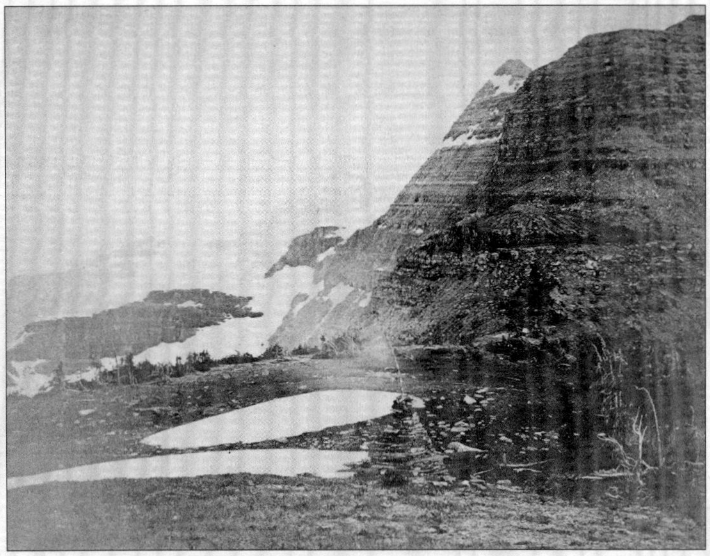

The photographs taken by the Royal Engineers include this one facing south into Montana. Mount Custer is on the right. Chapman Peak is in the centre. The set of pictures over 150 years shows the gradual recession of the glaciers around this peak. Cubanc79_27_1137355a, Bancroft Library

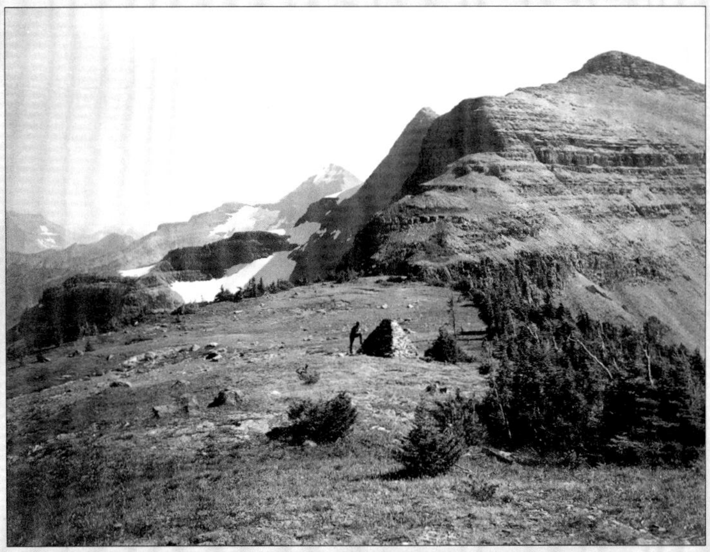

The US Geological Survey took this photograph in 1901 from a location close to the 1861 photograph. Wil00350, US Geological Survey

The Treaty of 1818 established the 49th parallel as the boundary between the United States and British North America from the Lake of the Woods to the Rocky Mountain Divide. In 1846 the Treaty of Oregon extended the boundary along the 49th parallel to the Pacific Ocean. (The boundary through the islands off the Pacific coast and through the Strait of Juan de Fuca was not settled until the 1871 Treaty of Washington.)

In 1857 the United States and Great Britain began surveying the 49th parallel from the Pacific coast to the Great Divide. The British surveying was done by the Royal Engineers. To document the surveying of the boundary, the engineers used trained photographers beginning in 1858. They were the first military organization to implement an organized system of photographic instruction and send its photographers on field assignments.

In 1861 the Royal Engineers started at Kootenay Lake and worked eastward, completing their work at the Continental Divide about 1.5 kilometres south of Akamina Pass in July. Originally labelled Monument 161, it is called Monument 272 today. Since it was the final monument on the survey, the Royal Engineers took a set of four photos, the first pictures of the Canadian Rockies.

One of the photographs was taken on the Canadian side of the border looking south. In 1901 the United States Geological Survey traversed the boundary in this area and took a photograph from a similar location. Between 1902 and 1908 more permanent monuments were established, but unfortunately it seems that no photographs were taken at the time. In 1915 one of Cautley's crew members took a picture of him surveying at Monument 272. In the boundary commission report, Wheeler described the location: "The intersection of the watershed with the International Boundary occurs on the flat summit of a little grassy col, with a few larch trees upon it, which makes a gap between two steep ridges of rock. No more suitable spot could have happened for the International Boundary to cross the main range of the Rockies, and the iron pillar erected there to a height of six feet [1.83 metres] is visible from many miles distant, both north and south."

The engineers were not pleased with the new technology, but the pictures they took are an invaluable record of the landscape. Today Monument 272, at the intersection of two national parks and a provincial park, remains a scenic and remote location with a photographic record that spans over 150 years.

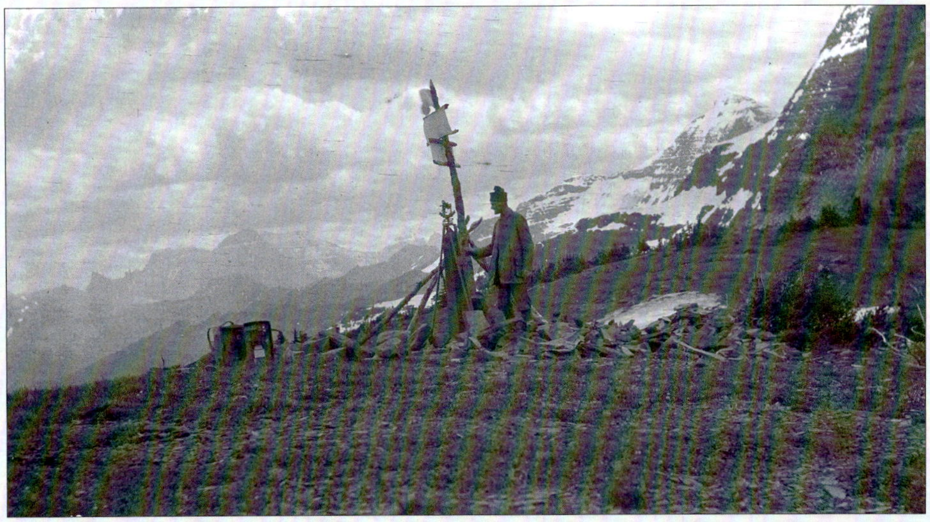

R.W. Cautley surveying at Monument 272. This photograph, using Cautley's camera, shows the new monument. It is taken closer to the monument than the 1901 picture but covers a similar landscape. e011166464, Library and Archives Canada

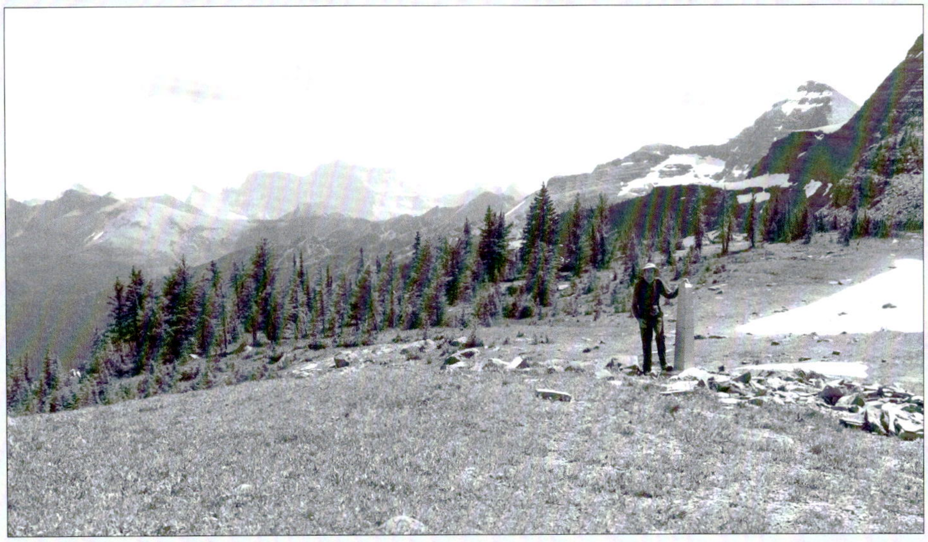

The 2016 photograph of the author at Monument 272 shows a significant loss of glaciation on the lower slopes of Chapman Peak. The encroachment of trees on the Montana side of the border is also evident. Evan Sherwood photo

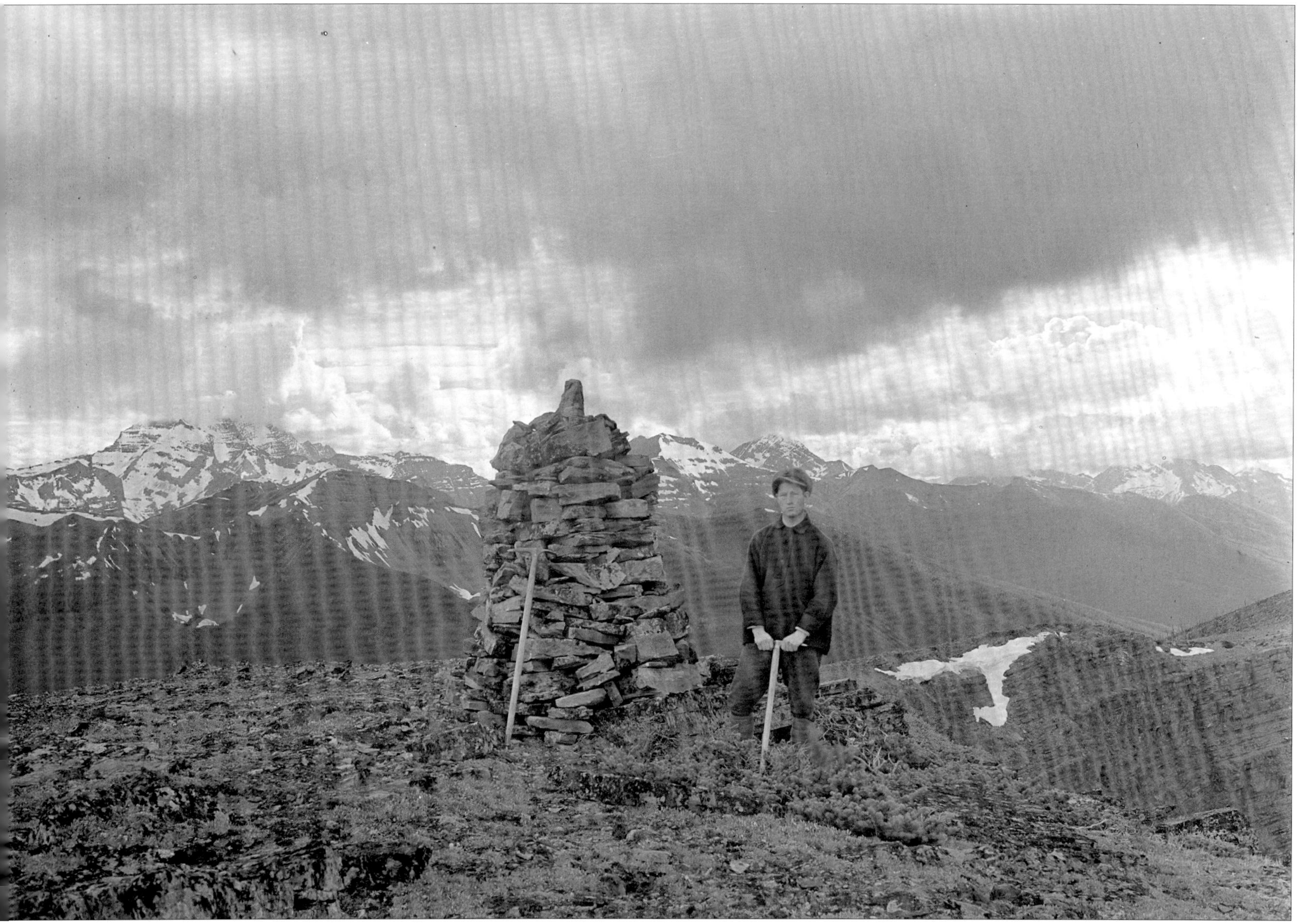

Wheeler photographed one of the members of his crew at station 12H at the top of Akamina Pass in early July. WHE1915_W15-29, Library and Archives Canada

1916 about the format and content of the report; the photographs to be used and how they would be printed; the size and scale of maps for the map atlas; and many other details.

After the meetings on May 28 Cautley took everyone to dinner at the Edmonton Club. On the return trip the next day, Wheeler spent time with Bridgland again and had supper at his house before taking the evening train back to Banff.

The first priority was to complete the survey of Akamina, the most southerly pass along the boundary. Since Cautley had more work than Wheeler did

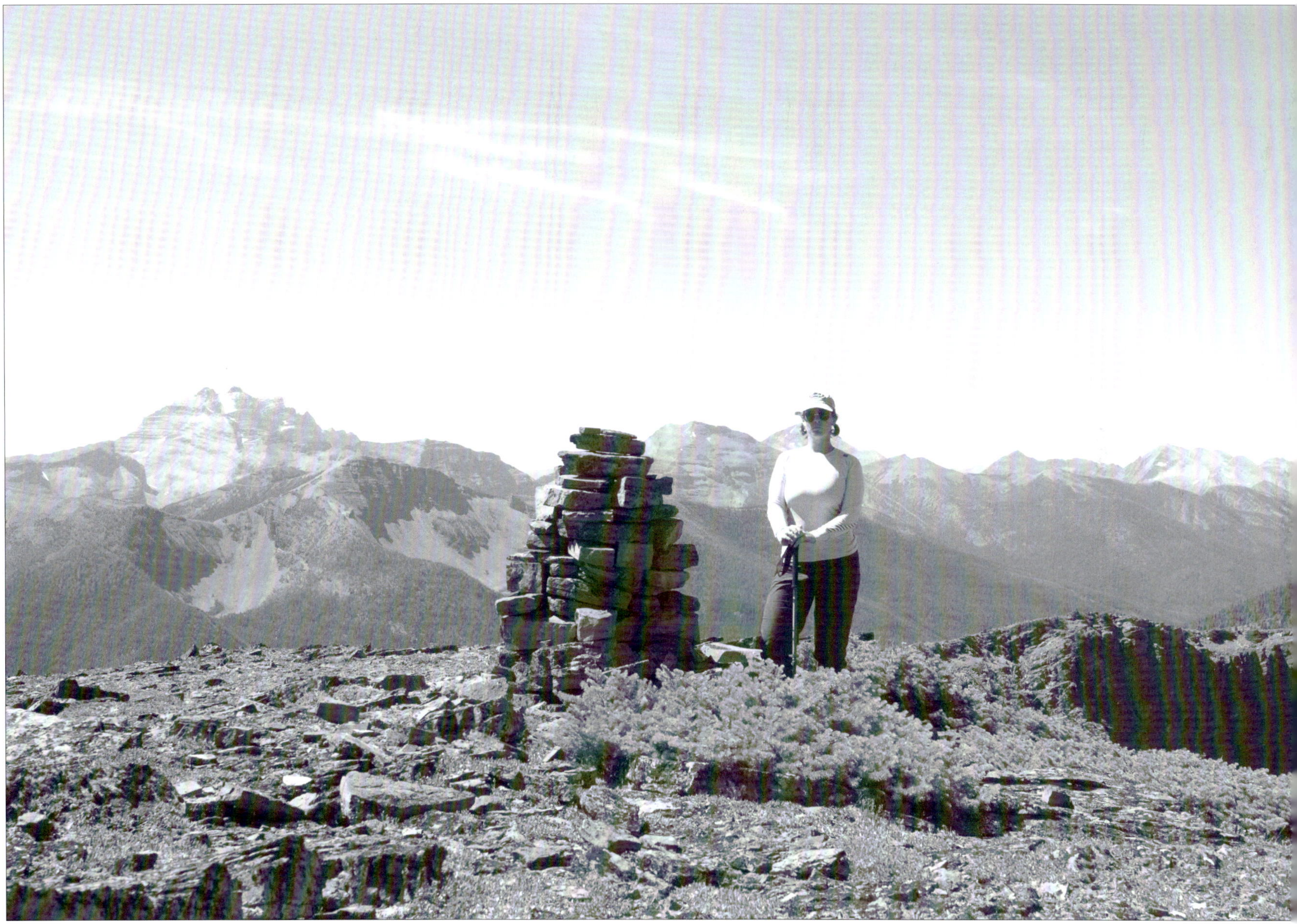

In this Mountain Legacy Project photograph, taken in 2005, the original cairn still existed. Only a small amount of snow remained on the peaks. B0022P_0084, Mountain Legacy Project

in Akamina Pass, he left Pincher Station on June 21 with his pack train and a wagon that he hired. Rain and muddy roads made travelling slow, and it took the crew three days to reach the pass. Since the preliminary line had already been established, he was able to start working immediately. It took three weeks to survey and construct seven monuments and four brass bolts and cairns. Cautley was able to connect with a Dominion survey station that was less than a kilometre away. From 9H, the last cairn on the southern side, Cautley surveyed to Monument 272 at the intersection of the Alberta-BC boundary and the United States.

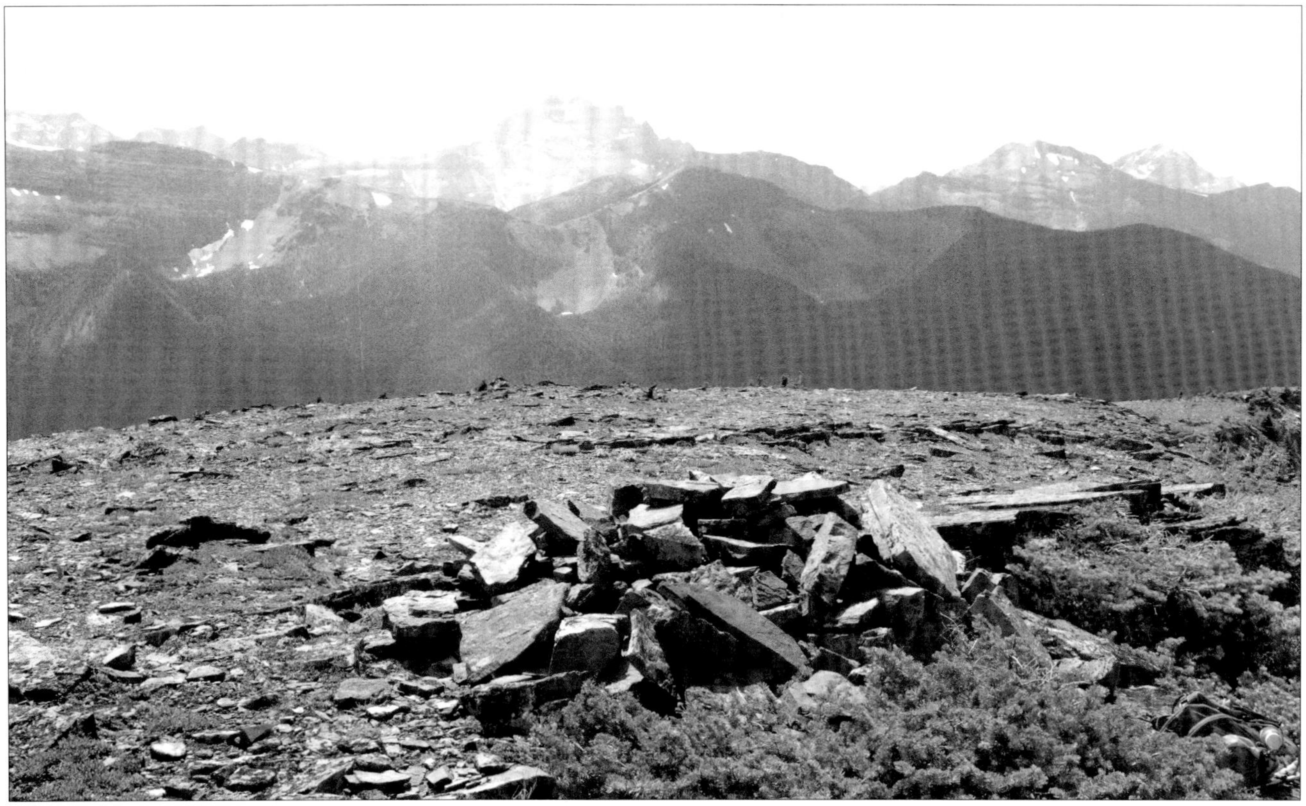

Monument 12H has collapsed since 2005. It was probably struck by lightning for the monument is in a prominent open location. Evan Sherwood photo

Cautley noted that mountain goats were numerous at Akamina Pass, and he described the bears they encountered: "A grizzly bear was seen trying to tear down Monument 8H; he sat up on the base of the monument and endeavoured to wrench the top off, failing which, he bit it and left deep tooth marks grooved in the metal covering. It is needless to state that these operations were watched through the transit at a safe distance. Brown bears also, were in evidence, and one that Mr. Wheeler came on suddenly was in such a hurry to get away that he rolled head over heels down a grassy slope."

Cautley completed his work at Akamina Pass on July 16, and on that day he and his crew started travelling toward Crowsnest Pass, following the same route that they had used when travelling south in 1914. At Michel, a coal mining town in BC at the western end of Crowsnest Pass, Cautley purchased supplies of food and cement. On July 27 the survey crew started north.

In preparation for the topographic crew's field season, Wheeler went to Crowsnest Pass in mid-June, stopping at Calgary to meet Bridgland. At Crowsnest Pass he made arrangements for supplies that would be needed when the crews passed through there later in the summer, and hired Jack Pidgeon as packer. On June 22 Campbell arrived in Banff. He and Wheeler went to the golf course to test the surveying equipment on June 25 and 28. Jack Stelfox returned as cook. Before departing Banff, Wheeler travelled to Lake Louise to check on preparations for the ACC camp at Paradise Valley. "At Laggan [Lake Louise] two train loads of 48th battalion went through—some officers I knew."

During the last week of June there was heavy rain and flooding, and the railway south from Calgary was closed for several days. On June 30, to reach Pincher Creek, Campbell and Jack Stelfox had to travel via Dunmore, near Medicine Hat , and then take the CPR's southern railway line. Wheeler departed from Banff the following morning. From Calgary he "left by 5 pm train for Pincher. First train going south for several days. Arrived at Pincher soon after 10pm." Wheeler stayed overnight at the Alexandra Hotel at Pincher Station.

The next day he and his crew left Pincher Creek at noon and got to Dry Fork, where they stayed at the Kinman homestead again. "Thunderstorm came on just as we were pitching camp. Thunder and hail. Managed to get things under shelter. Did not get them wet. Got tent up and Jack soon had supper ready.... Trail rotten—two lines of wire fence & a muck hole." Before departing the next morning he got "Mrs. Kinman to phone to Thornton for bread. Dropped map case on road and had to go back two miles for it." The crew camped at the property of well-known guide Bert Riggall, but he had gone to Pincher Creek. On July 4 they arrived at Akamina Pass. En route they met two park wardens and a gang who were going to start oil drilling at Oil City. Wheeler had difficulty finding a dry place for camping. He noted that the "mosquitos were very bad and the horses went crazy."

The crew spent the next day setting up camp, and on July 6 they started work on the south side of the pass, going down to Monument 272 on the International Boundary, where they set up a target for Cautley. Wheeler surveyed from a station close to the monument, while Campbell took photographs from a high station nearby. On July 7 Wheeler and Cautley met on the north side of the pass at 8H, the last concrete monument. From there the two men "went up divide line and selected place for 12H," Wheeler wrote. "First thing on reaching crest of hill we occupied 10H with camera & transit." Campbell and his crew constructed the cairns for these two stations, and on the way down Wheeler photographed them. Wheeler also noted that the packer, Jack Pidgeon, had the "horses all together in creek flat below camp. He stays there with them." Wheeler spent one more day at Akamina Pass, working on maps. "Had to give it up as I feared flies would spoil maps."

By July 9 Wheeler finished his work at Akamina Pass, and he and his crew went to the Blakiston valley, where he "camped about 5 miles [eight kilometres] up—just beyond Sheppard's camp. Stelfox caught two fish." This location was near where he had camped last September. From here Campbell and the rest of the crew started the topographic survey north toward Middle Kootenay Pass to complete the section along the boundary that remained unfinished from last fall. The next morning, Campbell and the crew went on a fly camp up the south branch of Blakiston Creek, while Wheeler and Jack Pidgeon with one pack horse departed for Pincher Creek. They stopped for lunch at a creek near Riggall's place, where they were joined

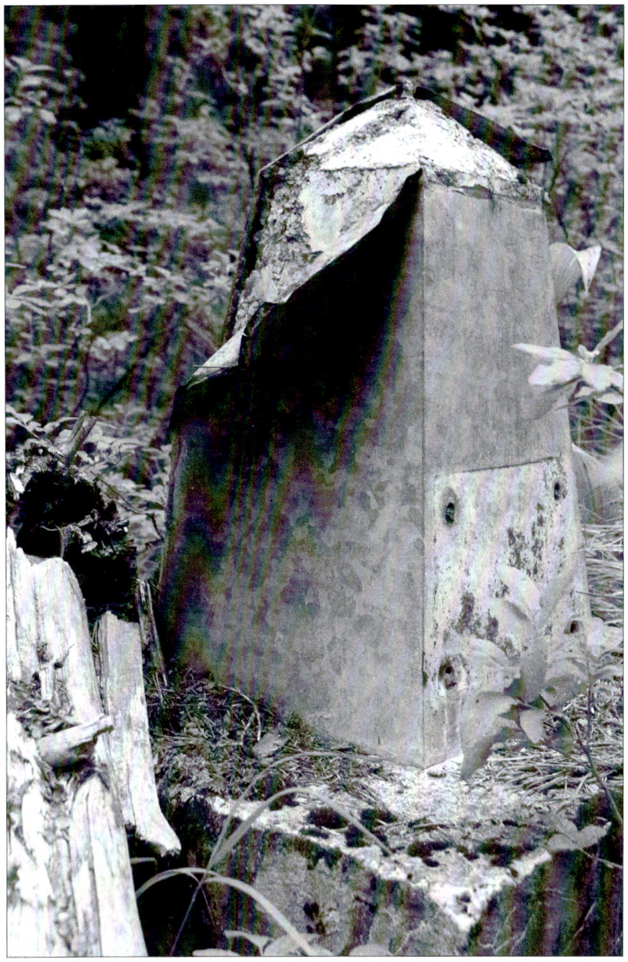

Despite the grizzly bear and over 100 years of mountain weather, Monument 8H still remains. Near the monument there is a small stream that drains into British Columbia. From this location Cautley surveyed a straight line to Monument 4H which was beside the wagon road going through Akamina Pass. Jay Sherwood photo

by Cautley's packer, Jacob (Jake) Koller, who was taking two pack horses to pick up supplies. Once again Wheeler tried to visit Bert Riggall, but he had gone with a fishing party. Wheeler stopped at the Twin Butte post office for mail, then went on to Dry Fork, where he stayed for the night. The next afternoon he arrived at Pincher Creek and then took the train to Crowsnest Pass. There Wheeler made arrangements to leave his outfit until he returned later in the summer.

Then he returned to Banff to get ready for the ACC camp. Wheeler had some anxiety when he heard a rumour that his son, Oliver, who had enlisted in the war, had been killed, but it turned out to be incorrect.

During the rest of July Campbell and his crew finished their work on the southern section of the boundary. There were two stations between Akamina and South Kootenay Pass. One was a Geological Survey station that enabled them to connect with that department's topographic and phototopographic survey. It was on a mountain named Festubert, commemorating a World War I battle in 1915.

From South Kootenay Pass it is about 40 kilometres along the actual line of the watershed to Middle Kootenay Pass. Jack Stelfox recalled meeting the famous frontiersman, conservationist and park ranger Kootenai Brown and his wife at their camp. The crew also met Bert Riggall, his clients, Russell Bennett and son from Minneapolis, and Mrs. Riggall, the cook, who were on a fishing trip in the upper Castle drainage. Campbell established nine stations in this section before reaching the location where he had stopped last fall. After completing work on July 25, Campbell and his crew proceeded to Crowsnest Pass, arriving on July 28.

The Alpine Club camp at Paradise Valley near Lake Louise finished on July 24, and Wheeler returned to Banff. On July 26 he left for Simpson Pass and camped that night near Peyto's claim. The next day he spent the morning "marking posts around Peyto's claims. Spent afternoon planting posts at location posts 1 and 2."

On July 30 Wheeler travelled to Crowsnest on the evening train. "Arrived at 12:20. Went to Summit Hotel and found a room—hotel in darkness." The next day he walked to the camp about 1.5 kilometres west of the pass. Campbell and the rest of the crew, except for the cook, were surveying a station on Mount Wilson. Wheeler brought Stelfox back with him to help order supplies for the rest of the survey.

There was a concern that Cautley's 1914 assistant, W.M. Carthew, had used an incorrect bearing while surveying Lot 8277. Carthew had enlisted in the war and was overseas, so Wheeler took his packer and one crew member with him on a three-day trip to trace the boundaries of the lot. While he was gone, Campbell and his crew completed their work immediately north of Crowsnest Pass.

Along the Alberta-BC boundary it is about 125 kilometres from Crowsnest Pass to Elk Pass at the head of the Elk River valley. The boundary commissioners intended to survey and monument one pass, North Fork, along the route. For their work on this section, Cautley's and Wheeler's crews travelled on the west side of the divide. Wheeler described this area in his government report.

> All this section of country on the west side of the divide, and on the east side between the High Rock and the Highwood and Livingstone Ranges, is underlaid by coal, towards the development of which much prospecting has been done on the west side of the divide in the Elk and tributary valleys. At intervals, camps with good log bunk-houses have been built along the road and in the side-valleys extending towards the crest of the main range. Caretakers are in charge of the camps, and their use as shelters is open to such travellers as may be on the move. This is a very great boon and one of which we were glad to take advantage; it speaks well for the courtesy and consideration of the company owning them.

The major difficulty was lack of a rail line from the Canadian Pacific Railway at present-day Sparwood up the Elk Valley to the coal areas. Wheeler wrote: "The Grain Belt Construction and Development Company has located a line of railway from Calgary in Alberta to Fernie in British Columbia which crosses the Elk Pass and follows the general course of the trail and road down Elk Valley on its east side." The Grain Belt Construction railway was never built, and there was such a large quantity of coal through the Crowsnest Pass and adjoining area that it would be about a half century before the coalfields in the Elk Valley would be mined.

Wheeler also noted: "The Elk Valley presents a broad fertile trough, originally well-timbered but with much open meadow land intermingled. A large proportion of the timber has been killed by forest fires." He commented that west of the divide "lies a minor trough paralleling, comprising the valleys of Alexander Creek, Fording River, and their tributaries. A road from Crowsnest leads up Alexander Creek to its forks, and then up each fork to camps where coal prospecting has been carried on to a considerable extent." Rather than following the road up the Elk Valley, "the inside line of travel" suited the crew's work well, Wheeler noted. "It enabled us to keep close to the continental watershed along the crest of the High Rock Range. Instead of following the West Fork of Alexander Creek, we followed the East Fork, where there certainly had been some travel, but a trail could hardly be said to exist."

In his government report Wheeler wrote: "From Crowsnest Pass to the north boundary of the Crowsnest Forest Reserve, situated on the east side of the continental divide, collaboration with M.P. Bridgland, DLS, who had made a photographic survey of the reserve, rendered a further survey for that side unnecessary." Also, in 1915, S.C. McLean was conducting a topographic survey for the Geological Survey of Canada in part of the region Wheeler was surveying. These surveys, and the trail clearing that Cautley's crew did, provided assistance to Wheeler in this rugged area.

On August 4, with Cautley's crew about a week ahead and working toward North Fork Pass, Wheeler's crew travelled about 20 kilometres up Alexander Creek. They passed the forks, following the east branch of Alexander Creek. While camped there, Cautley's packer arrived with a letter. The following day Campbell and a couple of men occupied a station above Alexander Creek, while Jack Pidgeon went back to Crowsnest Pass to pick up mail and more supplies that they would need later in the season, for this was the last community along their route. He returned the next day.

On August 7 Wheeler and Campbell surveyed two stations on Erickson Ridge. The next day the crew followed Cautley's trail. "Did not reach a campground until after 6pm. Then camped in a grove of spruce on very rocky ground. Very fine hot day. Horses and men very tired—went over two summits." On August 9: "With Jack Pidgeon and one packhorse started on Cautley's trail at 10am.…At 11:30 struck Jake & [Hicks] Cole, Cautley's packers, at lunch at point where trail to Dome Pass branches off—we followed this and about 2:30 arrived at Cautley's camp—he has been surveying the wrong pass. Jack pitched my tent and made things ship-shape, while I hunted up Cautley at summit of pass. Spent the afternoon and evening talking over boundary matters." (In his government report Wheeler wrote that Cautley had "arrived at an unnamed pass… which we have designated as Dome Pass." Today the official geographical name is Tornado Pass.)

Cautley had not been to this area before, so he was following directions from Wheeler. In his government report Wheeler wrote that the trail up the west side of North Fork Pass "was found littered by windfall and not very distinct, and there is little wonder it had been overlooked in the search for the pass on the west side of the divide. An indistinct hunting trail also leads over Dome Pass." The boundary commission report described the situation: "Mr. Cautley commenced work at Tornado Pass under the impression that it was North Fork Pass, and it was not until Mr. Wheeler arrived on the 9th August that he became aware of his mistake. In 1913, Mr. M.P. Bridgland, DLS, had made a phototopographical survey of the Crowsnest Forest, situated on the Alberta side of the watershed, and had then located North Fork Pass. Mr. Wheeler had a copy of Mr. Bridgland's map and was thus in a position to point out that North Fork Pass lay about three miles [five kilometres] southwest of Tornado Pass."

Once again, Cautley was in the wrong pass, but as with Akamina, it was a fortunate error, because Tornado Pass was a more suitable route through the Rockies in this section of the divide.

"In view of the facts that Mr. Cautley had already completed most of the preliminary work and that Tornado Pass has easy approaches on both sides—more so than the North Fork Pass—it was decided to complete the survey."

It took only a week to complete Tornado Pass, for there were just three monuments and three bolts with

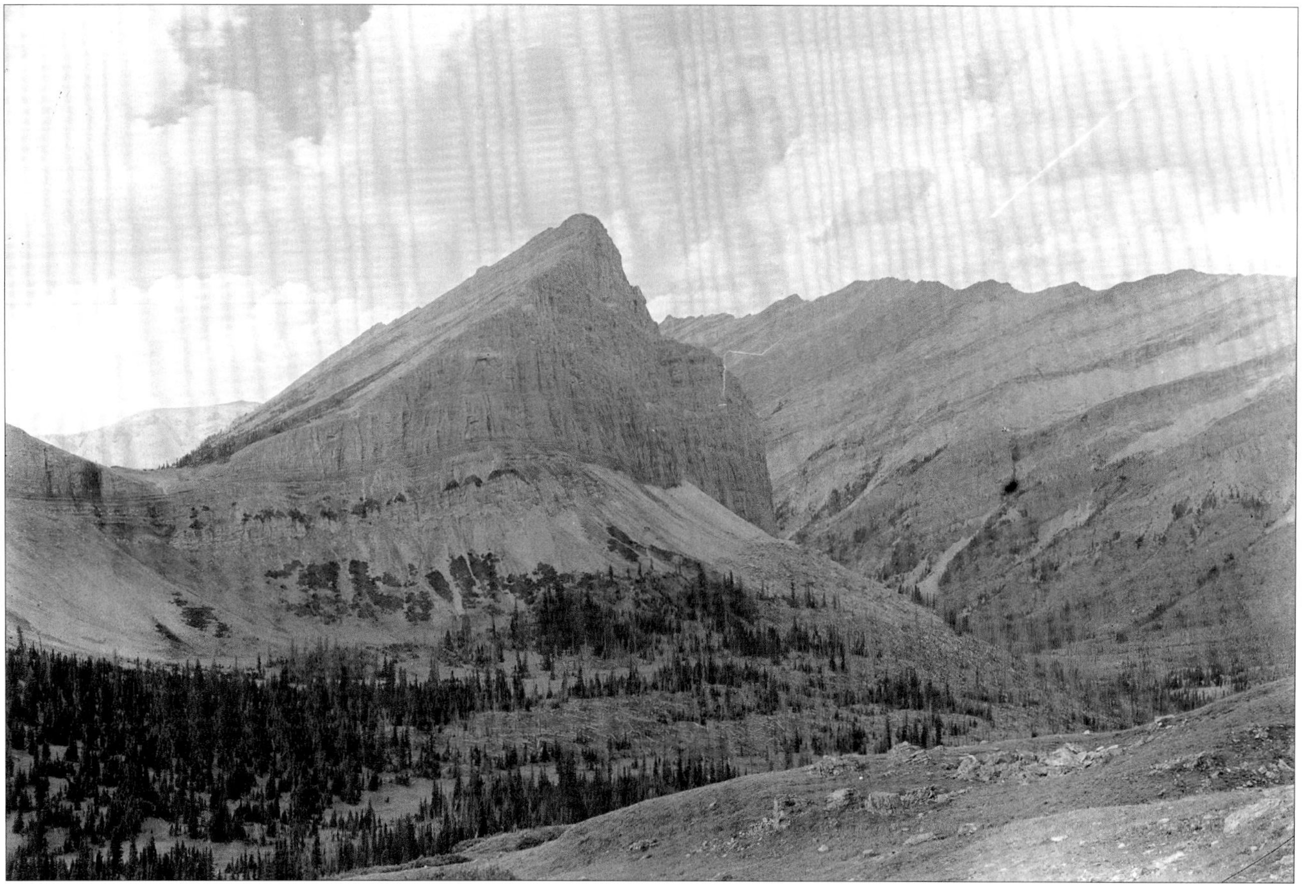

A view of Tornado Pass. WHE1915_W15-172, Library and Archives Canada

cairns established. Wheeler described the scenery at this location: "Dome Pass is of a delightfully alpine character, with open grass lands and groves of spruce on both sides of it. A narrow flat marks the pathway of the pass, and then steep slopes rise abruptly to towering precipices and crags of rock....With the exception of Simpson Pass, I know of none that is more charmingly picturesque or more grandly impressive in its surrounding." Cautley noted that he saw 17 bighorn sheep in the pass.

For the first two days, Wheeler and his crew established stations and surveyed from high locations around Tornado Pass. On August 11 Wheeler, armed with a stick and a small axe, went up a mountain to the southwest of the pass. In his diary he wrote that after reaching the shoulder he "tried a lead up rock for summit & failed. Then went up a snow slope. Lost little axe on the way. Had considerable difficulty without the axe. Reached summit at 2:30 pm, too late for Campbell who left his peak about same time." After resting on August 12, Wheeler and Campbell attempted to reach the summit of Tornado Mountain. They left at 7:00 a.m. In his diary Wheeler wrote about the climb: "Arrived at point about 12pm when could go no further without risking much danger. This point on watershed about 9500 or 9600 [2,895 to 2,925 metres]. Placed a bolt there and built a cairn over it. Soon after starting for home had severe hail storm with thunder & lightning falling rocks etc." The men waited until the storm eased before descending.

The next day S.C. McLean of the Geological Survey arrived and camped in the pass. He was making

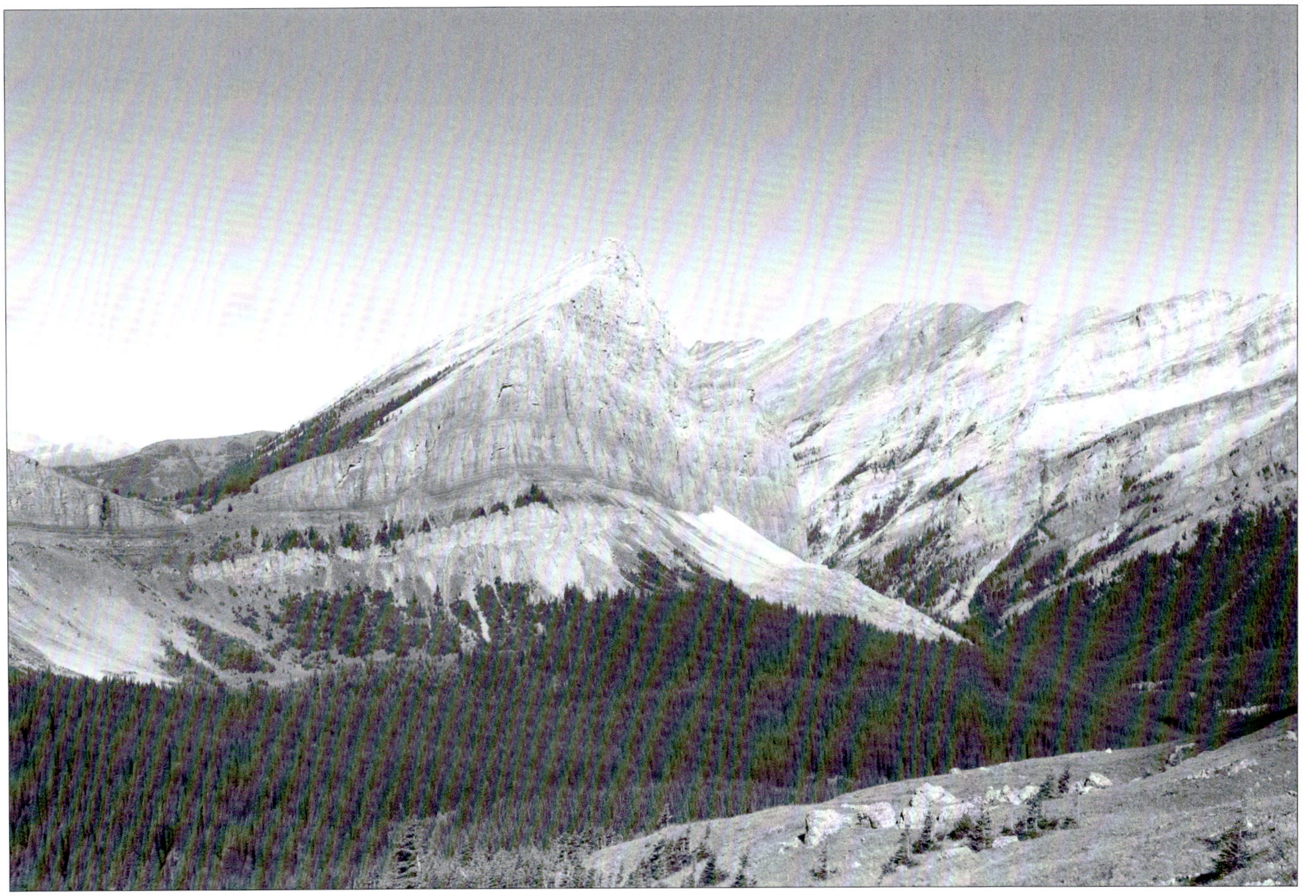

The Mountain Legacy Project photograph shows a significant change in the forest cover of the area. HB2_A0004418, Mountain Legacy Project

a triangulation survey related to a series of maps that would cover the coalfields in the Rocky Mountains from the International Boundary to the Elk Pass area. McLean spent the evening visiting with Wheeler and Cautley. August 15 was Sunday, so the men rested and continued their visitation.

On Monday both McLean and a couple of his crew, along with Wheeler and a few of his men, climbed Tornado Mountain. In his diary Wheeler wrote: "Found it an easy climb and arrived at top soon after 10am. Occupied station with camera and transit. Very bad thunderstorm during afternoon. Had lightning all around us at top of mountain & twice were highly electrified. Got finished about 7pm.…Got back to camp just before dark—8:30 pm. Did not feel very tired."

At 3,099 metres, Tornado Mountain is the highest peak in this section of the Rocky Mountains. The mountain was originally named Gould's Dome by Thomas Blakiston in the 1860s. However, Bridgland changed the name to Tornado in 1915 and transferred the name of Gould's Dome to a smaller mountain nearby. Wheeler wrote about the mountain in the boundary commission report.

> The precipices of Tornado Mountain rise fully 2500 feet [762 metres] and the gigantic rock buttresses that stand out, separated by huge, cavernous chimneys, are awe inspiring.…Tornado Mountain is a storm centre of the locality and, on the occasion of two ascents, the party had narrow escapes, first through a cloud-

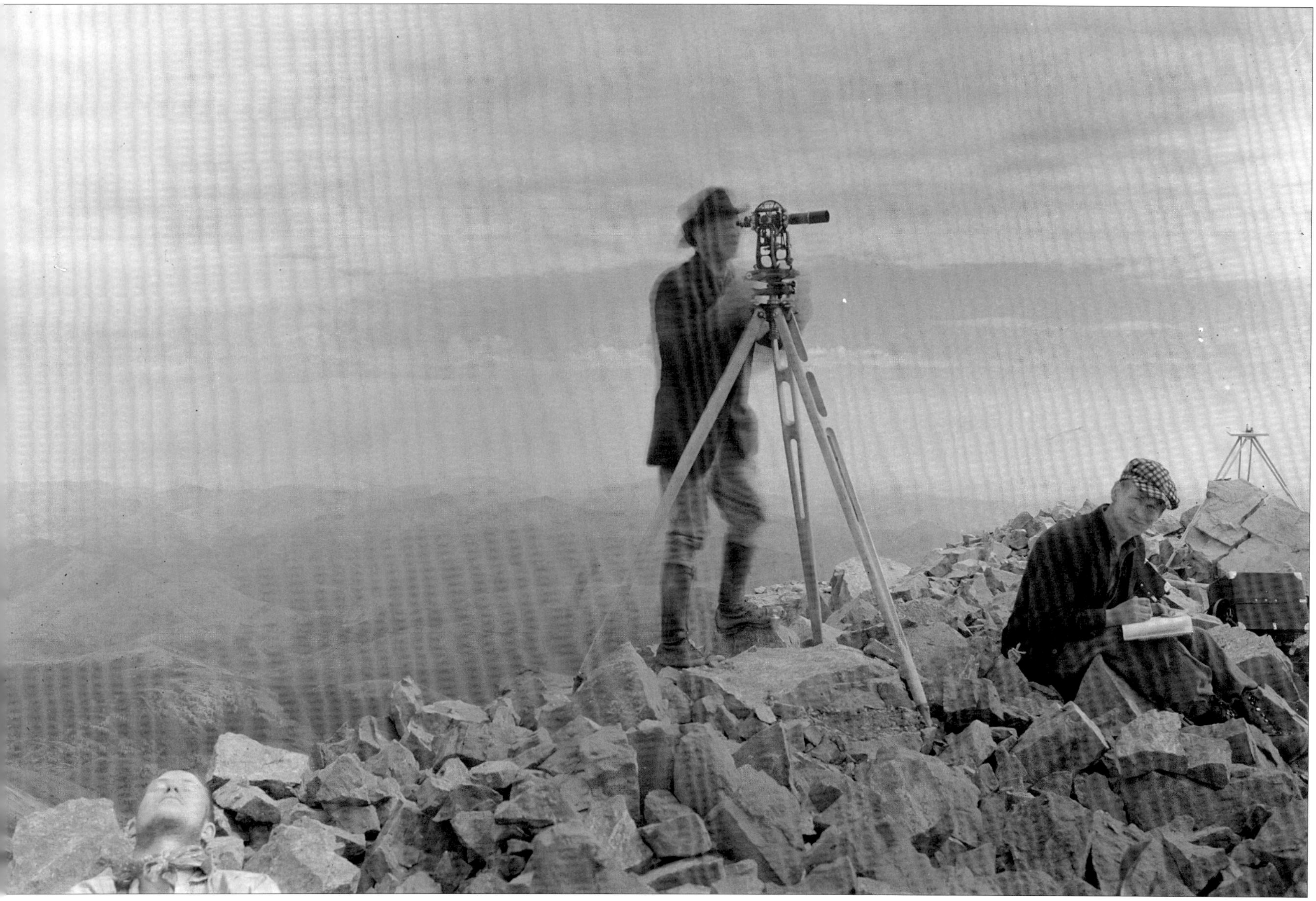

S.C. McLean of the Geological Survey (who unfortunately moved during the photograph) surveying on the summit of Tornado Mountain. His assistant is recording the notes. McLean's plane table, to be used for mapping, is in the background. WHE1915_W15-159, Library and Archives Canada

burst accompanied by sheets of hail, which caused the mountain to run wild, torrents of water cascading down its slopes in every direction, and rockfalls, loosened by the water, crashing on all sides; on the second occasion, a fierce electrical storm encircled the summit and severe shocks were felt by members of the party. For days at a time dark thunder clouds, rent by vivid flashes of lightning, were seen to gather around the summit and similar storms were encountered while on other adjacent heights.

Between Crowsnest Pass and Tornado Pass, Wheeler's crew occupied 19 transit and camera stations. While at Tornado Pass, both Cautley and Wheeler connected their surveys to one of the Dominion land survey posts, and they connected to the same post from North Fork Pass.

From Tornado Pass, the crews moved south to nearby North Fork Pass, where Cautley wrote to Deville on August 17.

> I have just arrived in North Fork Pass tonight. Owing to discrepancies in existing maps and the fact that all the mountain trails in this district have become much blocked by wind, fallen timber, I have had a good deal of trouble in getting here, and first arrived in Dome Pass, lying beneath Gould's Dome as shown in Mr. Bridgland's latest map, of which I did not have a copy but have since seen one in the possession of Mr. Wheeler—under the impression that it was North Fork Pass.…When Mr. Wheeler arrived there with Mr. Bridgland's map, I had already done considerable work in it & we decided that our Governments would desire the work to be completed.…From here we move to Elk River Pass as soon as possible.

Wheeler and his crew arrived the next day. On August 19 it was cloudy, so Cautley and Wheeler "went over both sides of pass and selected sites for monuments," Wheeler wrote in his diary. "Rest of day went cutting trail on west side N. Fork Pass." Inclement weather continued the next day, but on August 21 work resumed. Cautley had an accident that damaged his transit. He wrote to Deville: "A small piece of falling rock struck the instrument while it was being carried along the base of a rock slide. Vertical circle bent slightly. One reading glass for vertical circle broken but replaced. Micrometer A struck and thrown out of adjustment." Cautley was able to repair the instrument and continue using it. On August 22, while Campbell and one crew member put in some bolts and cairns at the top of North Fork Pass, Wheeler and one crew member climbed to one of Bridgland's cairns. "Read angles for Cautley & had just commenced a round for myself when clouds enveloped the mountains and thunderstorms broke all around. We waited till 5:30pm when we built a cairn & gave it up.…Reached camp 7:30pm very wet."

It took about a week to survey the boundary through this small pass. Cautley and Wheeler again established three monuments, along with four brass bolts and cairns. The boundary commission report provided a description of the area: "The summit of the pass consists of a rock ledge extending right across, from side to side. A somewhat curious feature is, that no water was discovered within half a mile [800 metres] of the summit and it was necessary, while making the survey, to camp about 600 feet [180 metres] below it, on the east side, where there was a small spring."

On August 25 Wheeler's crew moved camp to the Ewin Creek valley, about five kilometres north of the summit. Wheeler spent the next day working on surveying calculations while Campbell and another crew member explored the route down Ewin Creek to the Fording River. After a day surveying from a nearby station, the crew was in camp on August 28. In his diary Wheeler wrote: "Rheumatism very bad. Smoky during morning, cleared during afternoon." He spent the day writing letters and working on his accounts, for Pidgeon planned to go to Crowsnest Pass for mail in a few days.

The next day the crew moved camp about 10 kilometres down Ewin Creek and up the Fording River. From this camp Wheeler wrote to Dawson: "We are now working along the main watershed up the Fording and Elk River valleys, and expect to reach and complete the survey of the Elk and Tobermory Passes [today both are considered part of Elk Pass] by the end of September, when it will be necessary to close field work owing to the restricted appropriation.…Owing to all the old trails and valleys where there are no trails, being blocked by fallen timber, travelling is difficult and it is only possible to send for mail at long intervals." The men spent three days surveying at nearby stations, and the packer left with mail for Crowsnest Pass. In his diary Wheeler wrote: "Exploration shows that trail ahead is badly blocked by down timber."

On September 2 Wheeler's crew "packed up and moved camp to Kilmarnock Creek up Fording River valley—a fair trail counting the work Campbell and Joe [Fletcher had] done on it." Once again, they spent three days surveying at nearby stations. At one of these they saw three mountain goats, two adults and a kid. Wheeler spent one day exploring the trail ahead.

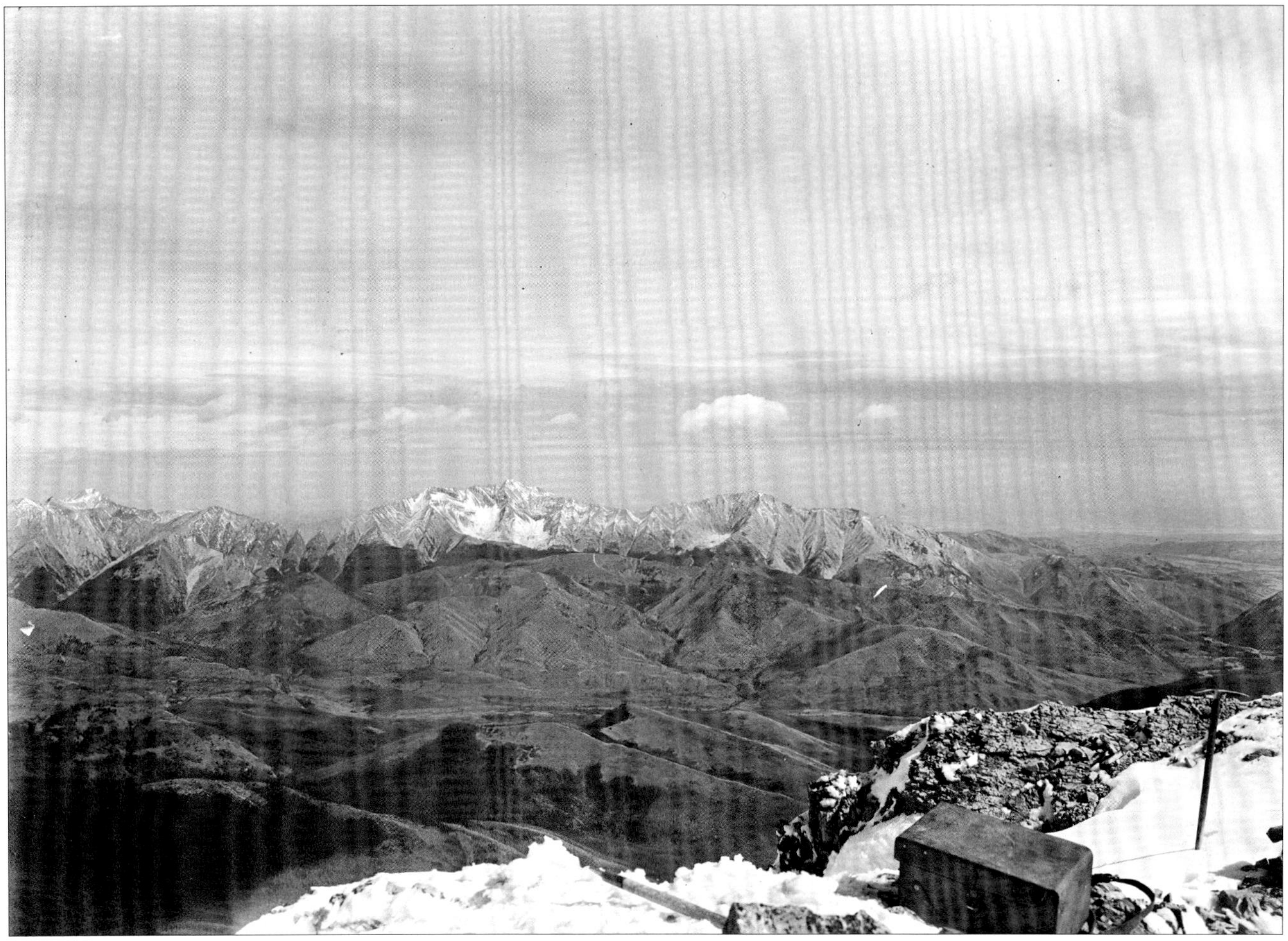

A view east from Mount Armstrong. The photograph was taken after a September snowfall. One of the boxes of surveying equipment is in the foreground. WHE1915_293-ne, Library and Archives Canada

"I went up the Fording River valley on old trail to junction of Henrietta. Found trail—a good one with a little cutting."

The next move was on September 6 to Henrietta Creek. In his government report Wheeler wrote: "On September 7 the first snow fell, and from then on the weather was very bad, snow falling frequently. In consequence, much time was lost owing to the impossibility of getting the photographs from which the maps are made." The crew stayed in camp on September 7. Wheeler wrote in his diary: "Got little stoves up in tent. Campbell went after the horses. Just before lunch had a visit from a man who teamed Cautley's stuff to end of Elk River Road. He and another are at the Northern Coal & Coke Co's camp close by on the Fording River. After lunch travelled for 3 or 4 miles [5 to 6 kilometres] up the Fording River. Good trail for about 2 miles [3.2 kilometres] to an unfinished shack." On September 10, after three days of snow, Wheeler "went with Joe & Gordon [Cameron] ahead and marked out & cleared trail. Campbell & Jack P[idgeon] moved camp about 6 miles [9.6 kilometres] up the valley up Fording R[iver] to junction."

In his diary entry for September 11 Wheeler wrote that the crew "moved to campground selected yesterday—up Fording River headwaters and creek from pass to Cataract Creek headwaters." The next day he observed: "Snowing quite heavy at intervals. Went up

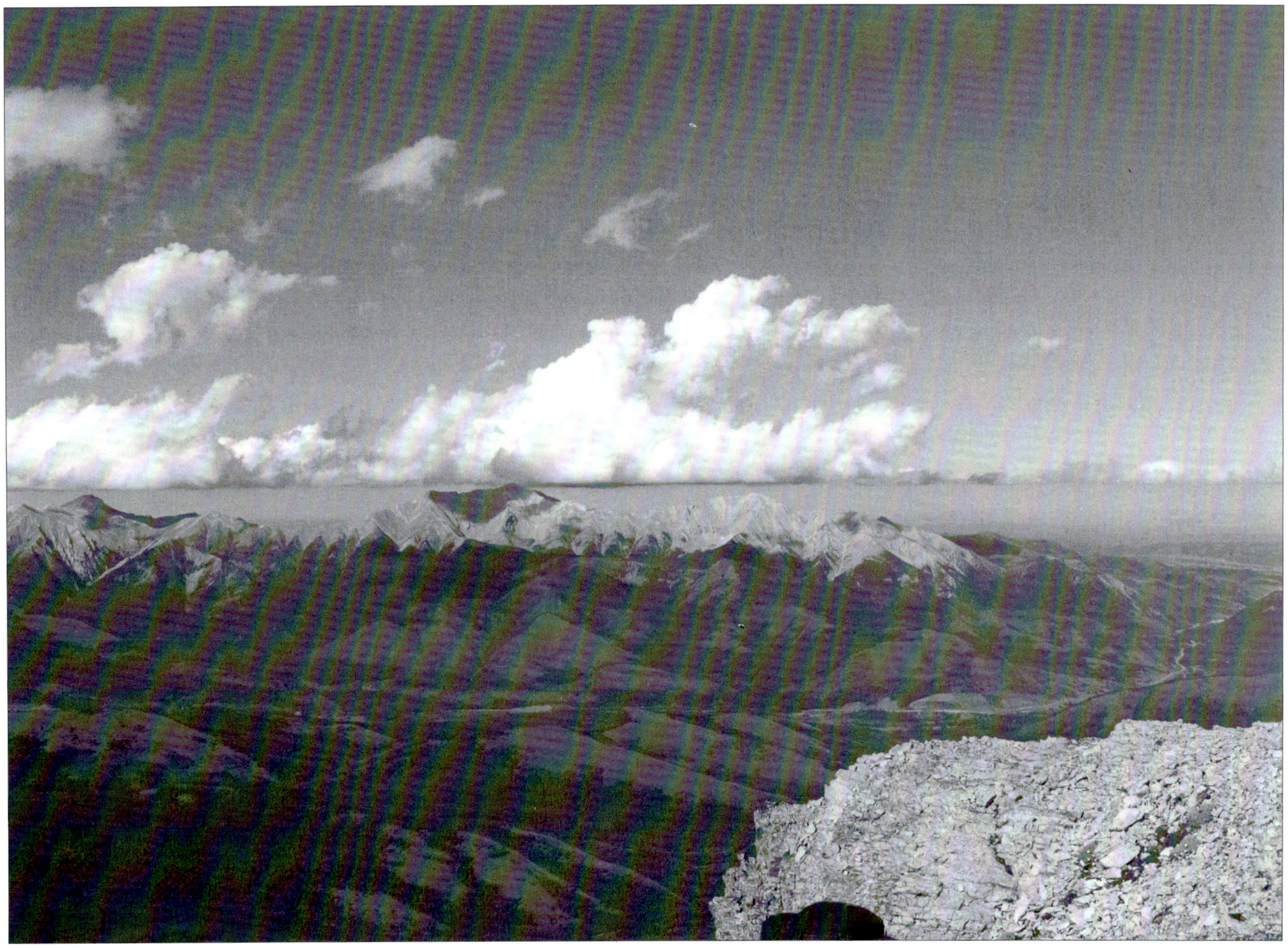

The Mountain Legacy photograph in 2009 shows changes to the forest cover. Highway 40 is also visible in the photograph. HB_1A0003686, Mountain Legacy Project

to see what pass to headwaters of Cataract Creek was like—snow very heavy on pass....Could see very little in any direction." By the time it cleared toward the evening there was at least 15 centimetres of snow on the ground. The men were finally able to resume work on September 13. Wheeler surveyed at Roscoe W., a Geological Survey station that McLean had occupied earlier in the summer. The next day Wheeler and two men explored the area around Fording River Pass while Campbell and the rest of the crew followed the trail to the Elk Valley road. In the afternoon Wheeler went to join his crew. "Soon after starting down trail met party coming back. They saw some Indians in Elk Valley." This was one of the few occasions when the boundary survey members met indigenous people, so it's unfortunate that Wheeler did not provide any detail. It was probably a group of Stoney hunters.

Inclement weather kept the men in camp on September 15. Wheeler, Campbell and Cameron spent the next day around Fording River Pass. "With Campbell & Gordon occupied Fording Pass E. Got a round of views & azimuth but clouds down low & some not very good. Got finished about 12. Went to summit of pass and explored same." In the boundary commissioner's report, Wheeler described Fording River Pass: "There are several steep ascents in the approaches from both sides and it is not suited for a serviceable road, on which account no monument survey was made of it."

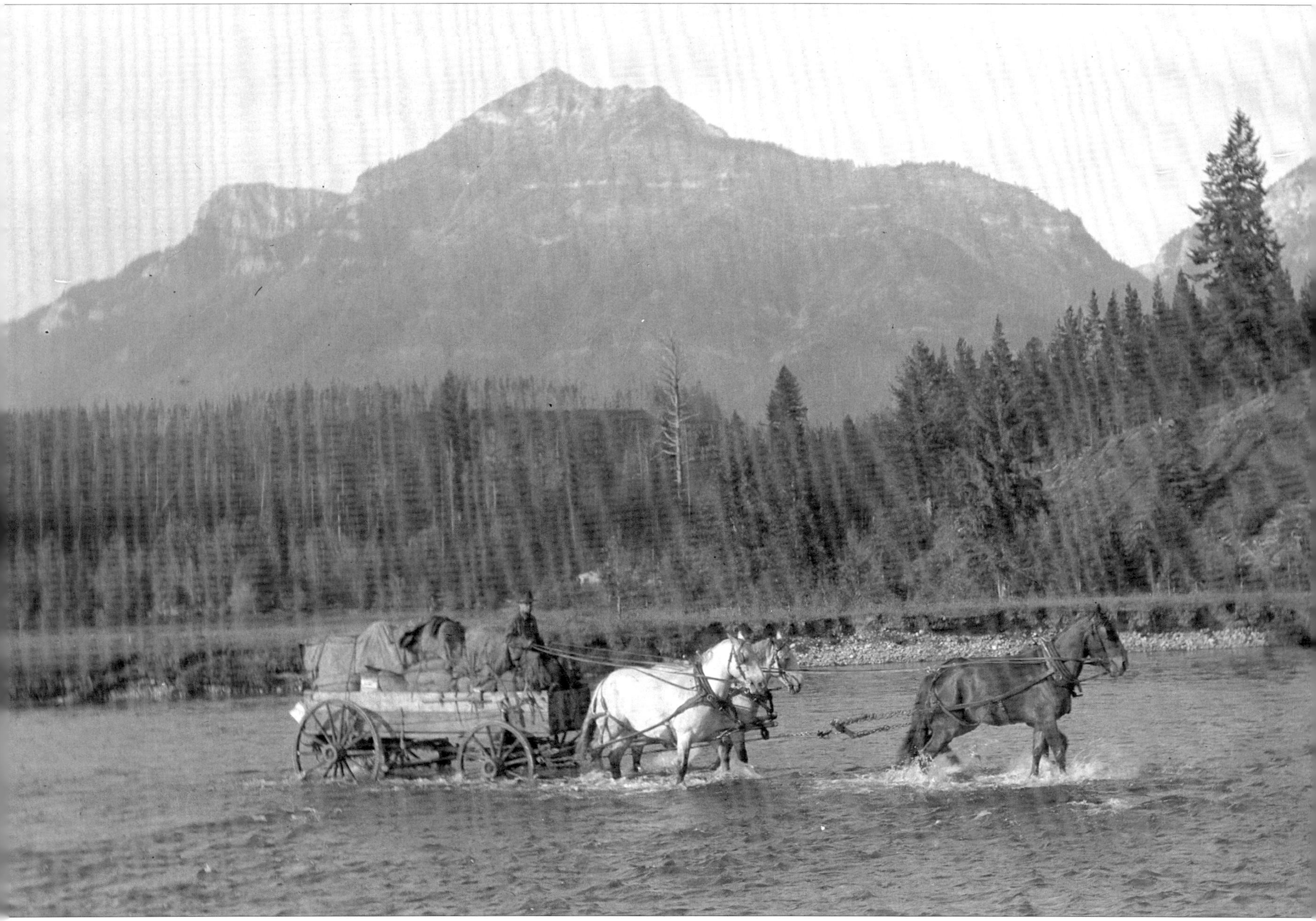

The wagon carrying supplies for Cautley's crew crossing the Elk River at Round Prairie. e011166470, Library and Archives Canada

Wheeler was now ready to go to Elk Pass and join Cautley. He and Jack Pidgeon left at 8:45 and arrived at 5:00 p.m. at Riverside, a Grain Belt Development Company camp in the Elk valley. On September 18 Wheeler and Pidgeon arrived at Cautley's camp at Elk Pass at noon.

Cautley finished surveying North Fork Pass on August 28. While Wheeler and his crew surveyed north to Fording River Pass, Cautley and his men proceeded to Elk Pass. Initially he and his crew travelled down Line Creek to the Elk River wagon road. From there Cautley replenished supplies at Michel and hired a teamster named Woods to freight them to the end of the wagon road. Then Cautley's crew travelled about 40 kilometres to Elk Pass, which they reached on September 6.

By the time Wheeler arrived, Cautley had completed the preliminary survey of Elk Pass.

> The Pass is in reality a twin pass with two very distinct summits which are separated by low timbered hills; these two passes are about 1½ miles [2.4 kilometres] apart, that to the west being about 240 feet [75 metres] lower than the other, and the intervening hill reaches a maximum elevation of 450 feet [137 metres] above the lower, or main pass, or 210 feet [64 metres] above the higher one.
>
> The summit of Elk Pass is a marshy meadow, which it was necessary to cross-section and take levels over before the point of commencement could be determined. There are also a number of wet muskegs which cross the line of watershed between the two passes, rendering the watershed more obscure than usual and the preliminary survey proportionately more difficult.

After arriving at Cautley's camp, Wheeler and Cautley spent the afternoon examining the proposed boundary line. Jack Pidgeon left the next day, and that night the horses he had left "stepped back to main camp." By September 20 Cautley and Wheeler had agreed on the boundary through Elk Pass, and the next day Wheeler wrote: "Cautley sent Hicks back with me to Weary Creek, supplying me with transport to that point. Left at 8:45, arrived at Riverside camp at 12:15. Left Riverside at 1:30, arrived at Weary Creek at 4:30."

On September 22 Hicks Cole returned to Cautley's camp. Meanwhile, Wheeler wrote: "Took my big eiderdown & a few things in rucksack and started on foot for main camp. Left at 9:50. At Aldrich Creek Camp where arrived at 11am met Jack P[idgeon] going out for me with three horses. He went on to Weary Creek Camp for my bed & I walked to main camp arriving at 3:30 pm.…Campbell party occupied N peak of the Sprinters."

Wheeler's crew remained in camp for the next two days because of inclement weather. On the 25th they occupied two stations that were close to each other. "Bright warm day—very good views and a lot of negs [negatives]." The next day they climbed "Roscoe—cold and windy ascending. Arrived at summit at 11:35. Wind dropped and it soon became warm but cloudy all day. Got good views and azimuths." This peak (now named Mount Courcelette after a World War I battle at that location) is 3,044 metres. The second-highest peak in the area after Tornado Mountain, it lies entirely within British Columbia. This was the first recorded ascent of the mountain.

In describing the phototopography in the area around Fording River Pass, the commission report stated that "a number of camera stations [were] occupied, but not very satisfactorily, as the whole country was covered by snow and was in a very poor condition for photographing, while dull days and clouds hanging low over the mountains added further to the difficulty of obtaining useful results."

Wheeler wrote in his government report: "On the 27th, finding it impossible under existing weather conditions to complete the location of the watershed line beyond the head of Fording River, the party crossed the summit to Aldridge Creek and followed the trail down that stream to the Elk Valley Road.…Twenty-one stations were occupied to carry the location of the boundary from Dome Pass to where the work was discontinued." This section would be completed in 1916. In his diary Wheeler wrote: "At Weary Creek saw the boss (Guillion) in charge camps and got some war news. Stopped for night at Riverside Camp. Took possession of camp, but I slept in my tent." The next day they arrived at Elk Pass and set up their camp about 400 metres from Cautley's.

Wheeler spent three days surveying around Elk Pass. He recorded that he placed three brass bolts and cairns at the highest stations in the pass. "Six stations have been occupied with camera and transit to gather information to map the pass. In all, for the season, fifty-nine stations were occupied and 364 photographic views were taken."

On October 2 Wheeler and his crew headed for the Kananaskis lakes on the return journey to Banff. In his

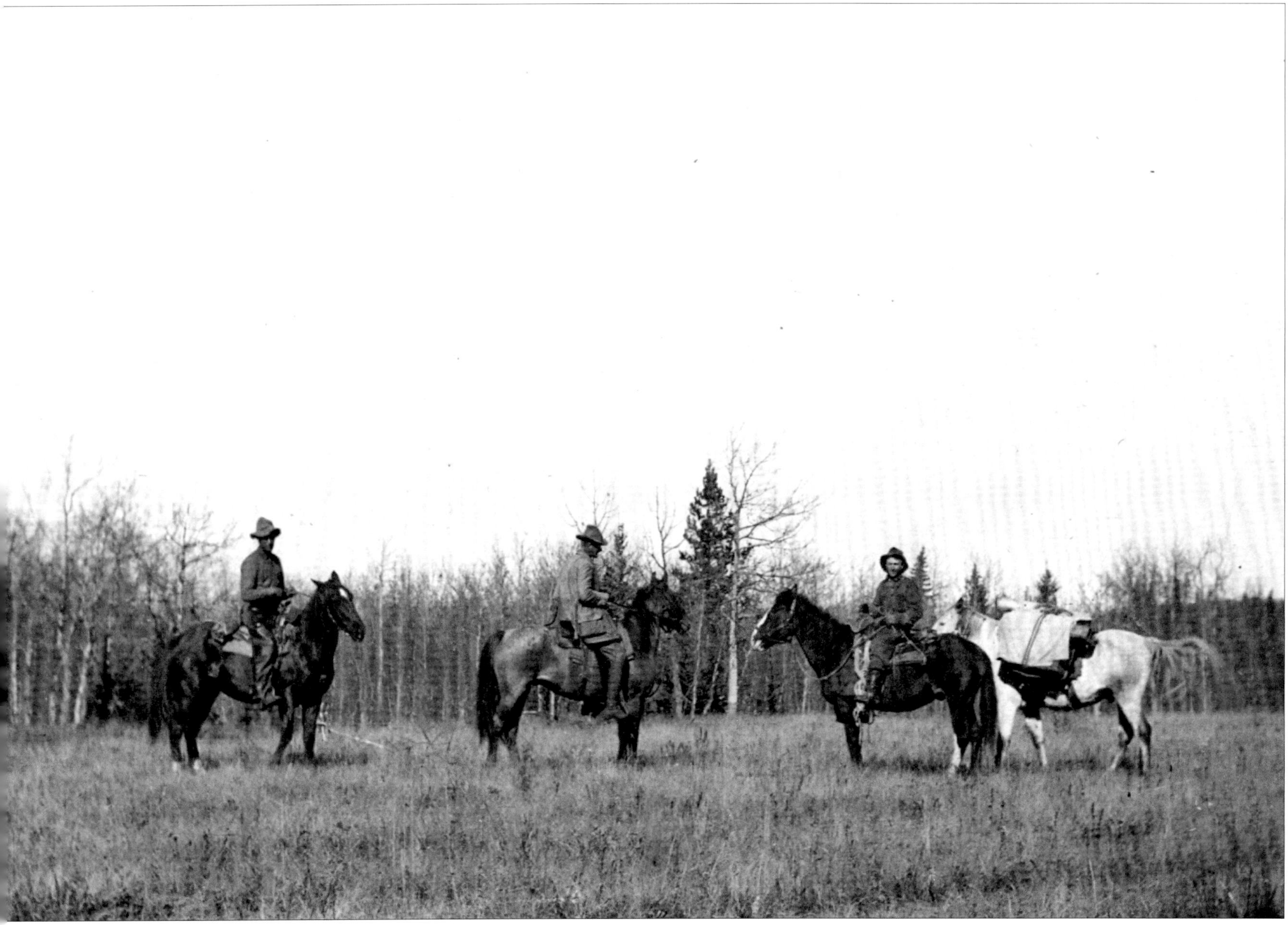

This photograph was taken on the last day of the field season about 15 kilometres from Morley. Packer Jacob Koller is on the left, Cautley is in the middle, and assistant packer Hicks Cole is on the right. Behind Cole is Johnny, the horse that carried the surveying equipment. J-00870, Royal BC Museum and Archives

diary he wrote: "We started down Lower Lake, crossed ford & in a snow storm passed the trail for Spray Lakes. Had to go on two miles [3.2 kilometres] for a camp." The next morning they "went back and found the trail up Kananaskis River," which they had passed in the dark. "Travelled all day up this valley & camped at 5pm about 2 miles from Mud Lake. Snowed while pitching camp." On October 5, after another snowstorm, Wheeler and Gordon Cameron walked to Banff, while the rest of the crew arrived the next day.

Cautley surveyed at Elk Pass until October 5. There were 13 monuments in Elk Pass, half of the total for the 1915 field season, and the distance measured across the pass was 6.4 kilometres. He wrote to Deville: "September weather in the mountains is always liable to be bad, and this month was particularly so. 11 inches [28 centimetres] of snow fell on the 9th September, and it snowed on 9 different days between this date and the 5th October, besides a great deal of rain, so that from the 9th September the ground was bare of snow for only a very few days." This made construction of the monuments difficult, as described in the commission report.

> It is necessary to take special precautions against frost when building concrete monuments during such weather; some of them were built under a tent put up for the purpose, but the most satisfactory way seemed to be to heat rocks in a log fire during the afternoon, put them in a shallow trench dug around the monument and, just before dark, cover them with dry soil; the monument and trench are then covered with canvas pack covers, the edges of which are weighted to the ground with stones and soil. When this has been done and the concrete mixed with warm water, the frost does not seem to hurt and the only possible trouble is that the concrete is liable to dry out rather too quickly.

Cautley connected the boundary survey to both the Dominion land survey and the four British Columbia lots in Elk Pass.

> Direct connection was made with the N.E. corner of Section 6, Township 19, Range 8 West of the 5th Meridian, the east boundary of which has been surveyed across the Boundary.
>
> Direct connection was also made with the surveys of Lots 8490, 8491, 8492 and 8493 of the British Columbia system, all of which are surveyed in such a way as to be partly in Alberta and partly in British Columbia. Lots 8492 and 8493, in particular, extend more than a mile [1.6 kilometres] on the Alberta side of the watershed—along the east boundary of Lot 8492 and the west boundary of Lot 8493 respectively—and it is difficult to understand how these surveys came to be made so far, and so palpably, over the watershed, since the above lines cross creeks which are plainly running into Alberta, and descend on the Alberta side, some hundreds of feet below the summit of the pass.

The adjustment of these lots now became the responsibility of the BC surveyor general.

After finishing Elk Pass, Cautley and his crew travelled to Morley, where the horses would winter. They arrived on October 11, Thanksgiving Day.

To finish the field season, Wheeler needed to take a trip to Crowsnest Pass. He left Banff on October 7, staying overnight in Calgary. The next day, Friday, he "left for Crowsnest by 5 pm train. Arrived at Crowsnest at 12:20 am—dance on." On Saturday he paid accounts, including cheques to the wives of Joe Fletcher and Jack Pidgeon, and shipped an old tent to Jack Stelfox. Wheeler was back at Banff for Thanksgiving Day. He spent the morning "putting away survey outfit and getting things dried & aired." In the afternoon he took a bath at the hot springs and for supper he had an "excellent kidney pie & Christmas pudding followed by a fine plum cake." The next day, before he returned to Edmonton, Cautley came to Banff to confer with Wheeler. Wheeler remained in Banff until the end of October, when he returned to Vancouver Island for the winter.

Snow and cold weather had ended the field season earlier than Cautley and Wheeler anticipated. But the two crews had completed most of their objectives for 1915, and the two surveyors anticipated that they would be able to complete the southern section of the boundary in 1916.

The Remonumentation of Elk Pass

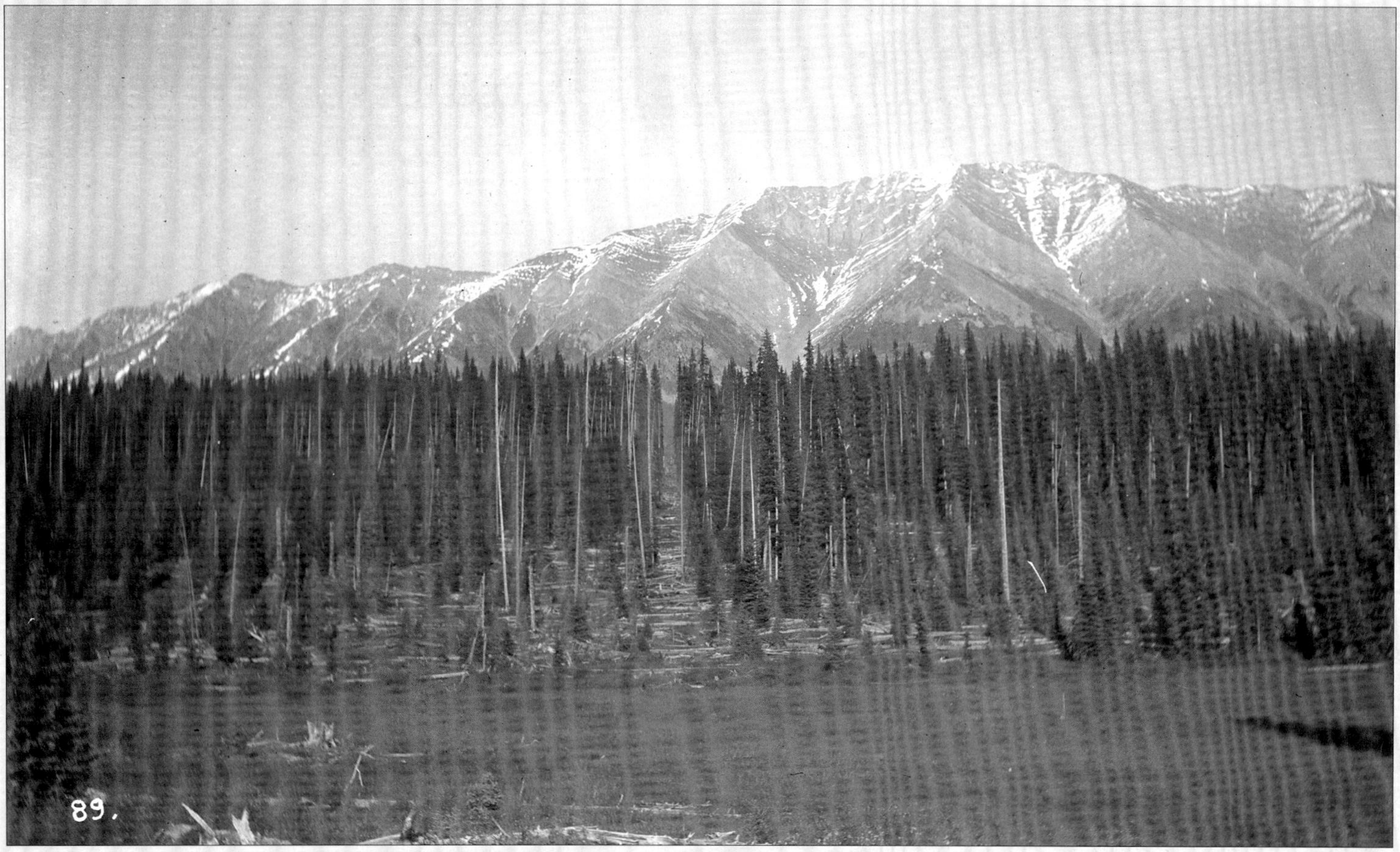

Cautley took this photograph looking east from Monument 1M. e011166471, Library and Archives Canada

The Alberta-BC Boundary Commission was re-established in the 1950s during the completion of the final section of the boundary survey. It still has one representative each from Alberta, British Columbia and the federal government and meets twice yearly. Mike Thomson, the surveyor general of British Columbia, is currently that province's representative.

One of the commission's important mandates is the ongoing preservation of the boundary's monuments. In 2011 a local volunteer organization reported on the deteriorating condition of the monuments in Elk Pass. Some of them had also been vandalized. Flooding in Alberta in 2013 did further damage. The boundary commission decided to remonument 10 stations through the main part of Elk Pass.

In 2015 Cima Geomatics of Calgary did the resurvey of this portion of Elk Pass. The restoration survey of the 10 monuments was done in July, and the survey of the measurements to the monuments was made in September. The company found physical evidence at all 10 stations, although some monuments had significant deterioration. In its report Cima Geomatics noted that "the position of each monument was determined from the existing original evidence. In all cases the concrete base of the monuments was found and exposed which revealed the edges of the base in good condition. From the edges of the square base the mid point was measured and the new monuments were referenced and placed at that point."

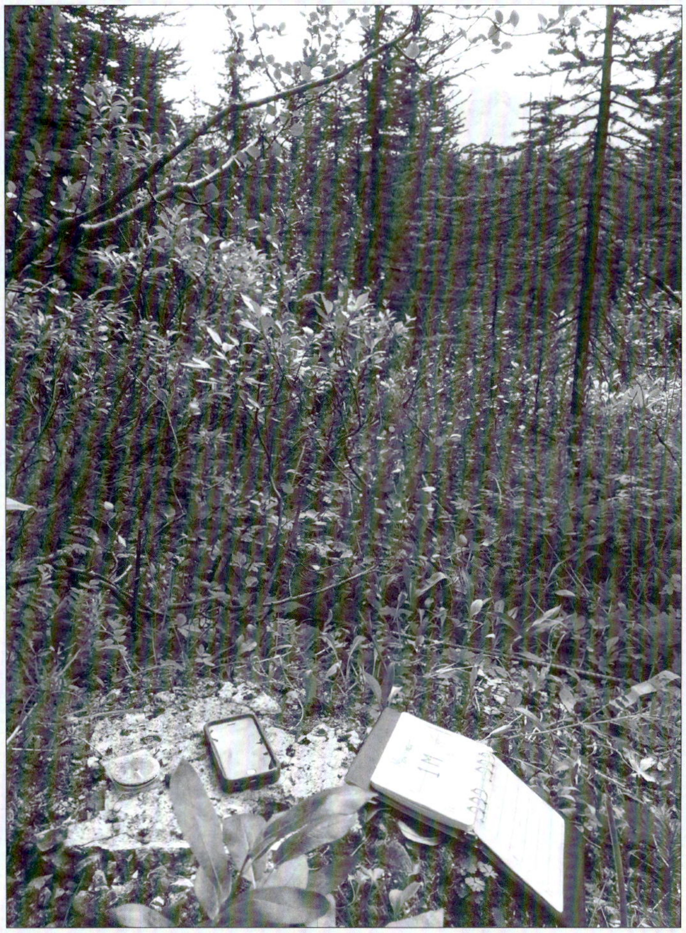

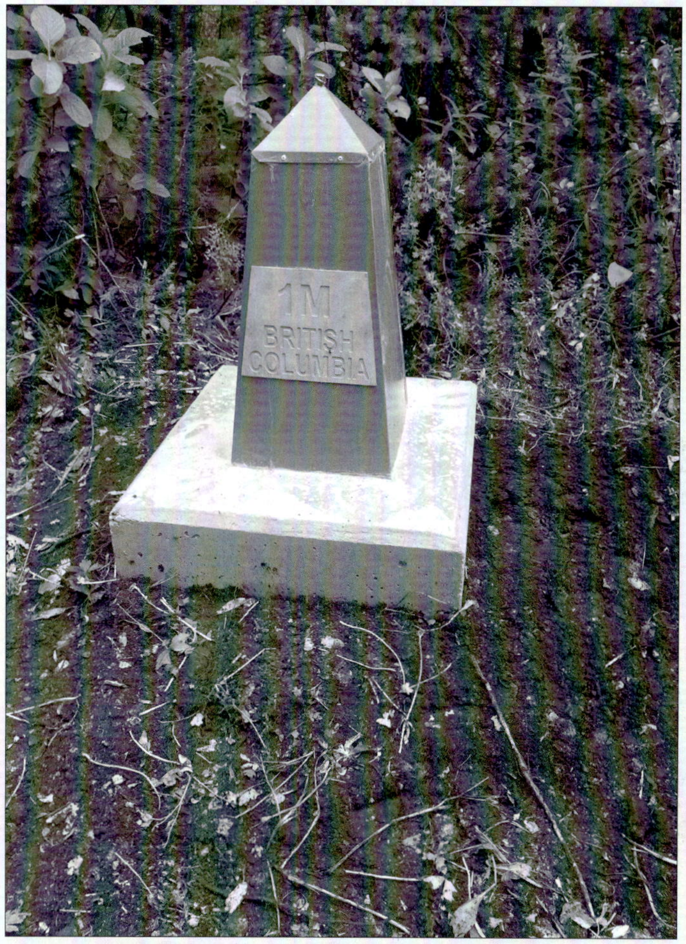

The remains of Monument 1M in 2015 and the restored one now on the site. Jamie Hume photo

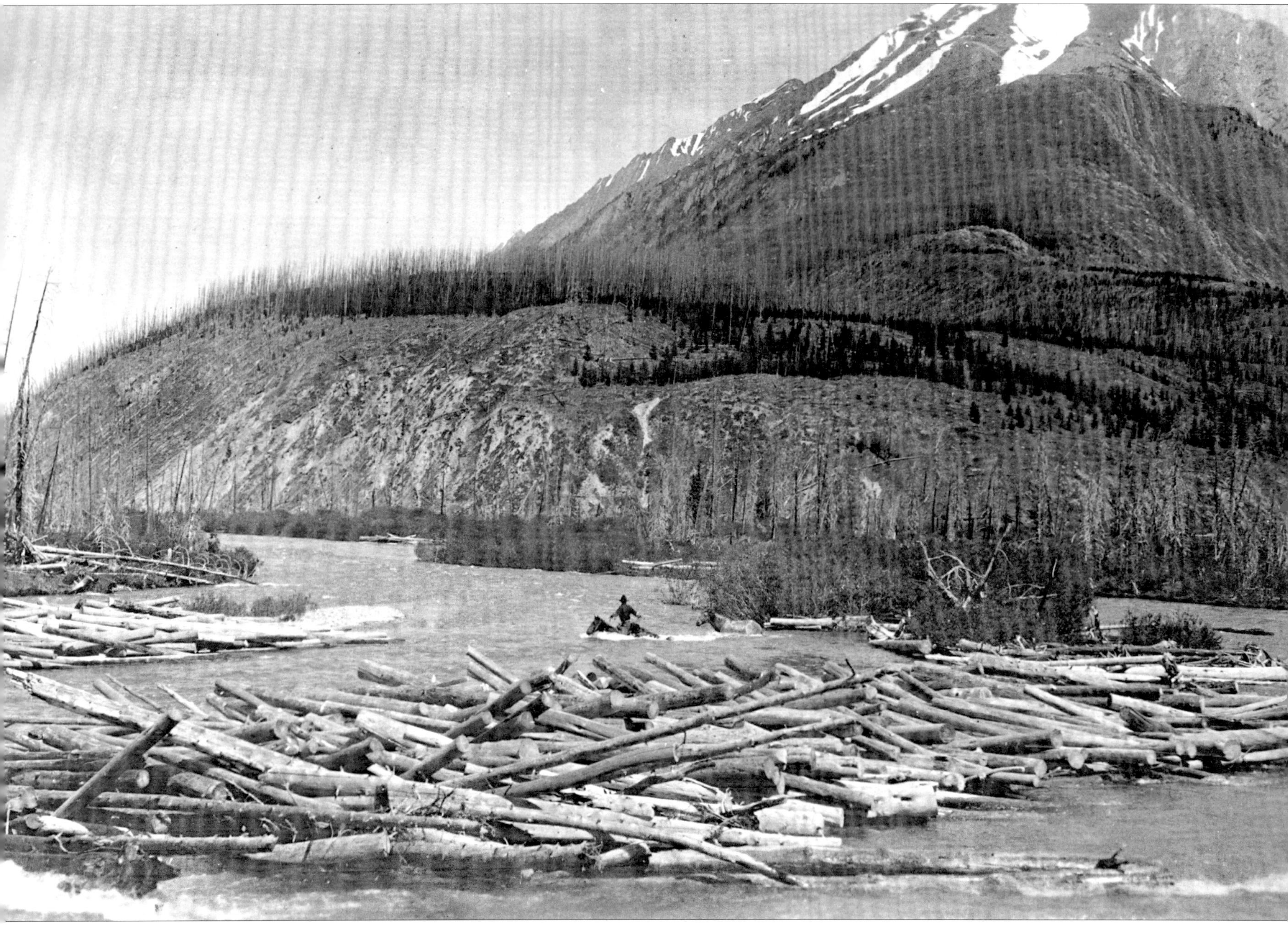

Fording the Spray River during the July floods. J-00874, Royal BC Museum and Archives

1916

The objective for the boundary survey in 1916 was to complete the first section, covering the area between the International Boundary and the Canadian Pacific Railway at Kicking Horse Pass. World War I was in its third year, but despite limited finances, there was a desire to continue the project by all three governments involved.

In a confidential letter to Deville on February 9, Dawson wrote:

> I also note your very pertinent question as to whether it is my intention to proceed with the survey of the Boundary this coming season. You are no doubt aware that three by-elections for members of the Cabinet are pending and that the term of the present House expires within a few months. You will appreciate that under these circumstances it is somewhat difficult for me to get any very definite information as to what appropriations I am likely to get this year. I can only undertake to advise you, as soon as I know myself, if the Boundary Survey is to be proceeded with. I anticipate that I will be given a limited amount for this survey.

The consensus was that the survey would be funded at the same level as in 1915, with each organization again contributing $6,000. However, there was disagreement over how these limited funds would be utilized.

In 1915 Cautley received more than half of the funds because of the cost of constructing the monuments. But he built only 26 monuments, less than half of his 1914 total. The passes where the boundary survey planned to work in 1916 were not large, so he would probably have about the same amount for the coming year. On the other hand, Wheeler wanted to have a second crew and phototopographic camera. He still had the section between Fording River Pass and Elk Pass to complete, along with the Great Divide north from Elk Pass to the Mount Assiniboine area. Wheeler also needed a draftsman for the winter office work. This was particularly important because the boundary commissioners had to make a report on the data gathered during the four years of surveying the first section.

Deville wrote to L.C. Charlesworth regarding Wheeler's request. Alberta's deputy minister of public works replied on February 11.

> So far as the Province of Alberta is concerned we had expected that the expenditure this year would not exceed $6,000.00 for this Province in accordance with the arrangements made last year and we have made provision for this amount in the estimate. I have so far received no intimation of any intention to discontinue the work this season.…I understand that Mr. Wheeler already finds it difficult to complete the necessary office work for the amount of work done in the field last season and if the field work is to be increased it seems to me that the office work must also increase and the arrangements that were made for controlling the total expenditure will all be undone. I am very strongly of the opinion that no greater amount of field work should be undertaken in any season than can be completed in the office for the same season and within the appropriation.

Charlesworth also reiterated the concern that he had expressed the previous year about the scope of Wheeler's surveying. "I must, however, mention the view taken by the Alberta authorities who, as you already know, consider that the actual marking of the survey on the ground in the passes is of greater importance than the topographical survey of the intervening watershed line." Deville suggested a compromise, believing that it would be fair to divide the funds equally between the two survey crews.

On February 22 Deville wrote to Charlesworth. While supporting the deputy minister of public works' viewpoint, Deville also stressed the importance of making a comprehensive survey. He wrote:

> [It is] well understood that the survey must be limited to one mile on each side of the watershed line or thereabouts, but the desire was expressed that it should be continuous, without gaps. This was not accomplished before 1915. While the survey expanded to a considerable distance from the boundary at some places, there are gaps at other places without any survey. Mr. Wheeler will have not only to make a continuous survey of the parts of the boundary surveyed during the coming years, but he will also have to fill in the gaps in parts of the boundary already surveyed. The important part of the boundary is evidently across the passes and the view of the Alberta authorities that its marking is of greater importance than the survey of the intervening watershed can not be disputed, but it would be regrettable not to make a complete survey of the whole boundary while there is an opportunity to do it.

In a letter to Wheeler on March 10 Deville stated: "The passes are the important portions of the boundary; if you are not able with the money placed at your disposal to supply detailed topography for the passes and also approximate topography for the intervening stretches of the watershed, it may be a question as to which of the two should be abandoned. I propose taking up the question a little later, when it is decided that the survey is to go on another year."

On April 4 Dawson sent Deville a telegram: "Personal estimates passed last night—$6,000 boundary survey." Deville ordered the plates for the phototopographic cameras two days later, and on April 12 he wrote Dawson: "I am glad to know that the survey can go on another year. As you will have seen from the report sent you on April 10th, some rearrangement of the work has become imperative." In his report Deville suggested a second crew for Wheeler; a limit of the office work to 150 days; a provision that both Cautley and Wheeler could employ draftsmen at a moderate salary; and that the balance of the appropriation be divided to keep both parties in the field for an equal number of days. From these recommendations Wheeler and Cautley formulated a working agreement, with Wheeler receiving slightly more than half of the $18,000.

Wheeler and Cautley not only needed to finish surveying the southern section of the interprovincial boundary, but also had to produce a public report. There was some discussion about the format of this report in 1915, but now they needed to make decisions. In a letter to Wheeler in October 1916, Deville expressed his displeasure that no written reports had been published yet. "The original intention was to commence by publishing the first three chapters. Every succeeding year publish new chapter with index.…It is evident now that the report for 1916 will also be required to complete the first section from the Kicking Horse Pass to the International Boundary. Four years will thus have elapsed before the first part of the report is sent to the printers. It seems to me that it would have been preferable to adhere to the original plan of issuing yearly reports."

The boundary commissioners and Deville decided to put the maps into a separate atlas. The format for the report, the method for illustrating and arranging the monuments at each pass, the style of printing photographs and many other details were arranged during the year.

As part of completing the southern section of the boundary survey, the commissioners realized that one small area remained unresolved. The boundary commissioners and Deville tried once again to get the Alberta government to agree on an equitable division of Phillipps Pass. However, the Alberta government refused to change its position.

The original plan for 1916 was for Cautley to survey and place monuments in three passes that were fairly close together: Kananaskis, Palliser and White Man. They were located between Elk Pass, surveyed in 1915, and Assiniboine Pass, surveyed by Wheeler in 1913. There were two Kananaskis passes. North Kananaskis was the main one, while South Kananaskis, a couple of kilometres away, was smaller and had a steeper approach. Wheeler and Cautley decided to begin the field season at the Kananaskis lakes. From this location, close to Elk Pass, Wheeler would finish the topographic

Charles Vincent Hope

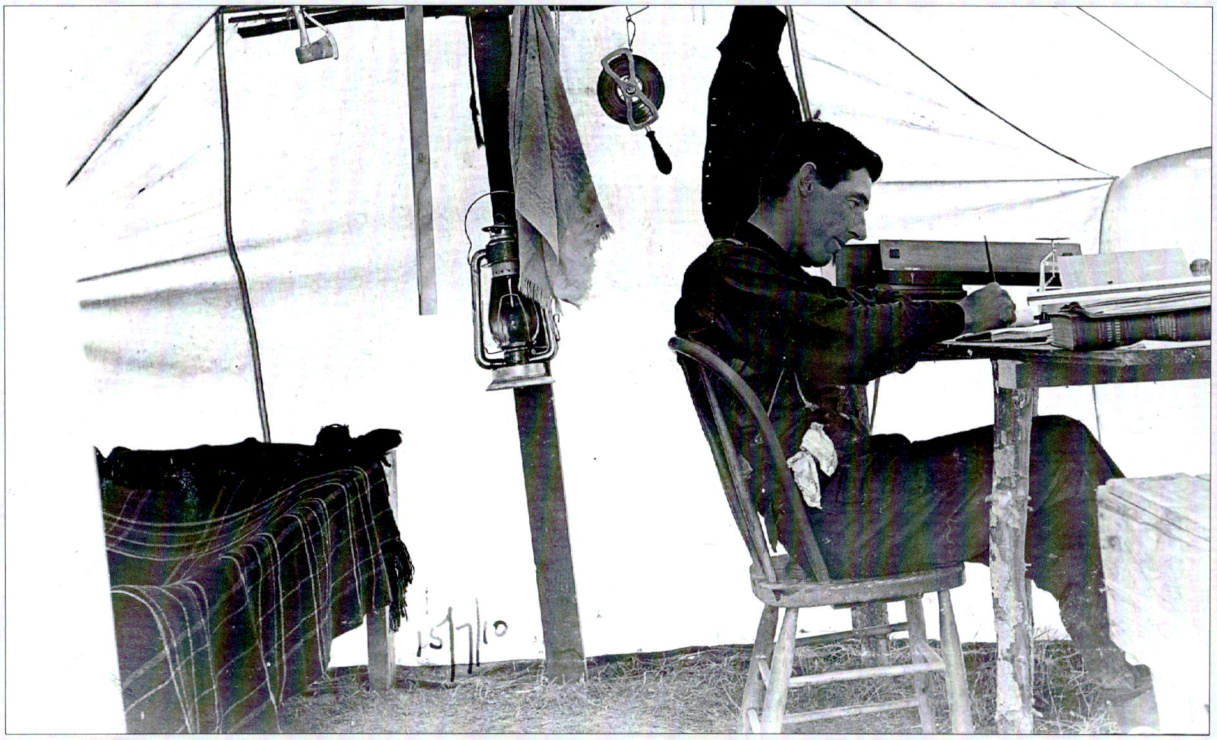

C.V. Hope working in his office tent during his railway bridge engineering work. C.V. Hope family collection

Charles Vincent Hope was born in England in 1879 and immigrated to western Canada in 1907. From 1910 to 1914 he was employed by the Grand Trunk and Canadian Northern railways as a civil engineer and worked on the construction of several railway bridges in central Alberta. Hope took photographs of the projects. The Jasper-Yellowhead Archives has a copy of Hope's photographs of the construction of the Canadian Northern bridge across the Athabasca River near Entrance in 1913.

During the 1916 field season, Hope took several photographs of crew members and the surveying, and Cautley included some of them in his personal photo album.

In February 1917 Hope enlisted in World War I, and he served with the Canadian Railway troops. He arrived at the Vimy sector about a week after the battle and remained in France until the spring of 1919.

After the war Hope resumed working with the Canadian Northern Railway (later Canadian National), and in the late 1920s he was an engineer during the completion of the Hudson Bay Railway in northern Manitoba.

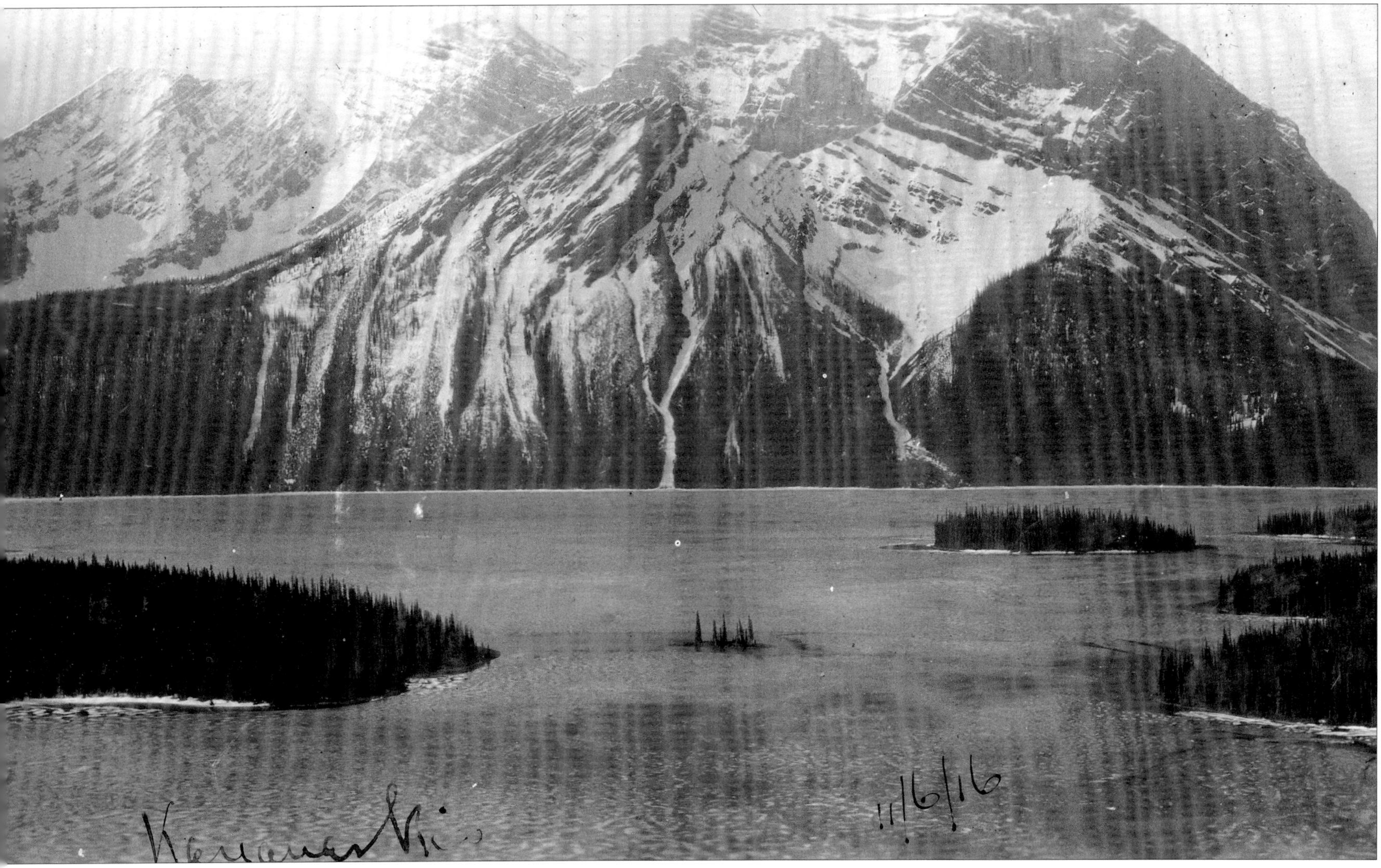

This picture taken on June 11 shows the high water level at Upper Kananaskis Lake beginning to submerge the shoreline and islands. C.V. Hope family collection

survey of the section between Fording River Pass and Elk Pass, before working northward. Cautley intended to survey the Kananaskis passes west of the lakes and then go to the two remaining passes

Cautley wanted to improve the quality of his photographs, so in 1916 he purchased a 3A Kodak Special fitted with a Cooke Series III lens. He also got Troughton & Sims, the company that manufactured his transit, to make a tripod head camera stand that would fit onto the same one he used for the transit.

To prepare for their fieldwork, Cautley and Wheeler met at Calgary on May 16. They had lunch together, visited with J.N. Wallace and spent time conferring. Their meeting continued all of the following day.

In early June Cautley and his crew assembled at Morley, where the horses had wintered. The men from Dowling Lake who had been on his 1915 crew returned: head packer Jacob Koller, assistant packer Hicks Cole and monument builder Chris Townsend. Cautley's assistant was Charles Hope, a railway engineer.

The crew proceeded up the Bow and Kananaskis Rivers to the Kananaskis lakes. In his memoir Cautley wrote: "Starting from Morley, on the Canadian Pacific Railway, on the 7th of June 1916, I got my outfit up the Kananaskis Trail as far as the upper end of Lower Kananaskis Lake. Beyond that, the trail was blocked with such deep snow that I couldn't go on. I therefore sent my two packers down to Morley to bring up a load of cement on the 12th of June."

Spring was late arriving that year, and there was still a considerable amount of snow in the mountains, so Cautley had to wait at Lower Kananaskis Lake until conditions improved. "The day after they left camp, the long-delayed warm weather arrived and caused all rivers and creeks to overrun their banks. All day and night we could hear avalanches thundering down from the precipitous mountains surrounding Upper Kananaskis Lake." The boundary commission report noted that "from the 15th June to the 15th July all rivers and larger creeks were dangerously high and overflowed their banks in many places."

Cautley described the events that followed for his packers. "Jake ran into trouble right away. The horses had wintered on the Kananaskis range and knew the country well. For this reason I had particularly told Jake to hobble the horses at night. Apparently he didn't do this. Anyway, he lost half the horses, and had to go on to Morley without them. When he started back, miles of the trail along the Kananaskis River was under eighteen inches [45 centimetres] of water."

Instead of stopping and waiting for the river to subside, Koller continued up the trail "until he reached a steep trail leading down to the abandoned Eau Claire lumber camp on a partly flooded river flat."

> A little bridge was broken at the bottom of the hill, and while the two men were fixing it, the loaded horses were backed up on the trail which overhung a raging rapid, and one of them got pushed off into the river. In some way, loaded as he was, this horse managed to swim over to an island.
>
> Next morning, Jake went about a mile up the river, to a place where the river was quiet, although swift, and swam across. He scrambled down along the foot of the bluffs on the other side of the river until he reached the horse, which he unpacked and unsaddled. Then he called out to Hicks to bring down a long rope, ready to throw to him, as he wasn't going all that way back. Hicks said that Jake waded into the river, and, as soon as he struck the swift water, was immediately swept off his feet and carried away: that he saw his head once and not again. His body was never found.

Hicks Cole searched unsuccessfully for Koller and then returned to Cautley's camp. "About 4:30 A.M. on the 23rd June, Hicks woke me up and told the above story, which I hadn't the slightest reason to disbelieve, particularly as I saw the horse next day, still on the island, with his load and harness hung on a tree, all of which was recovered in the fall."

Wheeler spent the early part of June completing his 1915 survey reports and making final preparations for the ACC camp. While he was doing this, A.J. Campbell and the crew departed from Banff on June 5. One of the members was A.S. (Spike) Thomson, who had previously worked for Wheeler as a draftsman. Thomson was on Wheeler's survey crew for 1916, 1917, 1919 and 1920, and he climbed many of the mountains with Wheeler and Campbell. He kept a diary, which he later copied and provided some additional retrospective notes. Thomson also took a camera. Ralph Rink also joined Wheeler's crew for the first time. He became Wheeler's packer for a few seasons, and after the boundary survey the two men formed a business that provided walking tours from Banff to Mount Assiniboine. Rink had a tepee that he usually set up at camp. Wheeler appeared to enjoy this accommodation, for he mentioned the tepee several times in his diary.

Thomson described the beginning of the field season: "We left for our first camp up the Spray on the site of the old Eau Claire Lumber camp.…Bob Irvine & I left the Club House about noon—ate our sandwiches about 1 pm beside the road leading to the lumber camp. Arriving at the Eau Claire about 2:15pm. Vermette the cook & [Roy] Duncan, a helper, arrived about 3pm, followed by A.J. [Campbell] about 4pm.…The pack string did not show up until 5pm—we helped drop the loads, then set to work to pitch camp."

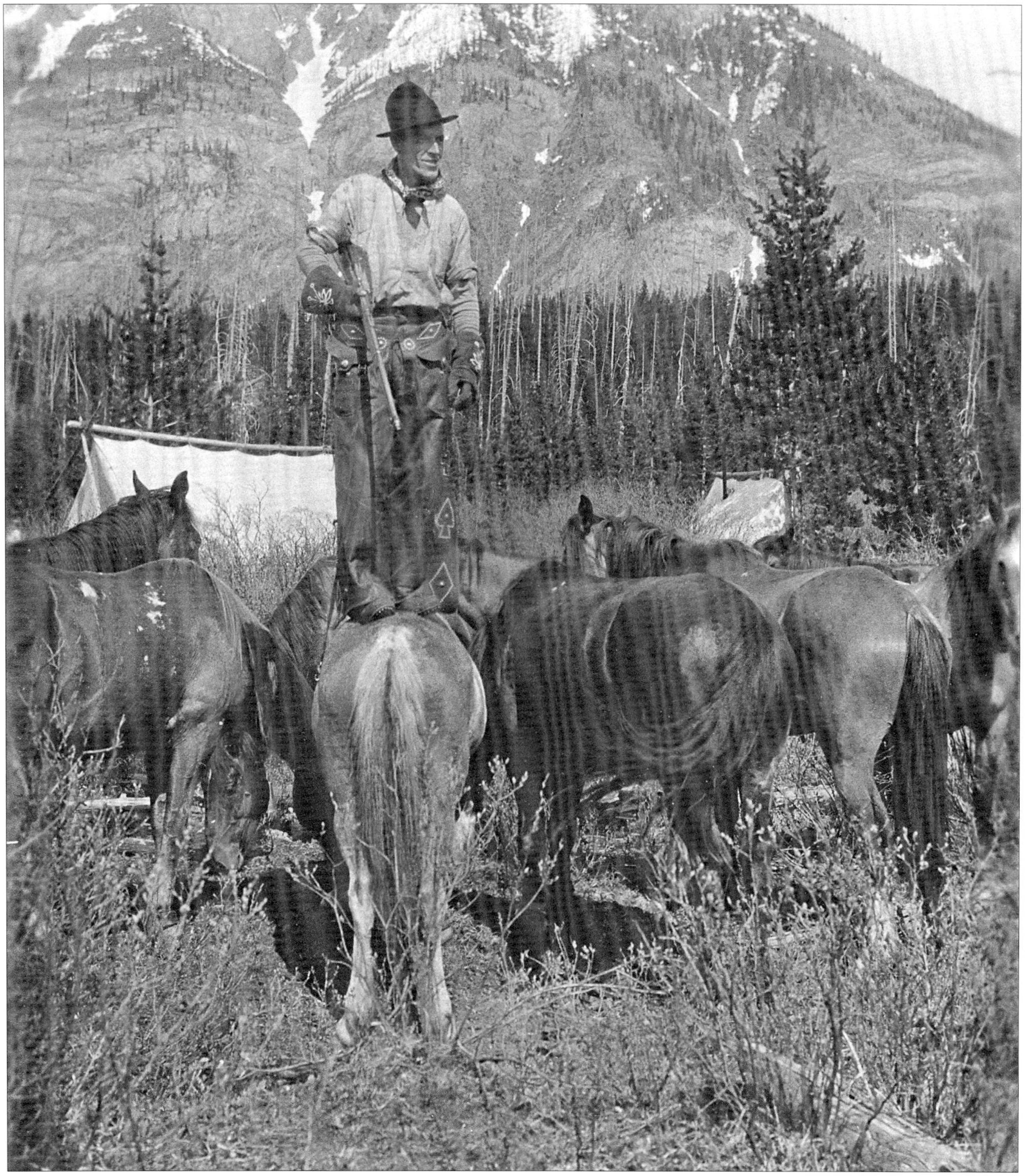

"Looking for horses, 6 am, Spray Lakes." PR1973.0534.0003, Provincial Archives of Alberta

The next day Ralph Rink and Curly Ford, the packers, left to establish a cache near the north end of the upper Spray lake, while the rest of the men got their equipment ready for use.

On June 8 the crew moved camp. "We forded to the east bank of the Spray opposite camp & found our trail leading up a small creek tributary to the Spray." They continued up the drainage, camping that night at White Man Gap (sometimes called Canmore Gap). "Trail well-travelled, gave us little trouble. From this camp we first noticed the snowline was not far above us."

The next day the crew moved to Mumford's cabin, situated at the north end of the lower Spray lake.

> We were now leaving the height of land. Though the valley still maintained a general direction southeasterly, the drainage began to fall away to the Spray Lakes. The trail still followed along the low benches of the westerly slopes of the Three Sisters Range. We skirted a small lake at the foot of one of the benches—near here our first mishap of the day, one of the horses shed a pack. We lost the best part of half an hour by the time we had gathered up the debris. I had him sewed up again neatly with a diamond [hitch].
>
> The valley floor was generally pretty open, but our trail about 100 to 200 feet [30 to 60 metres] above was mostly through light timber—some brulé. We had not gone far before event two of the day happened. Beside the trail along which we were travelling, there was a Government Telephone wire, strung along trees. In a recent storm, one of the trees had been blown down across the trail. Three of our horses got tangled up in the phone wire. Pandemonium followed till we could get in & steady the horses down. Some 400 feet [122 metres] of line had been torn down. Fortunately none of the horses' legs were damaged. It so happened that the wire had caught up in one of the packs followed by two others who milled around over the down wire. We managed to steer the rest

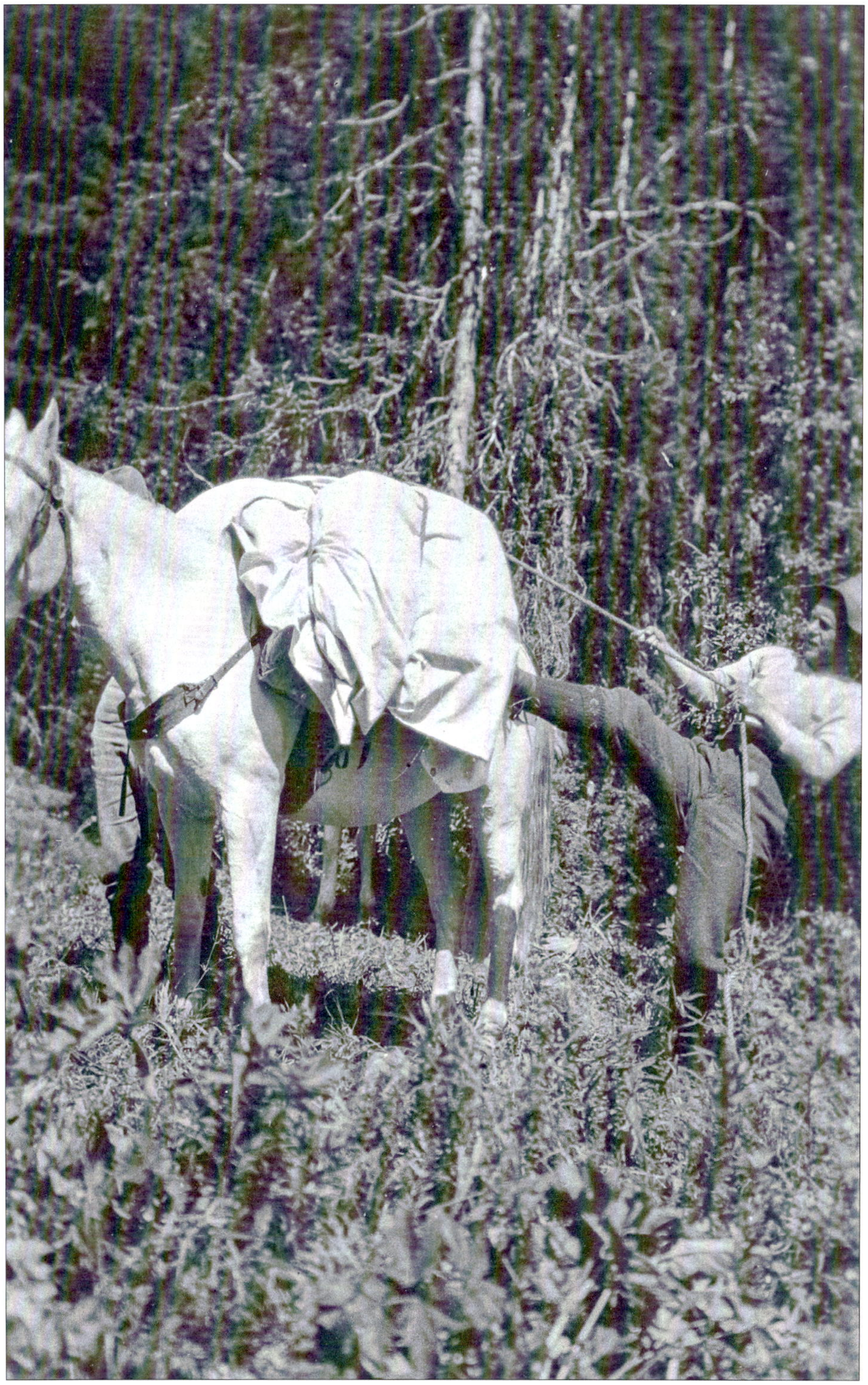

"A.J. Campbell – the final cinch." PR1973.0534.0002, Provincial Archives of Alberta

> of the horses away into the woods away from the danger area....
>
> Soon afterward we crossed a small stream about 30 or 40 links [six to eight metres], to its west side—flowing from the upper to the lower lake. There were grassy meadows in places between the lakes, snow on the ground & in the trees.

The men spent a few days at this location. While Campbell made some test exposures with the camera, Rink went back to Banff for more supplies and mail. He also took the cook, who was having health problems. The men spent Sunday evening telling stories. Thomson wrote: "Listened to a few hell-bent for leather yarns, interspersed with cahooting episodes on main street. We had several towns shot up by bed time."

According to Thomson, a fish hatchery had been established on the Spray Lakes. Mumford, the inspector of fisheries, arrived around nine the next evening with a small crew, and was not pleased to see the survey crew using the cabin. "In Wheeler's absence, A.J. [Campbell] was in charge & he received the impact—language known to pack horses." Mumford "did not know that we had obtained permission to use the shack before leaving Banff," so he and his crew left.

On June 13 Rink returned, accompanied by Wheeler and a cook named Tom Martin. Thomson noted that among the supplies Rink brought was a quart of rum.

The following day Wheeler's crew moved camp up Mud Lake trail, heading for the divide that would take them into the Kananaskis drainage. They went only a short distance before stopping to camp. Some of the crew went up the trail and found that snow blocked the route not far ahead. On June 15 some of the crew began shovelling a trail so the horses and men could proceed.

Thomson described the men's activities on June 16. "Ralph, Curly, Duncan & Bob away about 8am, with four saddle horses to continue to break trail up Mud [Smuts] Creek towards Mud Pass. A.J. and I remained in camp, started making snow shovels out of jackpine. Also, Wheeler, A.J. & myself took one of the cameras apart to check inner metal box....After lunch A.J. & I went to work on snow shovels again—we made 6 in all."

On the 17th the crew moved camp about eight kilometres up the Mud Creek trail, and the following day they resumed clearing the trail using their homemade snow shovels. There was about 60 centimetres of snow on the ground. They reached Mud Lake (today the Burstall Lakes) and then started working along the east shore. The next day the crew moved camp to the Burstall Lakes. It rained all of the 20th, so the men remained in camp. The warm weather and rain were melting the snow rapidly and Smuts Creek was rising.

On June 21 Wheeler's crew moved camp beyond Smith-Dorrien Pass and started down Smith-Dorrien Creek, a tributary of the Kananaskis River. Wheeler, Campbell, Irvine and Duncan cleared the trail toward Lower Kananaskis Lake. The next day, while some of the men went back to bring up the remainder of the supplies, Wheeler and Rink went to visit Cautley at the Kananaskis lakes. In his diary Wheeler wrote: "Crossed North Fork Kananaskis [Smith-Dorrien] seven times—first time had some trouble and beds and packs got wet. Arrived at C[autley]'s camp at 3pm. He had gone with his assistant to Elk Pass to photograph Mon[ument] M2. His pack train sent back to Morley—overdue several days. Pitched my camp with him."

Wheeler described the events of June 23. "About 6am Hicks Cole came in with the word that Jake Koller had been drowned and Cautley's pack train was back 20 miles [32 kilometres]. Breakfast at 7am. Ralph went back to meet Campbell and outfit. Loaned two horses to Cautley." Wheeler decided to make his camp across the ford on the trail to Elk Pass, since his crew would be working to the south. The rest of Wheeler's crew arrived that day. Thomson noted that the horses shook a couple of loads loose, and one horse got tangled in some trees that had fallen down.

In his memoir Cautley described his course of action after learning of Koller's death.

> Having taken a signed and witnessed statement from Hicks, I borrowed two horses from Mr. Wheeler's outfit. I asked my assistant, an English engineer named Hope, to accompany me, as I didn't like to ask one of the men to

take the risk. We started out at 1:00 pm. Twice we had to swim our horses across tributaries that had been knee-deep when we came up. We saw the horse on the island, and on the second night camped about fifteen miles [24 kilometres] from Morley. Next day we arrived at Morley in time to catch No. 1 train to Banff….

While I was shaving Frank Wellman, the storekeeper at Morley, came and told me that my assistant seemed a pretty sick man. "Oh," he said, "I'll be alright in the morning. Anyway, you want those horses shod." However, I told him that he was going to Banff with me, and that he just had time to shave before the train was due. Just three hours after I first knew that he was ill, I had him in Dr. Brett's hospital at Banff. He had an acute attack of appendicitis, but the two doctors agreed not to operate, but to keep him without food and packed in ice. They kept him this way for nine days, and he recovered so as to be able to rejoin me at Whiteman's Pass.

Cautley reported the accident to the Royal North-West Mounted Police, hired George Webb as second packer and returned to Morley. The Alberta commissioner wrote: "On our way back from Morley to camp, our lost horses came in to camp by themselves one night. One good little horse, loaded with cement, slipped into deep water at a place where the trail had been undermined during the flood, and was drowned."

On June 24 Wheeler, Thomson, Irvine and Duncan surveyed from a nearby mountain on the west side between the Kananaskis lakes. Campbell and Ford went with Cole to the accident scene to search for Koller's body, get the horse off the island and help bring up Cautley's pack train and goods. Cole rejoined Cautley at the scene of the accident.

The next day was Sunday, and the men did a variety of tasks. Campbell and Ford continued to search for Cautley's horses, while Thomson took a message from Wheeler to Cautley. Rink went back to their previous camp to bring forward supplies. On Monday Wheeler, with part of his crew and two members of Cautley's crew, went to the Elk Pass area. Wheeler and Irvine checked conditions at the east passage, while the rest of the men cleared and blazed a trail to the west passage of Elk Pass. It started to rain after lunch, so the men returned in mid-afternoon.

On June 27 Wheeler and his crew began surveying the section that had not been finished in 1915. They crossed Elk Pass at the west passage and then proceeded down to the Elk River, where they camped about 1.6 kilometres from Elk Lake. Thomson wrote: "Cautley's packers came over again this morning to say goodbye. Wheeler went over to see Cautley for final word with him." Thomson described an adventure at a creek crossing. "At one of the fords near the mouth of what is now Fox Creek we had dropped a 12" [30-centimetre] log across. I was about half way across, doing fine—balance normal. Then Tom decided to follow me. As he stepped on the end of the log it turned & I descended into the creek, feet first. I was apparently not very well acquainted with log birling. We sat down on the plinth of Mon[ument] 1M, ate our lunch—when I was able to dry out some." It was Bob Irvine's birthday, and after supper the men had "a little touch hot rum & cake."

The next day was spent working around camp and fishing at Lower Elk Lake. On June 29 a group of five men set out to climb and survey two stations on the north side of Elk Lake. Around mid-morning it began to snow, and the men returned to camp in mid-afternoon. The weather cleared the following day, so Wheeler took a small crew, including Thomson, to one station, while Campbell and some men established another. Wheeler's crew climbed the westerly slope of a high ridge on the west side of Elk Pass. They were unable to reach the top because of deep snow, but they surveyed from an open viewpoint at a station they called Elk Lake North.

Thomson described the surveying.

> During the setup I recorded for Wheeler. It was a snow setup. When about halfway through the circle left azimuths the readings jumped one minute apart. I called Wheeler's attention to it—there are evidently different ways of expressing appreciation—I was soon to be jarred out of my gentlemanly approach & told to do

Banff Crag and Canyon, July 1, 1916, p. 1

Drowned in the Kananaskis River
Jacob Koller gives up his life while following the line of duty

A sad accident took place last Thursday when Jacob Koller lost his life in a plucky attempt to rescue a packhorse which had swam across the river.

The accident occurred where the trail crosses the Eau Claire Flats about 30 miles [48 kilometres] from Morley. One of the packhorses had been crowded off the trail into deep water and had landed on an island on the opposite side of the river. It was while endeavoring to get the animal back that Koller was swept away by the swift current, in full view of the assistant packer who was unable to render the unfortunate man any help.

Koller was head packer for R.W. Cautley, DLS, who is commissioner for Alberta in the survey of the interprovincial boundary between Alberta and British Columbia and had been with him every season since the work was first started in 1913. At the time of the accident the pack outfit was taking supplies up to the main camp on Kananaskis Lake, 20 miles [32 kilometres] beyond the Eau Claire Flats. The assistant packer carried the sad news to the camp after spending some hours searching the banks of the river in the vain hope of finding that Koller had managed to regain the land. The Kananaskis was dangerously high at the time and the trail was flooded for miles and, in some places, washed out altogether.

The body has not been recovered up to date, and it is feared that it may not be found for a long time as the river is partially obstructed by drift wood in many places. However, the proper authorities have been notified and whatever is possible will be done.

Koller was a prosperous young man from the Dowling Lake district in eastern Alberta. He was unmarried and his parents resided with him on the farm. In appearance he was a tall, fine-looking young fellow, 26 years of age, and he was universally liked and regarded by all who knew him. His many friends will long regret his untimely end and sympathize most deeply with his bereaved family.

> as I was told. I had heard the innocent little click in one of the legs that often occurs with a snow setup. When the sun tends to warm the legs of the tripod, as a consequence the snow melts slightly, disturbing any one of the legs. However, A.O.W. realized then that I could use a transit & as will be noticed later on I let myself in for a job of operating the 2nd set of instruments.

From this station they were able to connect with some of their stations to the south that they had surveyed in 1915, to monuments in Elk Pass and to the station Campbell had established that day. They were also able to map the BC side of some of the high, glaciated peaks west of Elk Pass.

On July 1 Wheeler and Thomson surveyed from a low-elevation station that had a good view of the area. In his diary Wheeler wrote: "Pretty tired—going up and down in snow & brush very tiresome." Campbell and his crew went on a fly camp to Upper Elk Lake. They built a raft and spent a few days surveying some stations on the BC side of the divide west of Elk Pass. July 2 was Sunday with rain in the morning, so the men remained in camp. In his diary Thomson recorded: "Hicks, Cautley's packer, arrived camp shortly after lunch—brought in two of our packhorses that had strayed up through the Elk. He brought some papers along with him. Reported another horse lost up on the Kananaskis. News that Cautley's assistant had been taken out to Banff with appendicitis." Wheeler noted that the papers had "very little war news."

The next day Wheeler and his crew moved about 12 kilometres down the Elk River, where they camped at the site of the Riverside cabins. In his diary Wheeler noted: "Trail very wet and streams all overflowed. Got pretty wet in lower extremities." They spent July 4 there waiting for Campbell's party to arrive. Thomson described the cabins.

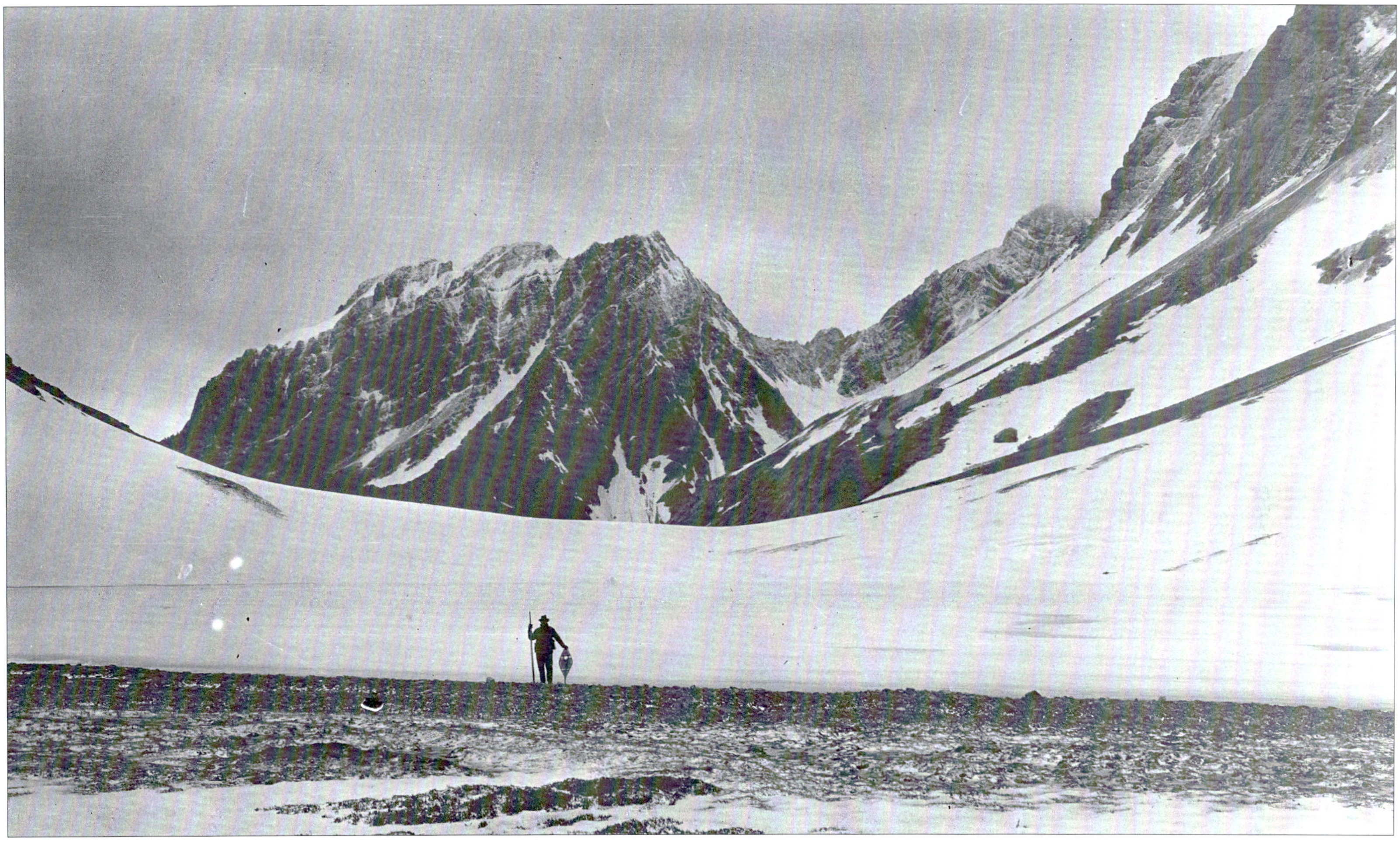

North Kananaskis Pass in early July. e011166473, Library and Archives Canada

We called these cabins the Riverside cabins. There were two and they were in excellent shape—built of logs 8-10", shake roofs. They consisted of a bunkhouse containing 8 or 10 bunks at one end, a cookhouse and dining room at the other. Separated by a wide entrance hallway, also covered over by a common roof. Door to bunkhouse and door to cookhouse and dining room. They were built by the Grain Belt Development Company of Calgary—to the east of these I climbed a sidehill of about 100'. I discovered a bore in the side of the hill—apparently for coal.

Event of the day—after supper A.O.W. & I went over to visit these cabins. They were definitely well built with windows & built in bunks. Stepping into the first bunkhouse we stood in the centre of the floor, when from under the bunks came porcupine—family and relations of 6. To get to the door they had to pass us—A.O.W. with his plus fours, stockings & romeos presented an excellent target. He jumped up, caught one of the cross beams or ties and hung by his hands, while I grabbed a slat from one of the bunks and was able to fend him off from A.O.W. However one big fellow—the daddy of them all—had his mind made up that he was going out the door and I was in his way & we closed in battle. He was a big joker, but I managed to hit

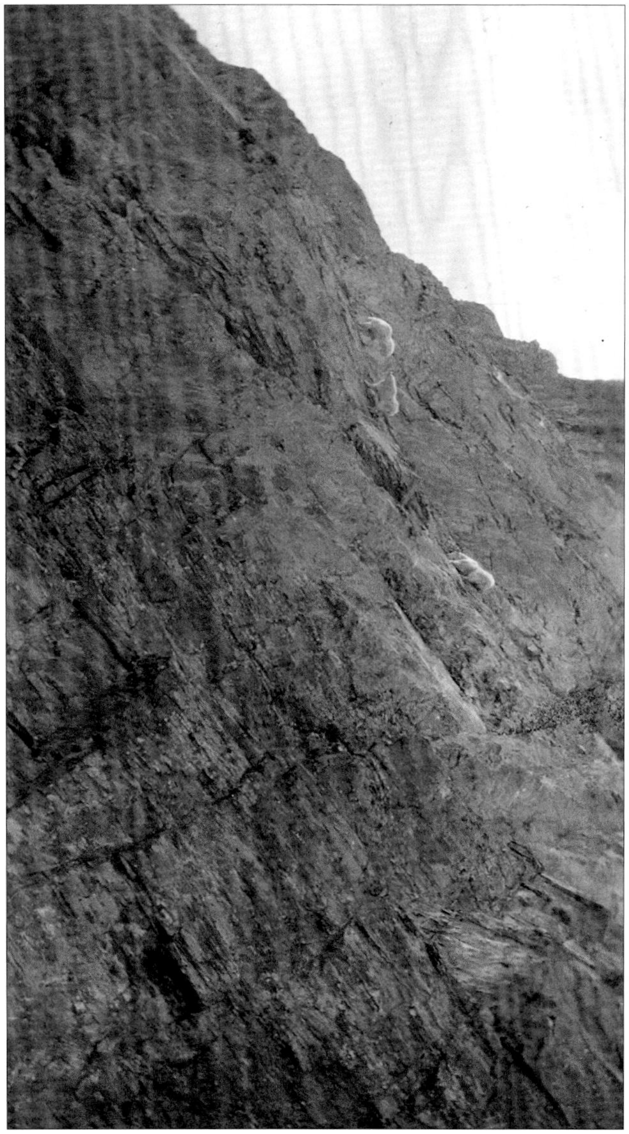

Mountain goats at White Man Pass. J-01027, Royal BC Museum and Archives

him a hard one across the nose, followed by a one-two and he keeled over on the floor. I turned around to find another directly behind me, who I was able to maneuver at the end of the bed pole into a favorable position to bust him hard on the nose, their vital spot. Meantime, during the encounter, the rest of the family and relations had made it out of the door or retreated unknown to me under one of the several bunks. All through the pandemonium, A.O.W. had clung tenaciously to the timber cross tie. Had he stayed on the ground he could very easily have had a rough time & further impeded my strategy. They gave some trouble around camp—more especially the packer's equipment. Good juicy leather cinches or saddle that are plugged with perspiration from the horses or leather instrument cases is their dessert.

July 5 was a clear day, so Wheeler and Thomson climbed a nearby mountain to the east and surveyed from a station they called Riverside East (later named Mount Odlum). This was a Geological Survey station probably established by McLean the previous summer. From it they could see several stations along the boundary that they had surveyed during the previous year, as well as Mount Assiniboine to the northwest. Thomson wrote: "Closer examination of the rocks revealed a number had been shattered by lightning.... There was much evidence of lightning strikes along the summit ridge." This station was not too far from Tornado Mountain, where Wheeler had encountered lightning twice the previous summer.

July 6 was also clear, and the two men surveyed a lower station called Riverside West, where they found an old cairn. They saw Campbell and his crew surveying from a mountain about eight kilometres away. Wheeler spent the next day getting ready to go to Banff, and Campbell's crew arrived around lunch.

After Wheeler's departure Cautley and his crew remained at the Kananaskis lakes. It was not until the fourth of July that Cautley was able to reach North Kananaskis Pass on snowshoes. The snow was generally a metre deep, but in places it was over four metres. (Two weeks later a Geological Survey crew travelled through the pass on horses.) Cautley found that North Kananaskis Pass did not need to be surveyed with monuments, for it was narrow, had steep approaches and was above timberline at over 2,300 metres.

The next day Cautley and his crew left for White Man Pass. They followed the route Wheeler travelled over the pass at Mud Lake and down to the Spray River, which they forded on July 7. The crossing was dangerous because the water was still high. Fortunately, there was a stream measurement cable and car just above the ford, so men and supplies were transported across the river there.

Cautley's crew travelled up the Spray and White Man Creek, reaching White Man Pass on July 8. This pass was part of the traditional indigenous travel network and provided the most direct connection between the Bow and Columbia River basins. It was also used by explorers and settlers in the 19th century. Cautley and his crew worked there until July 24, establishing four monuments. Although White Man Pass had historic significance, Cautley did not believe that it had any contemporary importance, either economically or as a transportation route.

Cautley's camp was in a meadow with one spruce tree about six metres away. On July 16, when Hope returned from Banff, lightning struck Cautley's camp. He wrote: "That evening I had been watching an approaching storm rolling up the pass from the west. It was an impressive sight. Except for intermittent forked lightning, it was almost dark and the black clouds seemed to rest on the summit when they reached it. Just then Hope arrived with the packers and we went into my tent. All of a sudden there was a blinding crash, and we both felt a shock and started to rub our lips vigorously. Immediately the tent was lit up and there was a roar of flames. Then the rain fell in sheets and put the fire out."

On July 8 Wheeler departed from the Elk River, taking Roy Duncan, who had quit, with him. He stopped at the Kananaskis lakes. "At Cautley's camp found a note and report on K[ananaskis] Pass. Report says not suitable for survey—from 9 miles [14 kilometres] up valley snow all over. He travelled on my snowshoes.…Reached Peyto's shack at lower ford at 3:45pm. Camped there for night. Used Ralph's tepee." Wheeler reached Banff on July 10 in the early evening.

After Wheeler left, Campbell and the crew moved camp about 12 kilometres down the Elk River to cabins below Weary Creek. They slept in their tents but used one of the cabins for cooking. The next day was Sunday, so the men remained in camp. On July 10 and 11 Campbell and his crew surveyed four stations accessible from their camp, and then on July 12 they moved to Fording River Pass. During the next two weeks the BC crew surveyed several stations on the Alberta side of the boundary, one of the few occasions on which they spent much time east of the divide or surveyed stations more than a few kilometres into the prairie province.

The next day they continued through the pass and travelled about 6.4 kilometres northeast down a branch of the Highwood River. Thomson described an incident that he called "the first of the 3 hat tricks of the season." It occurred about two kilometres from the pass, when the crew came out onto some open grassy slopes.

> When we were hit by strong winds—gale force—flowing in from the open foothills towards the pass it was with difficulty we were able to keep the horses heading into it. We were running with about 12 head, 3 saddles, 9 loads. They kept turning back and wanting to run with the wind. With AJ [Campbell] on the lead horse spotting the trail we split the string up. I brought up the trailing three—I was also in the saddle. One gust out of a clear blue sky caught AJ's hat. He was at the time nearly half a mile ahead of me between us a bunch of rebellious pack horses. Soaring into the air for a while it settled for elevation, passing me on the port beam chin high, making excellent progress back towards the pass. The nearest store being in Banff miles away a hat was a hat—if only a somewhat soiled lid. I abandoned my three head of horse [and] with the aid of speed proceeded to give chase. We made fair time running before the wind, the first one quarter-mile [400 metres] even stephen. However a huge boulder directly ahead on course [was] sufficiently high to further bounce the sky piece into the air, then to settle exhausted on the ground between gusts. I retrieved it resting peacefully among smaller & more friendly boulders.

From their campsite they surveyed two stations on July 14 and 15. Green Ridge was a low, timbered ridge about three kilometres to the southeast. The crew found an open meadow and "after considerable cutting" were able to get "a sufficient number of views to control the area to be mapped." They were able to see several of their 1915 stations, along with two from Bridgland's survey. There was insufficient rock to build a cairn, but they set a target, so they could sight on this

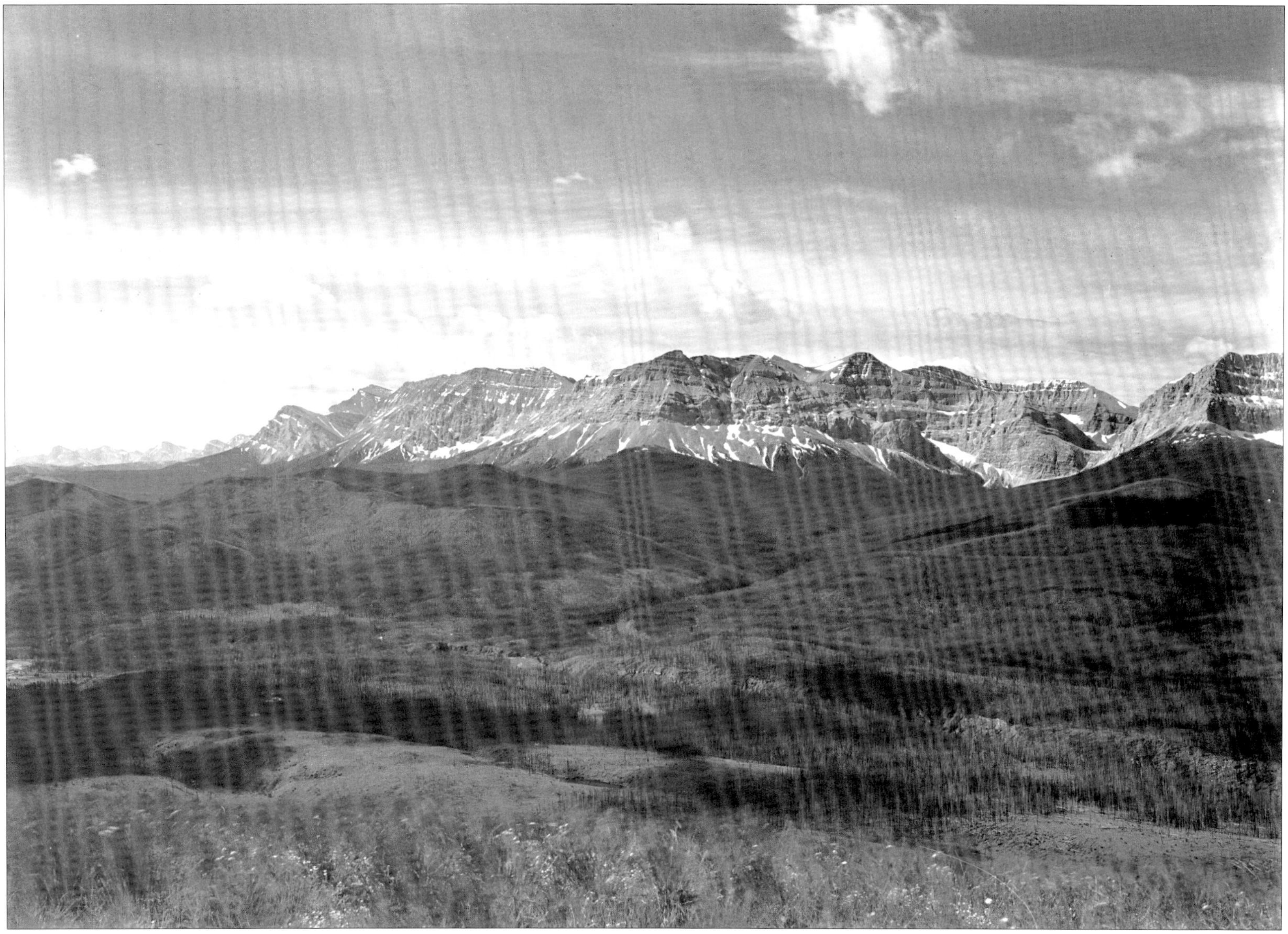

A view of the Rocky Mountains looking west from the Alberta side. This picture was taken on a station above the Highwood River named Grassy Hill. The Mountain Legacy Project has not yet done repeat photography on this section of the boundary survey, and smoky conditions this summer limited personal rephotography. e011183803, Library and Archives Canada

station. Their next station, Mosquito Hill, was about six kilometres from camp, south and east of Green Ridge. They found an open clearing again and once more connected their survey both with other stations from the boundary survey and with Bridgland's survey.

After a rest day on Sunday, Campbell, Thomson and Irvine climbed Mount Baril, a peak that is just under 3,000 metres. In his diary Thomson wrote: "It stands well out over the foothill country to the east—overlooks our stations Green Ridge & Mosquito Hill.... This station affords a fine panorama of outstanding peaks." Thomson commented that they could see across Fording Pass, along with the headwater tributaries of the Highwood River, and the nearby peaks along the divide. "This whole array of summits—pyramidal in shape, with a fine example of horizontal strata, are very inspiring. To the east, down across the foothills to the Highwood River, an old travelled route & beyond a sea of prairie." From these stations Campbell could also map the headwaters of the Oldman River flowing southeast. Thomson noted: "On the way up, around the 9500 foot [2895 metre] level, we saw a goat trail leading across the easterly face above the rock escarpment. A pathway for the sure-footed goat, but I doubt for man, it was so narrow."

In copying his journal, Thomson noted that the trail they followed from Fording Pass to the Highwood River was the same one that R.M. Patterson used in 1936 and described in the book *The Buffalo Head*. "There is reason to believe that it is an old Indian trail used by the Stoneys to the Elk [River valley]."

On the morning of July 18 the weather was unsettled, so the crew remained in camp until after lunch. Then the men went to a station about 1.6 kilometres north of camp that they named Coyote Hill because of the animals they could hear. Once again, they had a good view of several peaks along the divide.

The next day, Campbell's crew travelled about 12 kilometres down to the Highwood River, crossed the river and made camp on a grassy flat at the foot of an open bench, with feed for the horses. On July 20 they went downstream about four kilometres and occupied a station on an open grassy hill that they named Prairie Hill. There was sufficient rock to build a cairn. On the way back they found a Dominion survey iron pin for Section 36, Township 16, Range 6, so they set up the transit and read angles from that station. The next day they travelled up the wagon road about three kilometres to a station they named Grassy Hill.

Having completed their surveying from the foothills, Campbell and the crew travelled north up the wagon road along the Highwood River for about 15 kilometres. Along the way they met Ralph Rink, who was returning from Banff. July 23 was a Sunday and a day of rest, followed on Monday by two stations on the top of a ridge south of camp. From these stations Campbell was able to connect to two stations that they had surveyed earlier in the month when they were heading south. It enabled him to make a loop on this portion of the survey and check its accuracy.

On July 25 the crew resumed their journey north, and after about 11 kilometres they camped not far from the south end of Highwood Pass. The next morning the men climbed an open ridge west of camp. By the time they reached the top, the weather had turned inclement. "Took shelter on the westerly side of the ridge, lit a fire & waited for the clouds to clear." In the afternoon the weather got worse, so they cached the instruments under a rock cover and returned to camp. On July 27 the weather cleared by early afternoon and the men returned, surveying two stations on the ridge.

The next day the crew crossed Highwood Pass and returned to the Lower Kananaskis Lake campsite they had used at the beginning of the field season. Thomson noted that several outfits were camped in the area. The men spent the following day in camp, while their packers, Rink and Ford, went to Banff. Charlie Logan, a packer, visited them in the morning, and a forester named Bryant joined them for lunch.

On July 30 Campbell, Thomson and Irvine went on a short fly trip to the camp Campbell had established at Elk Lake at the end of June and early July. On the last day of the month the three men surveyed Bolt 8M on the summit of Mount Fox, elevation 2,973 metres, the final station at Elk Pass. Wheeler had been unable to establish this station the previous fall because the ground was frozen and snow-covered.

> Set up on the high point of the peak—dominating the west side of Elk Pass. Directly below us to the east Frozen Lake @ 7100 feet [2,165 metres], fed by a small glacier at the foot of precipitous slope of 2500 to 2600 feet [760 to 790 metres] directly below us. After lunch A.J. [Campbell] sent me down the ridge to Elk Lake North, our station of June 30th, to retrieve a bag of cement that had been cached near the cairn. After completing views and azimuths we drilled hole & cemented in Bolt 8M over which we built a six foot [1.83 metre] cairn.

Thomson's second hat-trick incident occurred that afternoon when "a strong breeze sprang up. The upsurge from the amphitheatre in which Frozen Lake lay was appreciable, in fact disturbing, to the extent that it took possession of A.J.'s hat, July 12 vintage, carried it 50 or 60 feet [15 to 18 metres] up into the air, to have fun, when suddenly the gust subsided, it returned to

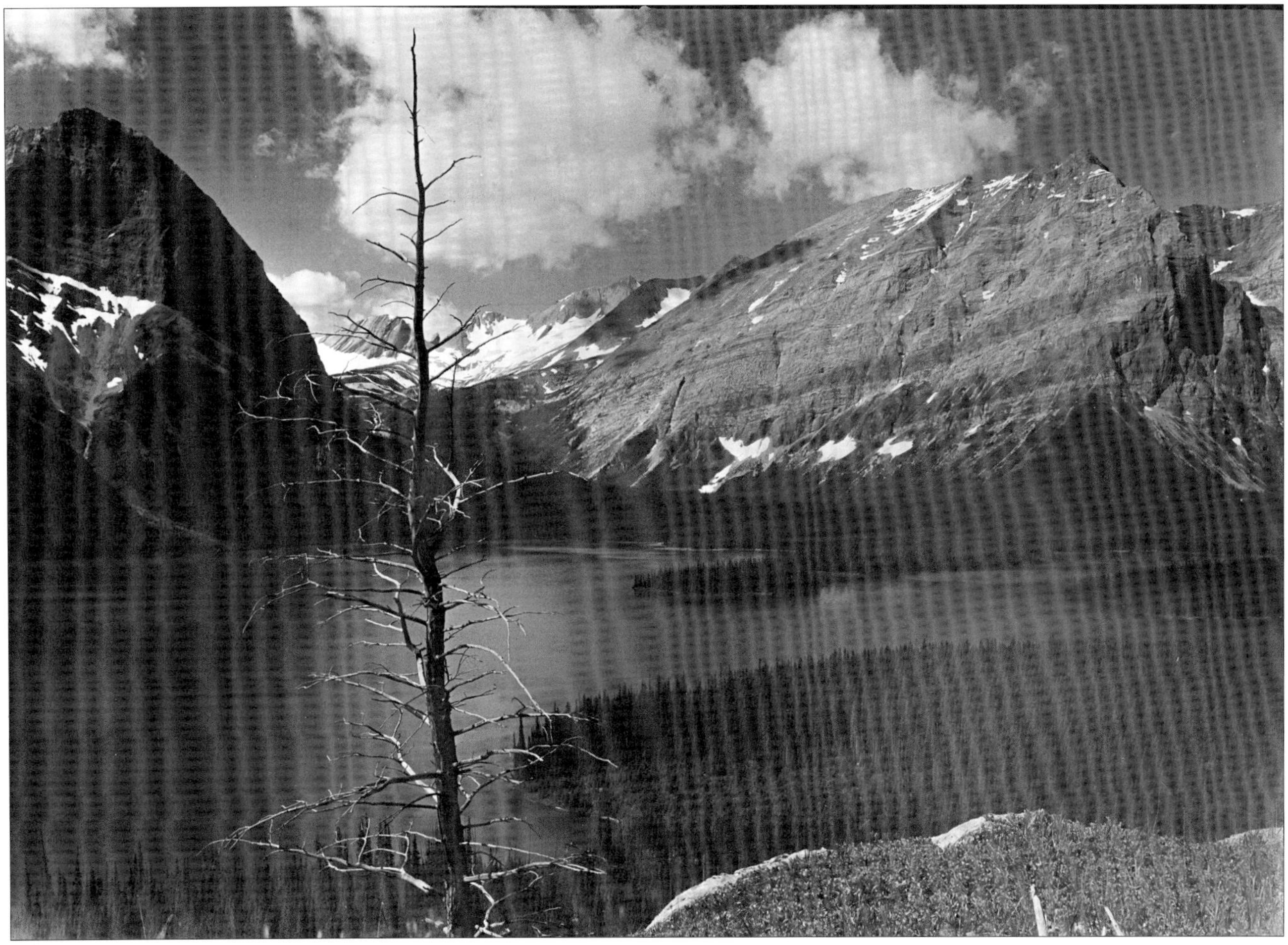

This photo from the Hogback panorama shows Mount Sarrail (left), Mangin Glacier, and Mount Lyautey. It is a part of a series of geographical features north of the lake that Wheeler named during World War I for French military leaders. The photograph is one of the earliest taken of Mangin Glacier, and shows that it was a sizeable glacier a century ago. e011183808, Library and Archives Canada

rest within 10 feet [three metres] or so of its master. Two of its lives extinct."

On August 1 the men loaded the supplies remaining from their cache and returned to their main camp, where they met a party who were taking their cook to the hospital in Banff.

> It appeared that they were camped further down the Elk, they had been troubled with porcupine as we had been at Riverside Camp (incident July 4th)....The cook had turned in for the night, snug, cozy, possibly in dreamland, when the interloper came through the flaps of the tent seeking that which was to be found. On waking suddenly, disturbed by the night visitor, he put his arm out of his sleeping robe to feel around for a match to light his candle. At this moment he got the full dose in his left arm. Poor chap looked pretty bleary. He still had 2, possibly 3 days trip to Banff.

Now, after occupying 20 triangulation and camera stations between Elk Pass and Fording River Pass, the British Columbia survey party was ready to head westward and north. The next day Campbell went to explore a route up the upper Kananaskis River, while Thomson and Irvine surveyed Hogback, a station on the ridge between the Upper and Lower Kananaskis Lakes. This

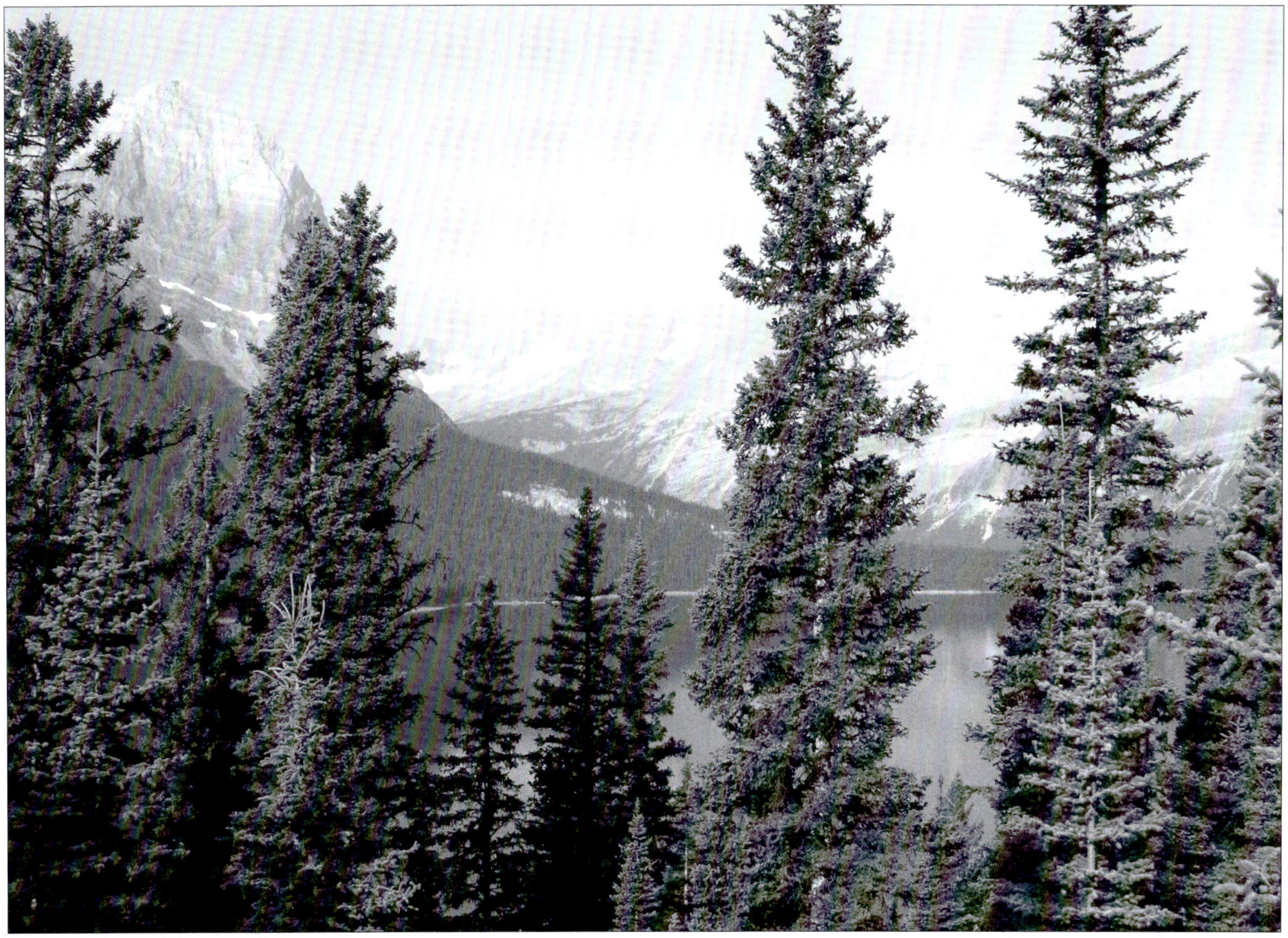

Today the boundary survey station named Hogback is the viewpoint on the Canadian Mt. Everest Expedition trail in Peter Lougheed Provincial Park. Tree growth partially obscures the open view the boundary surveyors had across Upper Kananaskis Lake in 1916, and raising the level of the lake with a dam has flooded the island. Photo Jay Sherwood

was one of McLean's Geological Survey stations.

On August 3 Campbell and his crew left on a five-day trip heading up the upper Kananaskis River. They established a camp near the junction of the upper Kananaskis River and the stream from South Kananaskis Pass. Thomson described their climb the next day: "Forded the Upper Kananaskis River, near the junction of a stream from the south fed by the Lyautey Glacier. Here we came to the foot of a rock slide that offered some good scrambling for about 400 feet [122 metres]. Another 1000 feet [300 metres] without difficulty to the tongue of Lyautey Glacier. Another 1000 feet brought us to the Névé. We worked across to the easterly side of the snowfield until we came to the wall under our intended station. Another 500 or 600 feet [150 to 180 metres] up a steep slope brought us to the summit ridge."

One of the nearby mountains was later named Mount Putnik. Thomson wrote that it was "an excellent example of what is known as the 'writing desk formation.' The westerly and southerly slopes appeared even though quite steep, possibly a 48 degree slope culminating in the main summit of Mt. Putnik. The north and east faces are very precipitous for about 2500 feet [760 metres]. From where we were on Lakeview it probably looked much worse than what it appeared." They had an excellent view of the area and the lighting was good for photographs. Thomson noted that it was one of the warmest days of the summer.

Following pages: Surveying from a station near the top of one of the passes. e011183810, Library and Archives Canada

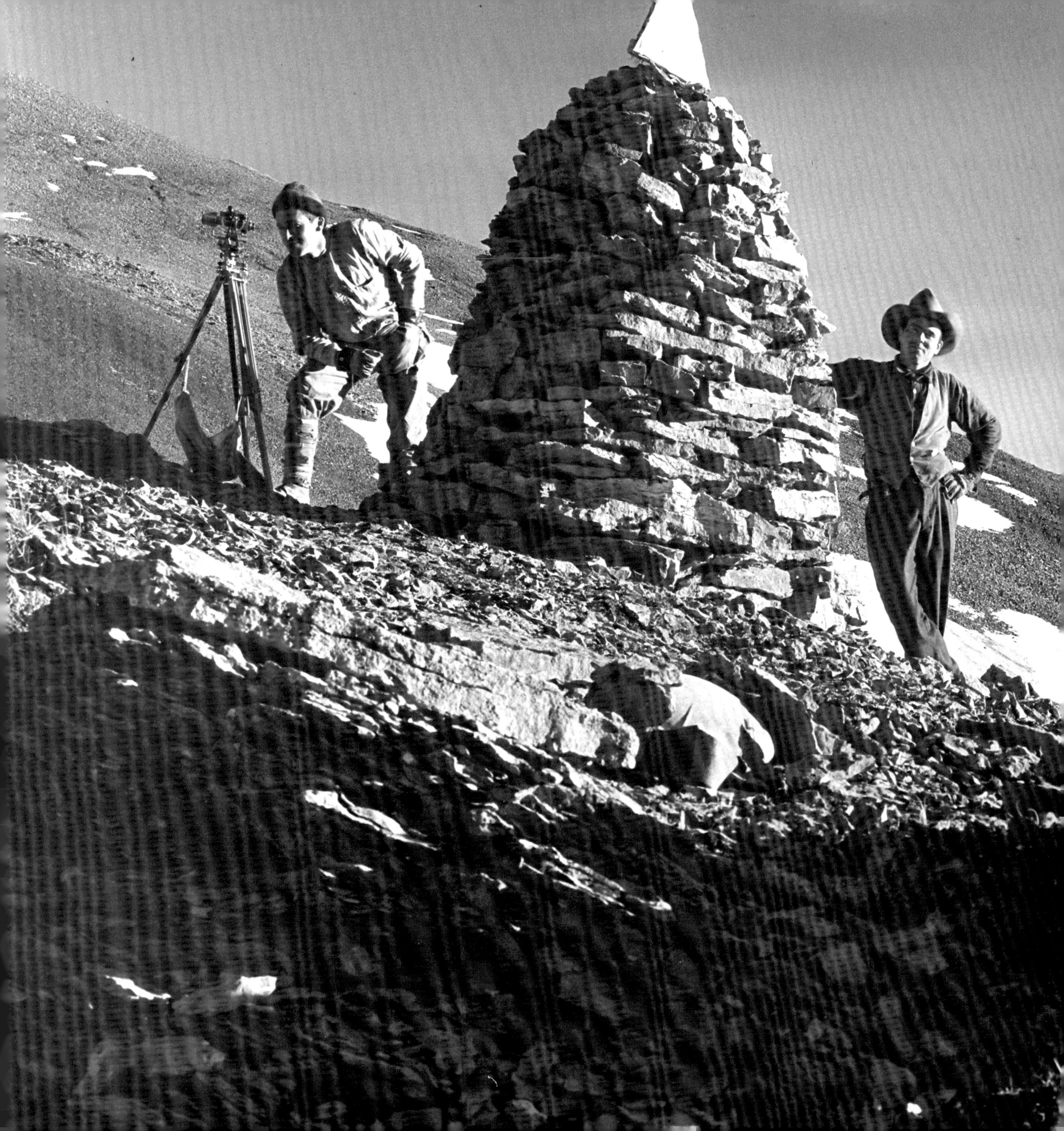

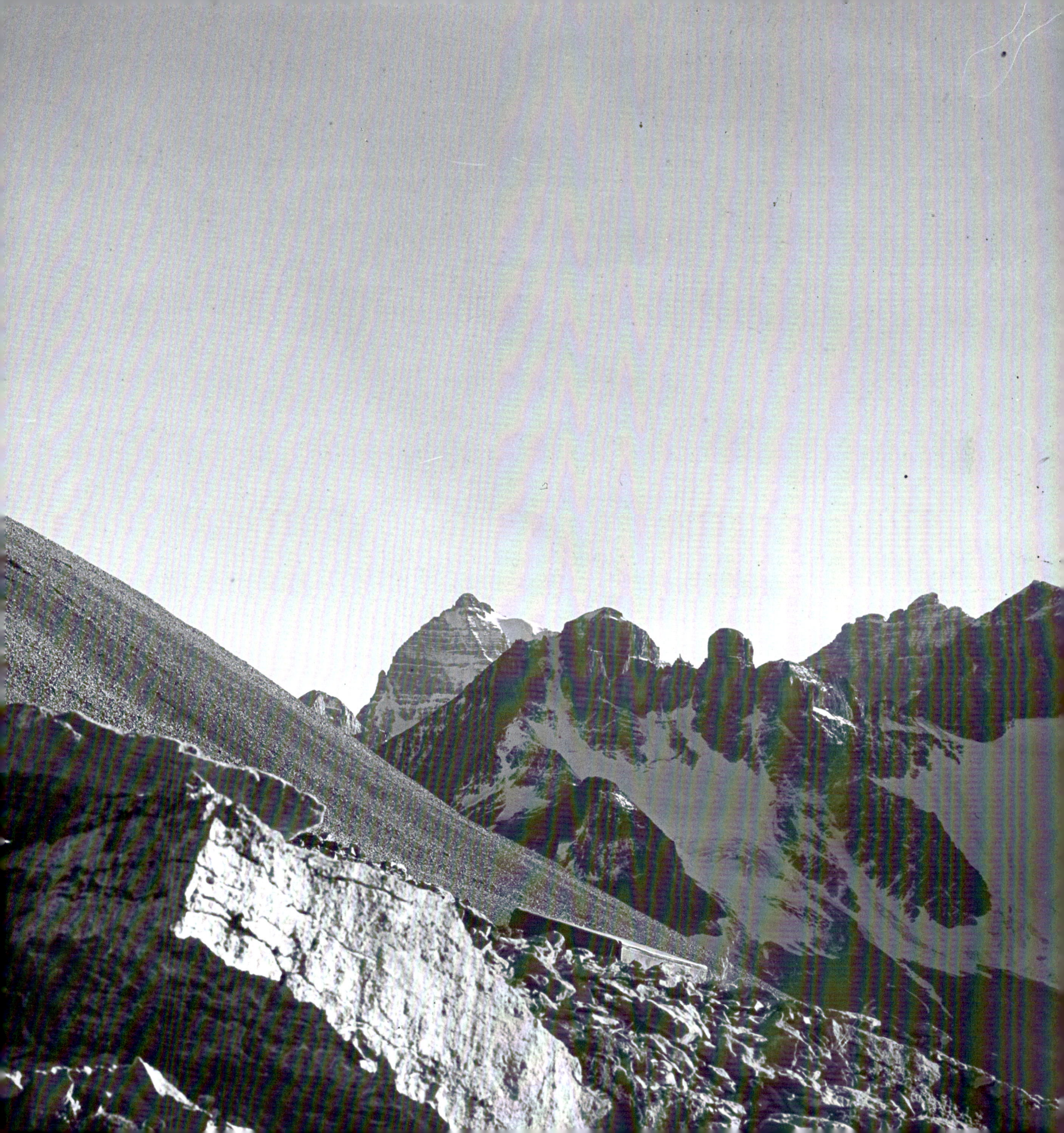

Thomson described how conditions changed on the mountains during the day and how it affected their return trip.

> In practice it was usually not bad going up the ice in the cool of the morning, but after the sun, during the heat of the day, had beaten down on the upper snowfield, travel invariably was poor, as not infrequently the whole surface of the glacier was running water or slush snow, hence one reason for using the lateral moraines. This we found to be the case through the years, particularly below the ice fall & among the seracs of the glacier snout.…Such conditions are to be experienced on almost any glacier, after a hot day.

The descent down the rocks was hazardous. Campbell was about 60 metres below Thomson and Irvine when they dislodged a boulder that rolled down the mountain slope, and Campbell had to jump into a ravine to avoid being hit. Thomson lost control coming down the slope and fell into the ravine, hitting his head and hurting his shoulder. "We were able to glissade the upper snowfield for about seven or eight hundred feet [213 to 244 metres], over smooth snow—left the glacier above the tongue & continued our descent down the easterly moraine."

The next day Campbell and Irvine occupied a nearby low-elevation station while Thomson remained in camp and did the cooking. On Sunday, August 6, at midday, the pack train arrived from Banff, bringing Gordon Weir, vice-principal of Hillhurst School in Calgary, as a replacement for Roy Duncan.

The following day the men climbed a nearby mountain. From the top they could see South Kananaskis Pass, and to the northwest they had their first view of Palliser Pass. In the distance they could see Mount Assiniboine, and on the far horizon peaks around Vermilion Pass. They also had views to the east and south to the peaks around Elk Pass and down into the Elk Valley. Altogether, Campbell and his crew surveyed 13 stations to cover the divide between Elk and South Kananaskis Passes. This rugged, glaciated section of the Great Divide has seven peaks that are over 3,000 metres high.

Campbell and his crew then moved to North Kananaskis Pass on August 8. The weather was inclement the next two days, limiting the work to setting a signal in the pass.

Meanwhile, Wheeler had returned from the Alpine Club camp in late July, and on August 2 he left Banff with the packers Rink and Irvine, and also Weir. The first evening Ford hurt his back, and two days later he had to return to Banff. By the second evening the men were at the Spray River crossing, where they met a park ranger named Pickering and arranged for him to accompany Wheeler to Palliser Pass. While Rink and Weir went to their campsite at the Kananaskis lakes, Wheeler and Pickering continued up the Spray River, reaching Cautley's camp at supper.

On July 25 Cautley and his crew travelled from White Man Pass to Palliser Pass. By early August the crew had almost completed their surveying, placing five monuments in the pass. In a letter to Deville, Cautley wrote: "Owing to the elevation of the Palliser Pass approximately 6700 feet [2,040 metres] and the steepness of approach for either side, it cannot be considered an important pass as a route of travel." He noted the benefit of his work: "The survey will afford a new measured base of approximately 2 miles [3.2 kilometres] on which Mr. Wheeler will be able to check his continuous survey." Around this time, Hicks Cole, Cautley's packer, and Chris Townsend, the monument builder (both from Dowling Lake, like Jacob Koller), left the crew, citing a desire to return home. Cautley had to find replacements for these two experienced men who had important positions on his crew.

Wheeler and Cautley spent much of August 5 inspecting the survey of Palliser Pass. They also looked at Cautley's preliminary map of White Man Pass. The next day Wheeler climbed a peak at the west end of the pass and Pickering returned to his cabin on Spray Lakes, taking mail with him.

On August 7 Wheeler and Cautley left to examine Assiniboine Pass. They "looked over the ground and decided to make survey. Climbed to timber line on west side and followed watershed to summit," Wheeler wrote in his diary. Assiniboine Pass was larger than either White Man or Palliser, and one of the main routes into the Mount Assiniboine area. Since

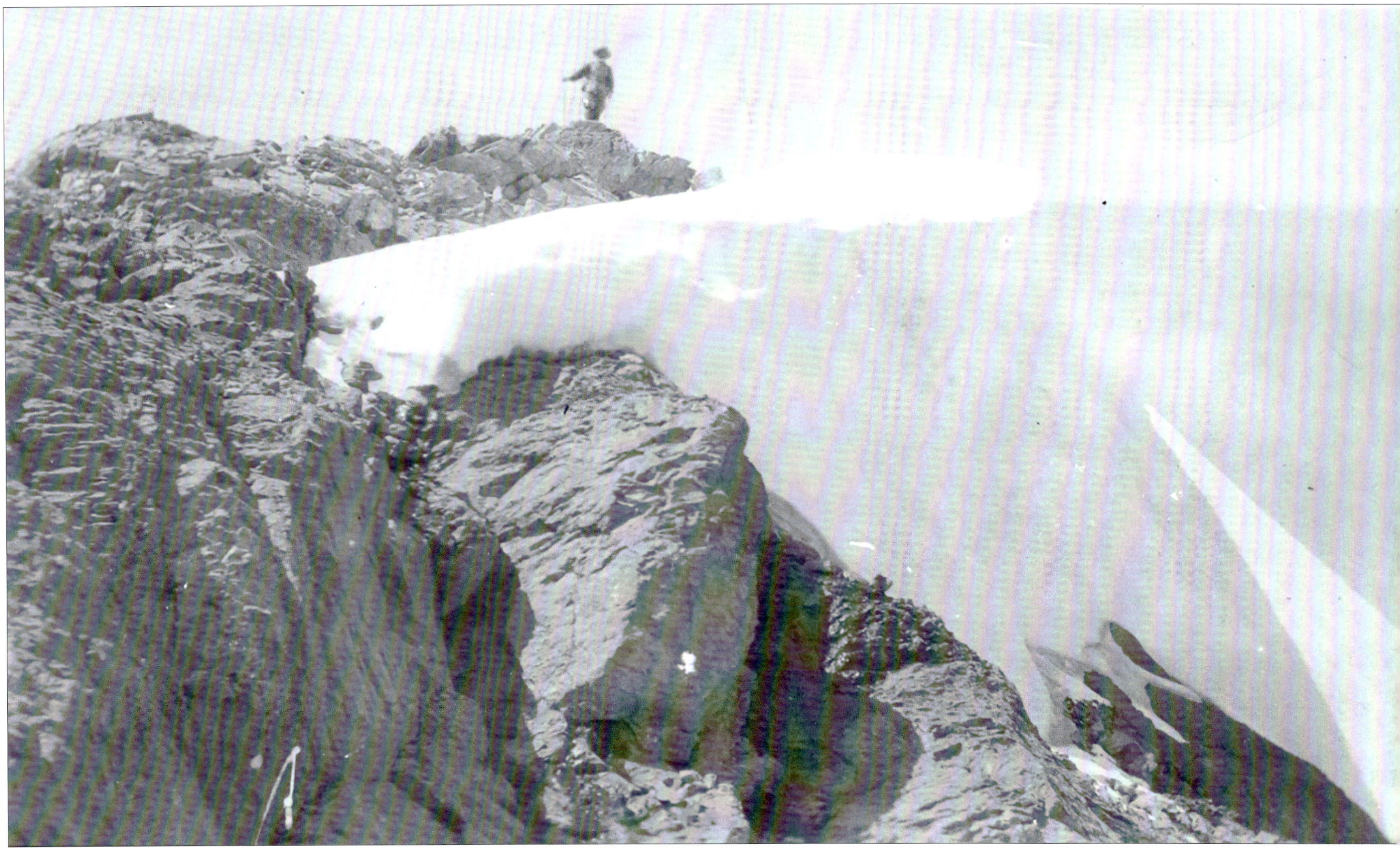

A.O. Wheeler on a mountain above Palliser Pass. J-01025, Royal BC Museum and Archives

the commissioners had decided not to survey the Kananaskis passes, they could replace it with this one. "We found it to be a wide timber pass of apparently more importance than North Kootenay, Dome, North Fork, White Man or Palliser Passes and decided that it would be necessary to survey it," Cautley wrote to Deville. When he sent a letter to Deville, Wheeler noted the size of the pass and "the fact that it is likely to be used as an established line of tourist travel in connection with Banff."

Cautley and Wheeler then returned down Bryant Creek. At the Spray River trail junction they found Rink and the new assistant packer, Arthur Crouch, waiting for them. The next day Cautley returned to Palliser Pass, while Rink, Crouch and Wheeler headed to the Kananaskis lakes, arriving at their camp in the mid-afternoon of August 10.

August 11 was an active day for the crew members. Campbell and Weir occupied a station north and east of North Kananaskis Pass. Irvine returned to the main camp at Lower Kananaskis Lake to bring back supplies. Thomson worked around camp, cutting wood for the cookstove and preparing food. In the early afternoon Irvine returned, along with Rink and Wheeler, who brought some fresh supplies. Wheeler inspected North Kananaskis Pass, climbing a slope to the south. He concurred with Cautley's decision not to survey and monument this location.

On August 12 Wheeler, Campbell, Irvine and Weir climbed Mount Beatty and surveyed from a station there. Rink went back to the Kananaskis lakes to bring up the remaining supplies, along with Crouch and Martin, the cook. The men arrived at North Kananaskis Pass late the next morning.

From this pass it was only a short distance along the divide to Palliser Pass, the next one to the north. The route went from North Kananaskis Pass down to the Palliser River, then a few kilometres up to the pass. However, the old trail was seldom used and in poor condition. While Wheeler and three men surveyed a station on August 13, Rink, Crouch and Martin crossed North Kananaskis Pass and headed for the Palliser River to establish a camp. They expected to return that evening but didn't do so. Wheeler's crew stayed around camp the next day, waiting for the packers to return with the horses. In his diary Wheeler wrote: "At 4:30 pm with Campbell went over pass and down to jct [junction] of valley with Palliser Pass valley where we found camp. They had only got here at 11 owing to bad trail. Beastly place to camp."

The next day Campbell and the crew cut trail toward Palliser Pass, while Wheeler and the packers returned to North Kananaskis Pass. Realizing that it would probably be difficult to get horses with supplies through on this route, Wheeler decided to have Rink take everything that wasn't needed back to their camp at the junction of the stream from South Kananaskis Pass.

Crouch took four pack horses with supplies to Campbell's camp.

From the camp on the Palliser River, Campbell, Crouch and Irvine surveyed some stations on the BC side of the divide and cut a trail to Palliser Pass. Wheeler took Thomson, Rink, Weir and four pack horses to survey the South Kananaskis Pass area. Thomson described the steep climb to Three Isle Lake on August 16: "There did not appear to be any alternative route (after looking around). Horses became restive, we decided to try the open face. A steep climb—we zig-zagged up some 600 or perhaps 700 feet [183 to 213 metres]. At times we barely made it—there seemed little foothold for the horses who began slipping on patches of bare rock. We reached the top of our climb not far from a fair-sized lake." They reached Three Isle Lake below the pass where they camped that night.

The next day they surveyed a station. While going up the mountain they encountered light snow, so the men stopped for a while under an overhanging rock. As the men approached the summit, the weather deteriorated, so they found a suitable place for surveying and taking photographs while there was sufficient light. "By the time we had read our rounds of azimuths & vertical angles, a thin powdery snow began to fall & the light was going fast," Thomson wrote.

Wheeler recorded that about 40 centimetres of snow fell on August 18. Thomson noted that they kept a fire going in their tepee. Inclement weather kept the men in camp the next day. Thomson wrote: "Ralph stepped out of camp around 2:30 pm to see if he could locate the horses, returned to camp about 4:30 pm without having seen any trace of them. Whichever way they had strayed, snow was covering up their tracks. We were now on our own. A.O.W. & I prepared a supper of Aunt Jemimas [pancakes] & biscuits. We were not yet out of food, conserving wisely on two meals a day." After another day in camp, there was sunshine on August 21, so Wheeler investigated South Kananaskis Pass and set a signal there. While looking for a trail down to the Palliser River, he found the horses feeding just west of the summit.

On August 22 Wheeler, Weir and Thomson surveyed at two stations around South Kananaskis Pass. Thomson wrote about the difficulty of surveying in the snow and Wheeler's predilection for surveying near the edge of a high location.

> Trouble with a snow set up—it melts, by and by a tell-tale creak on the tripod. One might say you have had it. You go back to zero—level up & start the round of azimuths over again. Sometimes at these awkward set ups A.O.W. would kick the tripod or stand too near a leg. Then things would be all different....Neither A.J. nor myself could see the necessity of setting up so close to a precipitous edge. But in this Wheeler was adamant. His argument in

> favor was that if set further back some of the photographic detail immediately below on the valley floor or on the slopes descending from the station would be lost.

Thomson described the scenery.

> Across the Palliser we got an excellent panorama of a remarkable group of mountains comprising of seven distinct peaks—glacier, precipitous wall, outlying ridges dominate the valley from which they rise. The name of King George was given to the highest summit—11,226 feet [3,422 metres]. Later the name "The Royal Group" was suggested & that names of the Royal Family placed upon the remaining peaks. Truly an impressive sight with almost perfect light.…We were certainly well-rewarded by our climb. Many high points of distant peaks to north and south were read. Looking northwesterly up the upper Palliser Valley it opened up the country in which we would be operating. We could see beyond Assiniboine group.

On the way down they surveyed a second station above Three Isle Lake. From this station they could connect the station at South Kananaskis Pass with the station they had surveyed earlier in the day, along with a Geological Survey station on Mount Back.

The next day Wheeler went to survey the station at South Kananaskis Pass, his final one on this section of the divide. Thomson recorded that they were almost out of food, but they knew that they would get resupplied once they reached the cache they had established on August 13 in the Palliser valley. When Wheeler finished, the crew headed down to the Palliser River. After passing Beatty Lake, their difficulties started. Thomson wrote:

> We began to drop & soon entered canyon, and for some 700 feet [213 metres] or more we traveled a steep scree slope. We zig-zag down through this canyon keeping to the north bank of the same creek from Beatty Lake. On this same steep side hill we soon ran into brulé for about three quarters of a mile. We kept contour along the slope—without vestige of a trail. Rounding a lower slope of Mt. Beatty we appeared to be well down onto the Palliser Valley, but still 1000 feet [305 metres] above the valley floor. During this last 1000 foot drop we were again compelled to lariat down to a stream that came in from the northeast, apparently from the North Kananaskis Pass. A further drop of about 200 feet [60 metres] brought us to the main camp and supply cache on the west side of the Palliser opposite the junction of the two trails from north and south passes.

Campbell's crew was at this camp. They had been on a fly camp and just returned the previous day. Thomson wrote: "It was in this camp we discover the porcupines had been busy—chewed through the back wall of the tent, some of A.O.W.'s personal effects and a camera case."

On August 24 the entire crew moved to Palliser Pass, arriving there just before lunch. Cautley had finished surveying there and was now working at Assiniboine Pass. In the afternoon Campbell surveyed at Monument 1E, the lowest point on the pass. The rest of the men set up camp across a stream from Cautley's camp, not far from the outlet of Belgium Lake on the Alberta side of the divide. Thomson wrote: "Wheeler had pitched his tent on a small rise, in the shelter of a small stand of trees overlooking our tents. Directly behind his tent was a tall dead snag. During the survey of the pass, Cautley had camped at the same spot. A violent thunderstorm hit the pass & this particular tree was struck by lightning. The flash seemed to spiral down the trunk of the tree, splitting the trunk & setting it on fire."

Wheeler's crew spent three days at Palliser Pass. They set and surveyed three bolts and cairns, occupied a Geological Survey station and established a station on a ridge near Mount Sir Douglas. Wheeler described the pass as "one of the most beautiful yet met with: open grassy meadows, groves of conifers, and several sky-blue glacial lakes lie amidst a setting of high snowy peaks and fine icefalls." He also wrote: "A faint trail from the Palliser Valley leads over the summit and

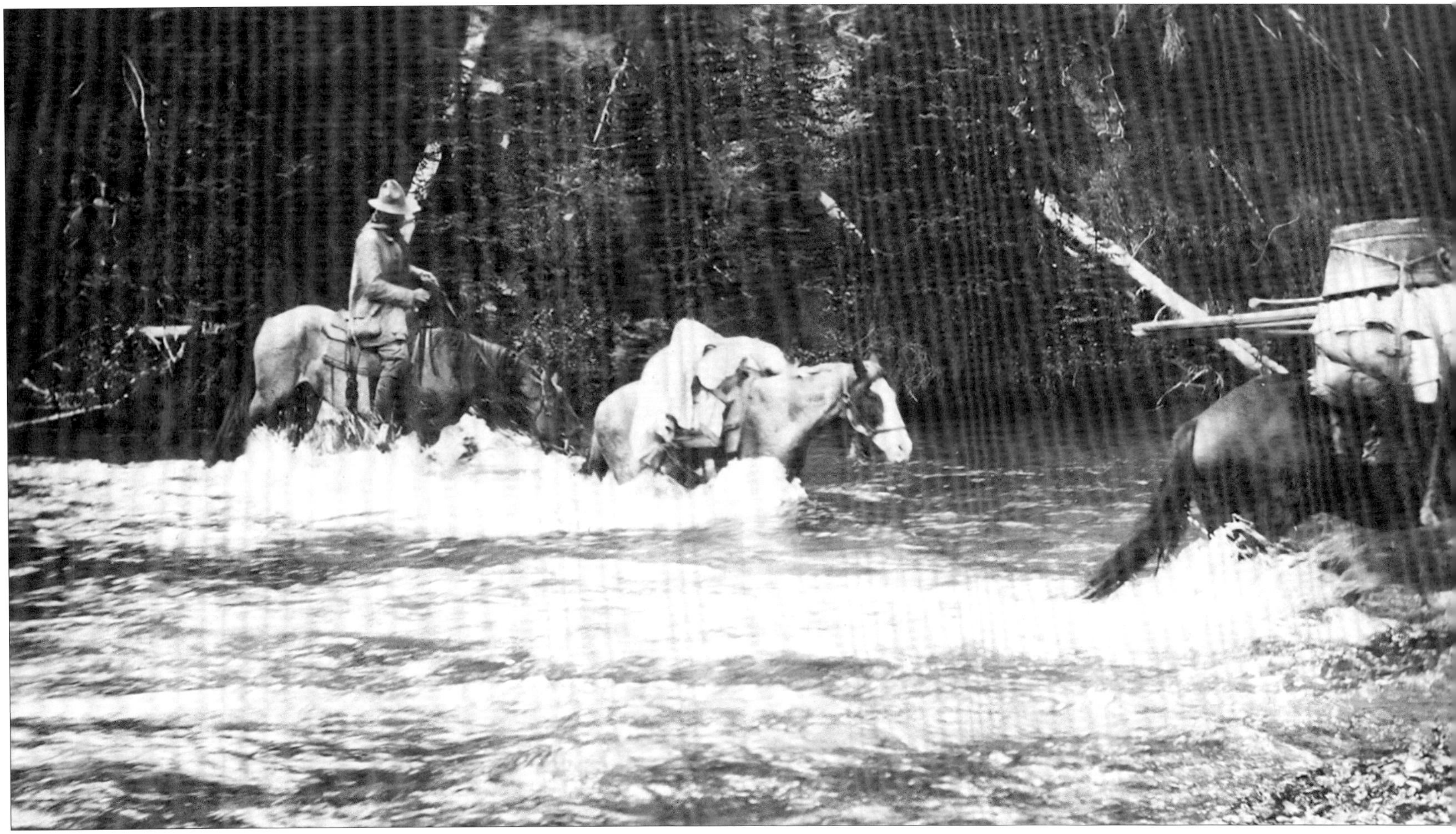

Cautley fording Bryant Creek. J-01026, Royal BC Museum and Archives

descends the slopes on the Alberta side to the valley of Spray River; that the pass was an Indian route of travel is indicated by the number of old tepee poles on both sides of the divide at camping spots along the trail."

On August 28 Wheeler's crew moved camp about 10 kilometres down the Spray River. They set up a main camp near the river and the cook stayed there, while the rest of the crew went on a fly camp to survey the Spray Pass area to the west above Leman Lake. The trail to Spray Pass was difficult to locate, so Wheeler and Campbell split up to see if they could find it. Campbell was unable to find the trail and also got separated from the rest of the crew. Wheeler wrote: "Ralph came along with pack train. We started on supposed trail but got on wrong side of canyon. Horses got tangled up on lake shore. I found trail & on getting horses back Frank [a horse] rolled down hill and got snagged. Got on trail and camped on west (BC) side of summit." The next morning, as Wheeler got ready to search for Campbell, he arrived, having spent the night at the main camp.

Wheeler and his crew spent the next two days surveying the Spray Pass area. On the second afternoon Wheeler returned to the main camp and made preparations for a short trip to Banff. He knew that Campbell would be moving to White Man Pass and there would be a rest day on Sunday. He also wanted to visit Cautley while he was surveying at Assiniboine Pass. Rink would accompany him on the trip.

On the last day of August Wheeler wrote: "Breakfast at 5 by candle light. Left by 7:15. Went to Assiniboine Pass, arrived around 3. Found Cautley at 1J. Ralph pitched tepee." During the same day, Campbell's crew moved back down to the main camp on the east side of the Spray River, a little north of the junction with the stream from Leman Lake. Campbell completed surveying the Palliser Pass area the next day. He occupied a station on the east side of the Spray to the north, while Thomson and Weir surveyed at a Geological Survey station on the east side of Spray, about five kilometres southeast of camp, along with a second station nearby on the same ridge. Thomson recorded that the station provided excellent coverage across Spray Pass, south to Palliser Pass and north to the White Man Pass area.

The first day of September Wheeler wrote: "Spent morning with Cautley looking over place for bolts on north side of pass. Lunch with Cautley then left for Healey Creek. Cautley accompanied us some distance into the Valley of the Rocks. Made campground on W. side of Citadel Peak near pond on divide." Wheeler and Rink arrived in Banff the next afternoon, while Campbell and his crew moved camp to White Man Pass. It was fortunate that they got their camp established, for a period of stormy weather followed. There was rain on Sunday, September 3. Labour Day was a "wild stormy day, accompanied by snow and sleet," Thomson wrote. "Clouds low. We stayed in camp all day, lay in or on our bedrolls."

Campbell and his crew were not able to resume surveying until September 6. It took only three days to survey White Man Pass. They established four bolts and cairns at the top of the pass and surveyed a couple of other stations. One of the bolts coincided with a Geological Survey station. Wheeler and Rink left Banff on the afternoon of September 5 and arrived at White Man Pass two days later. Wheeler spent September 8 going over Cautley's line and surveyed from his main station at the lowest point in the pass. Snow and sleet started late in the day and continued throughout September 9. For his diary entry that day Thomson wrote: "I spent my 29th birthday, sitting in my bedrobe in a 10x12 [three-by-four-metre] tent." Wheeler wrote about White Man Pass: "A well-beaten trail leads across it and there are many signs of its having been much used by Indians in the early days."

On September 10 Wheeler and the crew started toward Assiniboine Pass, their final location for the season. The men had to clear the windfall that had come down during the stormy weather. They camped at Bryant Creek in the vicinity of the present-day campground. Frank, the horse, died from the injuries suffered during his fall. They remained at this camp the next day. Irvine returned to Banff because of illness, and Weir had to leave to start teaching. Crouch accompanied them.

On September 12 Wheeler, Campbell and Thomson surveyed from a sharp point overlooking Marvel Lake. They completed most of their work before a sleet storm arrived. Thomson described an adventure that occurred while they were surveying.

> It was on this station that Campbell attempted the hat trick for the third time of the season.... During summit operations Wheeler's hat blew off, circled around awhile, finally decided to roll down a fairly steep gully. With all the confidence of a splendid climber he [Campbell] slithered down this gully in pursuit of the hat that had by now come to rest near some rocks at the bottom of gully. From there on it was one steep drop off for several hundred feet....With one eye on A.J. I saw him go lower & lower, any moment expecting him to slip—the other eye I kept on the field book—I was booking the angles for Wheeler. He too was very disturbed about his hat.
>
> Campbell reached the hat in a precarious spot.
>
> He stooped down to reach at arm's length, & in doing so his footing slipped, dislodging a rock which as luck would have it bounced on the hat & sent it further on its way down this gully, over the precipice out of sight. Then slowly he climbed back up to the station. I thought the whole effort somewhat break neck, for one solitary hat. At the foot of the gully one slip & we would have been short our key man. During this performance I stayed up beside Wheeler

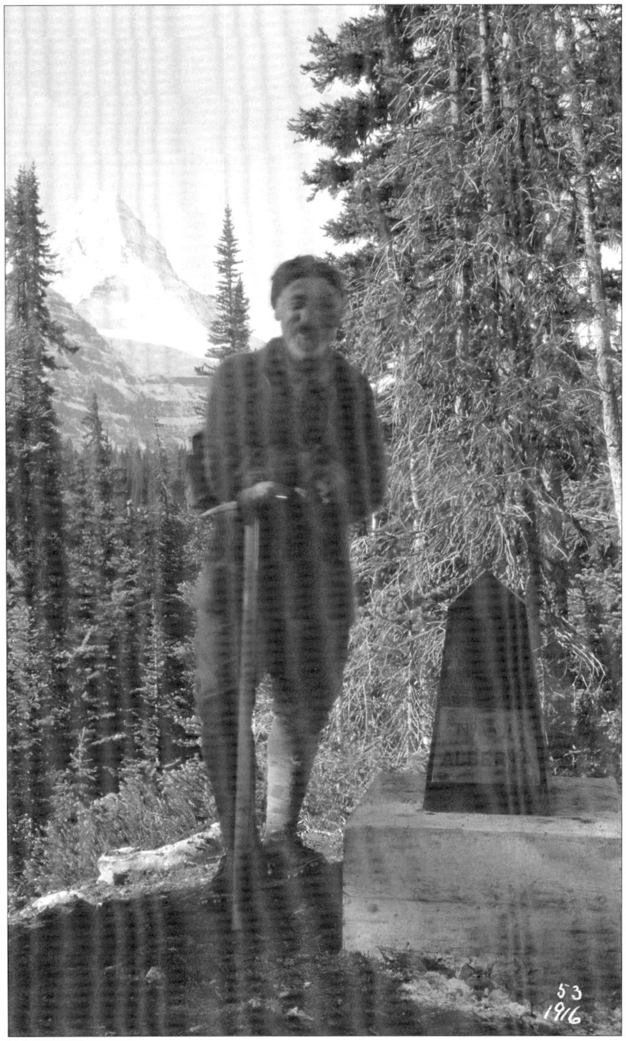

A.O. Wheeler at Assiniboine Pass. e011166481, Library and Archives Canada

> at the instrument—continued to read & book angles. He was a very tired man this day—he had spared himself little on his last trip to Banff. Another highlight, with one anxious eye on A.J. I watched Wheeler step back from the instrument, presumably to take a rest. As he straightened up, he had overlooked the fact he was now under the overhang above him. As he did so, said rock did not permit him to stretch to full height and minus hat rammed his head into the jagged rock above. That just about knocked him out. I jumped to his assistance when I saw him stagger—there was little room to spare at this set & the gullies on either side were steep—a fall could have been disastrous.

The next day Wheeler and Thomson surveyed two stations, while the rest of the crew moved to Assiniboine Pass. Although Wheeler had surveyed around Mount Assiniboine in 1913, he had established only a few stations, and there were some areas where he needed more detail. The two stations that the men did that day "added considerably to the control of Marvel Lake," according to Thomson.

After finishing their surveying, Wheeler and Thomson walked to Assiniboine Pass, where they met Campbell and Cautley. Thomson described the scene.

> It turned out a lovely clear evening. The four of us walked along the trail to a camp that had been established by Ralph and company near the junction of the Simpson Pass trail from the north. Cautley & Wheeler were ahead, A.J. & I fairly close behind....I had said before that Wheeler was a tired man & in the course of our stroll through the...alpland & majestic scenery, Cautley, a very good conversationalist, suddenly put his arm around Wheeler, drew him close & said perhaps (we say most likely)—"You know, Wheeler, a good prize fighter gets out of the ring before he is knocked out." Apart from Wheeler taking on a deeper complexion, that he was some embarrassed was evident. He made no effort to pull away, as he had a good deal of respect for Cautley, but for once he was stymied by perhaps a more versatile man who knew how to pass a remark.

On the 14th, Wheeler and Cautley spent the day looking over the work in Assiniboine Pass while Campbell and Thomson surveyed a station and Cautley's crew completed their work. The next day Cautley's crew began their return trip. Mount Assiniboine is the highest peak in the southern section of the boundary survey. One area of the divide around the mountain that Wheeler had not mapped was the western side, so he and his crew travelled down the Mitchell River.

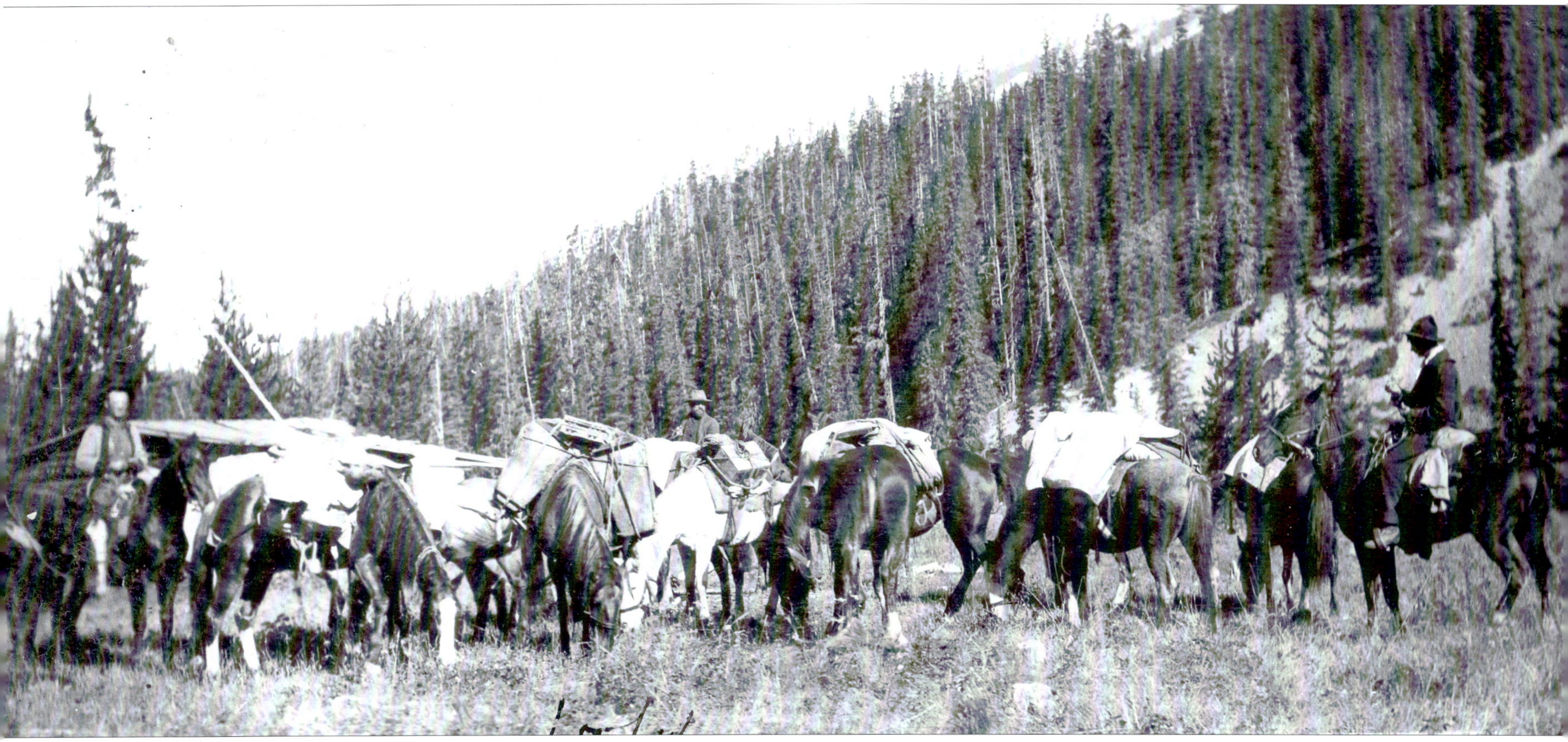

Cautley's pack train loaded and ready to travel. C.V. Hope family collection

Thomson recorded that about 12 kilometres from Assiniboine Pass they "came upon an old Indian camp, with the customary tepee poles." The men camped a few kilometres farther down the valley.

Fortunately the weather was good, and during the next two days the crew surveyed a couple of stations. At one of them they found a note that Conrad Kain had been there with a group of people from the Alpine Club in July of that year. After surveying a third station above their camp on the morning of September 18, Wheeler and crew returned to Assiniboine Pass. Crouch had returned from Banff and rejoined the crew. While he was waiting for Wheeler's crew to return, he had encountered a grizzly bear nearby.

The crew had the next day off, while Wheeler surveyed at stations 1J and 7J. The two packers assisted him by clearing the line in some places. During the next two days Wheeler, Campbell and the crew set four bolts, surveyed at these stations and built cairns. For their final cairn, on Cave Mountain they constructed their largest one of the season: 1.8 metres at the base and 2.15 metres high, with a wooden picket that extended up another 0.45 metres. Thomson described the view in his diary: "Across the pass to the south & southwest an excellent view of the Assiniboine group—inspiring to artist of nature & lover of mountain grandeur....The Assiniboine that had been in the back of our minds all summer, we were now about to leave." Wheeler also wrote about the scenery in his government report: "The Assiniboine Pass and vicinity are very beautiful. There are wide stretches of open alplands mingled with groves and belts of spruce, balsam and larch. Fifteen or more lakes, some of large size and all of wonderful blue and green colour, surround the group of mountains of which Assiniboine is the central massif. Snowfields, glaciers, and icefalls are on all sides and, as

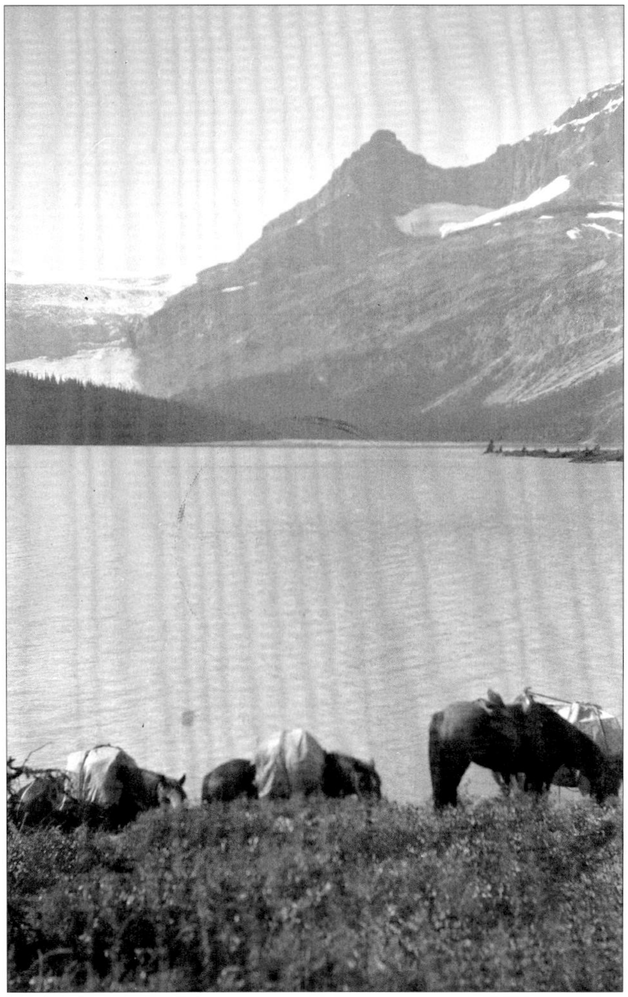

During his fall exploratory trip to Howse Pass, Cautley passed by Bow Lake where he took this picture. e011166482, Library and Archives Canada

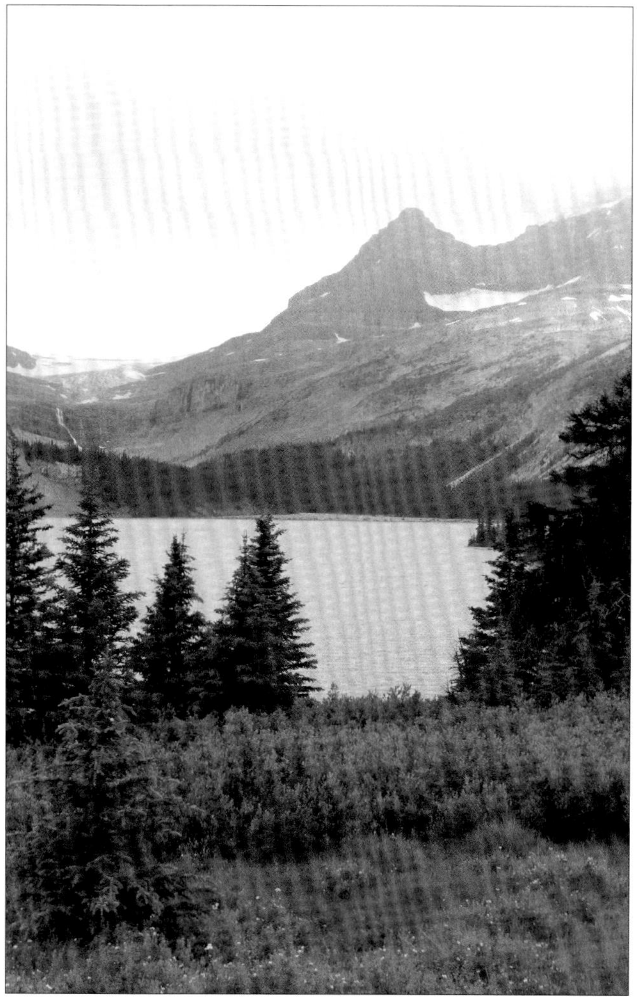

A picture in 2016 shows a largely similar landscape in the background. There are more trees in the foreground. Jay Sherwood photo

a scenic asset to the country, the region cannot be surpassed. Tourists from all over the world visit it yearly and the number will greatly increase in the future."

On September 22 the crew started the return trip to Banff via the Bryant Creek and Spray River route. Wheeler had one more station that he wanted to survey near the divide between the Spray and Kananaskis drainages, so he took Campbell and Crouch with him. Thomson, Rink and Martin went to Mumford's cabin again, but this time Rink put up the tepee. After surveying a station the next morning, Wheeler and the men returned to the main trail to Banff. They followed it to a campsite north of the upper Spray lake, where Rink had set up camp. On September 24 Wheeler's crew arrived in Banff in the early afternoon.

After Cautley finished the field season, he had one more objective to complete. In 1917 the boundary survey would work north from Kicking Horse Pass and the first surveying would be at Howse Pass. The boundary commission report stated: "In accordance with the plans of the Commission, Mr. Cautley then proceeded with one man and six horses to make an examination of Howse Pass with a view to ascertain-

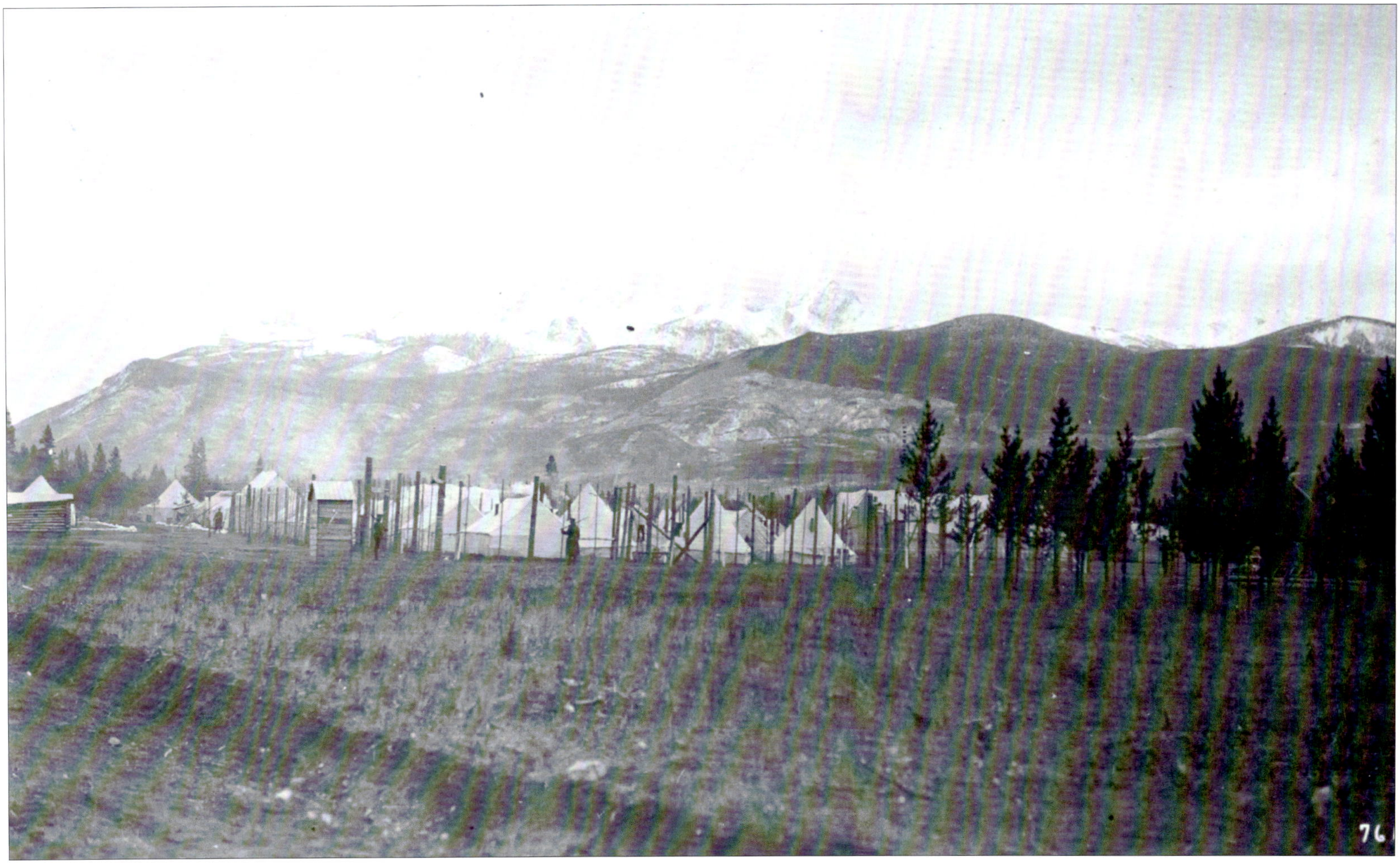

Cautley took this photograph of the Castle Mountain internment camp when he passed the site on his journey to Howse Pass. During World War I the Canadian government established internment camps for men who were categorized as enemy aliens—citizens of countries with whom Canada was at war. Most of the people housed in the internment camps were Ukrainian. The Castle Mountain internment camp started in 1915. It was the largest in the Canadian Rockies and the main one in Alberta. The men who were held there worked on infrastructure projects for the national parks and in Banff. The men lived in tents in primitive conditions and abuse was widespread. They spent the winters of 1915 and 1916 in Banff. The camp closed in August 1917. Today there is a commemorative plaque, statue, and interpretive signs at the site of the Castle Mountain internment camp along the Bow Valley Parkway. J-00873 Royal BC Museum and Archives

ing the best means of getting there with supplies." From Lake Louise, Cautley followed the present-day Icefields Parkway over Bow Pass and down the Mistaya River. He found that the crossing of the Mistaya at high water in June would be difficult and dangerous. The route up the North Saskatchewan River would also be hazardous at that time of year. Cautley's return trip from Howse Pass to Field, BC, was via the Blaeberry River, Amiskwi Pass and the Amiskwi River trail. Although the route was shorter in distance, it was higher in elevation, but Cautley found that it was practical for horses.

The first section of the Alberta-BC boundary survey was now finished. Next year Wheeler and Cautley would begin surveying a more remote portion of the Great Divide.

Climbing Mt. Fitzwilliam. A2251, Provincial Archives of Alberta

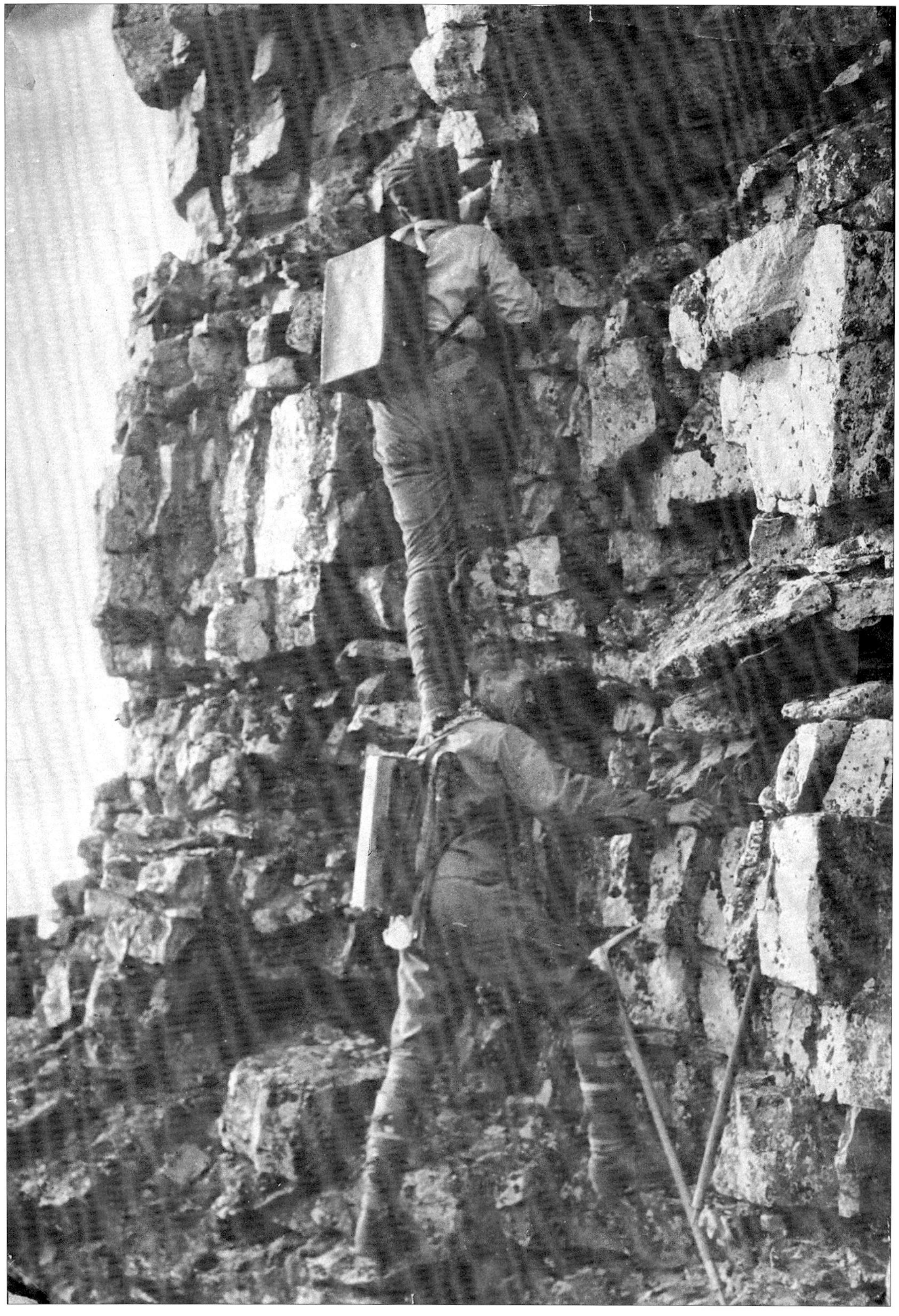

1917

The boundary survey now prepared to head into the rugged and remote terrain north of Kicking Horse Pass. From the beginning, all three governments participating in the boundary survey wanted to have Yellowhead Pass, west of Jasper, delineated. It was an important transportation route and both the Grand Trunk Pacific and Canadian Northern had constructed rail lines through the pass. But the governments had been reluctant to send the survey crews there when there was no other work in that section of the boundary that was urgent. In 1917 the survey of Yellowhead Pass became a top priority of the boundary survey.

Another factor became significant in deciding the plan of action for the boundary survey north of Kicking Horse Pass: more settlers were coming into the Peace River area to farm, and it was important for administrative purposes to locate the boundary through this largely agrarian area. This work would be done by Cautley and his crew, and the Alberta government believed that it would be the best utilization of their personnel. During the winter of 1916–17 the Alberta government urged Deville to begin surveying the second part of the boundary survey, the 120th meridian. The BC government also realized that it was important to define the boundary in the Peace River region. In a letter to Wheeler and Cautley on March 14, Deville wrote: "There is no urgent need of the demarcation of the boundary between the Canadian Pacific Railway and the Yellowhead pass, but it is urgently needed at the latter place and more especially across the Peace River district. In this district considerable settlement has taken place on both sides of the boundary and the need of a survey is imperative."

But the 120th meridian was a longitude line, and it would take time to establish a starting point for Cautley's surveying. The location would have to be along a telegraph line near the 120th meridian. There would have to be many observations on the sun and the stars, as well as signals sent along the telegraph line from locations with established longitude. The specialized work in establishing a survey station with an accurate longitude was done by Dominion Observatory personnel. In 1912 and 1913, F.A. McDiarmid from the Dominion Observatory came to BC and established longitude in a few locations. One of these was used by the BC government to survey the 124th meridian between 52° north and 55° north. On May 26 the Dominion Observatory sent a telegram to BC's surveyor general that McDiarmid was available to come to BC in the summer of 1917, but by the time he would arrive in the Peace River region and complete his work, only a portion of the field season would remain. McDiarmid established a station near Pouce Coupe about 10 kilometres from the 120th meridian.

The three governments involved in the boundary survey decided that for 1917 Wheeler and Cautley would work together one more season. The two crews would survey Yellowhead Pass and also Howse Pass, the first major pass north of Kicking Horse. This pass had historic importance for both the indigenous people and the fur traders, and there was a possibility that it could become a transportation route. On the BC side of Howse Pass the timber resources had economic value.

Although the surveying of the 120th meridian could not begin until 1918, the planning could start. There would need to be an initial order-in-council by the federal government authorizing the survey of the 120th meridian as part of the boundary survey, and an invitation to the two provinces to participate in the survey of this section of the boundary. After this was completed, a second order-in-council made the survey of the 120th meridian official.

Between 1903 and 1905 Wheeler had made a phototopographic survey along the Railway Belt in BC for the Dominion government. It included the terrain for about 30 kilometres north of Kicking Horse Pass along the boundary. Phototopographic surveying was

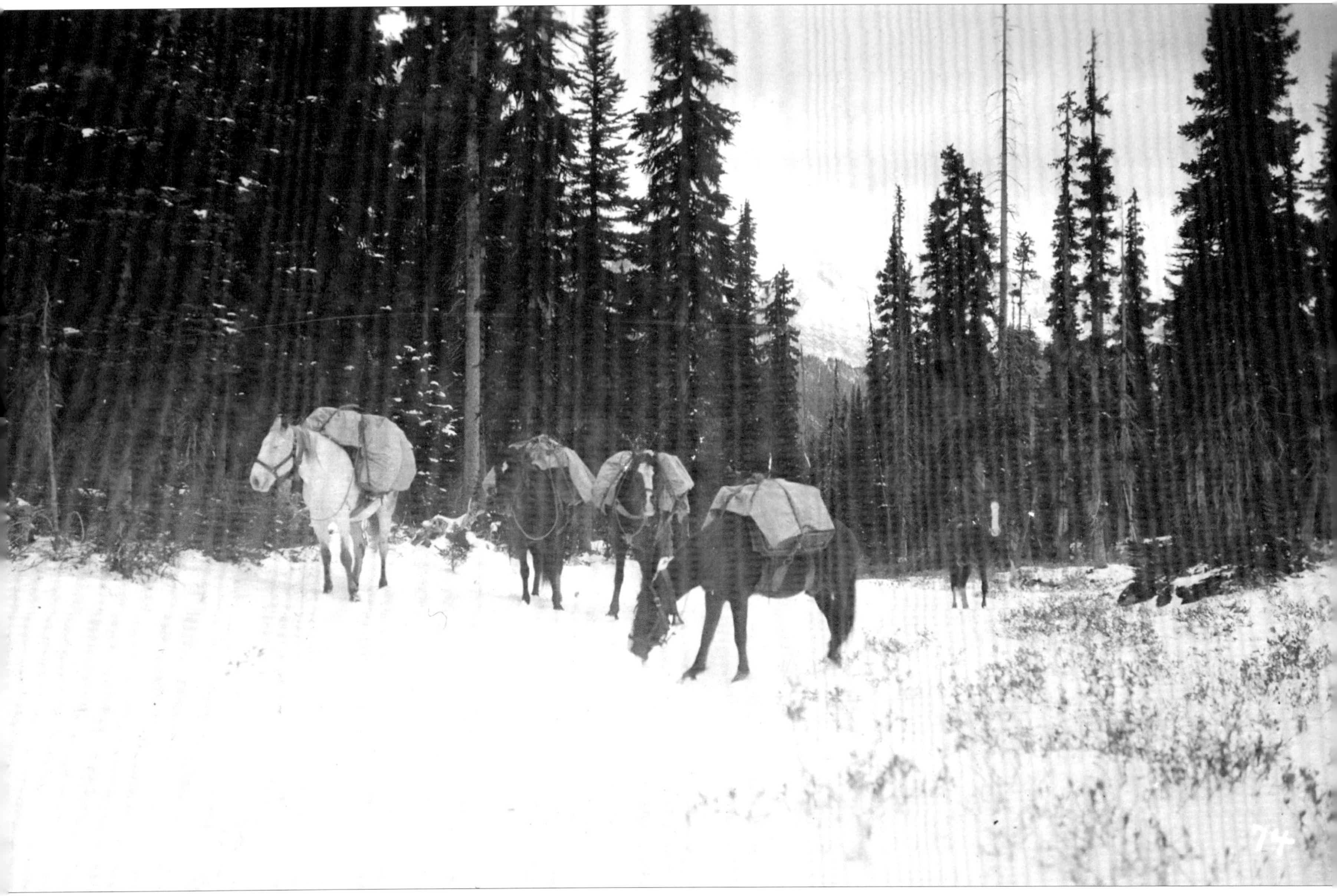

Horses at the summit of Amiskwi Pass. J-00871, Royal BC Museum and Archives

also done on the Alberta side north of Kicking Horse Pass. This enabled Wheeler to survey at Howse Pass with Cautley and then connect back to the previously established stations. In addition, Cautley had already determined the best route to reach the Howse Pass area during early summer when the waterways would still be high from spring runoff.

The amount of money allocated for the boundary survey remained the same. World War I was entering its fourth year, and it was becoming more difficult to find people who were capable of performing the rugged work necessary for the boundary survey. This was particularly applicable to Cautley, who had to assemble an entirely new crew. His assistant, C.V. Hope, had enlisted in the war, but T. Rochester Brown, his 1915 assistant, was available. Fortunately for Wheeler, all of the crew that he had during the second half of 1916 returned, except for the assistant packer; this position was filled by Frank Wallis. In 1908 Wallis had immigrated to western Canada from Kentucky with his sister and her family. He came to Banff and started working as a packer.

Cautley and his crew departed from Field on June 20. At Amiskwi Pass they encountered about 60 centimetres of snow still on the ground. It took the crew two days to clear and shovel out the trail for about five kilometres so the horses could get through. Cautley and his men arrived at Howse Pass on June 26 and he began the preliminary survey, getting ready for Wheeler's arrival. Howse Pass, which was about 100 metres lower than Kicking Horse Pass, was heavily timbered, so Cautley's crew had to cut the survey line across the entire pass.

Wheeler arrived in Banff in mid-May and spent the next month preparing for the Alpine Club camp and working on the boundary survey. He still had items to complete for the first volume of the boundary commissioner's report before he went into the field. On June 9 Cautley came to Banff to plan the field season with Wheeler. A.J. Campbell and Spike Thomson arrived on June 20, and the next day they went to test the cameras. Thomson, who kept a diary again, wrote: "A.J. & I went down to the golf course to test the cameras near 1st green. Set the three targets up on trees about 300 yds [100 metres] away over near bank of the Bow River."

Campbell and the crew departed for Field on June 26. Wheeler left on the evening train and arrived at Field around midnight. "Walked to camp—found my bed all ready and gladly turned in." Spike Thomson remained in Banff for the first part of the field season to complete the maps needed for the boundary survey report, label the photo albums and finish other items.

The next day Wheeler and his crew departed from Field, stopping for the night at the campsite that Cautley had used. During the afternoon of June 28 they met Cautley's packers about 2.5 kilometres south of Amiskwi summit. In his diary Wheeler wrote: "Told no feed there so camped. Snow patches on ground everywhere. Cook cut his foot slightly." It snowed overnight and the weather remained inclement, so the men stayed in camp the next day. On June 30 Wheeler's crew crossed Amiskwi summit and descended to the

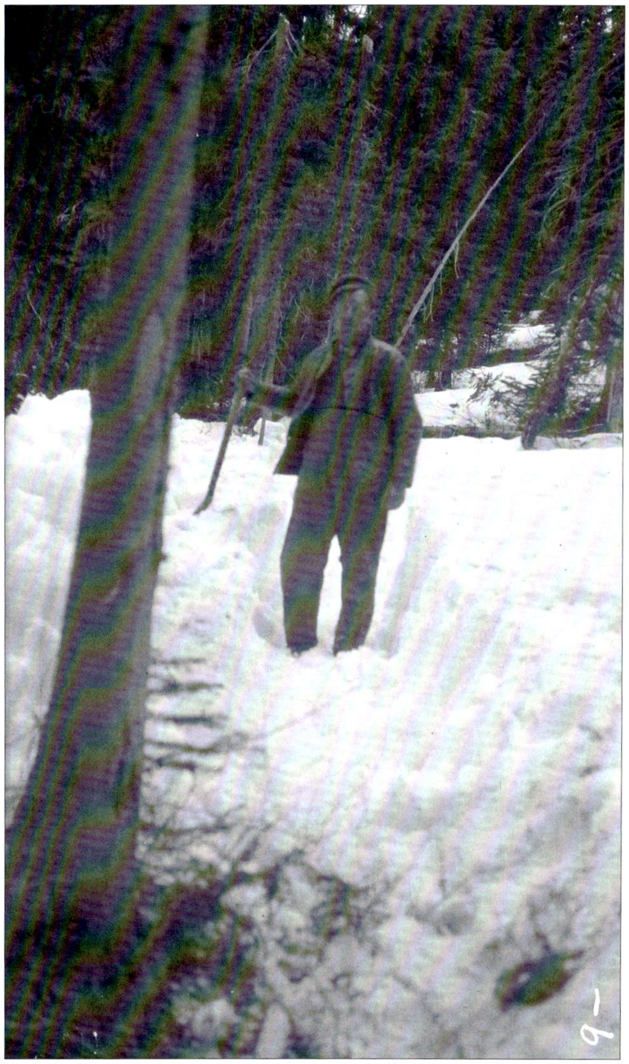

Shovelling out the trail across the pass. e011166460, Library and Archives Canada

Blaeberry River, where they camped. They arrived at Howse Pass at lunchtime the next day, camping near Cautley's crew. In the afternoon Wheeler went with Cautley to examine the boundary in the pass.

On July 2 Wheeler and his crew surveyed two stations. Then Wheeler went and joined Cautley at the north end of the pass. "Had a cup of tea with him and after fixed marking of watershed line. He then went to S. end of ridge and made signal."

The next afternoon Wheeler and another person (probably Campbell), accompanied by packer Ralph

Rink, went on a fly camp to timberline on the west side of Howse Pass. The clouds were low the next day so they couldn't climb. Unfortunately they "had only provisions for one day but had to make them do two." It cleared at night and the two men got an early start the next morning. "Reached top of mountain 9:30 am but had clouded over and was snowing. Clouds came lower with wet snow. Waited until 12 when built a cairn and returned to shelter camp.…Left camera, transit and things."

On July 6 Wheeler returned to the main camp. After lunch he quickly organized his whole crew for a fly camp to Amiskwi Pass. They left at 3:00 and arrived at 8:00 p.m. The next day Wheeler and his crew climbed and surveyed at a station called Amiskwi Pass West. "Grand day and good views," he wrote. After surveying two more stations in the area on July 8, most of the crew returned to Howse Pass, while Wheeler, Campbell and Gordon Weir went back to the July 3 location. "At the fly camp we found that porcupines had played the devil." The following day Wheeler successfully surveyed at the station. "Got glorious round of views," he wrote. By the end of the day the three men were back at Howse Pass, and Wheeler "went to where Cautley was observing—talked things over with him."

After a day of rest, Wheeler, Campbell and Weir joined Cautley for two days at the upper stations of Howse Pass. "With Cautley went over his trail up mt. [mountain] on west side of pass to site of Monuments 4N and 6N. Ralph took horses over trail and left Frank to make fly camp for us. Campbell & Weir were there when Cautley & I arrived. We agreed on site of monuments. With Cautley we then went up to site of 8N and occupied two other cairn stations. Stayed the night at fly camp." On July 13 the men planned to climb a large peak, but Wheeler "was afraid of the snow so occupied the point below it to the east. Got back to fly camp at 4 and then down to main camp. Campbell and Weir remained to put in bolt at 8N." That evening Wheeler "saw Cautley and made final arrangements with him." The next day Wheeler, accompanied by Rink, returned to Banff, leaving Campbell to finish the remaining stations at Howse Pass.

By July 16 Wheeler and Rink were back in Banff. For the next two days Wheeler and Thomson finished the surveying material for the report and Rink returned to Field. On July 19 Wheeler and Thomson took the morning westbound train. Wheeler got off at Hector, near the divide, to go to the Alpine Club camp at Cataract Valley, while Thomson continued to Field, where Rink met him.

The two men had lunch together at the Strand Hotel, then played a game of billiards before loading up the horses back of the hotel and leaving Field about 5:30. They had three pack horses and two saddle horses. Thomson described a scene that occurred along the route.

> Included in our commissary 6 bottles of Scotch we had raised from the proprietor of the Field Hotel. Crossed the wooden bridge over the Kicking Horse River & headed up Emerald Creek. We had traveled about two hours when a sudden event took our minds off scenery and trail.
>
> Bob, one of our steady & more reliable pack horses, whom we had chosen to carry the valuable consignment of Scotch, ran into a hornet's nest & took off willy-nilly at random. Under the stimulus of hornet serum showed remarkable agility. The other two loads didn't seem fussy so long as they got out of sight. As Ralph was in the lead he had apparently got by the nest without disturbing it. As I was bringing up the rear I was witness to the pandemonium that followed. A holler to Ralph brought him back to where there seemed more hornets than room. By this time the ponies were out of sight in the timber. We decided to track Bob down first, our concern more than hornets was our 6 bottles of the water of life. In loading Bob we had placed 1 bottle of hooch (under the top cover) in the X trees of the pack saddle—the remainder in the side packs. A diligent search of some 10 minutes brought us to Bob resting between two trees about 3 feet [1 metre] apart. The path was narrow & the pack was wide. He was not in pain & seemed content. In trying

> to force his way between the trees he all but shed his pack. Alas, the bottle of the good old brew from which we had previously taken a nip had not survived. Closer examination—the elixir of life had trickled down over Bob to act as a healing balm for hornet stings. Soon we had the three horses rounded up & packs secure. We had lost an hour & it was now getting dusk.

The men soon found a campsite with feed, but they hobbled the horses to prevent them from returning to Field.

The next day Rink and Thomson travelled almost to the summit of Amiskwi Pass, camping by a cache Campbell had left to be picked up. "We had brought along some fresh meat from Field. Two T-bone steaks—with the help of some potatoes & canned [goods] we had raised from Campbell's cache. By majority vote we opened up another bottle of whiskey. High up in those lovely alplands in a world of our own, we dined gorgeously & plenteously. With the best part of a bottle of Scotch less, seems we ended up higher than the surrounding country. Finally got the tepee up, stacked our saddles & gear under pack covers, set the cache in order, turned in by the light of the moon. A campground to be remembered." The next day the two men arrived at Howse Pass.

July 22 was Sunday and Thomson spent the morning visiting Cautley in his tent. He wrote: "Cautley & I brought ourselves up to date on 1917 yarns." Thomson also noted: "Cautley a well-educated man, an excellent conversationalist."

The British Columbia crew had now completed their surveying from Howse Pass south. Altogether, they established nine stations, along with four brass bolts and cairns in Howse Pass. In his BC government report, Wheeler described the BC side of the boundary near Howse Pass. "There is a lot of spruce and fir timber, valuable for commercial purposes, directly at the summit of the pass and along the sides of the valley of Blaeberry River, flowing south and west to the Columbia. Timber limits have been taken up here, but the getting-out of the timber would be a difficult and expensive process, probably requiring a railway to connect with the main stream of Blaeberry River." Wheeler also noted the contrast between the two sides of the pass. "On the Alberta side of the watershed the wide gravel bed of a branch of the Saskatchewan River lies only an eighth of a mile [200 metres] beyond the summit of the pass."

On July 23 Campbell and his crew headed north over Howse Pass down Conway Creek, which flows into the Howse River. They travelled about 10 kilometres from the pass, camping on a grassy flat.

The next day Thomson, Campbell and Weir occupied Chimney Bluff. They reached the foot of a big slide, then went up the slide to the foot of a steep wall. Thomson wrote:

> After a half hour search we came across a chimney that offered a possible route to the summit—a distance of 4 to 500 feet [122 to 152 metres]. We decided a try, quite steep—but as we saw it—nothing that would impede progress seriously. The scree slope at the foot of the wall had become very loose & fine. As we entered the chimney the slope gave way. As I was last on the rope, I soon had Gordon sitting in my lap & together we started downhill. In short time I was locked in knee deep & the whole slope on the move. The situation did not look too hot—how far we had traveled, probably 50 feet [15 metres]. A.J. brought us to a halt with a belay beside some rocks. Soon all was well & we made the summit.…We did not attempt a descent of the chimney but returned by a route on the south side—we discovered a goat trail.

In the evening Thomson and Campbell set up a canvas canoe they had brought along, thinking it might be useful for river crossings or possibly lake travel.

On July 25 the crew travelled down the Howse River to the junction of the North Saskatchewan River. Along the way:

> A.J. & I decided to put the canvas canoe we assembled yesterday in the water & try our luck. Unfortunately, the river had dropped & it was not easy to find the deep channel.…Many bars were showing or partially showing & the canoe

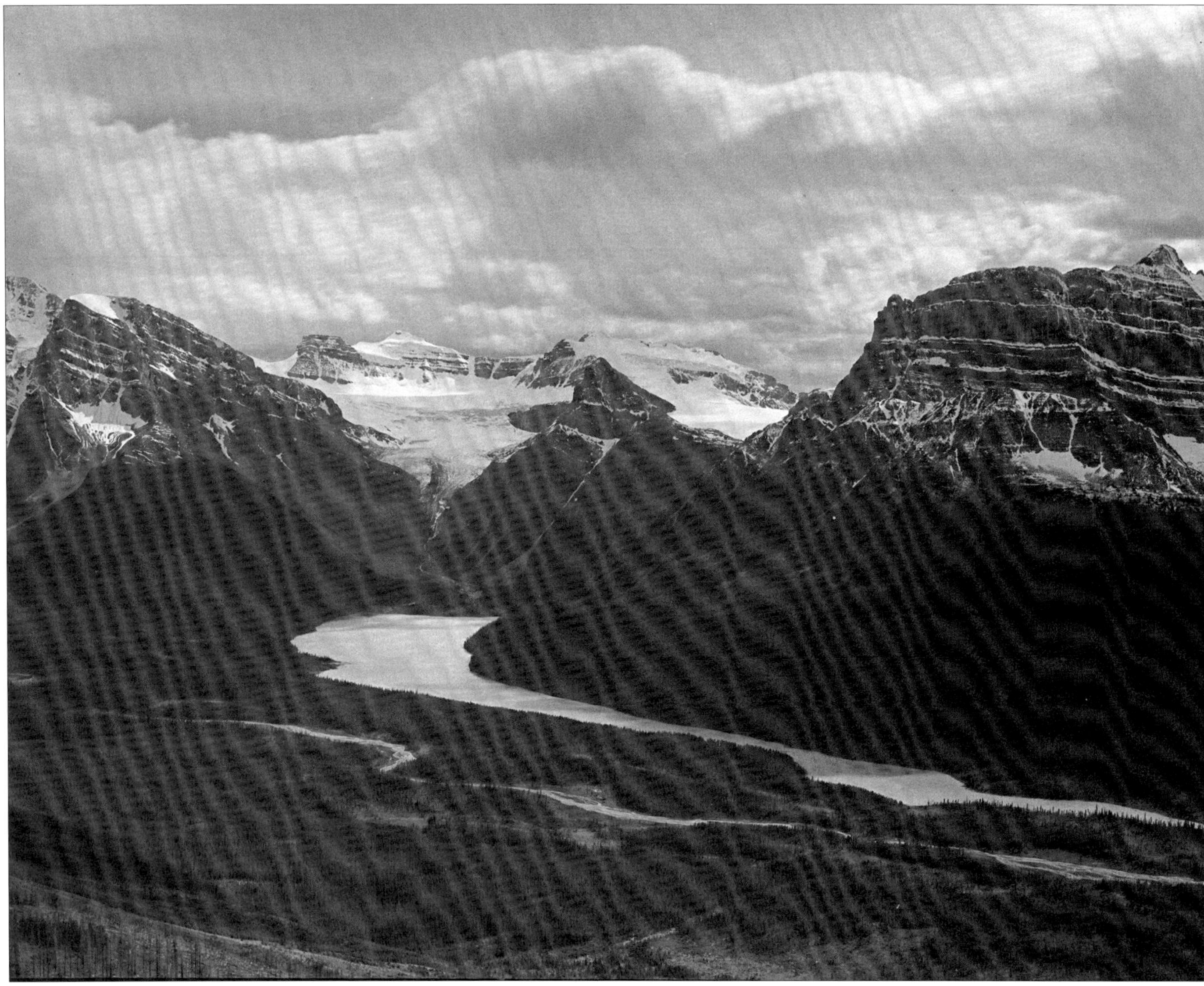

Part of the panorama of the Rocky Mountains taken from Mistaya station on the Alberta side of the Great Divide. e011183813 and e011183814, Library and Archives Canada

frequently grounded on the hard bottom. After about an hour's travel the river narrowed suddenly & we ran into a small canyon, the walls on either side reaching 50 to 60 feet [15 to 18 metres] high. The river became swifter about halfway in the canyon. Several large boulders showed up, making navigation doubtful. One in particular—the wash from the canyon wall forced us to broach a big fellow. Fortunately we did not capsize, the current swept us off back into the stream. There was little I could do as front paddle. As the canoe was flexible it was an uncanny sensation to feel it twist & bend with the current. We were soon out into open flats again, hunting a navigable channel & continued to ground. We turned the canoe end for end, but it was not long before we had a hole in both ends & we were getting sloppy. The canoe was now taking aboard water faster than we could take care of it. We decided it was time to abandon ship.

Their camp was on the south bank by the ford across the river. Saskatchewan River Crossing was a

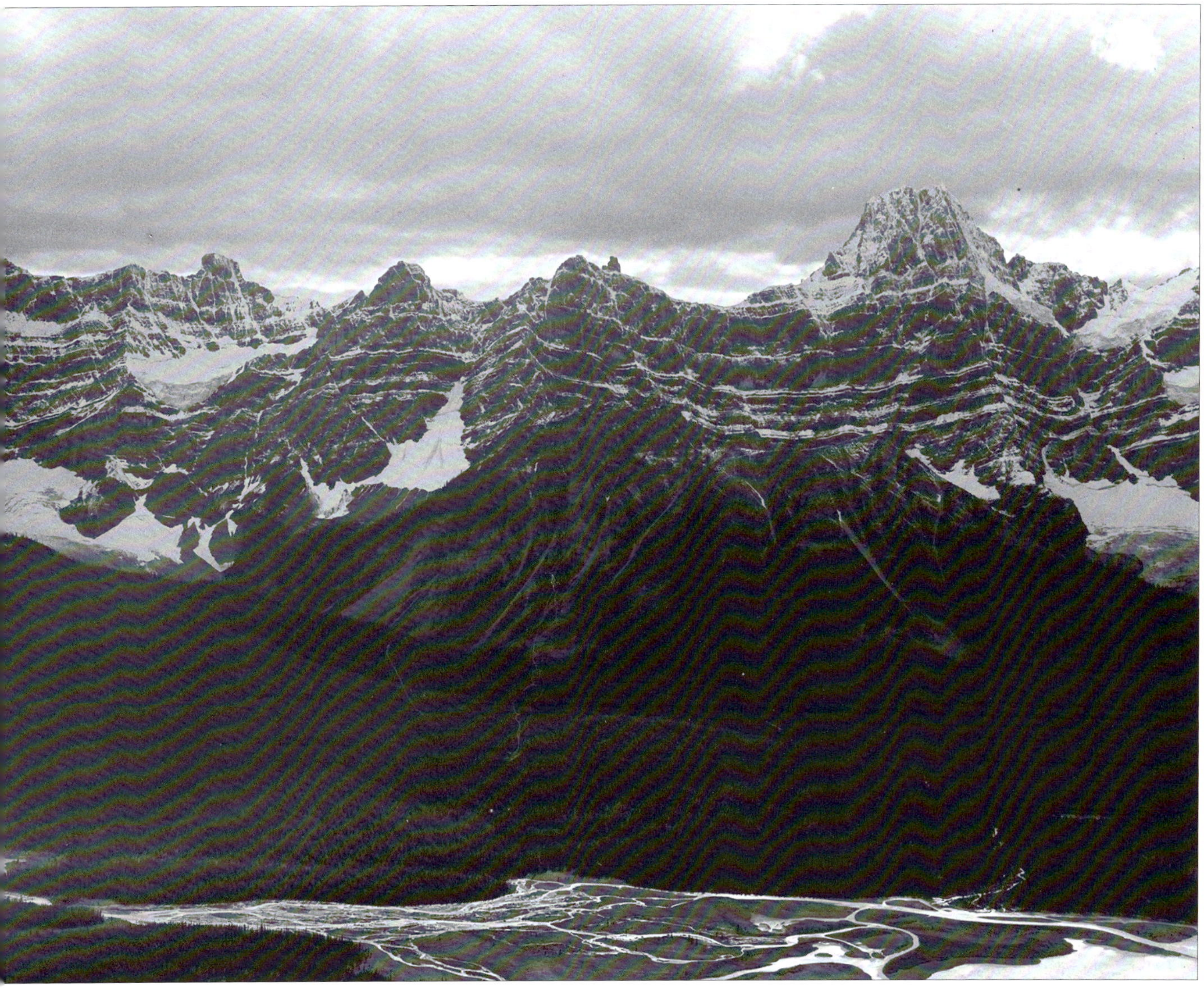

historic location along the North Saskatchewan River that was used by the indigenous people, fur traders and tourists. The section of the North Saskatchewan within Banff National Park is now a Canadian Heritage River. Thomson noted that there was "plenty of evidence that this camp ground had been used before."

Before proceeding to Yellowhead Pass, the British Columbia crew needed to survey some stations from the Alberta side of the divide in the vicinity of Howse Pass. On July 26 the men built a cache near their camp and took supplies for about a week. In his diary Thomson wrote: "We headed along south bank of the Saskatchewan to the Mistaya. Forded about 10 chains [200 metres] up from the mouth, crossing onto a big gravel bar, about 2 feet [60 centimetres] water to centre stream, worked downstream about 300 feet [91 metres], then turned sharply toward opposite (east) bank, fording what appeared to be the deep channel. At this stage of water the going was not too bad. Would guess about half flood. But current was swift. There were big boulders in the river bed which bothered the horses." Thomson noted that about 400 metres upstream from the ford there was a cable crossing that appeared to have been built recently.

The crew travelled up the east side of the Mistaya to Waterfowl Lakes, largely following the present route of the Icefields Parkway. They camped about a kilometre below the upper lake. The weather became cold and rainy, and the men remained at this camp for the next four days. Thomson spent the time copying a duplicate set of notes. The upcoming ford of the North Saskatchewan River was the most dangerous part of the trip. Campbell and Thomson planned to pack a set of notes and a transit on two separate horses in case there was an accident.

On July 31 the weather finally cleared. The crew made a cache and went on a quick two-day trip toward Bow Summit. On the first day they surveyed two stations. The mountains on the east side of the valley were easily accessible and provided excellent views across the valley to the Great Divide. Their camp was about eight kilometres north of Bow Summit.

The next day Campbell, Thomson and Weir surveyed at a station on the shoulder of Weed Mountain. Thomson wrote that they were on a "point of eminence commanding a fine panorama of the Mistaya valley—lakes, glaciers & mountains to the south beyond Bow Pass—to the west the high peaks of the Continental Divide—to the north the valley of the North Saskatchewan hemmed in by high mountain ranges on either side. Further still in the distance the lofty peaks that guard (form the gateway) to the Columbia Icefield. A view almost unparalleled for its combination of grandeur & extent."

On August 2 the crew returned down the Mistaya, camping about 10 kilometres from the mouth of the river. They reached the river crossing early the next afternoon, crossed to the west bank, loaded up the supplies from their cache and returned to their campsite of July 25.

While Campbell and his crew surveyed up the Mistaya River, Cautley and his crew completed their survey of Howse Pass on July 27. They constructed and surveyed seven monuments. The boundary commissioner's report described Cautley's difficulties: "The survey of Howse Pass proved to be an arduous

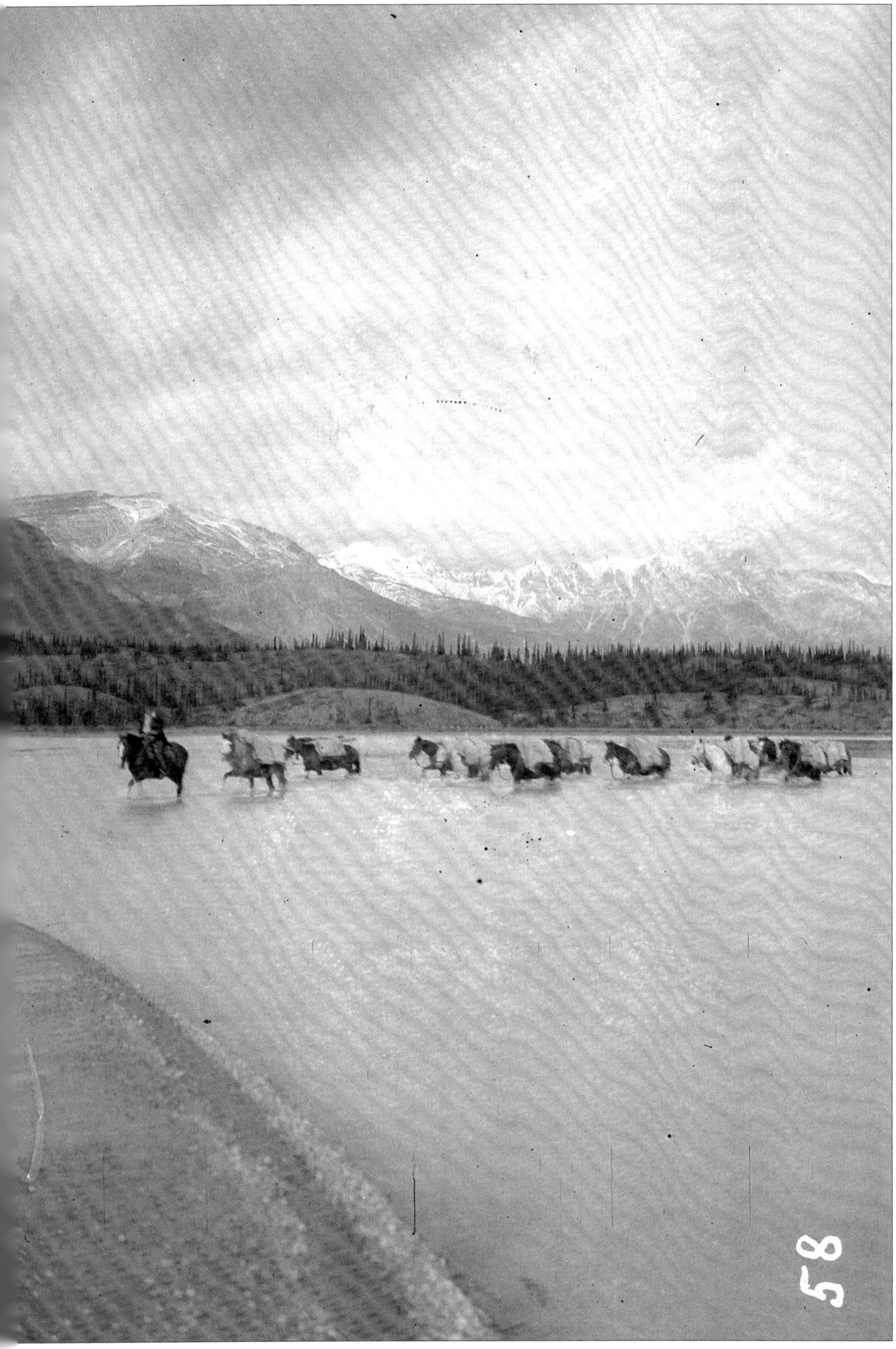

Fording the North Saskatchewan River. e011166499, Library and Archives Canada

undertaking from the point of view of Mr. Cautley's division; first because it is very heavily timbered for 1600 feet [488 metres] above the floor of the valley with spruce measuring up to forty-three inches [1.1 metres] in diameter; and secondly, because the mountain sides are so steep and so broken by precipitous rock ledges that great difficulty was experienced in locating and constructing trails by which horses could pack up monument material."

Cautley's crew left for Yellowhead Pass on July 28. Cautley did not provide much detail about the trip except for the crossing of the river.

> Crossing the big ford at the junction of the North and South branches of the Saskatchewan River was quite an experience. The River is divided into several big channels. The horsemen would ride into the first channel to test it for depth. If it began to look like swimming, they would come back and try again higher up or lower down, until they found a ford not more than four feet deep [1.2 metres], which would enable the pack horses to cross without getting their packs wet. Having crossed the first channel, it might be necessary to go a quarter of a mile [400 metres] up the intervening gravel bar between it and the next channel before finding a four foot ford, and so on. From bank to bank, the big ford must be about half a mile [800 metres] wide, but, for all its great width, it is fairly safe, because all the channels run over gravel bottoms, in which the variations in depth are gradual, and in which there are no boulders. It is boulders that make fording swift streams dangerous. Horses soon get used to fording, with the current foaming round their shoulders, but if they stumble over a boulder, the current is apt to roll them over sideways.

Cautley reached Yellowhead Pass on August 10 after a trip of about 225 kilometres and began the preliminary survey of the pass before the arrival of Wheeler's crew five days later.

In his diary for August 3 Thomson wrote: "In evening A.J., Ralph & Frank out trying to locate a crossing, eventually successful. Approximately half a mile to the north bank."

Like Cautley, Thomson provided a detailed description of their river crossing the next day.

> We split the string up, each taking about 4 to 5 horses—Ralph took off with a lead horse a little downstream from camp—into slack but fairly deep water, then headed out for centre stream. The rest of us followed suit in turn. As we approached centre stream, it became shallower til we struck a bar. The river water was very milky—carrying a lot of sediment & shall we say had to feel our way. After reaching the centre bar we turned abruptly upstream for perhaps 200 yds [183 metres] or even more, then again turned toward the north shore, through another deep channel to a second bar, repeated the process of following the bar upstream, gradually working toward the north shore. Turning sharply across, what might be considered the deepest channel, we climbed out on to the north shore of Saskatchewan, some distance west of the junction of the North Fork. The whole pack string intact, not a single stray. We were anywhere from 20 minutes to half an hour in making the crossing. At this time of the year, the river is not particularly high—the spring peak has run off. In flood it would be unwise to cross....
>
> We chose two of the steadiest or likely horses. Put one set of instruments & the original set of notes on one. The other carried the 2nd set of instruments & the duplicate set of notes as a safeguard against complete loss. The water reached the side packs at times, but apart from the odd wet bedroll, no damage to food or equipment. The packs were set high—instruments, exposed & unexposed plates, notes, as top packs, well-protected.

The men travelled up the west bank of the North Saskatchewan for about 500 metres, then crossed to the east side. Thomson noted that they were on a historic route used by the indigenous people for hunting. The

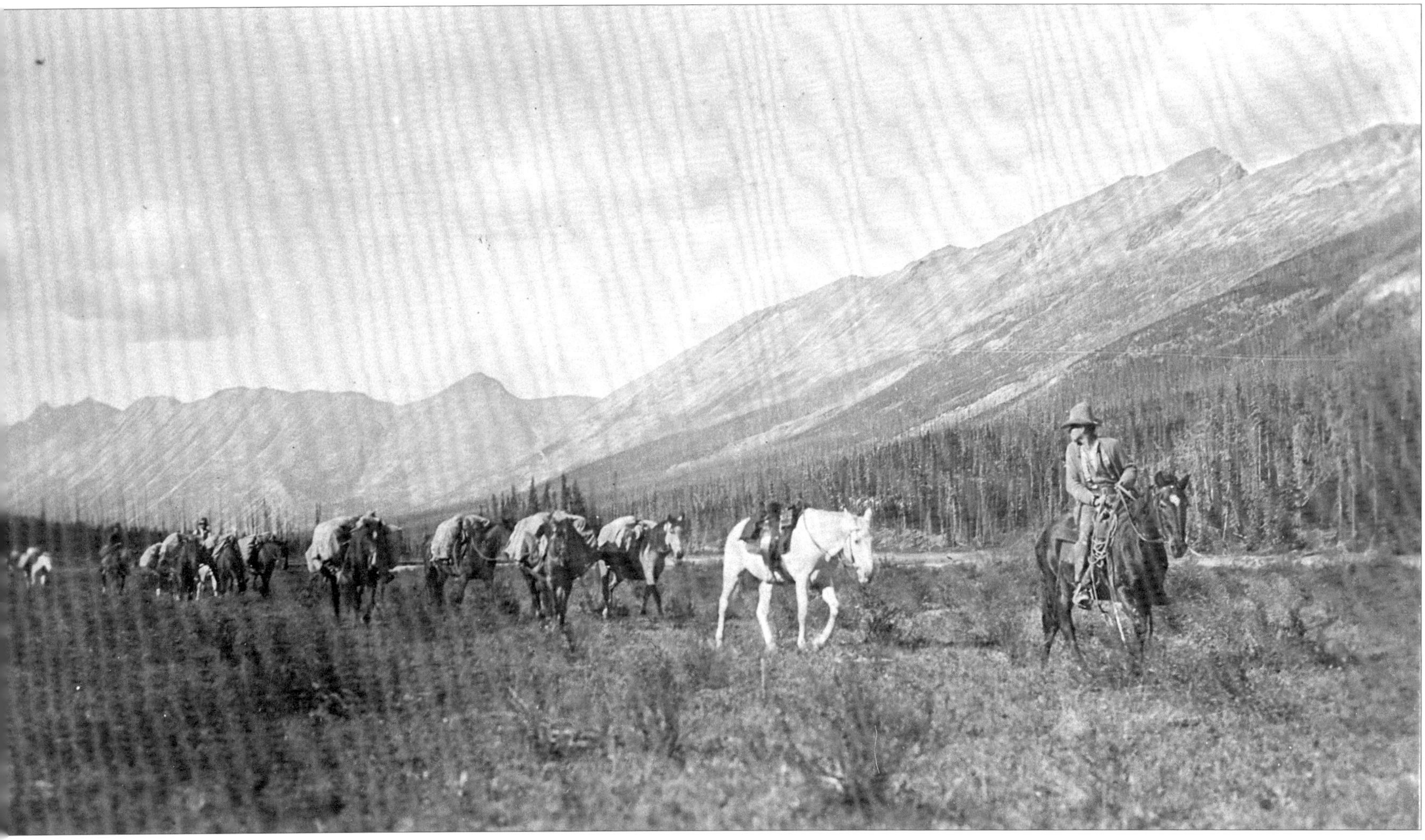

Pack train travelling along the Sunwapta River valley. A10723, Provincial Archives of Alberta

crew proceeded up the North Saskatchewan River, camping that night on the Graveyard Flats across from the confluence of the Alexandra River.

On August 5 the crew continued travelling up the North Saskatchewan, climbed the Big Hill, passed Panther Falls and reached Camp Parker. Their camp was in the timber near Nigel Creek. The route that they followed up the North Saskatchewan was generally similar to the present route of the Icefields Parkway. Thomson noted that Cautley had registered there on August 1. It rained the next morning, so the crew remained in camp and put up the stove. "The gang cut a panel on a spruce tree near the cook tent. I decorated same. Crossed ice axes & coiled rope. Names of party members. A bucking horse or two. Tree was alongside one which the Cautley party had registered." Thomson observed that several other parties had registered at this site over the years.

The men moved to the south side of Wilcox Pass on August 7 and stayed at the same camp Cautley had used. They were just north of Sunwapta Pass, the divide between the North Saskatchewan and Athabasca River watersheds. Thomson noted that a short distance above their camp was a fine view of the Columbia Icefield.

In 1917 the route across the headwaters of the Sunwapta River stayed high to avoid the canyon below the Athabasca Glacier. On August 8 Campbell and the crew crossed Wilcox Pass and then proceeded to Tangle Creek, where the trail dropped steeply to the Sunwapta River. They camped that night on a grassy flat along the riverbank.

As the crew proceeded down the Sunwapta the next day, they encountered a hornet's nest along the trail. Although they spotted it before running into the nest, a couple of horses got stung and took off in different directions. None of the men got stung, and they soon had the horses lined up again. They remained for two days at their next campsite along the river because of rain, and then on August 11 they reached the Athabasca River, another Canadian Heritage River. They camped about seven kilometres down the river.

The following day they continued down the Athabasca, crossed over the bridge at the falls and travelled down to the bridge over the Whirlpool River, camping on the north side below the bridge. On August 13 Wheeler met his crew. Thomson wrote about the day's events. He, Campbell and Weir left ahead of the pack train. Along the route they "came upon an old camp ground with the remains of tepee poles." Thomson continued: "It is possible that this portion of the trail over which we are travelling was once used by the fur brigades on their way up to Athabasca Pass." After about two hours of travelling they "came to a fork in the trail, where Wheeler had placed a sign with instructions to 'keep left' and hit out on a wagon road about ¾ to 1 mile [1.2 to 1.6 kilometres] further on. Down the wagon road a way further another sign directing us to a bridge near which AOW and party were camped." This campsite was near the trail leading up the Astoria River to Mount Edith Cavell. Wheeler was there with his brother-in-law James Macoun (son of botanist John Macoun) and his wife. While Weir took some pictures, Campbell and Thomson remained with Wheeler. Once the pack horses arrived, all of the crew, except for Wheeler and Campbell, left for the Miette River and set up camp at the flat by the bridge. Their camp was only about two kilometres from Jasper, so the men went into town for supper. In the evening Thomson and Campbell played billiards.

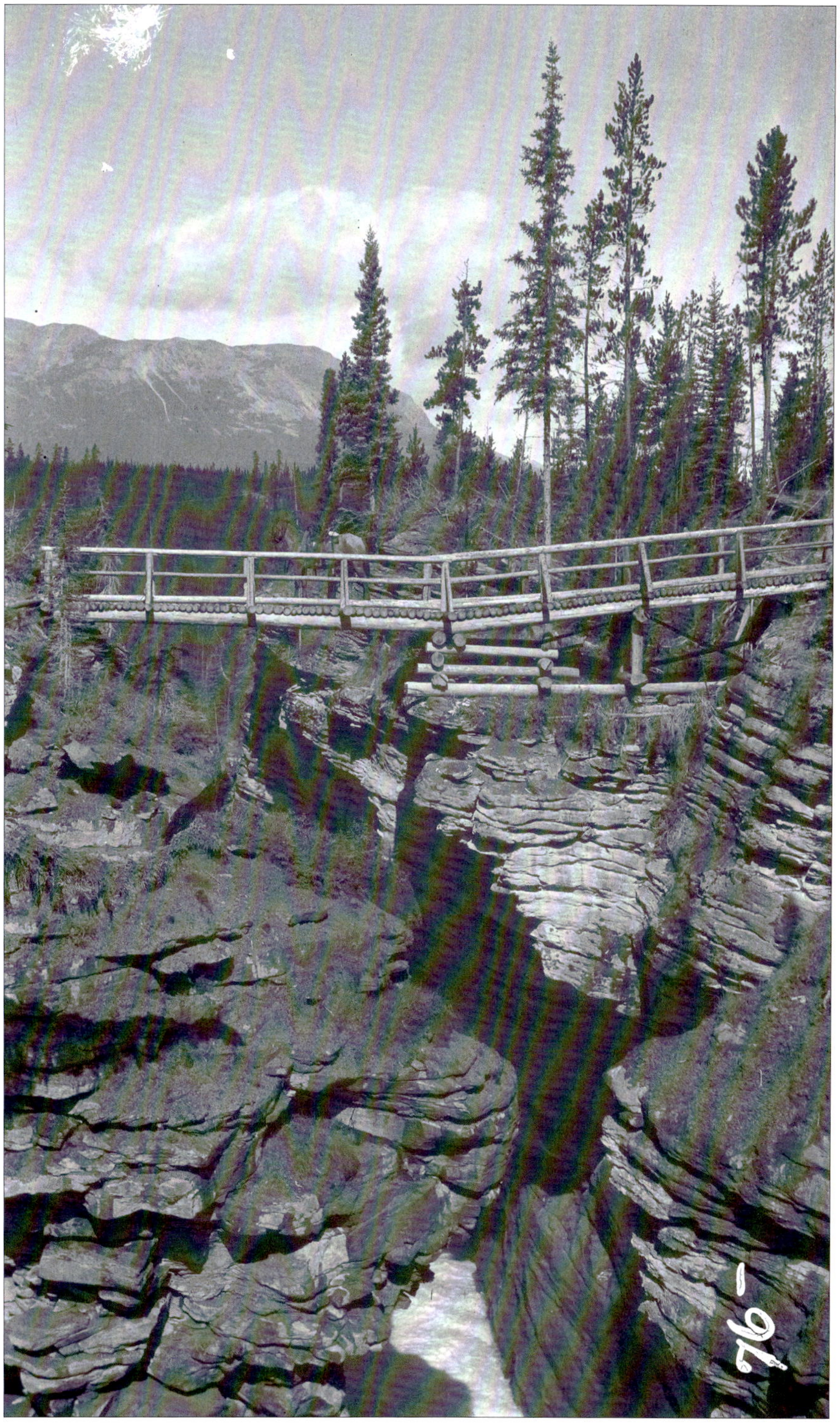

The bridge across the river at Athabasca Falls. e011166488, Library and Archives Canada

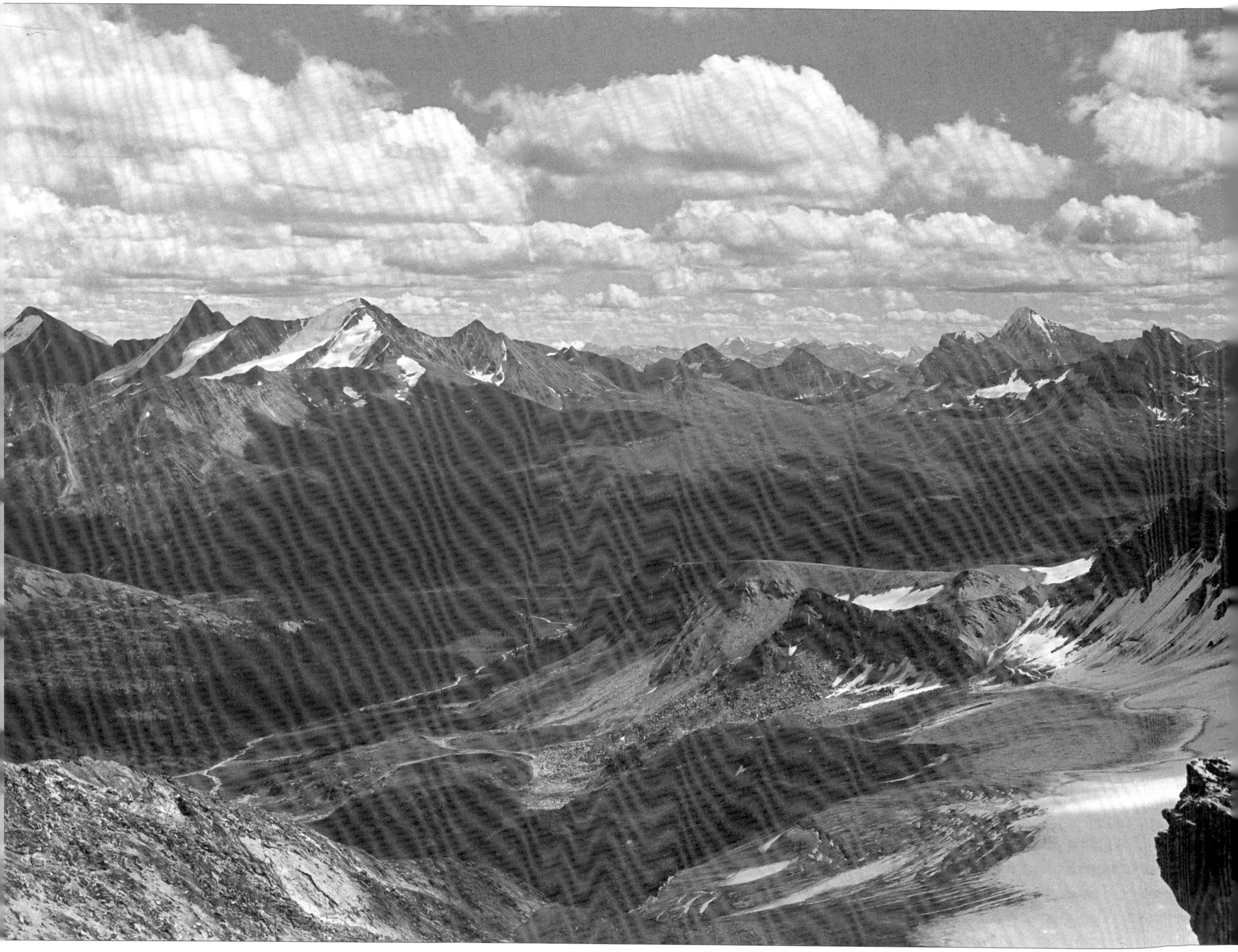

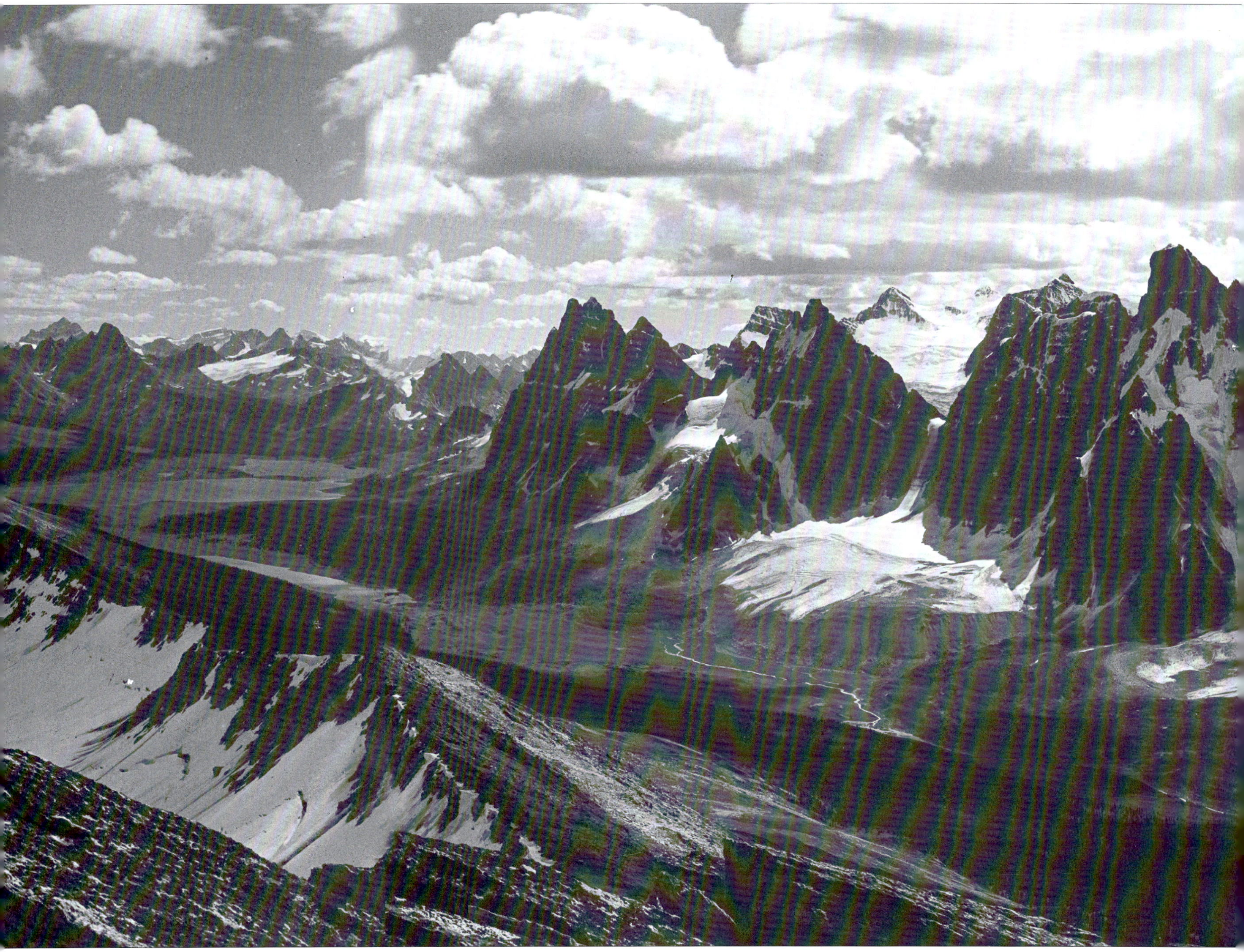

Part of the panorama taken from Vista Peak at the southern end of Yellowhead Pass, these two views look into the Tonquin valley.
e011183815 and e011183816, Library and Archives Canada

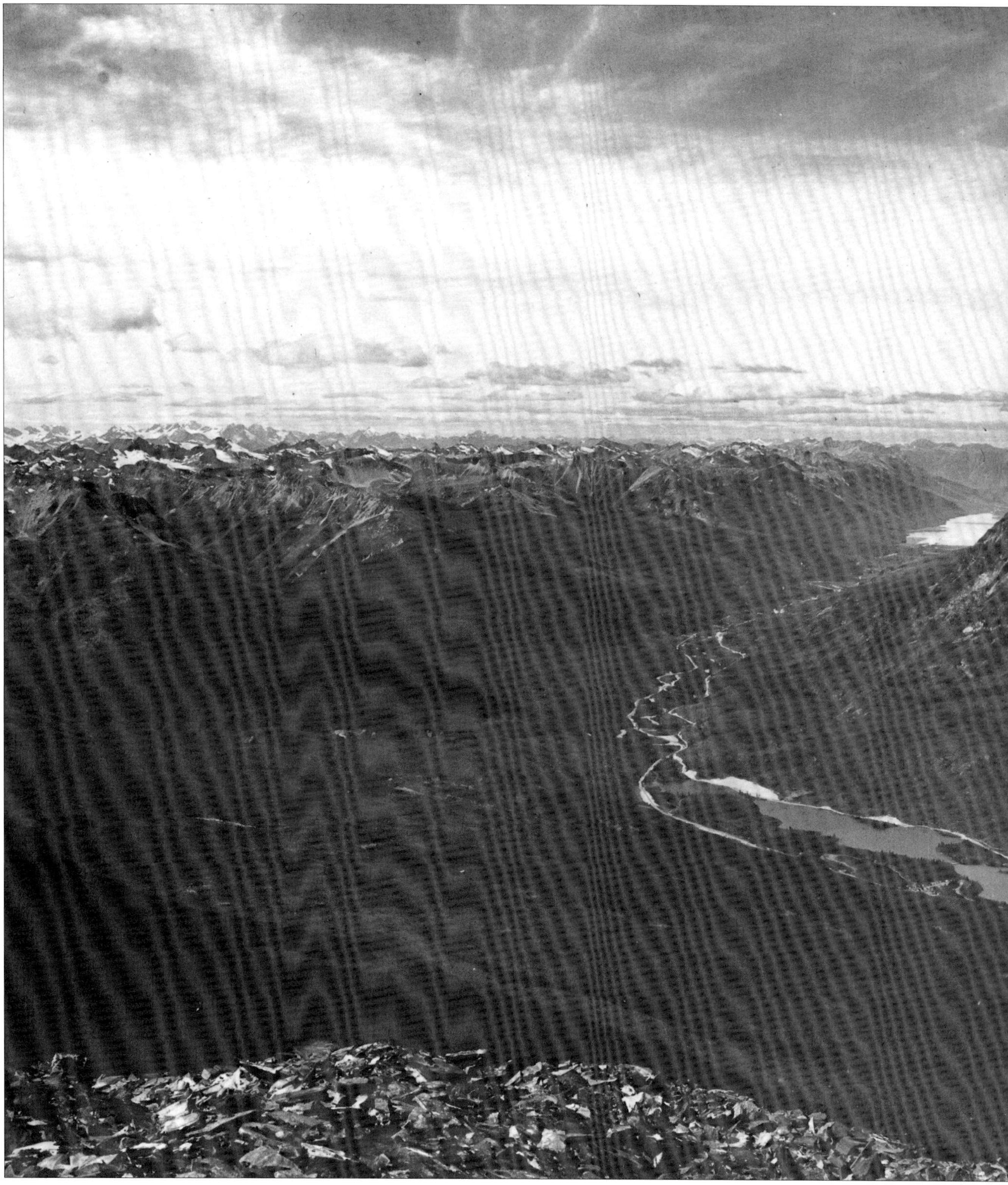

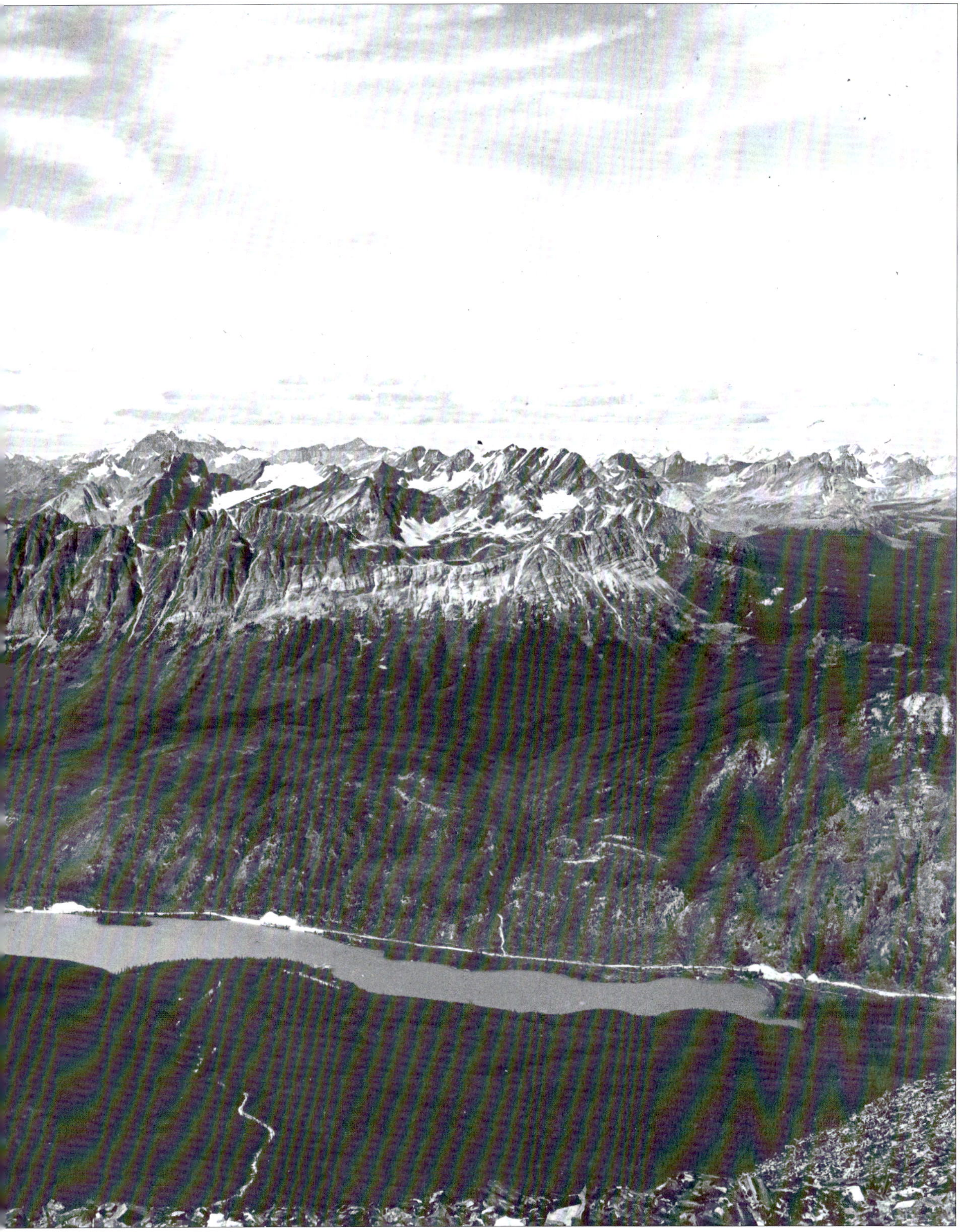

From Mount Fitzwilliam these photographs provide a view of Yellowhead Lake, Yellowhead Mountain behind it, the Fraser River below the outlet of the lake, and Moose Lake in the distance. The Grand Trunk Pacific rail line is visible on the north side of Yellowhead Lake, and both rail lines can be seen traversing the area below the lake outlet. e011183817 and e011183818, Library and Archives Canada.

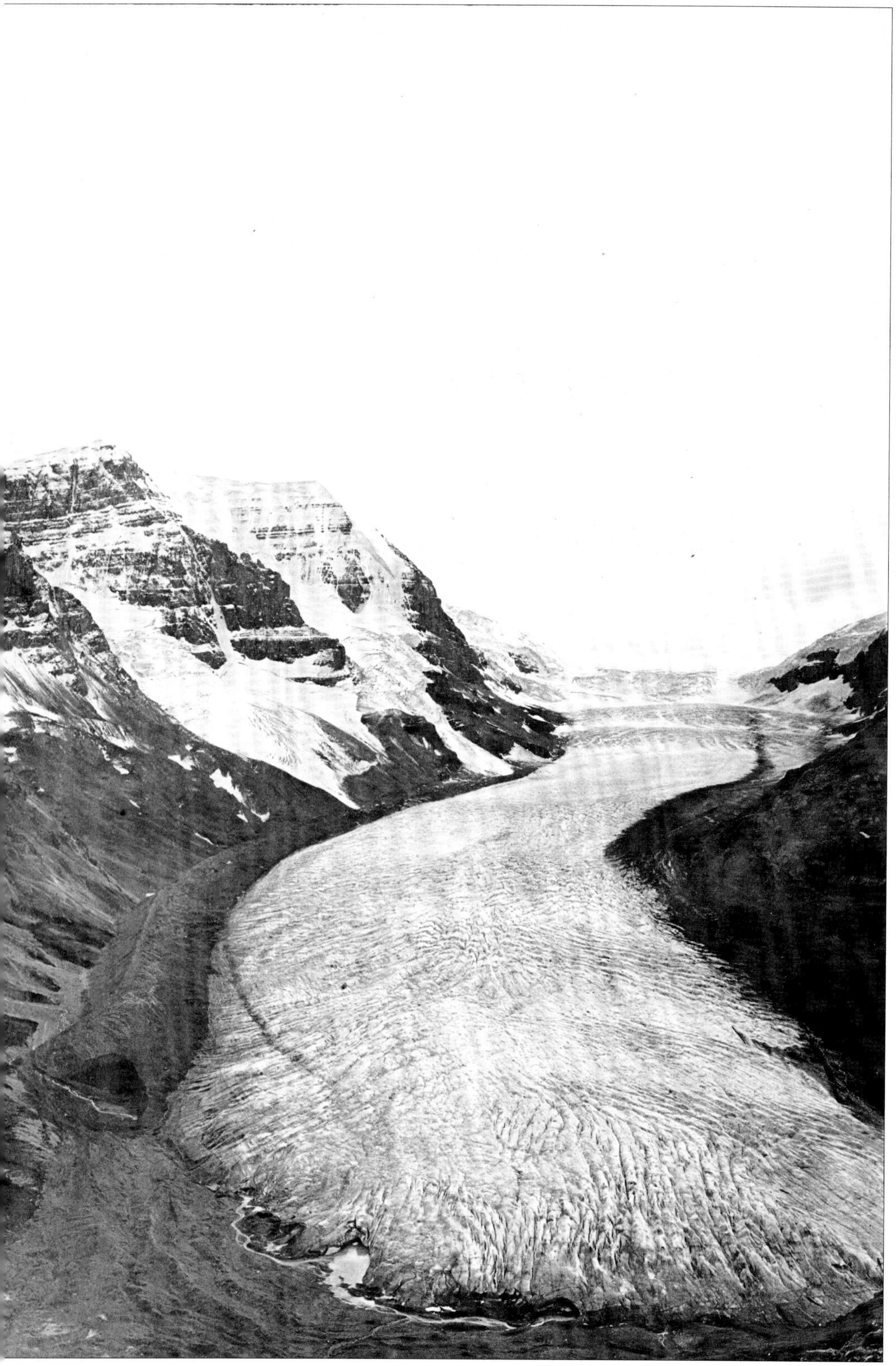

lowhead Mountain. There was snow throughout the day, with some sticking on the ground. Wheeler didn't anticipate the cold weather and had not brought the small folding stoves. Snowy weather kept the men in camp the next day.

On September 4 the surveying resumed, with Campbell and Weir doing one station, while Wheeler and Thomson surveyed a second one. The crew surveyed two stations the next day, working with the same partners.

Wheeler left for Cautley's camp on September 6. In his diary wrote: "Got Cautley's note—followed blazes till met his party. Cautley moved his camp to about a mile from ours—spent half a day with him. Moved back to camp at watershed E. end Yellowhead Mt." This was their August 30 camp. There was fog all of the next day, but after lunch Wheeler "went out on the line with Cautley," he wrote. "We did not get line far enough to decide number of bolts." The rest of the men stayed in camp.

Surveying resumed on September 8. Wheeler and Cautley fixed the position of monuments at the northern end of the pass, while Campbell, Thomson and Weir surveyed from Bolts 32S and 34S on the watershed summit of Yellowhead Bluff. The next day was Thomson's 30th birthday. Wheeler gave him an ice axe for a present, and the two men surveyed at Yellowhead Pass. Thomson wrote:

> AOW & I left camp about 9am. We took two horses, Bud & Roy. Put our instruments on Roy. We dropped into Cautley's camp on the way down for a short stay, then continued on down to the track, [and] left the horses in the corral at the old construction camp. We arrived at the bridge near the Miette about 11:30am. Ate lunch on the creek, then climbed up the hill & occupied Yellowhead Pass East target station, arriving about 12:30pm. The station situated on a bluff between 400 to 500 feet [122

Wheeler took this photograph of the Columbia Icefield from the Wilcox Pass area. The Mountain Legacy picture shows the extent of recession, both in length and thickness of the glacier during the past century. There is also evidence of the considerable human impact on the area. WHE1918282, Library and Archives Canada

to 152 metres] above the track. We took some exposures, not a complete panorama. We were on sidehill. Left about 4pm. We then went down and read azimuths at the Cautley picket in the pass.

They stayed that evening at Cautley's former camp in Yellowhead Pass. The next day Rink moved the main camp down to Dominion Prairie while Wheeler and his crew went on a fly camp to survey the final bolts on the south side of the pass. Wheeler chose the location for Bolts 33S, 35S and 37S. Bolt 37S on Miette Hill was a station established by Bridgland during his 1915 phototopographic survey around Jasper. During the next two days the British Columbia crew surveyed from these stations and rebuilt Bridgland's cairn. Wheeler also established a camera station at a lower elevation that provided a good view of the amphitheatre between Mount Fitzwilliam and Mount Kataka. After completing their work the men walked down the abandoned Grand Trunk railway line to Dominion Prairie.

On September 13 Wheeler finished odds and ends and paid off Thomson and Weir. The next day the rest of the crew returned to Jasper.

To finish the field season, Wheeler, Campbell, the cook, Tom Martin, and the two packers travelled with the horses back to Banff. On September 14 they went to Jasper, and at noon on the next day they departed south. By September 18 the men were on the upper part of the Sunwapta River. Wheeler recorded that it was a glorious day with fall colours on the foliage. "Camped in sight of snow-caps surrounding Wilcox Pass at 2:25 pm. Nice campground on side of gravel flat. Went back half a mile & took three views with survey camera." The next day they "went up Tangle Creek, made Sheep Camp at about 11:30, continued over Wilcox Pass. At summit of pass got camera and went west to heights above Sunwapta. Took nine views of surrounding peaks and glacier to west. Should be good." They camped south of Wilcox Pass and remained there the next day. In the afternoon Wheeler went to Athabasca Glacier to take some pictures. This trip was one of

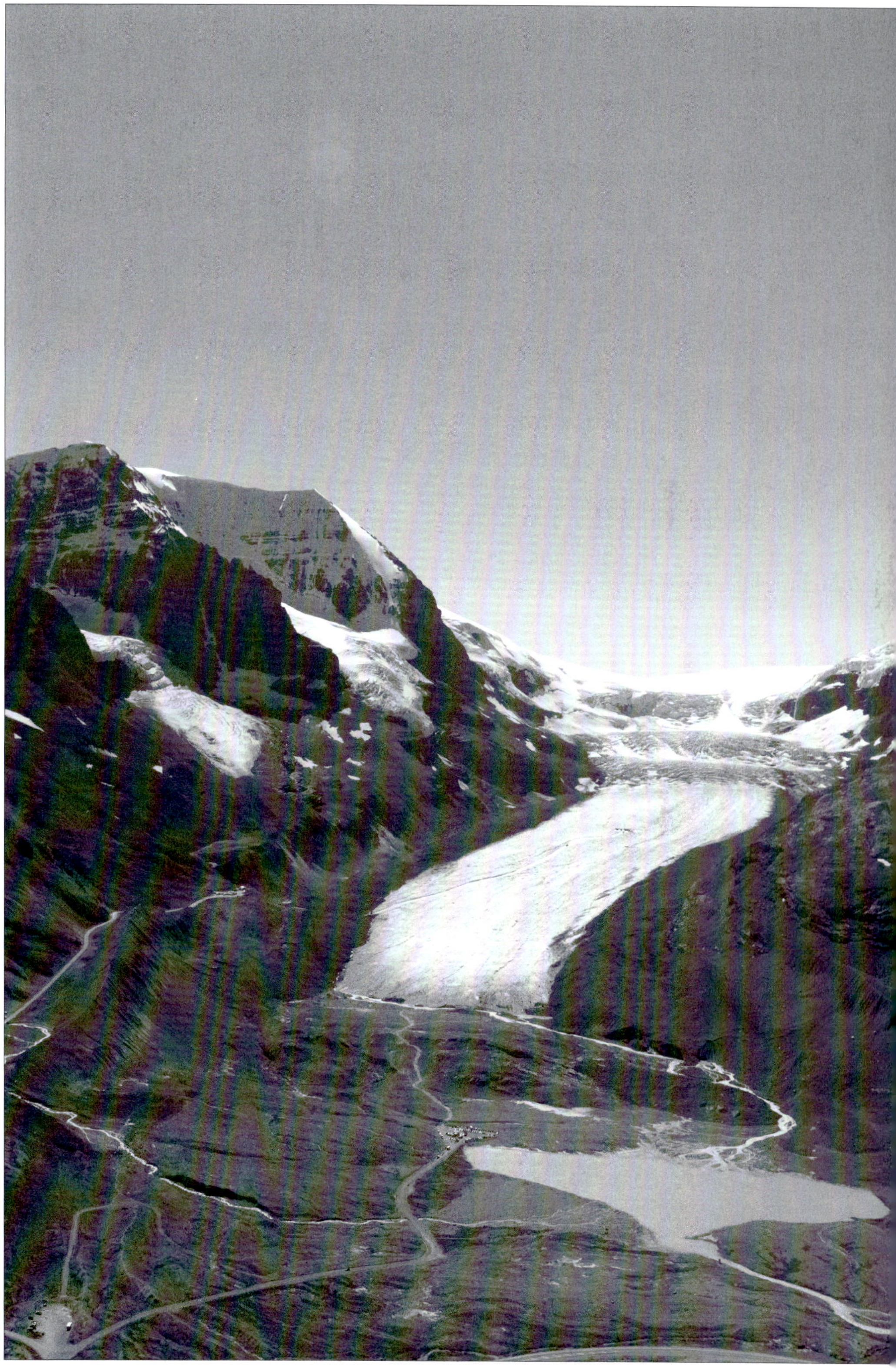

Courtesy Mountain Legacy Project MLP2011_282

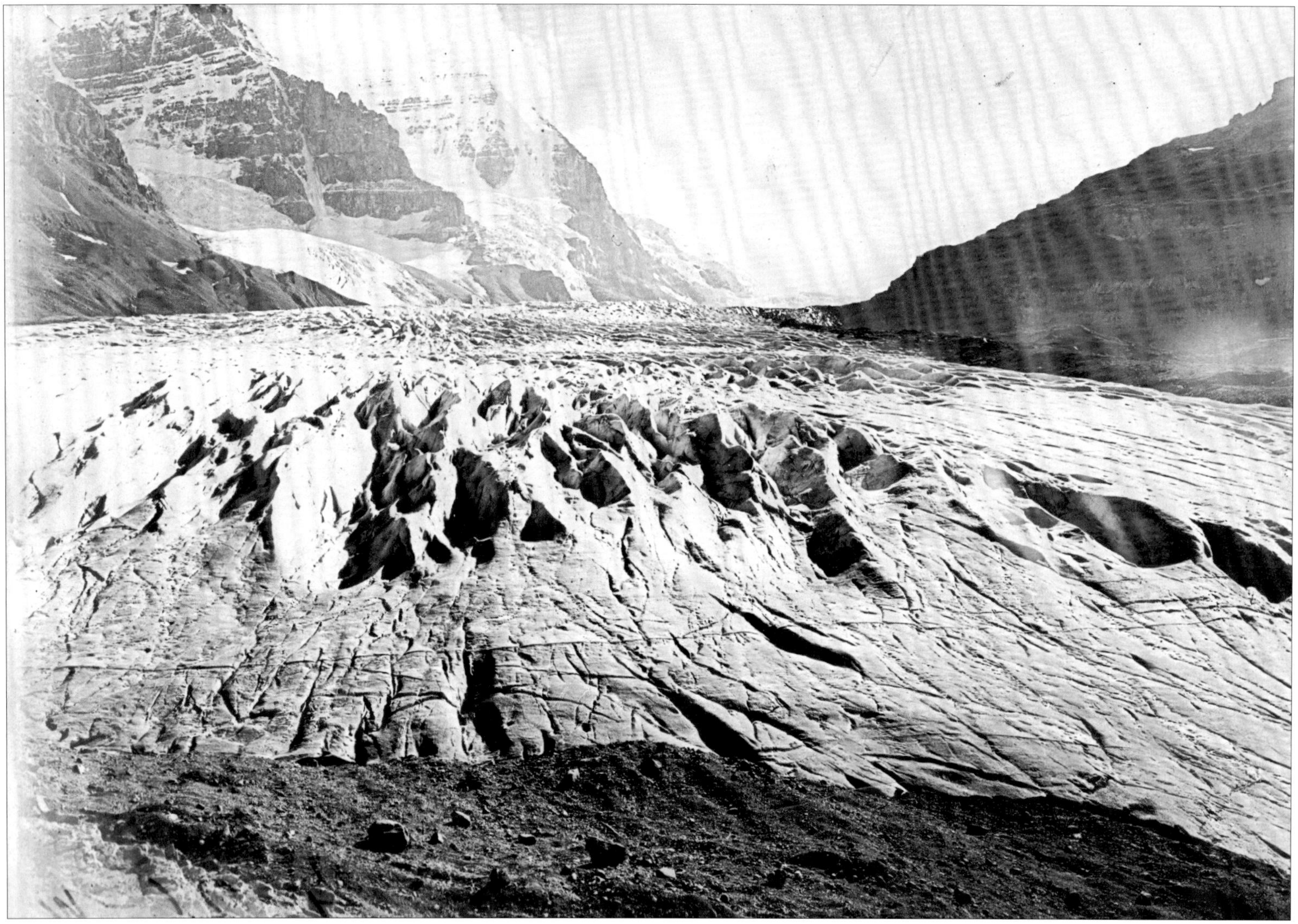

Wheeler also took a photograph from the toe of the Columbia Icefield. This location is north of Highway 93, providing an indication of how far the glacier has retreated. WHE1918291, Library and Archives Canada

the few occasions when Wheeler used the phototopographic camera to take pictures that did not directly pertain to the survey.

The beginning of fall was sunny. Wheeler wrote: "Traveled all day in magnificent scenery. Mt. Athabasca in view for a long time. Passed Panther Falls. Steep descent to gravel flats on main flow of Saskatchewan River—here flowing from splendid glacier. Hillside covered by yellow poplar brush a scene of yellow glory—browns, reds. Passed Graveyard camp." The next day they travelled down the North Saskatchewan to the mouth of the Mistaya. At this time of year the water level was low in the rivers, so the crossings were easy. On September 23 they followed up the Mistaya, camping about 10 kilometres above Waterfowl Lake.

The next day Campbell and Wheeler left for Bow Pass ahead of Rink and Wallis. In a short time they passed a Dominion government Parks and Forestry trail crew who were upgrading the route up to Bow Pass for more effective fire patrol. They turned the

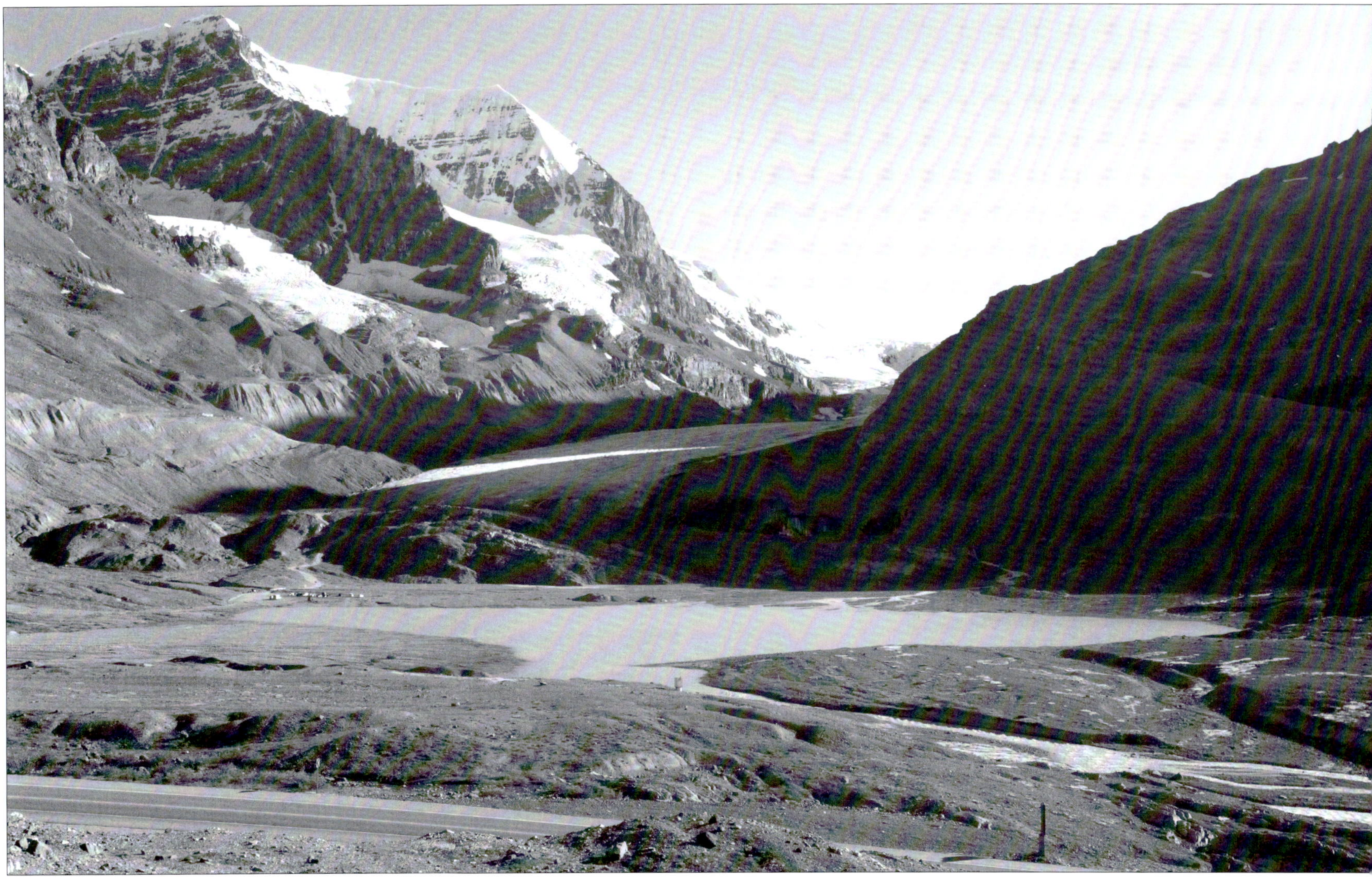

Courtesey Mountain Legacy Project MLP2011_291

horses loose, had lunch and began the ascent of Observation Peak. Wheeler wanted a station near Bow Pass where he could connect with his Railway Belt survey and the stations around Howse Pass. This would enable him to cover the area along the divide between Kicking Horse Pass and Howse Pass on both sides of the boundary. While the men were surveying, Rink and Wallis went to Bow Summit and set up camp. On the morning of September 26 they reached Lake Louise. Campbell, Wheeler and Martin took the train to Banff. Rink and Wallis began travelling to Banff with the horses, arriving the next day. The crew was fortunate to have good weather for almost their entire trip. In his government report Wheeler speculated about the future of this route. "It does not seem impossible that a good road could be constructed from steel to steel that would furnish a route over which the mountain scenic splendours, and they are truly wonderful, would attract crowds of tourists and thus be the source of very considerable revenue to the country when the time is ripe."

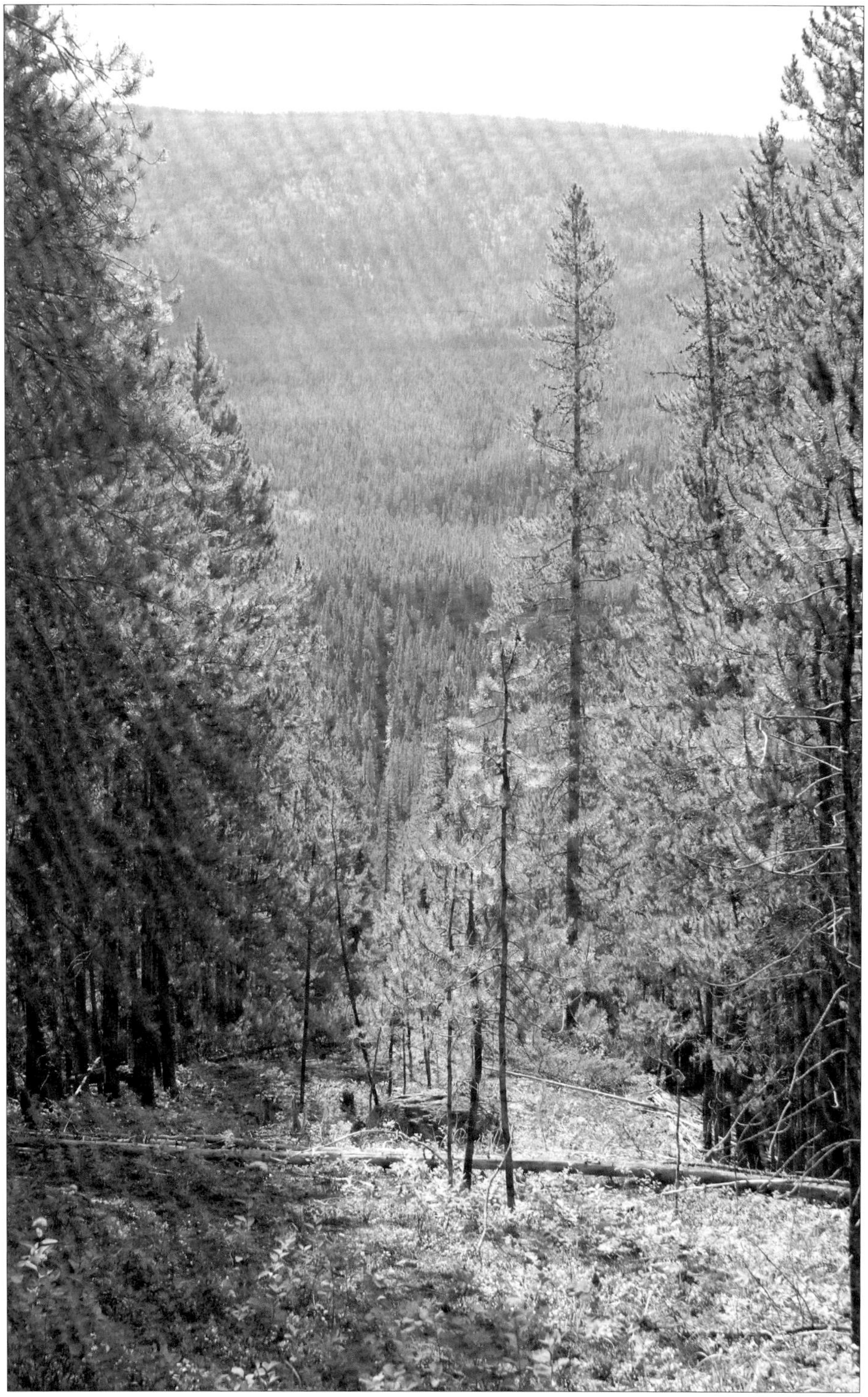

This picture shows the cut line of the boundary through Yellowhead Pass. Although faint in most places, it is visible and can be followed through the pass. Jay Sherwood photo

Cautley completed his surveying at Yellowhead Pass on October 18, establishing 32 monuments and five brass bolts. In addition to the five brass bolts, Wheeler's crew surveyed at five stations in the vicinity of the pass, three south toward Tonquin Pass and eight north of Yellowhead Pass. They mapped the pass, along with the boundary, for about 15 kilometres both to the south and north. Yellowhead was the most extensive pass on the Alberta-BC boundary survey except for Crowsnest. The boundary commission report noted that the boundary followed a very erratic course through the pass, with the direct distance being about 13 kilometres while the boundary line was about 18. The pass is at a low elevation, 1,131 metres, and the cement and gravel needed for 15 of the monuments had to be packed up more than 750 metres in elevation. Almost all of the boundary through the pass is below timberline, which necessitated extensive cutting of the boundary line. Wheeler wrote in his government report: "The country is little traveled over by prospectors and hunters and pack trails had to be opened up to give access to the various stations occupied, entailing a considerable expenditure of time."

While surveying in the pass, Cautley made one of his few connections with a BC survey. He did not anticipate tying into this survey, so he did not have the survey notes or plan. Cautley wrote to the BC surveyor general requesting these documents and any information from the surveyor, Maitland Lockhart Gordon, BCLS #18. The surveyor general sent the documents along with this note: "I regret to say that the surveyor of this lot, Mr. Gordon, BCLS, has been killed while serving in his Majesty's Forces." It was a reminder of the impact of World War I on the BC land surveyors, who had 24 men killed during the conflict.

In the 1917 field season Wheeler and Cautley surveyed the two main passes along the Great Divide from the Lake Louise to Jasper area, and they made the lengthy journey from Howse Pass to Yellowhead Pass, following a route similar to today's Icefields Parkway.

During its first five years, the Alberta–British Columbia boundary survey covered the southern part of the Great Divide. Despite the rugged terrain, financial restraints caused by World War I, and shortage of qualified personnel, A.O. Wheeler, R.W. Cautley

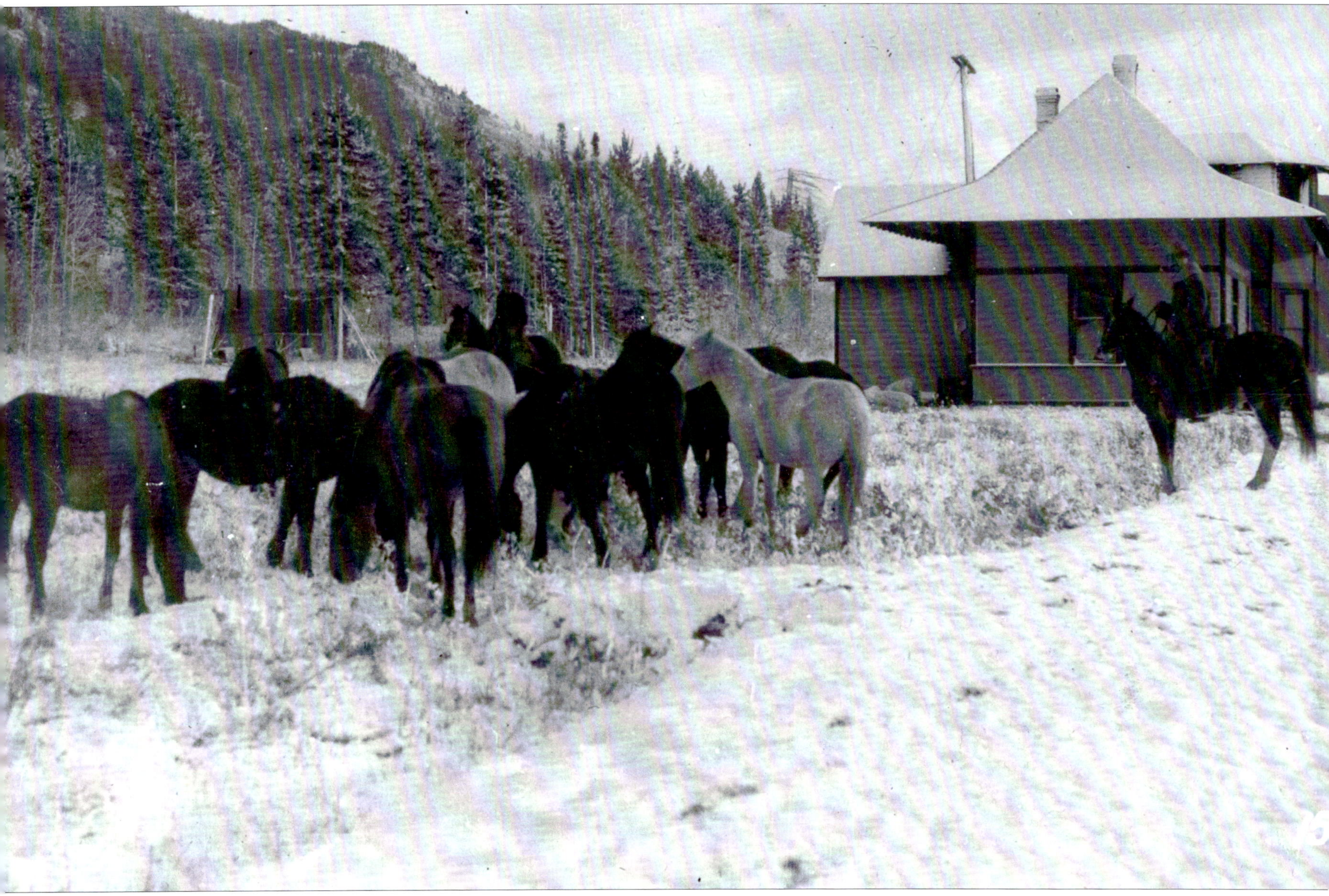

Cautley anticipated that he would begin surveying the 120th meridian in 1918, so he wintered his horses with the Otto brothers in Jasper. Cautley wrote: "Horses leaving Lucerne for Jasper to winter 19th October 1917." J-00872, Royal BC Museum and Archives

and their assistants succeeded in producing an accurate survey and maintaining the project during these five difficult years. The boundary survey delineated the major passes with concrete monuments (many of them still existing today); produced the first continuous detailed maps of the Rocky Mountains; and compiled a record of about 2,000 photographs that show the landscape at the time and can be used for comparative purposes today.

In the second part of the boundary survey, from 1918 to 1924, Wheeler would continue to survey the Great Divide while Cautley would primarily delineate the 120th meridian from the Great Divide through the Peace River region.

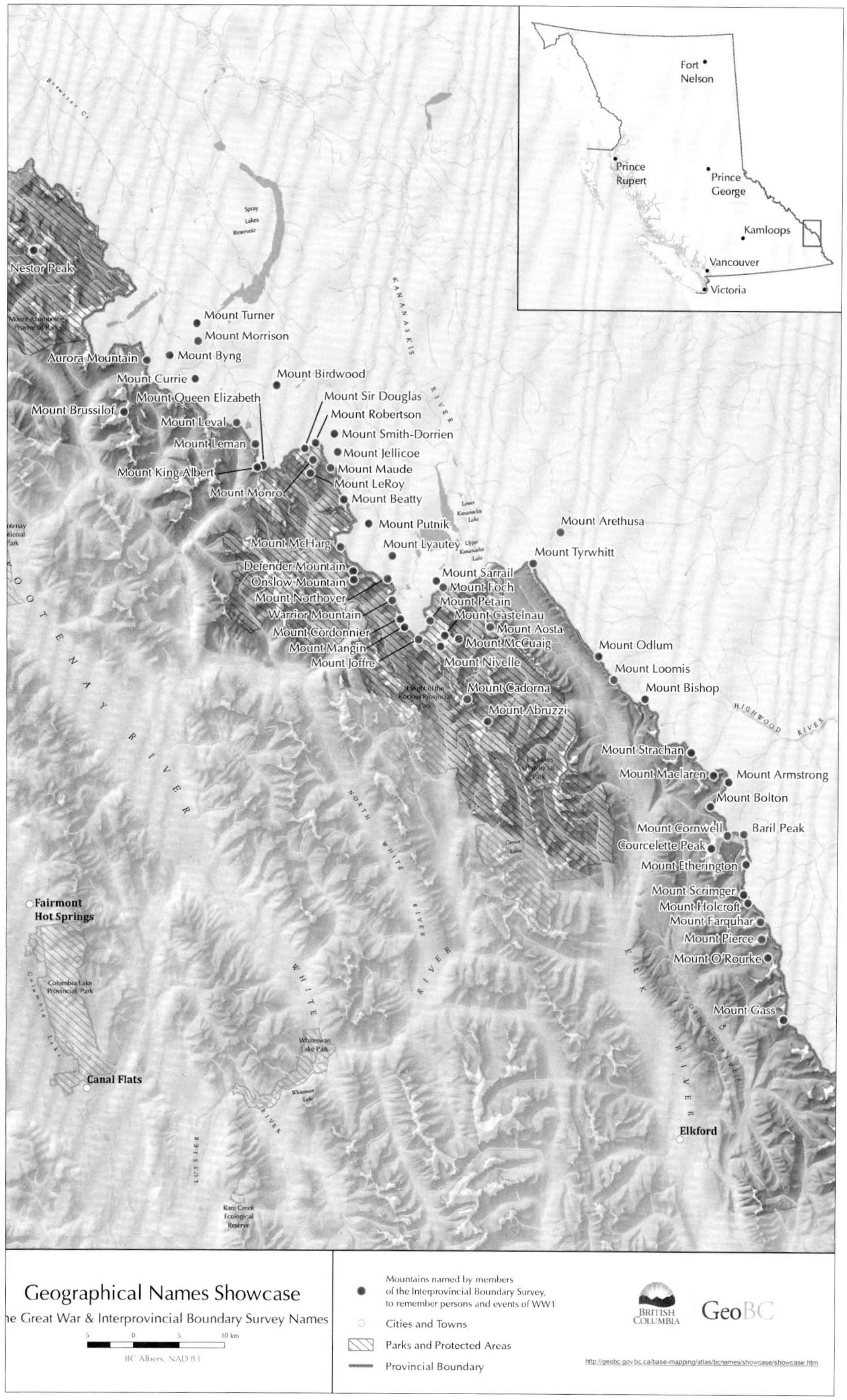

The Geographical Names Department of the BC government produced this map of mountains named by the Alberta–British Columbia boundary survey that recognize people and events of World War I. There are additional features like waterways that also have a World War I connection. In 1917 the Geographic Board of Canada designated the section of the Great Divide between Bow Valley and Crowsnest Pass for commemorative war names. The map shows how extensively the war influenced the naming of the landscape along the Great Divide. The Great War & Interprovincial Boundary Survey Names. Map produced by BC Geographic Names Department.

Geographical Names

Since A.O. Wheeler did the topography for the Alberta-BC boundary survey, he also had the opportunity to name the geographic features along the Great Divide.

Wheeler subscribed to the "empty land" theory regarding the geographical features in the area he was surveying. Since very few of them had official names, Wheeler believed that his position as BC commissioner and his survey work along the divide gave him the right to name the features he mapped. Although the names had to be officially approved by the Geographic Board of Canada, it generally accepted Wheeler's recommendations.

Wheeler seldom consulted anyone about naming the geographical features, and he ignored the principle of naming peaks to reflect the natural or human history of the area. As previously noted, Paul Wallace described how Wheeler arbitrarily gave Egyptian-related names to an area between Vermilion and Simpson Passes. Unlike 19th-century scientists and explorers, Wheeler and his survey party rarely met indigenous people who could provide names for the features of the Rocky Mountains, but he made no effort to consult them when making his maps.

The boundary survey occurred throughout World War I, and in patriotic fervour, many of the geographic names Wheeler gave were related to the conflict. Several of them had no direct connection with Canada's involvement in the war. The first large set of World War I names approved by the Geographic Board of Canada started in December 1916 and continued through 1918, with a few additional names in the following years. Most of the features named by Wheeler are located between Crowsnest Pass and White Man Pass, with the largest concentration in the vicinity of the Kananaskis lakes / Elk Pass area. In *Canmore & Kananaskis History Explorer*, Ernie Lakusta notes that Wheeler named 38 of the 44 mountains in Peter Lougheed Provincial Park, which is located in the upper Kananaskis valley.

In 1916 Wheeler and the BC crew surveyed many of the mountains from the area south of Elk Pass to White Man Pass. This was the same year that the Battle of Jutland, a large naval battle, occurred. Lakusta notes that Wheeler named over 25 features in the Kananaskis area for ships and personnel involved in this battle.

In some locations Wheeler named a group of mountains using a specific theme. In the boundary commissioner's report, Wheeler described the area west of Elk Pass and the naming he used. "Within the above described area of high mountains, wide glaciers and deep forested valleys bounded by Elk Pass and River, Mt. Joffre and the flanking icefields and the Upper Kananaskis River and Lake, are many striking peaks, five of which are over 10,000 feet [3,048 metres] and two over 9,900 feet [3,018 metres] in altitude: they are all dominated by the great peak named Mt. Joffre and have been given the names of distinguished generals who have rendered such names immortal through their splendid services to France in the great world war now in progress." Marshal Foch and General Mangin are some of the other French commanders who have mountains named for them.

Features commemorating other Allied commanders include Mount Brussilof and Brussilof Creek, named for the famous Russian general. Around Upper Elk Lake, Wheeler named some features that he surveyed in 1916 for Italian military commanders. Mount Putnik is named in recognition of a Serbian commander.

The British Military Group is farther north, from South Kananaskis Pass to the Palliser Pass area. The highest peak in this group, at 3,406 metres, is Mount Sir Douglas, named for Field Marshal Sir Douglas Haig. Wheeler wrote that "others not quite so lofty have been named after commanders in the British navy and army who have made for themselves great war records in the service of the Empire." Among these peaks are Mount Jellicoe, named for Admiral Lord Jellicoe; Mount French, named for Field Marshal J.D.P. French;

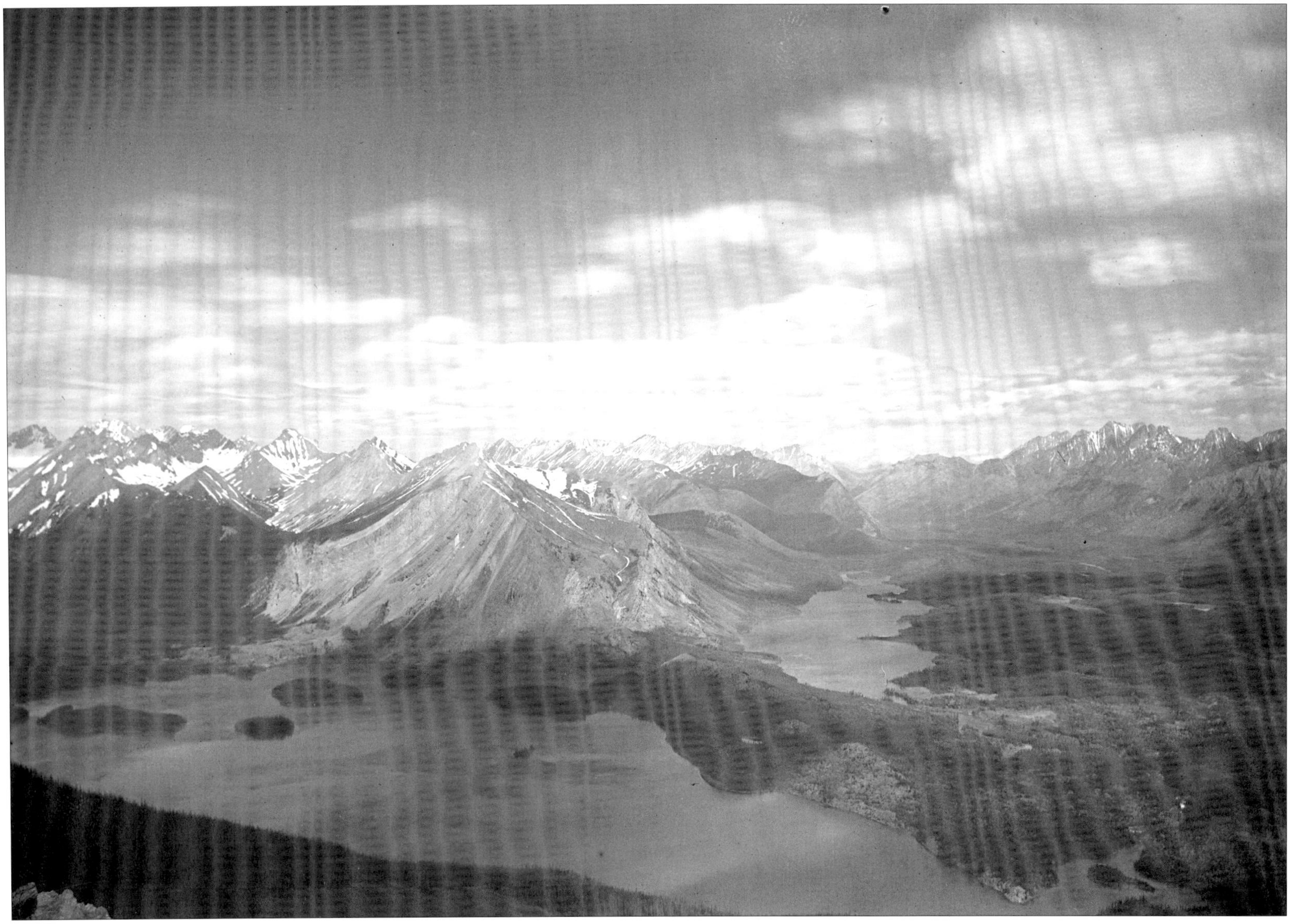

In 1914, as part of the initial survey of Elk Pass, A.J. Campbell took this photograph of Upper Kananaskis Lake. Wheeler named five islands in Upper Kananaskis Lake for British naval ships sunk in 1914. The sixth was named Schooner. WHE1914_6, Library and Archives Canada

and Mount Beatty, recognizing the British admiral Sir David Beatty. The BC Boundary Commission made the first recorded climb of this mountain.

Wheeler named some mountains for people with obtuse connections to Canada. Mount Smuts, named for J.C. Smuts, commander of British troops in Africa during World War I; Mount Allenby, recognizing Field Marshal Viscount Allenby, commander of the British Army in Palestine; and Mount Murray, commemorating the commander of British forces in Egypt in 1916 and 1917, are good examples.

South of Elk Pass, Wheeler named several peaks in the Highwood Pass range for British admirals and ships involved in the Battle of Jutland. Several peaks in the Smith-Dorrien drainage northwest of the Kananaskis lakes are named for Royal Navy battleships.

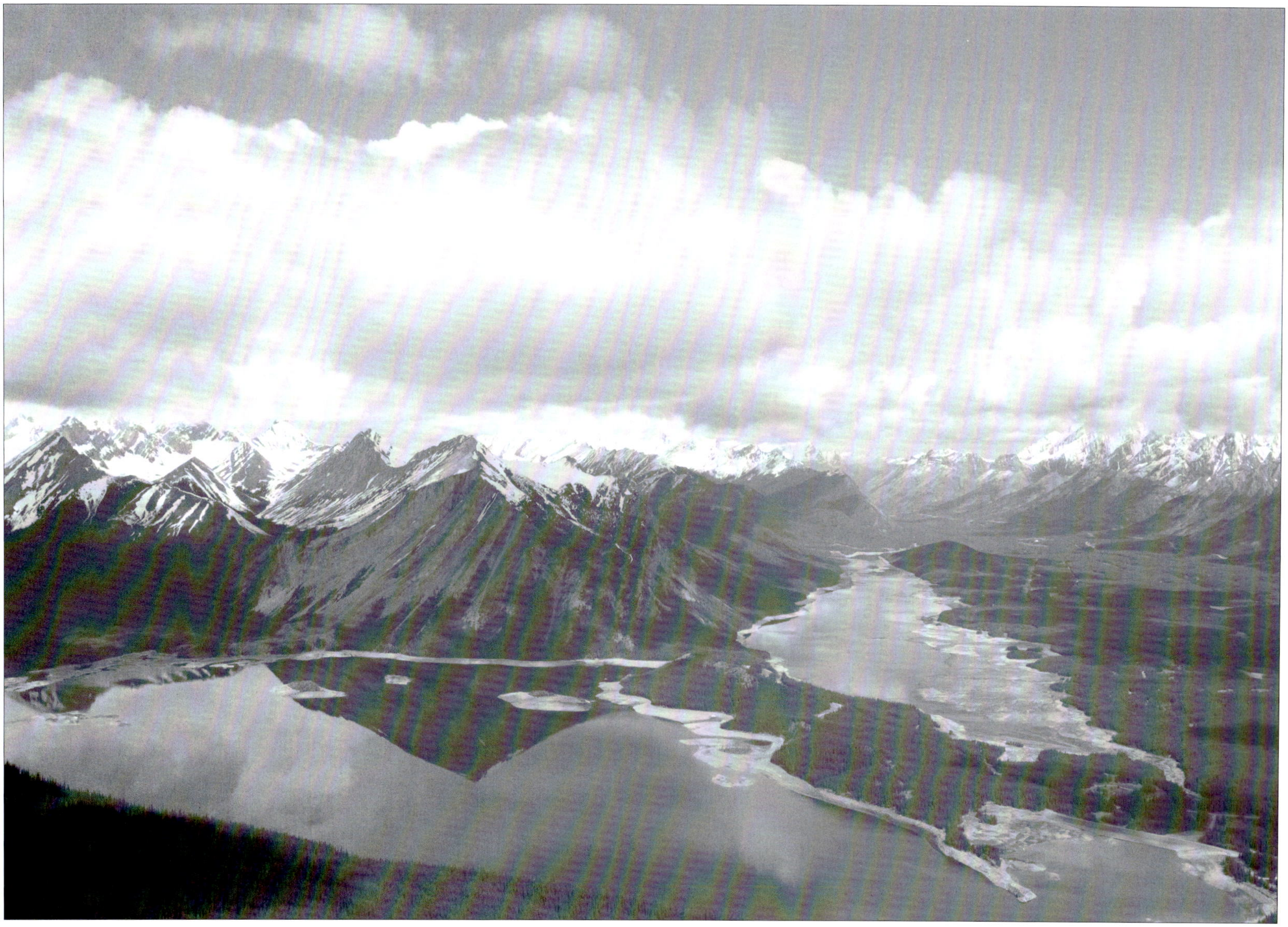

The landscape around Upper Kananaskis Lake has changed dramatically in the past century. In the early 1930s Calgary Power constructed an initial dam that raised the level of the lake, and another larger one in the early 1940s. This submerged all but the tops of a few islands. The dam has also had an impact on Lower Kananaskis Lake. Local rancher and guide George Pocaterra wrote that these lakes were "completely spoiled by the power dams, and the drowning of the marvellously beautiful islands." MLP2007_W14-6, Mountain Legacy Project

Some Canadian commanders are recognized with peaks like Mount Currie (General Arthur Currie), Mount Byng (Lord Julian Byng), Mount Burstall (Henry Burstall), Mount Loomis (F.V.W. Loomis, commander of the Western Canadian Infantry Brigade), Mount Farquhar (F.D. Farquhar, commander of the Princess Patricia's Light Infantry, who died during the war) and Mount McHarg (W. Hart-McHarg, lieutenant colonel of the First BC Regiment, killed in the war).

There are features named for battles or towns near locations where Canadian troops were in combat during the war. Examples include: La Coulotte Peak, St. Eloi Mountain and St. Eloi Brook, Courcelette Peak, Langemarck Mountain and Gravenstafel Ridge.

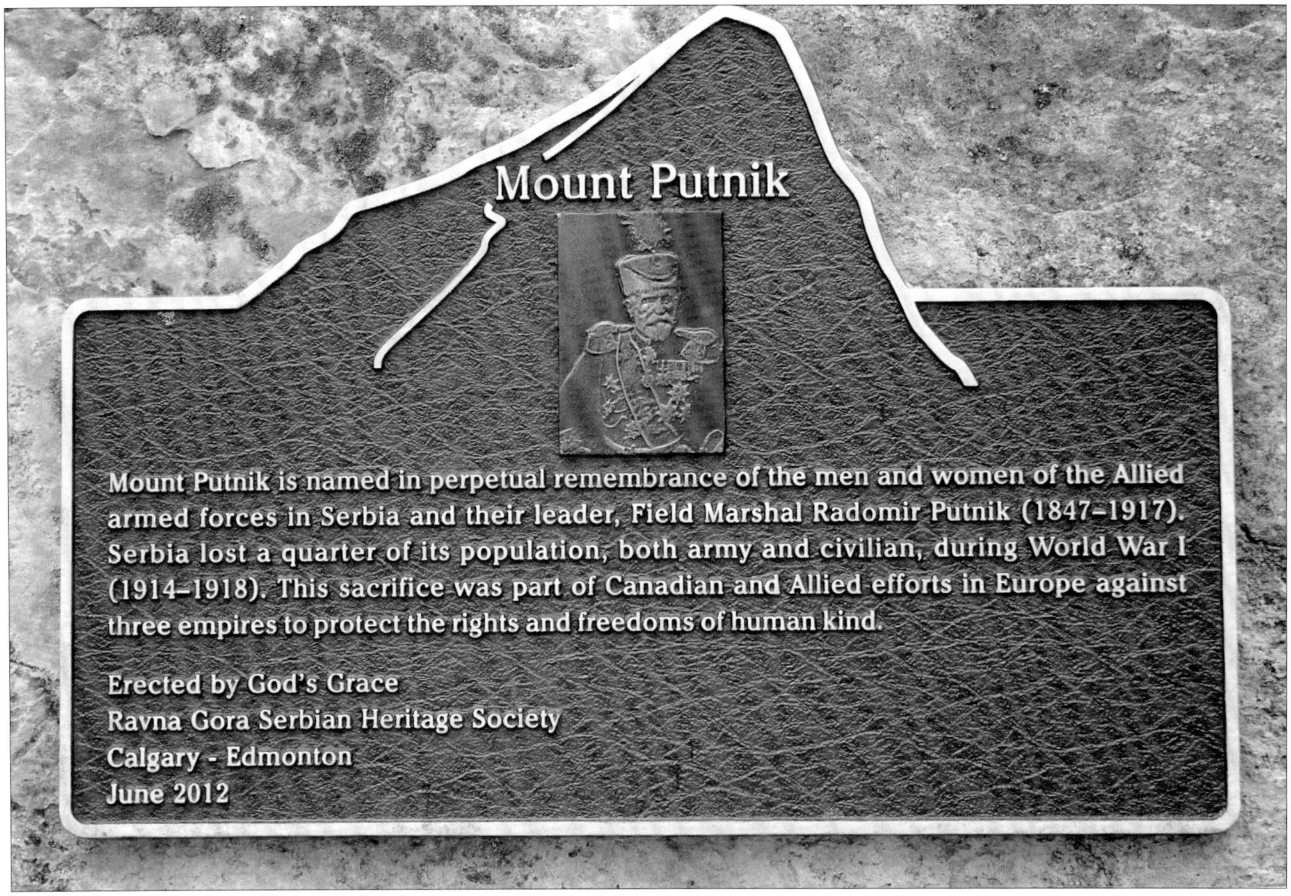

This commemorative plaque at Upper Kananaskis Lake recognizes Field Marshal Radomir Putnik and the Allied forces in Serbia. The outline of the mountain is above its name. Photo Jay Sherwood

Festubert Mountain is named for a village where Canadian troops fought in 1915. This mountain is just north of Akamina Pass, where Wheeler surveyed during that year, and is the southernmost geographic feature along the Great Divide that has a World War I connection.

Most of the soldiers from British Columbia and Alberta who won Victoria Cross medals have features near the Great Divide named for them, such as Mount Northover, Mount Strachan, Mount Scrimger and Mount O'Rourke. The famous Canadian airman Billy Bishop has Mount Bishop named for him. In addition to Cautley's assistant, W.M. Carthew, other people in the field of surveying who died during World War I have features named for them. Baril Peak, Mount Bolton, Mount Holcroft and Mount Armstrong commemorate members of the federal surveyor general's staff killed during the war, while Mount Gass is named for a Dominion land surveyor who died in combat.

The Royal Group, a cluster of high peaks on the west side of the Palliser River valley, includes Mount King George and Mount Queen Mary, named for King George V of England and his wife, and peaks named for each of their children. In the boundary commissioner's report Wheeler described this group.

> Directly west across the [Palliser] valley, which it flanks, is a very remarkable group of mountains comprising seven distinct peaks, the highest having an altitude of 11,226 feet [3,422 metres]; it is much in evidence, and its towers

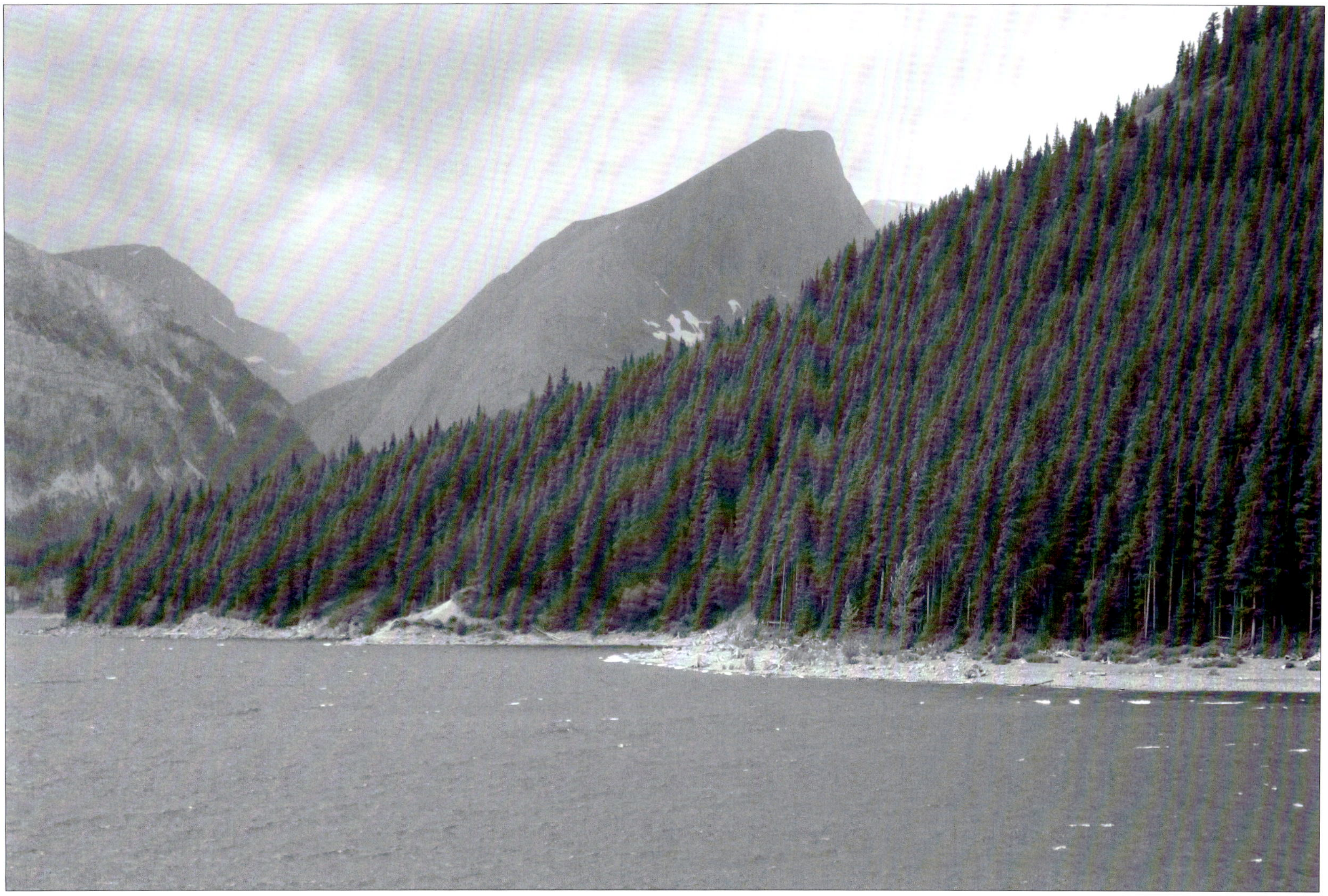

Mount Putnik is situated south of Upper Kananaskis Lake. Photo Jay Sherwood

and precipitous walls, its glaciers and outlying ridges dominate the landscape from all directions. It was first noticed in 1913 by the Topographical division from Wonder Peak, close to Mt. Assiniboine, and the name of "Mt. King George" was then given to the highest summit. The Commissioners now suggest that the title of "The Royal Group" be applied to this collection of peaks and that the names of the Royal Family be placed upon its several summits. [Mount Prince John, named for the youngest son, is a prominence on the same mountain as Mount Queen Mary.]

Spike Thomson's description of the view of the Royal Group from the South Kananaskis Pass area is included in the 1916 chapter.

Adjacent to Palliser Pass the Belgians are commemorated with Mount King Albert and Mount Queen Elizabeth (her actual named was spelled Elisabeth), Belgium Lake and Leman Lake, named for Gérard Leman, a Belgian general.

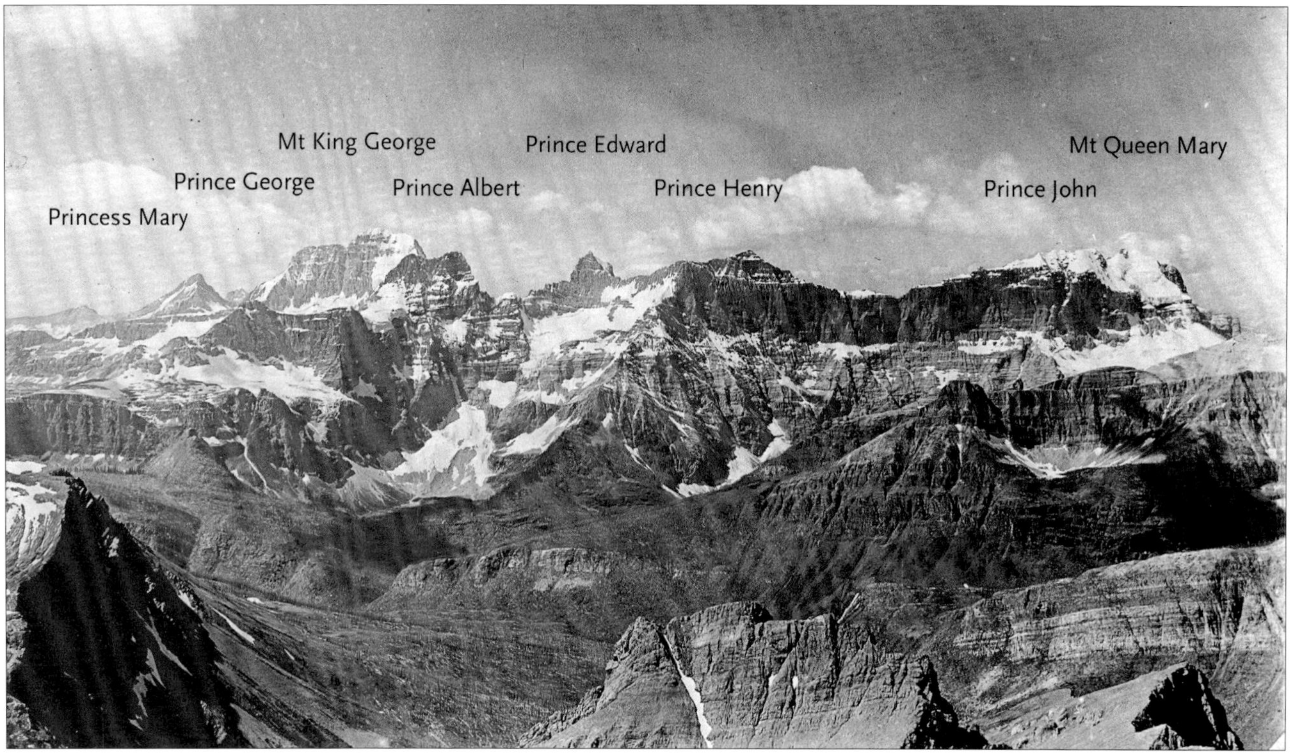

Spike Thomson's photographs included this picture of the Royal Group with the mountains labelled. PR1973.0534.0010, Provincial Archives of Alberta

Wheeler named Mount Pengelly, the maiden name of A.J. Campbell's wife, to commemorate his assistant, and Mount Cautley in the Assiniboine area for the Alberta commissioner. Cautley had mixed feelings about having a peak named for him. "The Geographic Board of Canada was kind enough to name the mountain on the south side of the pass after me. In theory, I know that it is perfectly absurd that one of the Creator's stupendous mountains should be named after any man, but I was awfully pleased at this particular negation of my theory."

One name that Wheeler used remains controversial today. Mount Pétain, Pétain Creek and Pétain Glacier commemorate a French general and marshal famous in World War I who betrayed his country in World War II by serving in the Vichy regime. Several provinces in Canada have features named for Pétain. After World War II some people petitioned to have Pétain's name removed from these features, but the Geographic Board of Canada decided that this would occur only if all of the affected jurisdictions agreed. To date this has not happened.

Along or near the Great Divide, Wheeler named over 100 geographical features related to World War I. Naturalist and author R.M. Patterson lived for a few years on a ranch near the Great Divide. In a book titled *The Buffalo Head*, he wrote: "The Rockies must sadly be the worst-named range in the world." He also stated: "If you look carefully at the map you can find there, enthroned in stone, a collaborator, a traitor to his country, sundry generals of dubious merit and a demagogue." Most people share Patterson's view. The geographical names that came from the Alberta-BC boundary survey are generally considered to be a negative aspect of the project. It is unfortunate that the geographic names for the Rocky Mountains do not better reflect the natural and human history of this spectacular feature of the Canadian landscape.

Afterword

The 150th anniversary of Canada is an opportune time to look back to an important geographical and scientific project that was in progress a century ago. One marvels at the fortitude of the surveyors and crews who spent four to five months in the field, often under difficult circumstances, and produced such accurate work with the technology available. Their maps, and especially their extensive photographic record, still have relevance today. The quality and detail of the photographs enable scientists to gain an understanding of the ecology of the Rocky Mountains a century ago. In some locations the change is obvious and dramatic, while in others it is more subtle. It will be impossible to rephotograph all of the locations from the boundary survey, but one hopes that the work (largely funded by the Alberta government) will continue, and that the government and scientists from British Columbia will participate more fully.

The rephotography of the early 21st century is a snapshot of what the Rocky Mountains look like now. But what will this mountain range look like at the 250th anniversary of the country? Will there be any glaciers remaining and how will the hydrology of the area be affected? What factors will influence the ecology of the region? How will the wildlife that inhabit the Rocky Mountains and the people who live in or visit the region be impacted by changes in the mountain landscape? Will a 200-year photographic record provide further information about the future of these spectacular peaks? When one looks at the Great Divide or thinks about this prominent feature of the western Canadian landscape, not only is the present to be considered, but both its past and its future.

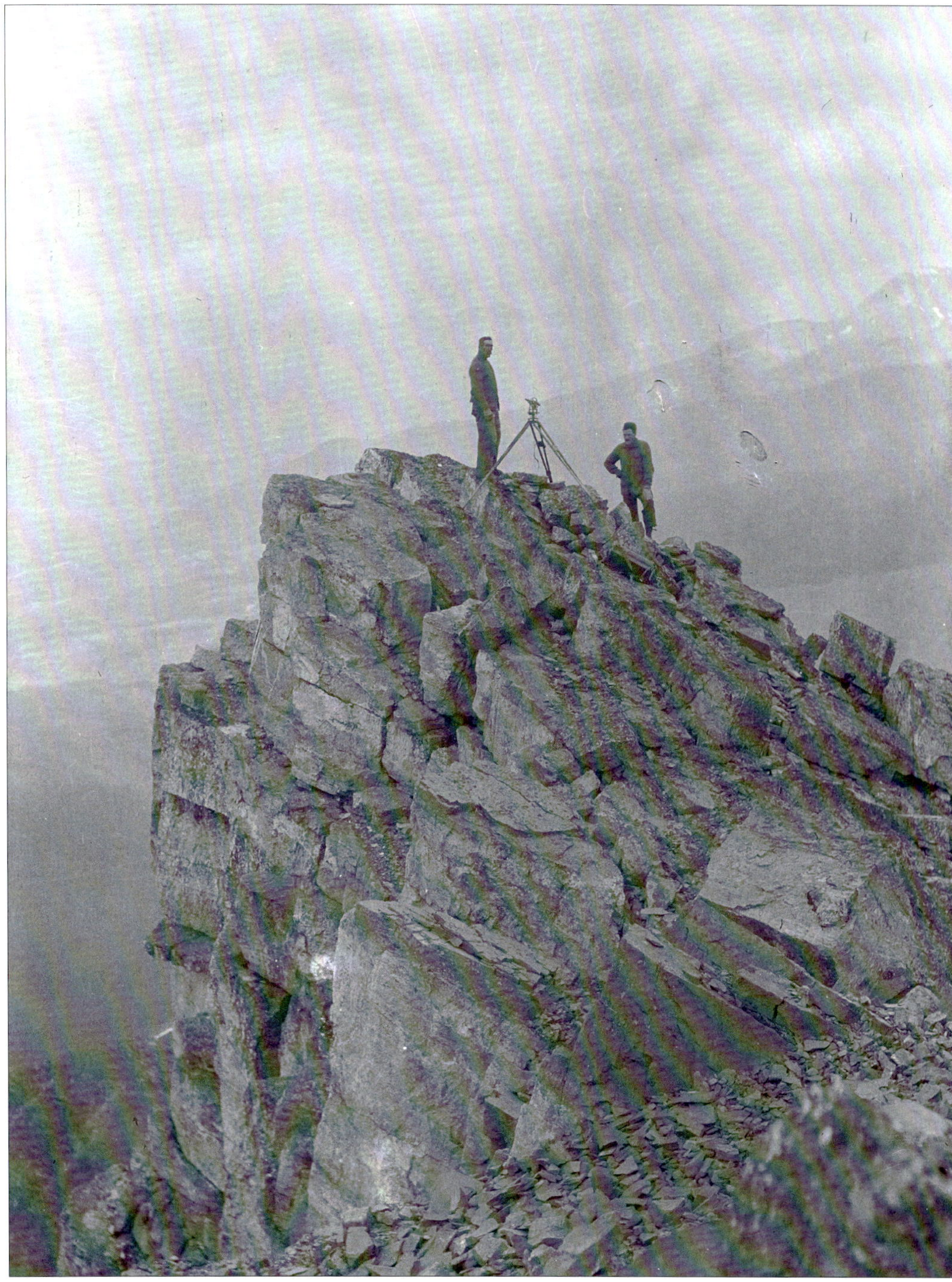

Surveying at a station at the top of Vermilion Pass. Library and Archives Canada e011166492

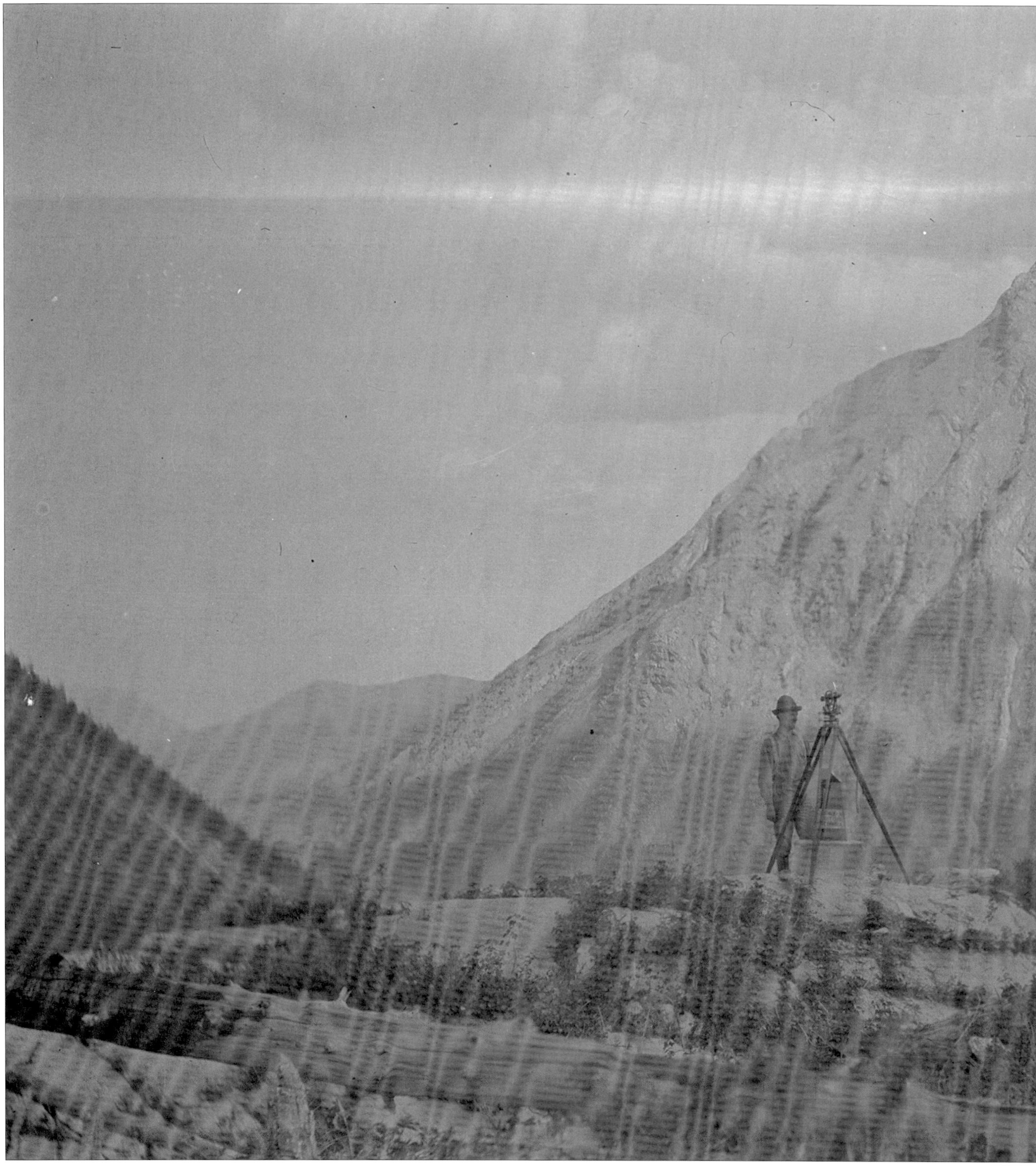

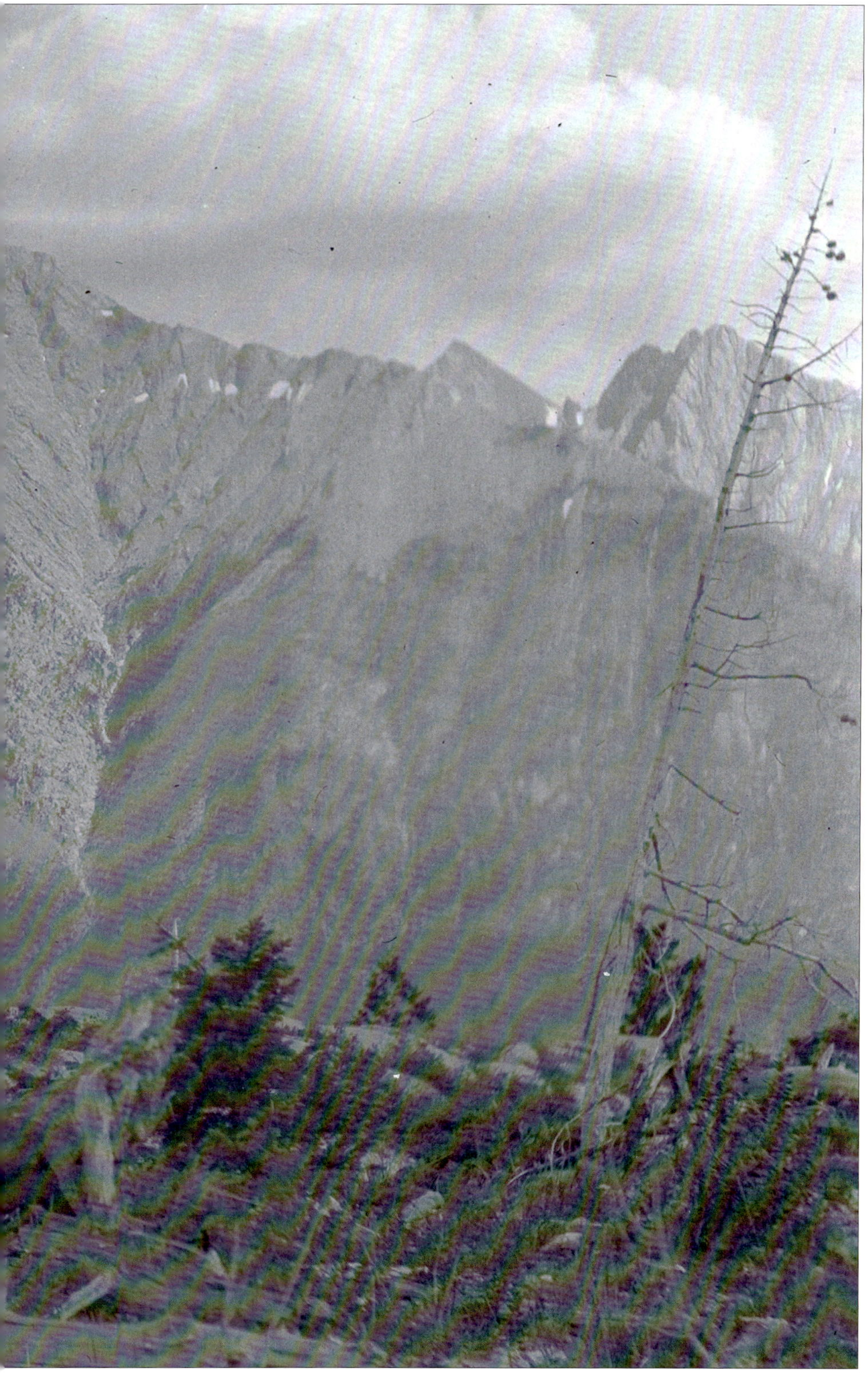

Surveying in the Crowsnest Pass.
LAC, e011166463

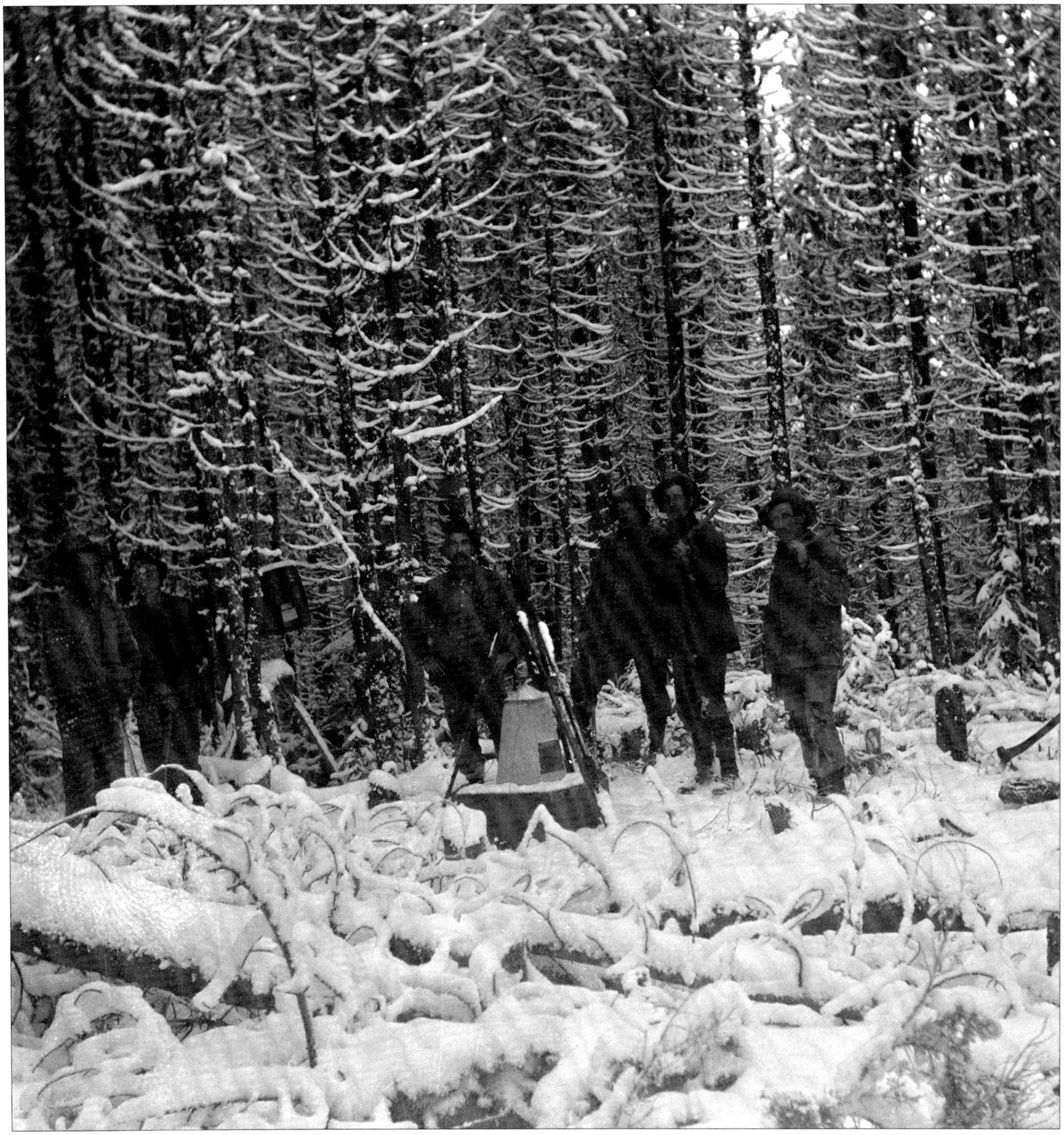

At a station in Elk Pass in the early fall. LAC, e011166472

Survey Crews

This list of members of the boundary survey is based on several sources of information. Cautley recorded the names of his crew in most of his field records. The list of Wheeler's crewmen is based on Wheeler's diaries and the accounts of a few of his crew, along with payrolls that exist for some years.

1913—Alberta
Cautley, R.W., chief surveyor
Smith, William, cook—to Aug. 11
Ward, William, cook—Aug. 12
Paquin, Hank, packer
Townsend, Chris, monument builder
Burton, Percy W., chainman
Piggott, Andrew, chainman
Davis, Fred, rodman
Koller, Jacob, axeman
Fielding, Smith, axeman

1913—British Columbia
Wheeler, A.O., chief surveyor
Campbell, A.J., assistant
Stelfox, Jack, cook
Logan, Bob, packer
Kain, Conrad
Brinkman, A.H.
Wallace, Paul

1914—ALBERTA
Cautley, R.W., chief surveyor
Carthew, W.M., assistant
Thompson, Joseph, cook
Henin, Sam, first packer
Koller, Jacob, second packer
Burns, Robert, monument builder
Burton, Percy W., chainman
Schultz, Charles, axeman—to Sept. 1
Schultz, John, axeman
Rider, George, axeman

1914—British Columbia
Wheeler, A.O., chief surveyor
Campbell, A.J., assistant
Hoggard, Ernest, cook
Woodworth, Benjamin, packer—to Sept. 2
Schultz, Charles, packer—Sept. 2
Kain, Conrad—to July 16
Westmoreland, Horace—to Aug. 12
Schultz, Roy
Aubernethy, Pete
Fletcher, Joe—July 17 to Aug. 31

1915—Alberta
Cautley, R.W., chief surveyor
Brown, T.R., assistant
Whitley, Hermon, cook
Koller, Jacob, first packer
Cole, Hicks, second packer
Townsend, Chris, monument builder
Schultz, John, axeman
Schultz, Roy, axeman

1916—Alberta
Cautley, R.W., chief surveyor
Hope, C.V., assistant
Whitley, Hermon, cook
Koller, Jacob, first packer—drowned June 22
Cole, Hicks, second packer, first packer—to Aug. 3
Webb, George, second packer, first packer—Aug. 3
Benson, Jake, second packer—Aug. 3
Dalen, Knute, axeman
MacDonald, Hugh, axeman

1917—Alberta
Cautley, R.W., chief surveyor
Brown, T.R., assistant
Jensen, Carl, cook—to Aug. 13
Miller, R.C., cook—Aug. 18
Stewart, Charles, first packer—to Aug. 28
Laird, Archie, second packer, first packer—Aug. 27
Ball, Frank, axeman, second packer—Aug. 18
Platz, Marcus, monument builder
Wilson, Edward, axeman
Fisher, Harry, axeman

1915—British Columbia
Wheeler, A.O., chief surveyor
Campbell, A.J., assistant
Stelfox, Jack, cook
Pidgeon, Jack, packer
Fletcher, Joe
Cameron, Gordon

1916—British Columbia
Wheeler, A.O., chief surveyor
Campbell, A.J., assistant
Martin, Tom, cook
Rink, Ralph, first packer
Ford, Harley, second packer—to Aug. 6
Crouch, Arthur, second packer—Aug. 6
Thomson, A.S.
Irvine, Bob—to Sept. 11
Duncan, Roy—to July 7
Weir, Gordon—Aug. 4 to Sept. 11

1917—British Columbia
Wheeler, A.O., chief surveyor
Campbell, A.J., assistant
Martin, Tom, cook
Rink, Ralph, first packer
Wallis, Frank, second packer
Thomson, A.S.
Weir, Gordon

Acknowledgements

I have received more assistance for *Surveying the Great Divide* than for any of the previous books, and this support was crucial for producing it. I would like to express my thanks to everyone who helped in any way.

Mike Thomson, surveyor general of British Columbia, provided funding for a month of research at Library and Archives Canada in Ottawa and various archives in Alberta, as well as assistance for many of Cautley's images used in the book. Peter Sullivan, surveyor general of Canada, also provided financial assistance, along with the Association of British Columbia Land Surveyors. I appreciate their support. Eric Higgs, director of the Mountain Legacy Project (MLP), furnished most of Wheeler's images, and made available the rephotography images from the boundary survey that MLP has taken during the past decade. Mary Sanseverino and other members of the MLP also contributed their expertise.

My thanks go to the staff at the various archives I visited for their courteous assistance. This includes the Whyte Museum, Glenbow Museum, Provincial Archives of Alberta, Royal BC Museum and Archives and Library and Archives Canada. I would particularly like to thank Jean Matheson and Jill Delaney at Library and Archives Canada for their work with the visual images, along with Elizabeth Kundert-Cameron and Lena Goon at the Whyte Museum for their assistance with A.O. Wheeler's material.

Several organizations assisted with this book. My thanks go to BC's Land Title and Survey Authority for making its material available, and to Dave Swaile and Calvin Woelke in particular. The Alberta surveyor general's office made its records accessible, and Ed Titanich was of invaluable assistance during my research there. Carla Jack, BC's provincial toponymist, provided invaluable information related to the names of geographical features along the boundary.

Individuals who helped me include Barb and Mike Helm, who once again gave me a home away from home when I was in Ottawa, a kindness I have always appreciated. Rob Watt shared his extensive knowledge of the boundary survey in the Waterton area. Mary Andrews, whose father, Gerry, was BC's boundary commissioner from 1951 to 1968, gave me some of her father's material related to the boundary. Jamie Hume provided me with images taken during his company's remonumentation of Elk Pass in 2015. Robert Allen assisted me with the technical aspects of the surveying.

I appreciate the support of descendants of the boundary survey crew members. Jay Hope made his grandfather's photo album available, and I am pleased to be able to include some of these pictures in the book. Jack Stelfox's descendants gave me copies of his recollections of working on the boundary survey. I also had an opportunity to visit Spike Thomson's son, and Alan Campbell's grandson.

I would like to express thanks to my family. Once again my wife, Linda, helped me in a myriad of ways. My son, Evan, accompanied me on a rephotography trip to the Rockies for two weeks in July 2015. I enjoyed his companionship and appreciated his assistance.

My thanks also go to Vici Johnstone of Caitlin Press for publishing this book.

Sources

Archives

Alberta Archives

A.S. Thomson fonds

Royal BC Museum and Archives

E/C/E31, Cautley, Robert, Highlights of Memory (memoir)

MS 733, Spike Thomson diaries, 1916–17

MS2259, BC Land Surveyors

198002-017, vols. 4–7, R.W. Cautley's personal photo albums, 1913–17

BC Geographic Names Office

Geographic Names record cards and files

Glenbow Museum

M1277, Paul Wallace fonds

Land Title and Survey Authority of British Columbia

Surveyor general's correspondence files, A.O. Wheeler, 1913–17

Library and Archives Canada

RG88, registry records related to the Alberta-BC boundary survey from the office of the Dominion surveyor general, E.G. Deville

vol. 136, file 13105, Wheeler, 1912–17

vol. 141, file 13668, Cautley, 1913–15

vol. 145, file 15322, Wheeler, 1914

vol. 145, file 15323, Cautley, 1914

vol. 148, file 15604, Wheeler, 1915 (photo index)

vol. 149, file 16123, Wheeler, 1916

vol. 151, file 16493, Cautley, 1917

vol. 151, file 16522, Wheeler, 1917

vol. 330, file 5674, Crowsnest Pass boundary, 1899–1902

vol. 330, file 6770, Crowsnest Pass and CPR, 1904–26

vol. 342, file 13105, correspondence with BC, 1912–18

vol. 346, file 13611, correspondence with BC, 1913–15

vol. 346, file 13668, correspondence with BC, 1913–15

vol. 356, file 16032, boundary commissioner reports, 1916–25

vol. 360, file 16426, boundary survey records, 1916–18

Whyte Museum

M234, Horace Westmoreland file

M546, A.O. Wheeler diaries, 1913–17

V771, A.O. Wheeler photograph albums, 1913–17

Wallace, James Nevin. "The Passes of the Rocky Mountains along the Alberta Boundary." Calgary: Historical Society of Calgary, 1927.

Books

Barnett, Doug. *The Demarcation of Alberta's Boundaries*. 2003 (self-published).

Birrell, Dave. *50 Roadside Panoramas in the Canadian Rockies*. Calgary: Rocky Mountain Books, 2000.

Fraser, Esther. *Wheeler*. Banff: Summerthought, 1978.

Hart, E.J. *Ain't It Hell: Bill Peyto's "Mountain Journal."* Banff: EJH Literary Enterprises, 1995.

Kain, Conrad. *Letters from a Mountain Guide, 1906–1933*. Edited by Zac Robinson. Edmonton: University of Alberta Press, 2014.

____. *Where the Clouds Can Go*. Vancouver: Rocky Mountain Books, 2009.

Lakusta, Ernie. *Canmore and Kananaskis History Explorer*. Canmore: Altitude Publishing, 2002.

Larmour, Judy. *Laying Down the Lines*. Edmonton: Brindle and Glass, 2005.

MacLaren, I.S. *Mapper of Mountains: M.P. Bridgland in the Canadian Rockies, 1902–1930*. Edmonton: University of Alberta Press, 2005.

Palmquist, Peter E., and Thomas Kailbourn. *Pioneer Photographers of the Far West*. Palo Alto: Stanford University Press, 2000.

Report of the Commission Appointed to Delimit the Boundary between the Provinces of Alberta and British Columbia: Part 1: From 1913 to 1916. Ottawa: Office of the Surveyor General, 1917.

Report of the Commission Appointed to Delimit the Boundary between the Provinces of Alberta and British Columbia: Part 2: 1917 to 1921 from Kicking Horse Pass to Yellowhead Pass. Ottawa: Office of the Surveyor General, 1924.

British Columbia Sessional Papers

1913—Wheeler, Arthur O. "Boundary Survey between the Provinces of British Columbia and Alberta." D317-322.

1914—Wheeler, Arthur O. "Boundary Survey between the Provinces of British Columbia and Alberta." D221-226.

1915—Wheeler, Arthur O. "Survey of the Boundary between the Provinces of Alberta and British Columbia." B112-116.

1916—Wheeler, Arthur O. "Survey of the Boundary between the Provinces of Alberta and British Columbia." L76-80.

1917—Wheeler, Arthur O. "Survey of the Boundary between the Provinces of Alberta and British Columbia." H64-67.

Family Material

C.V. Hope family collection—photo album

Jack Stelfox family collection—reminiscences

Newspapers, Magazines and Reports

Banff Crag and Canyon. "Drowned in the Kananaskis River." July 1, 1916.

Cautley, R.W. "Characteristics of Passes in the Canadian Rockies." *Canadian Alpine Journal* 12 (1922): 155–162.

Edmonton Bulletin. "Sad Drowning Accident at Cooking Lake." August 19, 1913.

Edmonton Journal. "Boat is upset." August 18, 1913.

Hume, A. James. "Alberta–British Columbia Boundary Commission: Survey Report—Elk Pass Boundary Monument Report." 2016.

Senior, C. Norman. "He Climbed Every Mountain, Forded Every Stream: Alan Campbell Surveyed the Rocky Mountain Boundary between Alberta and British Columbia." *Victoria Daily Colonist*, January 8, 1967.

Swaile, Dave. "Elk Pass Boundary Restoration Survey." *Link Magazine*, August 2016, 45–48.

_____. Wheeler, A.O. "Passes of the Great Divide." *Canadian Alpine Journal* 16 (1928): 150–176.

Wheeler, A.O. "The Application of Photography to the Mapping of the Canadian Rocky Mountains." *Canadian Alpine Journal* 11 (1920): 76–96.

Wheeler, J.O. "The Wheeler Family in the Mapping of the Canadian Cordillera." Proceedings of the Association of Canadian Map Libraries 28 (1978): 18–34.

Websites

Mountain Legacy Project, mountainlegacy.ca

Natural Resources Canada, clss.nrcan.gc.ca

Postscript note

As this book was being finished, a large and intense wild fire burned through Akamina Pass. The fire altered the ecosystem and landscape of this pass. Wheeler and Cautley produced an excellent photographic record of the Akamina Pass area in 1915. During recent years, the Mountain Legacy Project and the author have taken several repeat photographs there. In the future, scientists will be using Wheeler and Cautley's photographs in Akamina Pass as the basis of documenting the regeneration of the ecosystem and landscape changes in this scenic location.

Index

Bold indicates photo or illustration

E

F

G

H

I

J

K

L

M

U

V

W

Y